AF866731

How Payments Work

The Hidden Infrastructure Behind Cards, Bank Rails, Wallets, and Modern Fintech

Artem Smirnov

Copyright © 2026 Artem Smirnov

All rights reserved.

No part of this publication may be reproduced, stored in a retrieval system, or transmitted in any form or by any means without the prior written permission of the copyright owner, except for brief quotations and other uses permitted by applicable copyright law.

First edition, 2026

Published by Artemis Press

Hardcover ISBN: 978-3-00-088500-6

This book is provided for educational and informational purposes only. It does not constitute legal, financial, investment, tax, regulatory, compliance, or other professional advice. Laws, regulations, payment-network rules, tech-nical standards, and product features change over time. Readers should con-sult current official sources and qualified professionals before relying on the information for business, legal, compliance, or investment decisions.

All trademarks, service marks, product names, and company names men-tioned in this book are the property of their respective owners. Their use is for identification and educational purposes only and does not imply endorsement by or affiliation with the trademark owners.

Table of Contents

Preface

In the last decade, the payments industry has gone through significant changes. Contactless replaced the magnetic stripe at the point of sale. Real-time payment rails launched across dozens of countries. Card networks extended their infrastructure into digital wallets and tokenized credentials. Buy now, pay later grew from a niche product into a mainstream checkout option. Stablecoins and central bank digital currencies moved from academic proposals into live pilots and, in some markets, production systems. Embedded finance turned software companies into payment providers almost overnight.

Behind these changes are forces that have been building for years. Smartphones became payment devices for hundreds of millions of people. Regulators in Europe, India, Brazil, and the UK opened banking infrastructure to third-party providers, creating new competitive dynamics. The cost of processing fell far enough that new entrants could build payment products without owning the underlying rails. And the expectations of both consumers and businesses have shifted: a payment that takes three days to settle or a checkout that requires re-entering card details is no longer acceptable in most markets.

The buzzwords that fill the payment space are a sign of real change. But as payments professionals, we need more than product names and flow diagrams. We need a technically accurate and commercially realistic picture of the system behind them: who participates and why, how information moves before money does, where risk sits at each stage, and why the same transaction looks completely different depending on which side of it you are on.

Fortunately, terminology changes faster than the underlying mechanisms. Authorization remains distinct from clearing and settlement. Acquirers continue to assess merchant risk. Bank transfers rely on a different trust model from card transactions. A wallet token, however modern it appears, still connects to an underlying card or account relationship. New payment methods receive new names, but they must answer familiar questions: who can initiate the payment, who can reverse it, who bears the fraud risk, who holds the funds, and who reconciles the records?

Once you understand those mechanisms, new payment products become easier to place within a familiar structure. You can evaluate a provider's claims more critically, reason about architectural trade-offs, and diagnose failures without treating every new system as a mystery.

This book provides the foundation that many payments professionals spend years acquiring through work on separate projects, systems, and incidents. It examines the institutions and infrastructure that make modern payments work: card networks, issuers, acquirers, processors, bank rails, wallets, authentication flows, dispute processes, ledgers, compliance controls, and newer developments such as embedded finance, stablecoins, and CBDCs.

It is not a tutorial for a single provider, API, card network, or country, nor is it a legal textbook or an exhaustive catalog of rules and exceptions. Instead, we will look inside payment systems, separate roles that are often bundled together, and trace flows that are usually hidden behind a simple customer experience. The aim is to explain not only what happens but why the system works that way and what to ask when evaluating a new payment product, provider, or architecture.

After reading this book, you will understand how payment systems work under the hood and be able to reason about authorization, settlement, risk, compliance, reconciliation, and product design with greater confidence. You will also see how cards, bank transfers, wallets, open banking, and fintech platforms fit into the same larger picture.

We will begin with the payment experience most people already know: tapping a card at checkout. From there, we will follow the messages, records, money, and responsibilities that turn that simple action into a working payment system.

Who Should Read This Book

This book is for anyone who wants to understand how payments, banking rails, and fintech infrastructure work beneath the surface. It is written both for people entering the industry and for professionals who already work in one part of it but want to see the larger picture.

It will be particularly useful to product managers, engineers, solution architects, business analysts, operations specialists, consultants, founders, and students preparing for a career in payments or fintech.

No previous payment experience is required. The explanations begin with familiar actions, such as tapping a card, paying online, receiving a refund, or sending a bank transfer, and build the system step by step. You do not need to know how to code or have worked at a bank, although a general comfort with technical and business concepts will help.

Readers who already specialize in payments can use the book to connect their area with the neighboring layers. An issuing specialist can develop a clearer picture of acquiring. Someone working with bank transfers can understand how card networks differ. A product manager can connect the customer journey to authorization, clearing, settlement, fraud, and reconciliation. An engineer can see what an API request represents inside the wider payment system. A founder can understand the roles of sponsor banks, processors, networks, and Banking-as-a-Service providers.

This is not a setup guide for a specific provider or API; provider documentation is better suited to that purpose. The book explains the system behind the documentation, making individual products, integrations, and technical choices easier to understand.

Scope of This Book

This book focuses on the mechanisms of card payments, bank rails, alternative payment methods, and fintech infrastructure.

We begin with card payments because cards are one of the clearest ways to see the payments ecosystem in action. A single card transaction brings together a cardholder, merchant, issuer, acquirer, payment network, processors, terminals, authentication flows, fraud systems, clearing records, settlement obligations, fees, and disputes. Once that structure is visible, many other payment systems become easier to compare.

The book then expands beyond cards into bank transfers, direct debits, open banking, real-time payment systems, wallets, BNPL, stablecoins, CBDCs, Banking-as-a-Service, embedded finance, and the infrastructure choices behind fintech products.

The focus is on how these systems work conceptually and operationally. We look at roles, flows, incentives, trade-offs, and failure modes. We do not try to reproduce every rulebook, certification requirement, legal detail, or country-specific exception. Those details change by market and over time, and they are better handled through official documentation, legal advice, network rules, and provider-specific material.

The book also does not try to teach every implementation detail. You will see message types, data fields, protocols, and examples where they help explain the mechanism, but this is not a coding manual or an API reference. The aim is to give you the mental model needed to understand what an API call, authorization response, transaction record, token, chargeback notice, settlement file, or ledger entry represents inside the payment system.

Some topics receive more attention than others. Card payments get the most detailed treatment because they combine technical, financial, regulatory, and commercial layers in a compact form. Bank rails and alternative payment methods are covered in enough depth for readers to compare them with cards and understand their role in fintech architecture. Regulation, security, and compliance are included where they shape product design and operational responsibility, but they are not treated as standalone legal subjects.

The book is deliberately practical. It is written for people who need to reason about payment systems, not just memorize terminology.

Outline of This Book

The book is arranged into ten parts.

In Part I, we start with the foundations of card payments. We follow a simple card transaction, identify the main parties, examine the providers around them, explain merchant acquiring, introduce card networks and rulebooks, and look at the economics of a card payment.

In Part II, we move inside the card. We trace how payment cards evolved, what information a card contains, how magnetic stripes and EMV chips work, why contactless payments changed the point-of-sale experience, and how mobile wallets and virtual cards changed the idea of a card credential.

In Part III, we focus on card authentication. We separate authentication from authorization, explain PINs, CVV, and CVC codes, EMV cryptograms, 3-D Secure, Strong Customer Authentication, and the shift from static card data toward dynamic and risk-based controls.

In Part IV, we examine card products and business models. Debit, credit, charge, prepaid, commercial, co-branded, fleet, and gift cards may use similar rails, but they serve different account structures, risk models, and commercial goals.

In Part V, we follow the lifecycle of a card transaction. Authorization, clearing, settlement, posting, reconciliation, refunds, reversals, disputes, chargebacks, and accounting entries are treated as separate stages rather than one vague idea called "payment."

In Part VI, we look at transaction types and variations. Card-present and card-not-present payments, recurring billing, card-on-file transactions, merchant-initiated transactions, currency conversion, cross-border payments, and authorization response codes all show how the same system behaves in different contexts.

In Part VII, we turn to security, compliance, and regulation. We cover fraud, PCI DSS, tokenization, AML and sanctions screening, data protection, and PSD2. The emphasis is on how these requirements shape payment flows and product architecture.

In Part VIII, we move beyond cards into bank rails. We compare card payments with bank transfers, explain ACH, SEPA, SWIFT, correspondent banking, ISO 20022, open banking, and real-time payment systems.

In Part IX, we examine alternative payment methods. Wallets, account-to-account payments, BNPL, direct carrier billing, vouchers, cash-based payments, and local methods show that *payment method* is not a single category but a family of distinct trust, risk, and settlement models.

In Part X, we look at fintech business models and infrastructure. Banking-as-a-Service, embedded finance, ledger design, stablecoins, crypto payment flows, CBDCs, orchestration, fraud tooling, artificial intelligence, and the future of payment systems are all easier to understand once the earlier parts have built the foundation.

You can read the book from beginning to end, which is the best way to build the full model. You can also return to individual chapters when you need a refresher on a specific topic. The glossary at the end is included for that reason: payments have a large vocabulary, and a good understanding often starts with knowing what a term is trying to name.

The book begins with the most familiar payment object: a card at checkout.

Part I

Card Payment Foundations

Chapter 1: What Is a Card Payment?

Card payments look simple. You tap the card, hear a beep from the terminal, and get a receipt. Most people do this hundreds of times a year without thinking about it. But very few know what really happens in that moment between the tap and the beep. This book explains the payment system behind that moment.

Meet Emma. She is on vacation in Italy. One afternoon, she sits down at a small restaurant on a town square. She orders pizza and a glass of wine, and the bill comes to €14. She pulls a Visa card out of her wallet, issued by her bank in California, and taps it on the terminal the waiter brings to the table. A few seconds later, the receipt prints.

How does a card from a bank in California work in a restaurant in Italy?

The more you think about it, the stranger it gets. The terminal has never connected to Emma's bank. It doesn't know whether her card is real, whether her account has the money, or whether the card has been blocked or stolen. The card itself isn't the answer – it doesn't hold her money. Somehow, in a few seconds, the terminal got those answers anyway.

The obvious answer would be that the terminal asked Emma's bank directly. But it didn't, and it couldn't have. The terminal has no link to a bank in California, and there's no global directory it could look her up in. With tens of thousands of banks in the world, connecting each one to all the others would mean hundreds of millions of links, each with its own contracts, message formats, security rules, and dispute procedures – a system no one could build, run, or trust.

Card payments are designed to feel like a single action – tap, beep, done – but behind that is a layered system of intermediaries, message standards, risk checks, and settlement obligations. Several institutions are communicating to route the request, look up the issuer, check the account, reserve funds, calculate fees, and record the transaction for later settlement. Each one sees only its own part. The cardholder sees the approval on the terminal — and almost nothing else.

The Five Parties

A card payment usually involves five parties. Each one does different work, carries different risks, and earns money in a different way.

Emma is the *cardholder*. She holds the card, makes the purchase, and is ultimately responsible for paying for it. Whether she taps in a restaurant, enters card details on a website, or buys a subscription from her phone, her role is the same.

The *merchant* is whoever Emma is paying — in this case, the restaurant. Merchants sell goods or services and accept cards as payment. The merchant could be a small café, a global airline, a streaming platform, or an online marketplace.

When Emma taps, the merchant sends the request to its own bank — the *acquirer*, also called the *acquiring bank*. The acquirer gives the merchant access to the card system, receives the transaction from the merchant, and passes it forward. The acquirer is the merchant's gateway, but it cannot approve the transaction on its own. It has no view of Emma's account, no idea of her balance, and no way to know whether her card is active, blocked, or stolen.

Between the acquirer and Emma's bank is the *payment network*, sometimes called a card scheme in Europe. The network is the shared infrastructure that lets thousands of acquirers and issuers reach each other. Visa and Mastercard are the most widely known. American Express, Discover, JCB, UnionPay, RuPay, and many domestic networks fill out the rest. The network doesn't hold anyone's money. It routes the message, enforces the rules, and ensures both sides speak the same language.

The request finally reaches Emma's bank, the issuer. The *issuer* is the institution that gave Emma her card in the first place. It maintains the account behind the card, checks the funds, evaluates risk, and decides whether to approve or decline the transaction. If the issuer says yes, the answer travels back the way it came.

Five parties, one transaction. The next step is seeing how they actually talk to each other when Emma taps her card.

The Transaction Flow

This five-party system starts working as soon as Emma taps her card.

The terminal reads the card or digital wallet and creates an authorization request. The request includes the amount, currency, merchant details, terminal information, and the card or token data needed to identify the account. It first goes to the merchant's acquirer, sometimes through a payment processor, gateway, or payment service provider.

The acquirer cannot approve the transaction itself. It has no access to Emma's account and no control over her card, so the request goes onward to the network that connects to the issuer.

To do this, the acquirer needs to know which payment network to send the request to. The card number helps with that. The first few digits, called the Bank Identification Number (BIN), show which bank and network issued the card. It's like the country code at the start of a phone number. Before you can talk to someone, the system needs to know where to route the call.

The payment network is the shared routing layer between acquirers and issuers. It receives the request and determines which issuer should make the decision. The network doesn't hold Emma's money or maintain a wallet for every cardholder. Its job is to move information quickly and reliably between the acquirer and issuer, using common message standards and rules.

The issuer receives the request and decides what to do. It checks whether the card is valid, whether there is enough money or credit, whether the transaction follows account rules, and whether anything looks suspicious.

If the issuer approves the transaction, it sends an approval message. If not, it sends a decline with a response code. The message then travels back through the same chain in reverse: issuer, payment network, acquirer, and finally the merchant.

The terminal receives the answer, beeps, and prints the receipt.

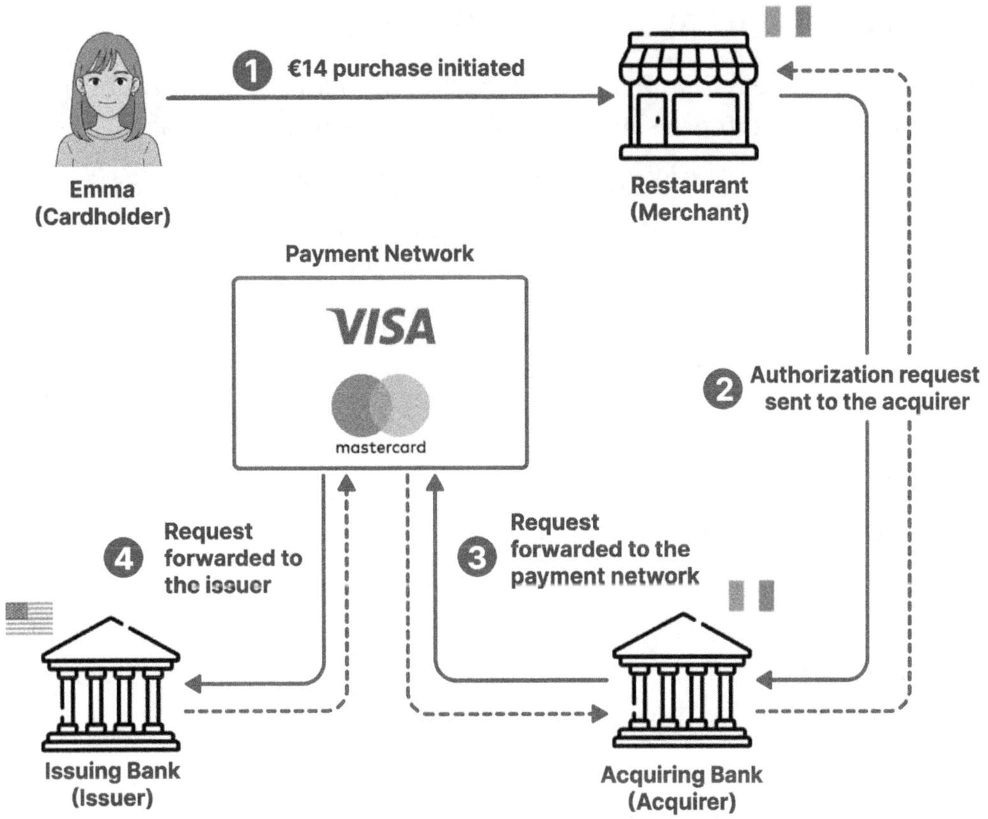

Figure 1.1: The basic card authorization flow.

The Routing Problem

The network structure solves a routing problem: with thousands of banks, millions of merchants, and billions of cards, direct connections between every bank and every merchant would make the system unmanageable. Each new participant would need new contracts, technical setups, operating procedures, security rules, and dispute processes.

The payment network reduces that complexity. An issuer connects to the network and can receive transactions from many acquirers. An acquirer connects to the network and can send transactions to many issuers. The network handles routing, message standards, and shared rules so both sides can work together without a direct relationship.

That is why Emma's California card works at a restaurant in Tuscany, a hotel in Tokyo, a grocery store in Nairobi, or an online shop in Berlin. The merchant does not need a direct link to Emma's bank. It needs access to an acquirer and a network that can reach the issuer.

Authorization and Payment Finality

The word "Approved" displayed on the terminal means the issuer accepted the transaction request. It does not mean the restaurant has been paid.

Authorization is the real-time decision to approve or decline a transaction. The issuer has answered the system's immediate question: should this card, for this amount, at this merchant, right now, be accepted?

In many card transactions, an approval creates an authorization hold when the issuer reserves capacity for the transaction. A hold temporarily lowers the cardholder's available balance or credit limit until the transaction is completed or released. For a debit card, the hold lowers Emma's available balance; for a credit card, it lowers her available credit. To Emma, the money can look gone, even though the transaction is not final inside the system.

The next stage is clearing. This is when the merchant presents the transaction through the payment network so it can be posted, matched, fee-calculated, and prepared for settlement. Settlement then moves funds between financial institutions to complete the transaction financially.

The system separates these steps because each one has a different goal. Authorization needs to be fast since Emma is waiting at the table. Clearing must be accurate because it creates the official transaction record. Settlement has to move money efficiently between banks, often for many transactions at once. Trying to do all of that before the receipt prints would make the system slower, more fragile, and harder to operate. We will return to authorization, clearing, and settlement in Chapters 23–25, where each stage is treated as a separate part of the transaction lifecycle.

That is the basic outline of a card payment: the cardholder sees a purchase, the merchant sees a sale, the issuer sees a request to approve or decline, the acquirer sees a merchant transaction it may later have to fund, reconcile, or defend, and the network sees a message that must be routed under shared rules.

No single party sees the whole payment in the same way. In Chapter 2, we keep the same payment in view, but separate what it means to each participant before later chapters add providers, economics, card products, and transaction mechanics.

Chapter 2: The Five Parties behind a Card Payment

In Chapter 1, we followed Emma's restaurant payment through the card system: merchant, acquirer, payment network, issuer, and back again. That path shows where the message travels. But it does not show what the transaction means to each party.

The same €14 pizza is an evening out for Emma, a sale for the restaurant, a risk decision for the issuer, a merchant transaction for the acquirer, and a routed message for the network.

This chapter examines each payment party in turn, clarifying their direct relationships: what each party sees in the payment process, the decisions they control, and the risks their role entails.

The Cardholder and the Issuer

The cardholder and the issuer are directly linked by an account or card agreement. This is the most personal relationship in the card payment chain because it is built around one customer's finances. The issuer either holds the cardholder's money or provides credit. The rest of the payment system supports this direct relationship.

When a cardholder uses their card, they depend on the issuer's decision, which shapes their experience. Seeing "Approved" at the terminal signals an authorized payment, while a pending charge in the banking app indicates that the money is on hold. If the payment is declined, the transaction has been refused. Although most cardholders rarely think about dealing with their bank, every transaction briefly connects them to it.

Cardholders make only a few visible decisions: which card to use, whether to complete extra authentication, and whether to dispute a transaction later.

Although cardholders face limited risks, the most common ones involve unauthorized use – such as stolen cards, leaked numbers, or fraudulent charges. Consumer protection generally restricts their losses. Still, handling fraud demands time and effort, and reimbursement is sometimes delayed during investigations. The same issuer relationship can also expose cardholders to costs that are not obvious at checkout: foreign transaction fees, late fees, ATM surcharges, and, for credit cards, interest on unpaid balances.

The issuer decides whether to approve or decline a transaction using information only it has. The issuer knows if the card is active, suspended, expired, or reported lost. It also knows the account balance or credit limit, the cardholder's recent transactions, and their usual spending habits. The issuer can notice if something about the transaction is unusual, such as a new country, a different type of merchant, or a sudden series of small purchases that could indicate a stolen card is being tested. For each authorization, the issuer has only a few seconds to approve, decline, or request additional verification.

The issuer faces specific risks. With credit cards, there's the risk that the cardholder never pays, while both debit and credit products bring exposure to fraud and operational hurdles. When fraud occurs, the issuer often bears the loss, but responsibility may shift based on payment method, network rules, or local laws. Alongside those transaction-level risks, issuers must keep their authorization systems running at all times and remain compliant with regulations.

The cardholder-issuer relationship is the only one in this model that is built around an individual customer over time.

The Merchant and the Acquirer

A payment acceptance agreement connects the merchant and acquirer. That agreement lets the merchant process card payments.

For merchants, card payments mean getting authorization and then waiting to be paid. The terminal might say "Approved," but the money does not arrive immediately. The acquirer pays the merchant later under the merchant agreement.

Most merchant decisions occur before the customer arrives. Merchants select whether to accept cards, which networks to support, which acquirer or payment provider to use, and what commercial terms to agree to. A small restaurant tends to prioritize simple pricing and reliable terminals. A large retailer has enough scale to negotiate for lower fees, faster payouts, and backup acquiring arrangements.

Once signed up, the merchant manages the system daily. When a customer pays, the merchant sends the authorization and later completes the transaction. The merchant also chooses when to issue refunds, challenge chargebacks, or abandon or retry transactions that take too long.

Merchants face real risks too. An approved sale does not always guarantee finality: a transaction may remain incomplete, or a later chargeback may reverse funds that seemed to belong to the merchant. Fraud risk varies by payment channel and authentication method, so some transactions are easier to defend than others. Too many chargebacks may lead the acquirer to raise fees, increase reserves, or terminate the agreement.

The acquirer provides the merchant with access to the card system and serves as the merchant's partner in accepting card payments. The acquirer onboards each merchant, connects it to the network, receives settlement funds, and pays the merchant under the merchant agreement.

Much of acquiring is merchant risk management. Before onboarding, the acquirer decides if the merchant is acceptable. Afterward, it monitors transaction patterns, sets fees and reserves, and intervenes when chargebacks, fraud, or suspicious activity rise to a level that requires action.

The acquirer's biggest exposure is the merchant itself. If a merchant closes down while there are still chargebacks to settle, the acquirer is exposed to the remaining chargeback losses. A dishonest merchant can process legitimate-looking transactions, take the payout, and disappear before the disputes catch up. That is why acquirers carefully review merchants, hold reserves, monitor transaction patterns, and sometimes end agreements when risk increases.

The relationship between merchant and acquirer is mostly about business and contracts, unlike the more personal cardholder-issuer relationship. Acquirers have many merchant customers, judge them based on business and risk factors, and manage them through fees, reserves, and rules.

The Payment Network

The payment network is the only party in the five-party model that does not manage the cardholder or the merchant directly. It does not hold cardholder accounts or run merchant accounts. Instead, it works with issuers, acquirers, processors, and other certified participants that follow its rules.

What the network mostly sees is the transaction message. When an acquirer sends a transaction through Visa or Mastercard, the request includes card or token data, the amount, merchant ID, terminal details, and security information. It does not include the cardholder's full bank balance or the merchant's full history. The network has enough information to route the request, apply its rules, and send the message to the correct issuer.

The issuer normally makes the approval decision. The network provides the routing, standards, and rule framework that allows the decision to travel through the system.

Its risks are mostly system-level risks: availability, compliance, rule integrity, and trust. If a major network goes down, the effect can spread across many markets. If participants ignore the rulebook, fraud can rise, and confidence can fall. Cardholders expect the card to work, merchants expect predictable dispute and fraud rules, and banks expect the system to keep running.

This is an institutional relationship. Issuers and acquirers join the network under its rules, pay fees, and follow procedures. The network connects issuers and acquirers without direct relationships between them.

> **Payment Network or Card Scheme?**
>
> This book usually uses the term *payment network*. In Europe, the term *card scheme* is also common. The terms are not always identical, but in this book, they refer to the shared system that handles routing, rules, standards, clearing, settlement, and dispute processes.

The five-party model is useful, but it still treats each party as if it performed its work directly. The next layer is the operating stack around those roles: processors, gateways, payment service providers, payment facilitators, and technology vendors.

Chapter 3: Processors, Gateways, and Payment Providers

The five-party model is the right starting point, but not the operating reality. A real card transaction usually passes through more hands than the cardholder, merchant, acquirer, payment network, and issuer.

A restaurant might use one company to run its terminal, another to handle online checkout, an acquirer to connect those to the card system, and a payment processor to handle the technical work behind the acquirer. On the cardholder's side, the issuer may rely on its own processor, a card-production vendor, a token service provider, and a 3-D Secure provider.

Those extra companies do not replace the five-party model. They work inside it: routing messages, running terminals, processing authorizations, manufacturing cards, authenticating users, scoring fraud, and managing tokens. In Chapter 2, we separated the five parties. Here, we look at the operating companies that make those roles work. Figure 3.1 shows the core acquiring and issuing stacks around a card transaction.

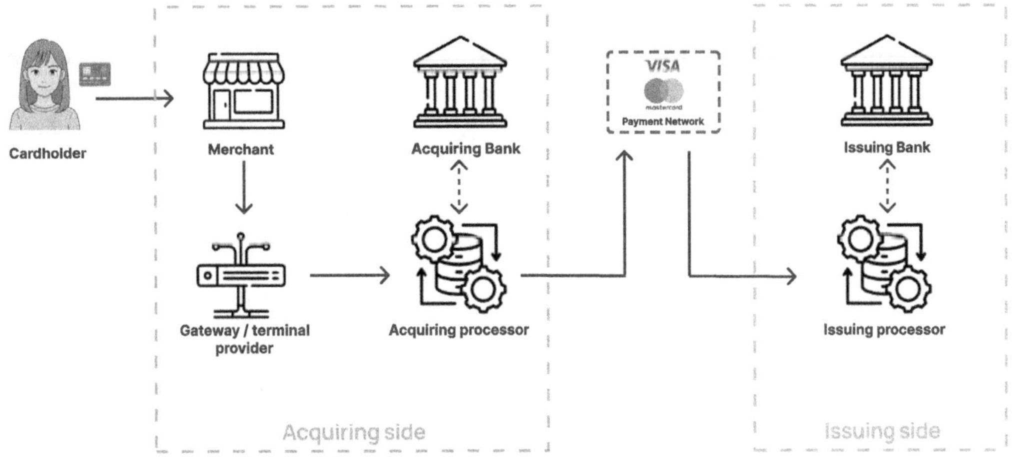

Figure 3.1: The core acquiring and issuing stacks around a card transaction.

Merchant-Side Stack

The merchant side of payments has the most layers in the ecosystem. A small business that wants to accept cards rarely works directly with an acquiring bank. It signs up with a payment provider, which handles the gateway, the processor-acquirer relationship, and the rest of the plumbing.

The first layer is the *payment gateway*, software that captures, secures, and routes payment data. On websites, the gateway appears as an embedded form, an application programming interface (API), or a back-end system that collects card data for authorization. In stores, terminal software captures and sends card data to a processor. Gateways handle encrypted data transmission, retries, tokenization, and basic fraud checks. Nearly all merchants use gateways directly or via a payment service provider. Authorize.Net is commonly used as a gateway, while Braintree is a PayPal-owned payments platform with gateway functionality. Stripe and Adyen bundle gateway-like functions with broader merchant services.

Next to the gateway is the acquiring processor, which manages the acquirer's side of transaction processing. It takes transactions from gateways or merchant platforms, formats them for payment networks, routes authorization requests, handles responses, and prepares data for settlement. Some acquiring banks use their own processors, but many hire specialist firms. Large providers such as Fiserv, FIS, Nexi, Worldline, and Global Payments operate at this level, though their specific roles vary by market and product. The acquirer manages the merchant relationship: pricing, underwriting, risk, and contracts. The processor turns those commercial and risk decisions into operational rules and system actions.

A payment service provider (PSP) bundles merchant services — gateway, processing, acquiring, reporting, fraud tools, and multiple payment methods — into a single integration. PSPs are popular for reducing integration work, allowing merchants to obtain all these features from a single provider instead of assembling them. Companies like Stripe, Adyen, Checkout.com, and Worldpay operate as PSPs, direct acquirers, or both, depending on the role they perform in a given market. Figure 3.2 compares the narrower gateway and processor functions with the broader bundle a PSP can provide.

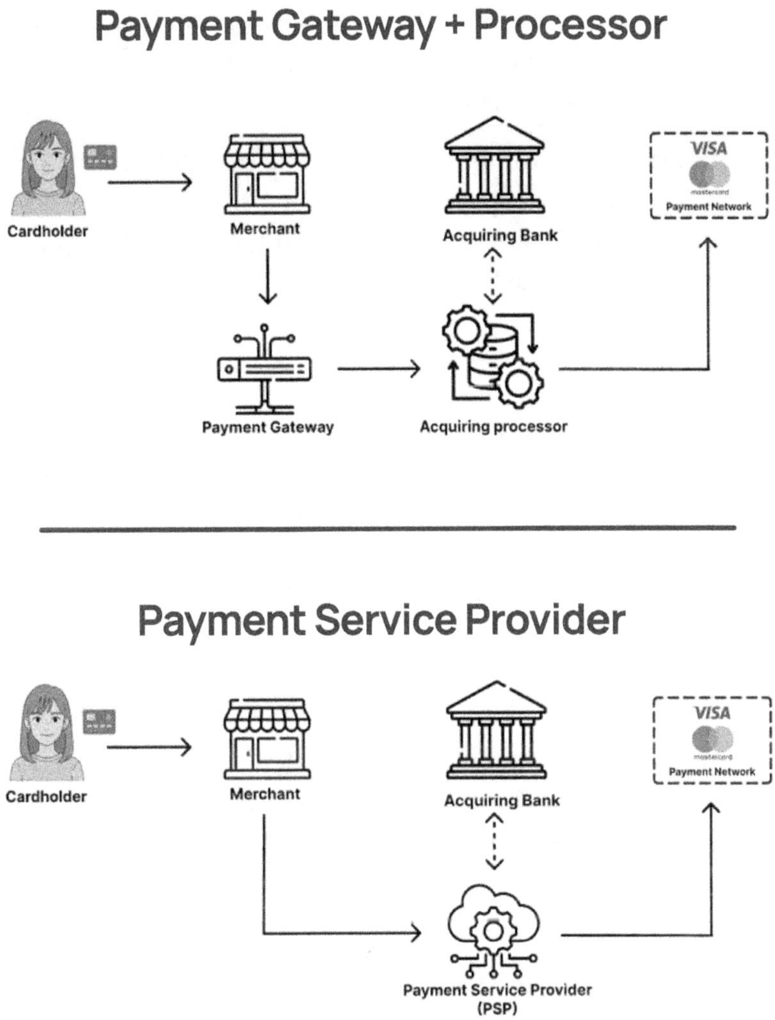

Figure 3.2: Gateway and processor functions compared with a payment service provider.

A payment facilitator (PayFac) changes onboarding by signing a master agreement with an acquirer and enrolling smaller businesses as sub-merchants. This lets sole traders, creators, and small businesses start accepting cards quickly, without waiting for a direct acquiring relationship. The PayFac takes on much of the operational onboarding, underwriting, monitoring, and compliance work under its master acquiring relationship.

That faster onboarding changes the risk profile. Any sub-merchant could cause fraud, chargebacks, customer complaints, or regulatory issues. If the PayFac accepts bad merchants too easily, the problems do not stay with those merchants. They affect the PayFac and eventually the acquirer as well.

This model lets small businesses accept cards, even if they do not qualify for or want a traditional merchant account. Square popularized this in the United States. Stripe often uses PayFac-style models, and PayPal took a similar approach before the term was widely used.

Gateway, acquiring processor, PSP, and PayFac are distinct roles within the payments ecosystem, each responsible for specific functions. One company can perform several of these roles at once, and the same company can serve different roles in different markets.

Issuer-Side Stack

The issuing side has fewer public-facing labels, but the operational load is just as heavy. Someone has to authorize transactions, manage card records, apply limits, handle personal identification number (PIN) services, produce cards, provision wallets, and report activity back to the issuer.

The main provider here is the *issuing processor*: the technical system that runs most issuer-side card operations, including authorization, balance and limit checks, card management, PIN services, transaction history, and reporting.

When an authorization request reaches the issuer in the five-party flow, the issuing processor often returns the real-time response. The processor follows the issuer's rules and returns an approval or a decline. Operationally, the processor may send the response, but the issuer remains responsible for the card program, the account relationship, and the policies behind those rules.

Many small and midsize banks do not manage their own card systems. Instead, they hire issuing processors that handle card portfolios for multiple banks. Companies such as FIS, Nexi, Fiserv, TSYS (now part of Global Payments), and Marqeta operate at this level. Some focus on traditional banks, some on fintechs and modern card programs, and some serve both. The distinction between the issuer and the issuing processor is important because policy decisions and technical work are handled by different organizations with different priorities and timelines.

Another important layer is card production. Most banks do not make their own cards. Specialized providers handle plastic card personalization, chip personalization, PIN mailers, virtual card credentials, and mobile wallet setup. Companies like Thales, IDEMIA, and Giesecke+Devrient lead this market worldwide.

A *sponsor bank*, also known as a BIN sponsor, gives regulated issuing access and a BIN range to fintechs that want to issue cards but do not have their own network membership or banking license. The fintech may manage the app, marketing, customer experience, and product design, but the sponsor bank is usually the legal issuer for regulatory and network reasons. Most early-stage fintechs that issue cards use this setup, with the sponsor bank's name in the BIN registry and the fintech's brand on the card and in the app.

The issuing side is simpler to map than the merchant side, but the responsibility still sits with the issuer. In this book, the term *issuer* refers to the organization responsible for the card program, even when other providers handle operational work.

Services around the Transaction

Some providers do not sit neatly on only one side of the transaction. They support functions that many participants need: fraud scoring, authentication, tokenization, terminal hardware, certification, and security.

Fraud and risk providers such as Feedzai, Riskified, Sift, or Forter offer real-time scoring, identity checks, and screening tools. Issuers, acquirers, PSPs, merchants, and networks all use fraud signals and risk tools, often from different vendors. Some providers focus on merchant-side fraud, issuer-side fraud, anti-money laundering, or broader crime controls, creating a specialist market around the tools banks and merchants need to combat fraud.

Providers of 3-D Secure (3DS) support online cardholder authentication. A 3DS flow may involve the merchant's PSP, a Directory Server run by the network, and an issuer-side access-control system. Specialist providers may operate access-control or 3DS systems for issuers, acquirers, PSPs, or merchants. In Chapter 40, we trace the full 3DS flow, including how issuer authentication is incorporated into the online card authorization path.

Token service providers replace real card numbers with tokens. A token can look like a card number but is restricted to a particular device, merchant, wallet, or use case. Mobile wallets such as Apple Pay and Google Pay rely on network tokenization services, including Visa Token Service and Mastercard Digital Enablement Service (MDES). Chapter 11 explains wallet tokenization in detail.

Terminal and point-of-sale (POS) providers design and manufacture hardware for payments, including card readers, point-of-sale terminals, kiosks, and mobile POS devices. Companies such as Verifone, Ingenico, and PAX Technology make the hardware found at merchant counters. Some, like Square, offer both hardware and the software that runs on it. Terminals are part of the merchant's setup, but they must be certified by the networks and work with the gateway and processor. These devices are physical endpoints for cryptographic protocols that connect the counter, kiosk, or phone to the global card system.

The common pattern is specialization: banks, merchants, and PSPs need these capabilities, but usually do not want to build specialist teams and certified systems in-house.

Provider Names and Functional Roles

The function a company performs matters more than its brand name. Stripe, Adyen, Worldpay, Fiserv, Marqeta, Visa, and Mastercard do not fit into just one category. Stripe can be a gateway, PSP, PayFac, or acquiring partner. Adyen can be both a PSP and an acquirer, and it also runs much of its own technical stack. Fiserv works in both issuing and acquiring processing. Marqeta is mainly known as an issuing processor. Visa and Mastercard are payment networks, but they also offer token services, fraud tools, and identity products.

When someone in payments says "we are using X," the best question to ask is "for what purpose?" The provider's name does not reveal which function they are performing in that situation. The same provider can be a vendor in one role and a competitor in another, depending on the customer and market.

Function	Main Job	Usually Works For
Payment gateway	Captures and secures payment data	Merchant or PSP
Acquiring processor	Formats, validates, routes, and processes merchant-side transactions	Acquirer or PSP
PSP	Bundles gateway, processing, acquiring access, reporting, and payment methods	Merchant
PayFac	Onboards sub-merchants under a master merchant relationship	Small merchants or platforms
Issuing processor	Runs issuer-side card processing: authorization, limits, lifecycle, PIN services, and reporting	Issuer or fintech program

Sponsor bank	Provides regulated issuing access and network membership	Fintech or platform
Token service provider	Replaces card numbers with tokens	Network, issuer, wallet, or merchant ecosystem
3DS provider	Supports online cardholder authentication flows	Issuer, acquirer, PSP, or merchant
Fraud and risk provider	Scores transactions, identities, devices, or behavior for risk	Merchant, PSP, acquirer, issuer, or network
Terminal / POS provider	Provides acceptance hardware and POS software	Merchant, acquirer, or PSP

Why the Layers Exist

Separating the functions this way makes the ecosystem's structure clearer. These layers exist for three reasons: specialization, scale and certification, and regulation.

The first reason is specialization. Each function in the ecosystem requires deep expertise in cryptographic protocols, network certifications, banking regulations, fraud modeling, and hardware security. Building any one of these well takes years. It would be inefficient for a single bank or merchant to build all of them, especially when specialist providers can serve many customers using the same infrastructure. Over the past sixty years, the card payment system has grown by spinning out, specializing, and then buying back these functions as services.

The second reason is scale and certification. A PSP that connects to many networks, processors, fraud vendors, and payment methods, and offers merchants a single API, gains a significant advantage from scale. The cost of certifying each integration is paid once and spread across many merchants. Smaller companies cannot match this scale, so they buy access instead. The same idea applies to issuing processors, token services, and 3DS providers: certification is expensive, but the cost per customer is low, so the market tends to favor providers who have already paid for certification.

The third reason is regulation and capital efficiency. Sponsor banks exist because banking licenses are costly and slow to get. PayFacs exist because onboarding merchants directly is expensive to do properly. These models make it cheaper to join the card system by moving work into specialized arrangements. The trade-off is complexity: when something goes wrong, responsibility is often spread across several companies rather than clearly resting with one.

The five-party model is the basic structure. The real ecosystem emerges when different companies build on that structure and compete over many years.

You don't need to remember every provider's name. Instead, focus on understanding each function, where it fits in the transaction, and the role a company plays in a given situation.

Chapter 4: Merchant Acquiring

Merchants do not directly use Visa or connect to Mastercard. Instead, they accept cards through an acquiring relationship. An acquiring relationship is a business arrangement with an acquirer that enables merchants to process card payments.

In Chapter 3, we outlined the providers involved in the five-party payment model. This chapter examines one critical component in depth: the acquiring relationship that enables a business to accept card payments as a merchant.

The Acquiring Relationship

An acquirer is a bank or other regulated financial institution licensed by networks such as Visa or Mastercard to enable merchants to accept card payments. Merchants connect to the acquirer either directly or through providers such as a PayFac. In all cases, merchants access the card system under the acquirer's rules, pricing, risk controls, and settlement processes.

The network holds the acquirer responsible for the merchant's activity, even when a PSP, PayFac, gateway, or processor sits between the acquirer and the merchant. Acquiring is therefore more than a technical connection. The acquirer decides whether to work with the merchant, sets the commercial terms, enables payment acceptance, pays the merchant upon settlement, holds reserves as needed, and monitors the merchant once transactions begin.

Merchant access usually follows one of two models. In a direct merchant account, the merchant signs its own agreement with the acquirer, receives its own merchant ID, and can see pricing and settlement details directly. Midsize retailers and large enterprises such as Walmart, Amazon, or Booking.com typically use this model, often with several acquirers across markets.

In an aggregated model, the merchant enters via a PSP or PayFac that maintains the primary acquiring relationship. The merchant is treated as a submerchant under that arrangement. This model is common among small e-commerce sites, sole traders, creators, and small businesses that use mobile readers, because onboarding can be faster and more automated.

Onboarding and Risk Assessment

Before a merchant can accept any card payments, the acquirer must decide whether to work with them. In principle, this could be a fast decision: anyone with a registered business and a bank account could plausibly accept cards. In practice, it never is.

The first step is Know Your Business (KYB). The acquirer checks if a business exists, is legally registered, and has the right licenses. It verifies that the listed operators actually run it. Acquirers review corporate documents, verify addresses, and check tax IDs against public records. Online-only stores get just as much scrutiny as physical ones, and sometimes even more.

Beneficial ownership is checked separately. AML rules require acquirers to identify who actually owns or controls the business. A common threshold is 25 percent ownership or more, though local rules set the exact trigger. Shell companies and front merchants are standard vehicles for laundering and fraud in card systems, so the check protects the acquirer from hidden ownership and disguised activity.

The acquirer also assesses the business model. What does the merchant sell? How quickly is the product delivered after payment? Does the merchant sell subscriptions, travel, event tickets, regulated products, gambling where allowed, adult content, debt collection, or other categories that attract extra scrutiny? Some categories are prohibited by network rules. Others are legal but restricted by the acquirer's own risk policy.

The main concern is future exposure. A merchant can accept payment now for items delivered months later, such as trips or subscriptions. If the merchant fails, customers may dispute transactions after the acquirer has already paid. Risky merchants face higher prices, bigger reserves, slower payouts, and strict monitoring.

For online merchants, reviewing the e-commerce website is part of the onboarding process. Network rules require clear terms and conditions, a visible refund policy, contact details, accurate product descriptions, and a secure checkout. The acquirer checks all these before approval and checks again when risk changes or during periodic review.

During onboarding, the acquirer assigns the merchant a *Merchant Category*

Code (MCC), a 4-digit code that identifies the business type. MCC affects interchange, cardholder controls, rewards, regulatory rules, and how acquirers compare similar merchants. For example, MCC checks can enforce "no gambling" card controls. Wrongly assigned MCCs lead to incorrect pricing, missed risks, and issues such as transaction laundering.

PayFacs do the same checks, but through a shorter process. A small business signs up through an app, uploads documents, and approval can come in hours or minutes. That speed changes the depth of the check, not the accountability. The PayFac remains accountable under its master account for the merchants it chooses to onboard.

Pricing Models

Once the merchant is accepted, the next question is price. The same transaction can be priced differently depending on the acquirer's model. The underlying costs can be similar, but the statement can present them separately or combine them into a single rate.

The main cost is the *Merchant Discount Rate (MDR)*. This is the price merchants pay to accept cards, shown as a percentage of each transaction, sometimes with a fixed fee added. Depending on the pricing model, MDR can include interchange, network fees, acquirer markup, and other costs as one rate or show them separately.

> **MDR vs. Merchant Discount Fee**
>
> Strictly speaking, the Merchant Discount Rate is the percentage rate applied to a transaction, while the *merchant discount fee* is the amount charged. In everyday payments language, *MDR* is often used more broadly to refer to the merchant's overall card acceptance price.

Acquirers usually present card pricing in one of three ways: blended pricing, interchange++, or tiered pricing.

With *blended pricing*, every transaction has the same MDR, regardless of card type or processing method. For example, a small merchant paying 2.5 percent on every transaction uses blended pricing. The acquirer covers the difference between cheaper transactions (such as regulated debit) and more expensive ones (such as premium credit or commercial cards). Blended pricing is easy to budget for and simple to invoice. It can also increase the acquirer's profit, especially if the merchant's transactions are cheaper than the blended rate, which is why it's common among small merchants.

With interchange++ (also called IC++ or interchange-plus-plus), the MDR is split into three parts on the merchant's statement: interchange paid to the issuer, network fees paid to the network, and the acquirer's markup. Larger merchants prefer IC++ because it shows exactly what they're paying for and lets them negotiate the markup, which is the part the acquirer controls.

Tiered pricing sits between blended and IC++. Merchants see a few rates: qualified, mid-qualified, and non-qualified. Transactions are sorted into tiers by card type and processing method. Tiered pricing is common in the US. It is also the least transparent of the three: the tiering logic sits with the acquirer, and the merchant rarely sees the underlying interchange. In the EU and UK, where interchange is regulated, tier differences are smaller, and IC++ and blended are more popular.

Headline card pricing is only part of the cost. Merchants also pay other fees, including statement, gateway, Payment Card Industry (PCI) compliance, terminal rental, batch processing, and chargeback fees. Such charges aren't part of MDR, but over the course of a year, they can exceed headline rates, especially for low-sales merchants.

Small and large merchants buy access to the same card system but want different things. Small businesses prefer simplicity and predictable rates. Large merchants want transparency, bargaining power, and control over routing, reporting, and cost.

In Chapter 6, we put MDR, interchange, network fees, and issuer incentives into the same transaction-level picture.

Merchant Acceptance Setup

After the merchant is accepted and the commercial terms are set, the acquirer or its partners set up the merchant to accept payments through one or more channels.

In-person merchants use certified POS terminals for chip, contactless, and sometimes magnetic stripe payments. The terminals can be branded, leased, or bought, but must be certified for card networks. Modern terminals also accept wallet payments like Apple Pay and Google Pay via near-field communication (NFC) and can connect with POS software for inventory, receipts, and reports.

Online merchants integrate payments via a payment gateway, using an API or a hosted checkout. The gateway collects card data securely and sends it to the processor. Smaller or less technical merchants can use payment links or hosted checkout pages handled entirely by the PSP. Card data never touches their systems, which simplifies PCI compliance.

For subscriptions and recurring billing, the acquirer supports card-on-file transactions. Merchants store tokens linked to the customer's card to charge on a set schedule. Recurring payments follow specific network rules and use transaction-type flags that distinguish them from one-time purchases.

Many merchants also add digital wallets and local payment methods, such as Apple Pay, Google Pay, iDEAL in the Netherlands, BLIK in Poland, or Pix in Brazil. These often sit alongside card acceptance in the same checkout, sometimes via the same PSP and sometimes via separate integrations.

The degree of a merchant's integration with their acquirer affects their bargaining power. A merchant using only one payment channel can easily switch if rates go up. But a merchant integrated across in-person, online, recurring, and local methods will find switching costly and slow. Acquirers know this and set renewal prices accordingly.

Payouts and Reserves

Once the merchant can accept payments, the next operational question is when the funds reach the merchant's bank account. For many card programs, settlement reaches the acquirer within one to two business days. Exact timing depends on network, market, currency, cut-off time, and transaction type. The merchant is paid after that, according to the acquirer's payout schedule.

Most merchants are paid on a set schedule. Transactions accumulate throughout the day, the acquirer batches them, and a net payout is sent to the merchant's bank account one to two business days after settlement. Faster payouts, sometimes even same-day, are available for an extra fee or for low-risk merchants. High-risk merchants often receive slower payouts as a risk-control measure, meaning the acquirer holds their funds for longer.

Merchant payouts usually follow one of two structures. In net settlement, the acquirer deducts its fees from each payout and remits the remaining amount to the merchant. The merchant gets a smaller deposit but has simpler accounting. This is common for small and midsize merchants. In gross settlement, the merchant receives the full transaction amount, and the acquirer issues separate invoices for the fees. Larger merchants often prefer gross settlement because it keeps their gross revenue clear and makes it easier to analyze fees, though they still have to pay the invoices.

In addition to payout timing, the acquirer reserves funds as a buffer against future losses. This is called the *reserve*. A *rolling reserve* means holding back a percentage of every transaction for a set period before releasing it. For example, 5 percent of card sales might be held for 180 days, though the amount and time can vary by merchant risk, market, and acquirer policy. The reserve grows as the merchant processes more transactions and is released gradually as the holding period ends. For instance, a merchant making $1 million a month with a 5 percent rolling reserve held for 180 days would have about $300,000 tied up once the reserve is fully built.

A *fixed reserve* is a lump sum the acquirer holds for the duration of the relationship, often required when onboarding high-risk merchants. The merchant either deposits this amount up front or has it deducted from early payouts until the target is reached, and the acquirer keeps it for the duration of the relationship.

A reserve can frustrate merchants because the sale has already been completed. From the acquirer's view, the risk remains: chargebacks can come months later, and if the merchant is out of business, the acquirer is still responsible. The reserve protects the acquirer while tying up the merchant's working capital. Reserves protect against losses after the sale. Ongoing monitoring tries to detect those risks before they grow.

Ongoing Risk Monitoring

The acquirer's relationship with a merchant doesn't end after onboarding. The acquirer continues to monitor the merchant's transaction patterns and responds if anything changes.

The headline metric is the chargeback ratio — the share of transactions that become chargebacks. Networks have monitoring programs with set limits for chargebacks, fraud, and other risks. Acquirers check each merchant against these limits and their own internal rules.

Each monitoring program sets thresholds for chargebacks, fraud, and other risk signals. If a merchant crosses the relevant limits, the acquirer can impose fines, require a remediation plan, hold larger reserves, restrict certain transaction types, or eventually terminate the relationship. A merchant that loses acquiring because of serious risk issues often struggles to find another acquirer, because the same warning signs tend to follow it.

Refund patterns are watched alongside chargebacks. A merchant with an abnormally high refund volume relative to others in the same MCC may have a generous return policy or be trying to suppress chargebacks by aggressively issuing refunds when customers complain. The intent is hard to prove from the data alone, but the pattern is visible, and persistent anomalies trigger reviews.

Volume spikes require attention regardless of direction. A merchant whose monthly card volume jumps from $50,000 to $500,000 in a week could be seeing a successful campaign, could have launched a new product, or could have had its acquiring credentials compromised by a fraudster running stolen cards through the merchant's account before the acquirer notices. A sudden volume drop can signal business problems, customer issues, or the merchant routing transactions to a different acquirer in preparation for cutting the relationship.

Transaction laundering is one of the more serious patterns acquirers watch for. A merchant approved for one MCC actually processes transactions for a different, higher-risk, restricted, or prohibited business: someone approved as "consulting services" runs volume for online gambling, counterfeit goods, or other categories the acquirer would never have approved. Detection is difficult and depends on cross-referencing transaction patterns, customer complaints, and intelligence from card-issuing banks that see the same transactions on the cardholder side.

The acquirer's relationship with the merchant is not approve-or-reject. It's a continuing assessment. A merchant whose risk profile changes, through their own behavior, through changes in their business, or through external pressure, can be re-priced, asked for a higher reserve, restricted to certain transaction types, or terminated.

Chapter 5: Card Networks and Their Rulebooks

Card payments work because thousands of institutions agree to act as if they were part of a single system.

Issuers need to recognize transactions from unfamiliar merchants, acquirers need to reach issuers they do not know, merchants want an acceptance mark customers trust, and cardholders want a card that works outside their own bank's network, city, or country.

The payment network makes this possible by providing a common operating layer that includes routing, messaging standards, rulebooks, certification, clearing, settlement, fees, and dispute resolution. In Chapter 1, we followed the route a transaction takes. Here, we examine why that route can be trusted.

Routing, Rules, and Shared Obligations

The most obvious job of a payment network is routing. When an acquirer sends an authorization request, it usually does not know the issuer directly. It only knows which network the card uses. The network receives the request, finds the appropriate issuer or processor, and sends the response back in the same way.

Routing, however, is only the surface layer. The real challenge is making sure everyone can understand and trust the messages being sent.

Authorization messages must include certain details, such as amount, currency, merchant category, terminal data, card or token data, and authentication data. Clearing records need enough information for posting, fees, reconciliation, and future disputes. Terminals must follow acceptance rules. Contactless transactions should work consistently. Online transactions need defined message formats for authentication, fraud signals, and authorization.

Certification works the same way. A terminal, processor, issuer platform, acquirer platform, or wallet integration has to prove it works correctly before going live with real transactions. Certification can be slow and frustrating, but it prevents a bigger problem: a global payment system that almost works the same way, but not quite.

Standardization is what lets the system scale. Acquirers do not need custom technical agreements with every issuer, and issuers do not need to support every acquirer's private message format. The network gives both sides a common routing and standards layer.

Rules behind the Brand

A payment network is also a rulebook. The network sets the rules that issuers, acquirers, processors, and merchants must follow. These rules go beyond message routing. They cover card issuance, merchant acceptance, authorization, clearing, settlement, dispute handling, fraud controls, and day-to-day responsibilities.

The rulebook is what turns a group of banks into a working payment system.

> **Rules Are Infrastructure**
>
> At checkout, the rules are invisible. The terminal only shows "Approved" or "Declined." But the message has force because participants have already agreed on what those words mean: when clearing must occur, how fees are calculated, what evidence counts in a dispute, and who bears the loss when something goes wrong. The rulebook turns a message into a shared obligation.

Without shared rules, an approval could mean different things to different participants. One issuer might see it as a firm promise, while another might treat it as tentative. One acquirer might send clearing records after a day, while another might send them after two weeks. One merchant might allow refunds for six months, another might not allow them at all. A cardholder might have dispute rights in one country but not in another.

The network sets a common framework for everyone. Participants can still differ by product, country, risk level, and business agreements, but they all work within the same structure.

The rules also decide who is responsible. If there is a dispute, who provides evidence? If a merchant accepts a card in a risky way, who pays for fraud? If an acquirer signs up a bad merchant, who answers to the network? If an issuer declines too many good transactions, what happens to acceptance? These questions are about responsibility when the system works, fails, or is misused.

The brand is the visible layer. A Visa or Mastercard logo on a card tells the merchant it can be accepted. The same logo on the merchant's window tells the cardholder the card will work there. The mark stands for the rules, standards, routing, settlement, and dispute processes both sides agree to follow, not merely for marketing.

Clearing, Settlement, and Disputes

After authorization, the rulebook continues to govern what the transaction becomes.

First, it sets the economic rules that make the system work across many issuers and acquirers. It publishes interchange structures, charges network fees, and defines how participants calculate obligations. Pricing becomes part of the common operating layer rather than a separate bilateral negotiation for every issuer-acquirer pair.

Second, the network manages the shared framework for clearing and settlement. After acquirers submit clearing records, the network validates them, applies rules and fees, sorts them by issuer, and calculates the net positions that participants must settle.

Third, the network sets up the process for handling disputes. A cardholder might claim they didn't make a transaction. A merchant might say the goods were delivered. An issuer might think the cardholder has a valid claim, while an acquirer might believe the merchant followed the rules. Without a shared process, every dispute would turn into a one-on-one argument.

The network sets the types of disputes allowed, the time limits, the evidence needed, the order of messages, and when liability can shift between issuer, acquirer, merchant, and cardholder. It gives issuers and acquirers a standardized way to handle disagreements without having to start from scratch each time.

In each case, the network reduces bilateral work. Issuers and acquirers do not have to negotiate separate fee logic, settlement procedures, or dispute processes with every counterparty. They join a shared operating layer and follow its rules.

Network Models

Not all card networks use the same business structure. American Express and Discover are often described as three-party schemes, especially in their traditional form. In that model, the scheme has direct relationships with both cardholders and merchants and can combine issuing, acquiring, and network functions within a single organization. The real difference is not simply the number of companies involved. A three-party transaction can still involve processors, merchant service providers, bank partners, co-brand programs, and international licensing. The difference is control: in a five-party model, the network coordinates independent issuers and acquirers; in a three-party model, the scheme can control more of the cardholder-merchant relationship directly.

> **Four-Party Scheme vs Five-Party Model**
>
> Visa and Mastercard are often described as four-party schemes. The four parties are the cardholder, merchant, issuer, and acquirer; the scheme provides the operating layer between them. This book treats the payment network as a visible fifth participant because routing, rules, clearing, settlement, and disputes are central to understanding how transactions work.

Network scope also differs. International networks such as Visa, Mastercard, American Express, JCB, Discover, and UnionPay are designed for cross-border acceptance. A merchant in Mexico can accept a card issued in Japan because both sides connect to the same global network.

Domestic schemes solve a different problem. They operate primarily within a single country and are often linked to local banks, domestic debit products, local regulations, or lower merchant costs. Examples include Girocard in Germany, Cartes Bancaires in France, eftpos in Australia, Interac in Canada, RuPay in India, mada in Saudi Arabia, and Elo in Brazil. Their legal structures, ownership, routing rules, and settlement processes differ, but they show that a card network is not limited to Visa or Mastercard.

Some cards are co-badged. A co-badged card carries two network brands on the same card, often a domestic scheme plus an international network. A local transaction may route through the domestic scheme, while a cross-border transaction may use Visa or Mastercard. Routing can depend on regulation, merchant choice, issuer preference, terminal configuration, and cardholder choice, where local rules allow it.

Network Effects and Switching Costs

A payment network gets more valuable as more people use it because each participant's incentive depends on the others: cardholders want cards that work in many places, merchants want to accept cards that many customers carry, issuers want broad acceptance, and acquirers want to offer the networks their merchants need.

Each side becomes more valuable as the other grows, making the network difficult to displace once it reaches scale.

The logo is just the visible layer. The real work is in the operating layer: routing, standards, rules, clearing, settlement, dispute handling, certification, fraud controls, and economic incentives. A new payment method might lower costs or improve speed, but matching a card network requires building acceptance, trust, risk management, merchant and issuer participation, dispute handling, certification, and operations at scale.

Card networks are hard to replace because the functions are bundled: brand, routing, rules, certification, settlement, dispute handling, and trust. A new method that beats them on one dimension, usually cost or speed, still has to rebuild the others. Most challengers have gotten further with the technology than with participation.

Chapter 6: The Economics of a Card Payment

Emma paid with her card, got her receipt, and left the restaurant. Authorization was only the initial step, and the restaurant did not receive the entire €14.

A small portion of what Emma paid was deducted before reaching the restaurant and was shared among at least two other parties. With billions of transactions daily, these small deductions add up to a huge financial business.

The fee split exists because each participant is doing different work. The cardholder pays for the purchase, the merchant accepts the card, and the acquirer, issuer, and payment network each play a role and get paid for it.

In Chapter 2, we looked at what each party sees and the risks. Here, those risks turn into fees and incentives.

The Fee Split

Emma paid €14 at a restaurant in Tuscany, but the restaurant got less. For easier math, the following examples use €100, but the same principles apply regardless of the amount.

If a customer pays €100 at a shop that accepts Visa, the acquirer deducts a fee (MDR) before depositing the rest into the merchant's account. The MDR is usually a percentage of the sale. In most markets MDR runs between 1 and 3 percent, higher for categories like airlines and gambling, lower for regulated debit transactions in the EU.

For a €100 purchase with a 2 percent MDR, the merchant pays €2 in fees and receives €98. That €2 is divided into two parts, and the split is the heart of card payment economics.

The smaller part, called the *acquirer markup*, is what the acquirer keeps. In this example, that's €0.30. This covers merchant onboarding, terminals or integrations, support, risk monitoring, payout operations, and the acquirer's margin.

The larger part, the *interchange fee*, is paid from the acquirer to the issuing bank. In this example, that's €1.70. The issuer does not bill for it separately. Interchange is embedded in MDR, and the acquirer routes the issuer's share through to the issuer on every transaction.

So, for a simplified €100 purchase: €98 goes to the merchant, €0.30 stays with the acquirer, and €1.70 is passed to the issuer as interchange. In this example, the MDR is the sum of acquirer markup and interchange. Figure 6.1 maps the simplified fee split and previews the other revenue flows discussed later in this chapter.

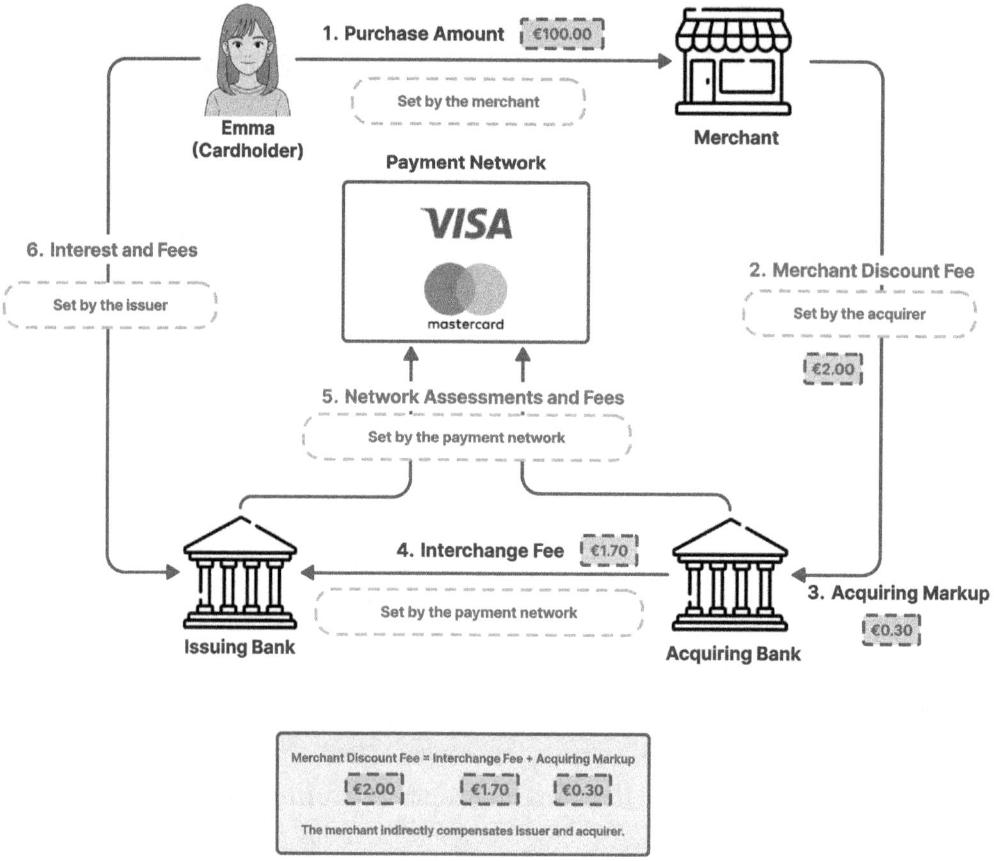

Figure 6.1: The main revenue flows around a €100 card payment.

Issuer Economics

In many card transactions, interchange is the largest component of a merchant's card acceptance costs. In the €100 example, the issuer gets more than the acquirer. This can seem odd, since the acquirer manages the merchant relationship and services, while the issuer is often a bank unknown to the merchant.

The split makes more sense when you look at the issuer's role. Interchange helps fund three things the issuer brings to the transaction: risk bearing, account infrastructure, and, for credit cards, short-term funding.

First, the issuer holds the risk of fraud losses. If a card is stolen and used without authorization, the issuer often absorbs the loss under network and consumer-protection rules. Because fraud is an expected part of card usage, issuers must be compensated for each legitimate transaction to cover these potential costs. Interchange helps fund that risk, even though the rate is not a direct invoice for any single issuer cost.

Second, the issuer runs the account infrastructure. It maintains customer accounts, sends statements, provides customer service, monitors for fraud, handles disputes, applies account controls, and replaces cards as needed. The acquirer has infrastructure too, but the issuer carries the long-term consumer relationship, which is expensive to maintain.

Third, for credit cards, the issuer fronts the money. The merchant is paid within one to three business days of the transaction. The cardholder does not repay the issuer until their statement is due, which could be a month later, and if they pay only the minimum, the issuer carries the debt longer than that. During that period, the issuer's capital is financing purchases. The interchange fee is compensation for that float, on top of any interest the issuer may eventually charge directly.

In the economics of a card payment, interchange is the issuer's transaction-level revenue for making the card usable, managing the account, and bearing part of the risk.

Who Sets Interchange

The interchange fee is set by the payment network, not by individual banks. For each network, region, card product, merchant category, transaction channel, and qualification, the rate is standardized rather than bilaterally negotiated between issuers and acquirers.

Standardizing rates is what lets the network scale. If every issuer-acquirer pair had to negotiate interchange separately, the system would collapse under the burden of its own coordination costs. Standardizing rates enables the network to operate at scale. The trade-off is that interchange isn't set by the market, but by the network, which wants to keep issuers motivated to issue cards and acquirers willing to accept them.

Regulators have intervened in many markets. In the European Union, the Interchange Fee Regulation (IFR) has capped many consumer card interchange fees since 2015: 0.2 percent for debit cards and 0.3 percent for credit cards. The cap applies to consumer card transactions within the EEA. Different rules may apply to commercial cards, some three-party arrangements, ATM withdrawals, or interregional transactions, including separate EU commitments for some non-EEA cards.

> **Interchange Caps and Incentives**
>
> When regulators cap interchange, the visible per-transaction fee falls. The cost rarely vanishes entirely. Issuers can increase other fees, cut rewards, or shift focus to products less impacted by the cap. Merchants might see one fee decrease and another rise. The system's economics usually adjust rather than collapse.

In the United States, the Durbin Amendment, passed as part of the Dodd-Frank Act in 2010 and implemented by the Federal Reserve as Regulation II, caps debit card interchange for banks with more than $10 billion in assets. The current cap is $0.21 plus 0.05 percent of the transaction value, with an additional $0.01 allowed for issuers that meet fraud-prevention standards. The Federal Reserve proposed reducing the cap in 2023, but under the current rule, the cap remains in place. US credit card interchange is not capped in the same way and varies by card type, merchant category, channel, and network rules.

In markets with no caps, interchange is set entirely by the networks. Rates vary by country, card type, and merchant category. In some markets, domestic schemes such as RuPay in India, Elo in Brazil, and other national networks compete with Visa and Mastercard, in part, on interchange.

Premium and rewards cards often have higher interchange than standard cards, especially if interchange is not tightly capped. Rewards programs are often funded by interchange. A 2 percent cashback card needs funding from interchange, annual fees, interest, partner deals, or merchant offers. More generous rewards put more pressure on the card's economics. That is one reason premium and commercial card products remain attractive to issuers, especially where parts of the portfolio fall outside consumer interchange caps.

Regulation changes the incentives in a predictable way. When interchange is capped, issuers earn less per transaction. They often respond by cutting rewards, raising annual fees, or focusing on commercial and premium cards that aren't capped. Whether merchants pass these savings to customers is debated. The answer depends on competition, merchant type, pricing structure, and the size of the regulatory change.

> **Honor-All-Cards Rules**
>
> A merchant that accepts Visa or Mastercard generally cannot choose only the cheapest cards from those networks. If the merchant accepts the brand, it usually has to accept the range of eligible cards carrying that brand, including premium rewards cards that cost more than basic debit cards. That rule gives issuers confidence that their cards will work wherever the brand is accepted, but it also limits merchants' ability to avoid accepting more expensive cards.

Network Fees

Interchange goes to the issuer, and the acquirer's markup stays with the acquirer. The payment network earns through separate network fees, often called *assessments* or scheme fees, that are charged to issuers, acquirers, processors, and other licensed participants. Depending on the merchant's pricing model, those fees are passed through separately or folded into the merchant's overall cost.

Each fee can look small on a single transaction. On a €100 transaction, the network's share is often only a few cents. But because there are so many transactions worldwide, even small fees add up to a huge business. Visa reported processing 257.5 billion transactions on its networks in fiscal 2025. Total Visa-branded payment and cash transactions processed by Visa or other networks reached 329 billion.

Network fees vary by transaction type, geography, and processing model.

They are less standardized and less transparent than interchange, which has led to years of criticism from merchants who find that, year after year, the scheme fees line item on their statements grows faster than their transaction volume.

The payment network does not normally hold cardholder deposits or merchant accounts. Its revenue comes from charging the institutions that use the network: issuers, acquirers, processors, and, in some cases, other licensed participants. It routes information in real time and coordinates settlement later, but its revenue comes from access, transaction processing, brand use, rules, risk tools, and other network services.

In three-party models, the economics work differently. The scheme handles issuing, acquiring, and network functions together, so there is no separate interchange flow between independent banks.

Cardholder Revenue and Credit Economics

Interchange is transaction-level issuer revenue, but it is not the issuer's only source of income. Some revenue comes directly from cardholders, and the mix depends heavily on whether the product is a debit or a credit card.

Debit cards draw on money already held in a checking account. The issuer earns interchange and can also earn account, ATM, or foreign-exchange fees, but there is usually no revolving credit balance. In markets with capped debit interchange, direct transaction revenue is thin. Debit cards can still be valuable because they keep customers active, support account usage, and help retain deposits.

Credit cards add additional revenue streams. Premium, travel, rewards, and business cards often carry annual fees. Foreign-currency purchases may include issuer foreign exchange (FX) markups or foreign transaction fees, often around 1 to 3 percent on standard consumer cards, although many premium and travel cards waive them. Cash advances often carry separate fees and usually start accruing interest immediately.

The largest difference is interest. If the cardholder does not pay the full statement balance by the due date, the issuer charges interest on the revolving balance. Rates vary by market and risk profile, but credit card APRs in many developed markets are high enough that interest is often the single largest revenue line in the credit card business.

The same rails, therefore, hide two different business models. Debit is often about account usage and customer retention. Credit adds funding, credit risk, interest income, rewards economics, and capital management. We return to debit, credit, charge, prepaid, and commercial cards in Part IV.

Merchant Incentives

A merchant paying €2 on every €100 has every reason to ask why. Cash has no MDR. Bank transfers are usually cheaper. But card acceptance is also a sales, operations, and risk decision, not only a payments decision.

Conversion is the first answer. Customers who expect to pay by card and can't will often walk away. In a restaurant, a customer can look for an ATM or choose another place. Online, the effect is sharper: a checkout that does not support the customer's preferred card can lose the sale immediately.

Cards also reduce cash handling. Cash has no MDR, but it has costs: counting, reconciliation, theft, bank deposits, armored transport for larger businesses, robbery risk, and the need to make change. For many merchants, the card fee replaces a set of operational costs that are less visible but still real.

Cards extend reach in a way cash cannot. Tourists, business travelers, and online buyers can pay with a familiar credential without local cash or a local bank account. In many card-present transactions, merchants also get a clearer framework for fraud liability than they would with cash or informal payment methods, though online transactions can shift more risk back to the merchant.

The MDR is a real cost. But the alternative is lost sales, higher cash-handling costs, more operational friction, and weaker access to international customers. For most merchants, accepting cards is less about liking the fee and more about avoiding the cost of not accepting them.

The balance is not perfect and is often contested by merchants, banks, networks, regulators, and consumer groups. But the system lasts because each participant has a reason to stay in it: merchants gain sales and operational convenience; acquirers earn merchant revenue; issuers receive interchange, interest, and customer engagement; networks get transaction volume and control over the rulebook; and cardholders get a payment method that works in many places.

With the parties, providers, network rules, and economics in place, Part II of this book turns to the object that brings a transaction into the system: the card itself.

Part II

Inside the Card

Chapter 7: The Evolution of the Card

A modern payment card is a small object that carries the history of card payments in its features: a logo, a number, an expiry date, a chip, a contactless symbol, and sometimes a metal body.

Cards did not acquire these features all at once. Each layer appeared because an older version of the card had reached a limit. Store credit was only valid at one merchant. Charge cards expanded acceptance but required a company to act as an intermediary between the customer and the merchant. Bank cards scaled issuance but needed shared rules and routing. Magnetic stripes made cards machine-readable but easy to copy. EMV chips made counterfeit fraud harder. Contactless shortened checkout. Mobile wallets and virtual cards reduced the reliance on plastic payment credentials.

Card history is easiest to follow as a sequence of constraints. The card changed whenever the system needed to solve a new problem: recognition, acceptance, scale, machine readability, fraud, speed, online use, or software issuance.

Figure 7.1: The evolution of the card.

1920s–1950s: Store Credit and Charge Plates

In the early 1900s, many payment credentials were tied to a single business. Retailers, hotels, oil companies, and other merchants offered store credit to their own customers, but the credential, whether a paper card, charge coin, or metal charge plate, usually worked only with the business that issued it. The merchant knew the customer, recorded the purchase, and billed the customer later. Back then, a *card* was not a ticket to a global payment system. It showed a credit relationship with one merchant.

Some early systems used charge plates, which were small metal plates stamped with the customer's details. At checkout, the cashier used a mechanical imprinter to press the plate's details onto a paper slip, making a record of the account. The merchant kept the slip, updated their records, and billed the customer later.

Charge plates solved a basic problem: they let a merchant recognize a customer and record a purchase without having to write everything by hand.

The limitation was that the solution worked only within a single merchant's business. A store's charge plate did not help the same customer pay at another store. It did not create a shared acceptance network, send anything to a bank, or request real-time approval from an issuer. Early cards were still linked to a local business relationship, so the next step was making a card useful at more than one merchant.

1950: Diners Club and Shared Acceptance

In 1950, Diners Club introduced what is widely treated as the first multipurpose charge card. Its original use case was narrow: restaurant and travel spending by business customers. But the underlying idea was much bigger.

The important change was acceptance across merchants: a cardholder could carry one card and use it at participating restaurants and hotels. The card company stood between the customer and the merchant, handling billing on one side and merchant payment on the other.

That changed the relationship between customer and merchant. Merchants no longer had to know each customer personally. Customers did not need a separate credit relationship with every merchant. The card company set up the acceptance, billed the customer, and paid the merchant after taking a fee.

Looking back, this was an early move toward separating the roles described in

Part I. The customer, merchant, and card company no longer had to repeat the same relationship at every store. A card could now be a portable credential accepted by many merchants.

Diners Club was a charge card, not a modern revolving credit card. Cardholders had to pay the full balance. But the business model already had three sides: merchants accepted the card because it brought in customers and made payments easier; cardholders liked the convenience; and the card company earned money by serving as the link between the two sides.

The card was no longer just proof of a relationship with one merchant. It was becoming a way to access a wider network of acceptance.

1958–1966: Bank Cards and the Network Model

The next step was scale. American Express launched its charge card in 1958, requiring cardholders to pay the balance in full each month. That same year, Bank of America launched BankAmericard, which helped establish the bank-issued credit card as a mass-market product. Together, these developments moved cards from merchant-specific or travel-and-entertainment products toward bank-issued network cards.

A single card company could build relationships with merchants and cardholders, but banks were better positioned to issue cards widely. Banks already managed customer accounts, checked credit risk, handled billing, and worked within the regulated financial system. If banks could issue cards that worked at many merchants, cards could grow from a travel-and-entertainment product into a mainstream payment tool.

By 1976, BankAmericard had become Visa. Mastercard grew out of the Interbank Card Association, formed in 1966. The card business was moving from local and national programs toward global network brands.

At this stage, the card began to resemble the system described in Part I. The cardholder had an issuer, the merchant had an acquirer, and the network provided the shared operating layer. The card was the visible item that allowed the transaction to enter the system: the credential connecting the cardholder, issuer, merchant, acquirer, and network.

The acceptance mark became more important, too. A Visa or Mastercard logo showed merchants that the card was part of a trusted system. It told cardholders that the merchant could accept their card. The logo stood for rules, routing, settlement, dispute processes, and business agreements, not merely for branding.

The card had moved from a merchant-specific identifier to a network credential.

1960s–1970s: Revolving Credit and Machine-Readable Cards

As bank card programs grew in the 1960s and 1970s, the card business changed in two ways at once. The card became a lending product, and it became easier for machines to read.

The business change was revolving credit. A charge card requires the cardholder to pay the full balance every month. A revolving credit card lets the cardholder carry a balance and pay interest on any amount not paid by the due date. This changed how card issuing worked financially.

For issuers, the card was no longer just a payment tool. It became a lending product. Issuers could earn interchange when the card was used, fees from cardholders, and interest on revolving balances. This made credit cards especially attractive to banks in markets where regulations allowed them to make a profit.

For cardholders, revolving credit changed the purpose of the card. It lets them avoid carrying cash and spread spending over time. The convenience came with risk: interest charges, late fees, and minimum payments could turn a payment tool into long-term debt.

At the same time, scale created a technical problem: manual processing started to slow things down. Early card transactions often used paper slips, embossed numbers, signatures, printed lists of stolen card numbers, and, later, manual or phone authorization. This process worked for small volumes, but it was slow, labor-intensive, and error-prone. The industry needed machines to automatically capture card details. The answer was the magnetic stripe.

A magnetic stripe on the back of the card could store the card number, expiry date, service code, and other details needed for a transaction. A terminal could read the stripe faster and more reliably than a clerk copying numbers by hand. This sped up checkout and helped move card payments toward electronic approval.

The Iron and the Magnetic Stripe

In the late 1960s and early 1970s, IBM engineers were trying to solve a surprisingly physical problem: how to bond magnetic tape to a plastic card without destroying the card.

Forrest Parry, one of the engineers working on the project, kept finding that the heat needed to attach the tape warped the plastic. According to the story, he came home frustrated, and his wife suggested trying a household iron. The iron applied enough heat to bond the tape without melting the card.

The anecdote is almost too neat, but it captures the real engineering challenge. The breakthrough was storing data on magnetic tape and making that data durable enough for wallets, counters, terminals, heat, pressure, and thousands of swipes.

The magnetic stripe was a major step forward. It made transactions faster, improved routing, reduced manual work, and helped cards become common at checkout. Its built-in weakness was that the data was static: if someone copied the stripe data, they could reuse it. This problem grew as fraudsters learned to skim cards and to make counterfeit magnetic stripe cards.

As counterfeit fraud increased, the industry needed a card that could do more than repeat the same data.

1970s: Electronic Authorization

By the 1970s, card payments were also moving toward electronic approval. Instead of relying on delayed checks, paper records, or manual calls, a terminal could send a transaction request through the acquiring side, across the network, and to the issuer. The issuer could then check the card status, available funds or credit, account rules, and fraud signals, and send back an approval or decline.

In Chapter 1, we introduced authorization as the issuer's real-time decision. Electronic authorization made that decision part of the checkout experience.

This change turned the card from a simple identifier into part of a real-time decision system. Even then, the card still did not hold the cardholder's money or pay the merchant instantly. But it carried the data needed to ask the issuer whether this transaction should be accepted.

Electronic authorization made card payments faster, safer, and easier to scale. It also made the network more important, since it had to reliably carry messages between institutions that didn't know each other directly.

The card had now become part of an information system.

1990s–2000s: EMV and Chip Cards

Before EMV became the global chip-card standard, France was an early leader in chip payment cards in the 1980s, with trials and broader deployment later that decade. That early migration showed where the industry was heading: the card could become an active security device rather than just a carrier of stored data.

EMV later turned that idea into a global card standard. The specifications emerged in the 1990s, while migration to chip cards unfolded over different timelines across markets.

> **What EMV Stands For**
>
> EMV originally stood for Europay, Mastercard, and Visa, the companies behind the first version of the standard. The name stayed even after the governance expanded. Today, EMVCo manages EMV specifications in collaboration with the major global card networks.

The historical shift was straightforward: instead of relying only on data read from the card, the terminal and chip could interact during the transaction. That made counterfeit card-present fraud harder in markets where chip cards became the norm.

EMV did not eliminate fraud. No payment technology does. Fraud moved toward weaker points: online transactions, social engineering, account takeover, merchant fraud, and markets or terminals where fallback remained available. But the card became harder to counterfeit at the point of sale.

2000s–2010s: Contactless Payments

By the 2000s, networks and issuers were pushing another change at the point of sale: contactless payments. The chip improved security, but inserting a card and waiting for the terminal-card interaction could be slower than swiping. In high-volume environments, even small delays reduce throughput. Transit gates, grocery stores, quick-service restaurants, stadiums, and convenience retail all depend on speed.

Contactless payments changed how people interacted with payment terminals: instead of inserting the card, the cardholder taps the card near the reader. The card and terminal communicate over NFC, a short-range radio technology. The transaction can still use EMV-style dynamic data, but the user experience is faster.

Mastercard PayPass and Visa payWave became two of the most visible branded contactless implementations in the 2000s. For merchants and cardholders, the brands gave a new behavior a simple label: tap to pay.

Contactless was more than just a convenience. It addressed a practical question: how can the system keep card-present payments secure while speeding up checkout?

That speed required new controls. Many markets introduced no-CVM thresholds, where low-value contactless transactions could proceed without PIN entry. Issuers and networks added limits, counters, step-up rules, and risk controls to decide when a cardholder should be asked for verification.

Contactless prompts can therefore seem inconsistent to cardholders. One tap might go through without a PIN, another might ask for a PIN, a mobile wallet tap might use Face ID or Touch ID, and a transit payment might work differently again.

The variation comes from risk controls: the system is trying to balance speed, fraud prevention, and cardholder verification.

2010s: Mobile Wallets and Tokenized Cards

In the 2010s, mobile wallets brought tokenized card payments into everyday consumer use. A mobile wallet does not simply store a photograph or a copy of the plastic card. It can present a device-specific payment credential while keeping the real card number away from merchants and terminals. This reduced a major weakness of plastic cards and basic online card entry: exposing the same card number in too many places.

Wallets also changed cardholder verification. Instead of proving cardholder presence by entering a PIN at the terminal, the cardholder can unlock the device with a face scan, fingerprint, or passcode. That's how a wallet transaction can be fast while still supporting strong cardholder verification.

Chapter 11 explains wallet tokenization in detail. At this point in history, the important shift is that wallets moved the card credential from plastic to a device.

Late 2010s–2020s: Virtual Cards

Virtual cards existed well before the late 2010s, especially in corporate, travel, procurement, and online payment use cases. What changed in the late 2010s and 2020s was the wider adoption of software-issued credentials across consumer fintech, business spend management, and instant card issuance.

The physical card remained useful for stores, ATMs, hotels, and travel. Its limits were becoming harder to ignore: it had to be manufactured, shipped, activated, replaced, and carried.

A virtual card separates the payment credential from the plastic card. It can be issued instantly in an app, used online immediately, and created for a specific purpose, merchant, employee, subscription, travel booking, or spending limit. It may have its own card number, expiry date, security code, and controls, even if no physical card is ever produced.

The card no longer has to be a physical object in a wallet. It can be issued, displayed, controlled, and replaced as a software credential.

A virtual card still uses card rails, has an issuer, enters authorization, clearing, and settlement, and follows network rules. What changes is the credential: it can be created, controlled, and replaced much more flexibly than plastic.

For businesses, virtual cards became especially useful. A company can issue a virtual card for a single supplier, campaign, employee, or transaction type. Controls can be applied to that specific card number. If it is compromised, it can be blocked or replaced without disrupting the whole account relationship.

Virtual cards continue the larger shift in card history: the credential now does more work than the plastic.

2020s: Tap-to-Phone and Software-Based Acceptance

By the late 2010s and early 2020s, the same software shift was also reaching the merchant side. For many years, accepting cards required special terminal hardware. Merchants needed a card reader, certification, connectivity, and a relationship with an acquirer or payment provider. That hardware is still common and important, but now card acceptance is also moving into software.

Tap-to-phone services, such as Apple's Tap to Pay on iPhone, allow a compatible smartphone or tablet to accept contactless card and wallet payments without a separate traditional terminal. For small merchants, this lowers the barrier to card acceptance. A sole trader, delivery worker, market seller, or mobile service provider can accept a tap using a device they already carry.

This changes the form factor, not the underlying payment structure. The acquiring relationship, network rules, and security requirements still remain. The acceptance device becomes software running on general-purpose hardware.

2020s and Beyond: Invisible and Biometric Payments

The newest phase is the gradual shift of card credentials into places where plastic cards are no longer presented: wearables, merchant apps, stored credentials, biometric checkout, and background payments.

A ride-hailing trip ends, and the charge happens in the background. A subscription renews without a checkout. A wearable taps at a terminal. A biometric system lets a customer pay with a palm or fingerprint linked to stored payment data. A merchant app saves the payment details and charges them later. In each case, the card is absent from the customer's hand, but the underlying payment method can still be a card or network token.

The modern card is no longer tied to one object. It can appear as a plastic card, a virtual card, a wallet token, a stored credential, a wearable, or a background payment method.

From Plastic to Credential

The history of cards is not a list of inventions. It is a sequence of trade-offs.

Store credit helped merchants identify trusted customers, but it did not scale beyond a single merchant. Diners Club widened acceptance, but it required an intermediary between the cardholder and the merchant. Bank card networks scaled issuance and acceptance, but they required shared rules, routing, settlement, and dispute processes. Magnetic stripes made cards machine-readable, but easier to copy. EMV made counterfeit card-present fraud harder, but added more complex terminal-card interaction. Contactless made checkout faster, but required new verification and risk controls. Wallets and virtual cards reduced dependence on plastic but introduced questions about token, device, and credential lifecycles. Each new layer solved one problem and exposed the next.

The card has lasted because the credential behind the plastic keeps changing. The system has adapted to new materials, data formats, security models, devices, and acceptance channels. The basic structure remains: the cardholder presents a credential, the merchant submits the transaction, and the issuer decides whether to accept it.

Chapter 8 moves from the card's history to the card in your hand: the details printed on it, the data stored in it, and the parts of the credential the cardholder never sees.

Chapter 8: Anatomy of a Card

Take a payment card out of your wallet and look at it for a few seconds.

You might see a bank name, a network logo, a card number, an expiry date, a chip, and a contactless symbol. On the back, there is often a magnetic stripe, a signature panel, a short security code, and a support phone number. Cards can be made of plastic or metal. Some hide the card number on the back, or show none at all. Virtual cards do not have a physical form.

Each feature of the card has a job: identifying the card, telling the merchant which network can process it, helping machines read it, supporting security checks, or preserving older acceptance methods that have not fully disappeared.

Cards as Payment Credentials

Before looking at the card number, chip, stripe, and security code, let's clarify what the card actually is.

Cash is easy to understand. A €20 note has value because the note itself is handed over. If a customer pays cash at a restaurant, the restaurant receives the money immediately.

A card works differently. It does not contain euros, dollars, or points. It does not give the merchant direct access to the cardholder's bank account or carry a live copy of the balance.

A card is a payment credential. It carries the data needed to start a transaction, but the issuer still decides whether to approve it. The card may link to a debit account, a credit line, a prepaid balance, a charge-card account, or another funding arrangement, but it does not move money on its own.

When the cardholder taps, inserts, swipes, or enters card details online, the merchant can initiate a request. If the issuer approves it, the transaction still has to be cleared and settled between institutions before the merchant is paid.

The card is just one way to present payment credentials. The same underlying account might be accessed via a physical card, a virtual card, a mobile-wallet token, or a stored credential. Each method allows you to use the account, but they differ in form and security.

Front-Side Features

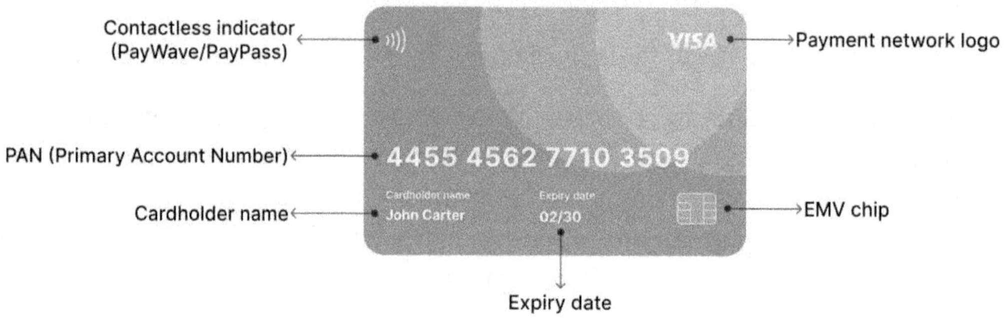

Figure 8.1: The front of a payment card.

The front of the card is designed for both people and machines. The issuer name identifies the bank or financial institution that issued the card. In a fintech program, the brand on the card may differ from the regulated institution that issues it. A fintech may control the app and customer experience while a sponsor bank or licensed issuer sits behind the program.

The network logo indicates where the card can be accepted and which network or scheme can process the transaction. Visa, Mastercard, American Express, Discover, JCB, UnionPay, RuPay, Girocard, Cartes Bancaires, and other schemes use acceptance marks to indicate that a card can be used on a specific network or domestic scheme. The logo is small, but it stands for routing, rules, certification, clearing, settlement, and dispute procedures.

Some cards show the cardholder's name. That wording is deliberate: cardholder, not card owner. In many card programs, the card remains the property of the issuer. The cardholder is the person or business authorized to use it.

Many modern cards move the cardholder's name, card number, and expiry date to the back of the card or remove them altogether, expecting the cardholder to view them in an app.

Most modern cards also show a chip contact plate. The visible gold or silver plate is not the whole chip. The contact interface allows the terminal to communicate with the chip beneath it.

If the card supports tap-to-pay, it usually bears the contactless symbol: four curved lines resembling a sideways Wi-Fi mark. The symbol tells the cardholder that the card can be tapped at a compatible terminal. The antenna that makes this possible is hidden inside the card body.

Card Number (PAN)

Figure 8.2: PAN structure.

Figure 8.2 separates the PAN into the issuer-identifying prefix, account identifier, and check digit. The long card number is formally known as the *Primary Account Number (PAN)*. Despite the name, the PAN is not necessarily the same as a bank account number. It's the main card number used inside the card payment system. Many Visa and Mastercard cards have 16 digits, but the PAN length can vary by network and product, typically ranging from 13 to 19 digits.

The PAN is structured, not just randomly assigned. The first digit, the Major Industry Identifier (MII), indicates the issuer's industry category. Visa cards often start with 4, many Mastercard cards with 5 or 2, and American Express cards with 3. However, modern ranges are more complex, so 1 digit no longer uniquely identifies a network.

The first 6–8 digits identify the issuer or card program. This range is known as either the *BIN (Bank Identification Number)* or the *IIN (Issuer Identification Number)*. These terms refer to the same identifier and act as the routing clue for the acquiring bank.

After the BIN/IIN comes the account identifier. This part distinguishes one card or card account from another within the issuer's number range. The exact structure is defined by the issuer and its processor.

The last digit, called the *check digit*, is calculated using the Luhn algorithm. Its purpose is not to prevent fraud, but to catch common input mistakes.

If a cardholder types a card number incorrectly at checkout, the Luhn check usually fails before the transaction ever reaches the issuer. The merchant or gateway can reject the malformed number immediately, rather than sending a useless authorization request through the system.

> **How the Luhn Check Works**
>
> When a card number is entered, the system can perform a quick mathematical check to see whether the number is structurally valid.
>
> Starting from the right, every second digit is doubled. If doubling produces a 2-digit number, the digits are added together (or equivalently, 9 is subtracted from values greater than 9). All digits are then summed.
>
> If the total is a multiple of 10, the number passes the Luhn check.
>
> For example, changing a single digit by mistake will usually cause the calculation to fail, allowing the error to be detected immediately.

The PAN is the card system's primary identifier. It can be printed, typed, read from a chip, encoded on a stripe, routed, checked, and, where needed, replaced by a token.

The PAN is also sensitive information. When combined with the expiry date and security code, it can be enough to attempt online fraud. Modern card security focuses on limiting where the real PAN is exposed.

Expiry Date

The expiry date looks like a minor detail: month and year, usually written as MM/YY. But it does several practical jobs.

First, it gives the issuer a renewal cycle. Cards wear out. Chips fail. Network rules change. Issuers redesign products. Security practices improve. The expiry date forces the card to be refreshed.

Second, it limits the life of exposed card details. If a card number and expiry date leak, that exact combination should eventually stop working. This isn't enough security on its own, but it reduces the useful lifetime of stolen data.

Third, the expiry date is part of transaction data. In many transaction types, the merchant or terminal sends the expiry date along with the PAN. If the date is wrong, the issuer may decline the transaction.

The card is usually valid through the last day of the month shown. A card marked 08/30 normally remains valid until the end of August 2030, unless the issuer blocks or replaces it earlier.

The expiry date applies to the card credential, not necessarily to the customer relationship. The card may expire while the underlying account continues. The issuer can send a replacement card with a new expiry date and, depending on the case, a new security code or a new PAN.

Back-Side Features

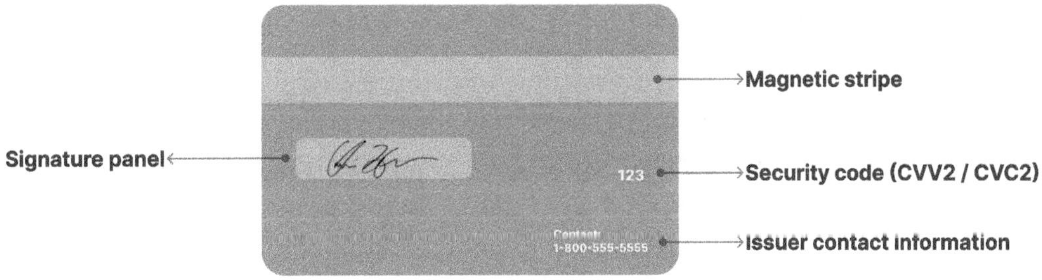

Figure 8.3: The back of a payment card.

The back of the card combines older technology, security information, and a way to contact the issuer.

The band across the back of the card is the magnetic stripe. For decades, it was the primary method terminals used to read card data at the point of sale. Even after EMV chips became common, many cards continued to carry a stripe for compatibility, as a fallback, or in markets where stripe acceptance remained available.

The signature panel comes from an older world of cardholder verification, where the cardholder signed the card, and the receipt, and the merchant compared the two. In practice, signature checking was inconsistent: some merchants scrutinized signatures, while many ignored them. Chip-and-PIN, contactless rules, online authentication, and issuer fraud systems now carry the weight that handwritten signatures once did.

The short security code (CVV2/CVC2) is used mainly for online, phone, and mail-order transactions. Its label and placement differ by network, but the purpose is the same: to provide a value printed or displayed separately from the PAN.

The back may also include issuer support information, such as a website, phone number, or instructions for reporting a lost or stolen card. That information is not part of the transaction itself, but it gives the cardholder a route to the issuer when the card is blocked, damaged, or questioned.

Magnetic Stripe

The *magnetic stripe* is a strip of magnetic material that stores card data in a machine-readable form. It usually contains three tracks, though modern card payments primarily use Track 1 and Track 2. Track 3 is rarely used in payment-card transactions. The stripe encodes the PAN, expiry date, service code, and a stripe-specific security value (CVV1).

The magnetic stripe was useful because it made card data easy for terminals to read. However, its weakness is that the data is mostly static. If someone copies the stripe data, they can use it again at places that still accept magnetic stripe transactions.

That same weakness explains its modern role: in card-present payments, the stripe is mostly a legacy fallback. It remains on many cards for compatibility, but its static data model is no longer secure.

EMV Chip

The *EMV chip* is the small secure component that changed card-present security. To the cardholder, the visible part is the metallic contact plate on the front of the card. Underneath that plate is a microprocessor. It can store application data and perform cryptographic operations during a transaction.

This is what makes it different from the magnetic stripe: a stripe gives the terminal the same data each time it's read. A chip can produce transaction-specific data that helps the issuer decide whether a genuine card is present.

The chip stores and uses several kinds of data: PAN, expiry date, application data, card configuration, and cryptographic material. Each issuer and network decides which applications and configuration data belong on the chip.

The chip supports both contact payments, where the card is inserted into the terminal, and contactless payments, where the card communicates via NFC. It can also support multiple payment applications. In some markets, a debit card may carry both a domestic application and an international network application on the same physical card.

Contactless Antenna

A contactless card has a part that the cardholder cannot see: an antenna embedded inside the card body. When the card is brought close to a compatible terminal, the card's antenna enables it to communicate with the terminal via NFC. The contactless symbol on the card tells the cardholder that this hidden interface is available and that the card can be tapped at a compatible reader.

Contactless cards also change how people use them. The cardholder does not hand over the card or leave it in a terminal. Instead, they tap and remove it quickly. This speed helped contactless payments become popular in places like transit, grocery stores, stadiums, cafés, and other locations where faster checkout changes the flow.

In Chapter 10, we follow that contactless interaction in detail.

Security Code

The security code gives the issuer an additional value to check when a terminal does not read the physical card. It helps show that the person entering the card details has access to information that merchants are not supposed to store after authorization.

Visa commonly refers to the printed code as the Card Verification Value 2 (CVV2), while Mastercard uses the Card Validation Code 2 (CVC2). American Express uses its own placement and naming conventions.

The security code is not a PIN or a password. Anyone who has access to the card, its image, or virtual card details can see it. It is a useful signal, but not a complete authentication method.

In Chapter 15, we separate the security-code family: CVV1 or CVC1 on the magnetic stripe, CVV2 or CVC2 for card-not-present use, and dynamic values used in some chip, contactless, or related transaction contexts.

Cardholder Name and Signature

The cardholder's name and signature may feel personal, but they are no longer the primary components of card security.

The name shows who is authorized to use the card. It may help with manual checks, travel bookings, corporate cards, business cards, receipts, and support. But most modern card transactions do not rely heavily on the name printed on the card.

> **The Name on the Card Is Usually Not Checked**
>
> Online checkout forms often ask for the name on the card, but standard card authorization typically does not verify that name. The issuer mainly checks data such as the PAN, expiry date, security code, card status, available funds or credit, fraud signals, and, where supported, address data. The name can still be useful later in merchant records, customer support, fraud review, or dispute evidence. But in most ordinary card authorizations, a typo in the name doesn't determine whether the transaction is approved or declined.

The signature is even weaker. It belongs to a world where the merchant could compare the receipt signature with the card signature. That process was slow, subjective, and often ignored.

The name and signature are still part of the card design because payment systems change slowly. Old practices do not disappear right away when better controls are introduced. They stay on cards, receipts, terminals, rules, and habits long after they stop being important.

Modern card security relies more on chip data, PIN, contactless limits, online authentication, tokenization, and issuer fraud monitoring.

Layers of a Card

The word *card* often hides several different layers. There is the physical object: the plastic or metal in the cardholder's hand. There is the card account: the issuer-side record that defines the card's status, limits, product type, expiry date, and authorization rules. There is a funding source behind it: a debit account, a credit line, a prepaid balance, a charge card account, or another funding arrangement. And there is the payment credential: the PAN, token, or wallet credential used to initiate a transaction.

These layers can change independently. A physical card can be replaced while the card account remains open. A debit card can point to the same deposit account after the plastic changes. A mobile wallet uses a token instead of the real PAN. A virtual card may exist without any plastic at all. A stored credential may keep a subscription running even after the cardholder no longer remembers the original checkout.

This distinction explains many everyday card experiences. A lost plastic card can be replaced without closing the account. A phone can be removed from a wallet without blocking the physical card. A card can expire while some recurring payments continue through account updater services. A card number can change while the customer relationship continues.

That is why *card* can refer to an object, a credential, a number, a set of rules, or an account relationship. The issuer connects those pieces.

A payment card gives different parties different information. The cardholder sees a familiar object. The merchant sees a network brand and acceptance method. The terminal reads a stripe, a chip, a contactless signal, or card details entered by the user. The issuer receives structured data that it can use for routing, security checks, and authorization.

The magnetic stripe and the EMV chip may sit on the same card, but they use very different security models. In Chapter 9, we examine that difference: the move from reusable stored data to transaction-specific proof.

Chapter 9: The Magnetic Stripe and the EMV Chip

A payment card can have both a magnetic stripe on the back and an EMV chip on the front, allowing terminals to read the card for a card-present transaction. The stripe returns stored data, while the chip generates transaction-specific proof. That difference fundamentally changed card-present security.

Before terminals could read cards electronically, card payments involved more manual work. A clerk imprinted the card onto a paper slip, checked a signature, looked up a printed list of stolen card numbers, or called for authorization. That worked when card acceptance was limited. It broke down as transaction volume grew.

The magnetic stripe changed what the terminal could do: read card data automatically instead of relying on a cashier to copy it by hand. A terminal could capture the card number, expiry date, service code, and other data directly from the stripe. This sped up checkout, reduced errors, and moved card payments from paper slips to electronic authorization.

Magnetic Stripe Data

The magnetic stripe usually has three tracks, though card payments primarily use Tracks 1 and 2.

Track 1 contains the PAN, cardholder name, expiry date, service code, and discretionary data. It has more room and can include alphabetic characters, which is why it can carry the cardholder's name.

Track 2 is the workhorse: compact, used for most authorization processing, carrying the PAN, expiry date, service code, and either CVV1 or CVC1.

Track 3 exists, but it's rarely used in modern payment-card transactions.

The *service code* is invisible to the cardholder but important to the terminal and issuer. It tells the system how the card can be used. For example, it can indicate whether the chip should be used when available, whether international transactions are allowed, and what type of authorization or cardholder verification is required.

CVV1 is hidden on the stripe and secures magnetic-stripe transactions. It differs from CVV2/CVC2, which are printed on the back of the card and are used for online purchases.

The stripe's strength became its weakness: it made card data easier for terminals to read, making it easier to copy. If a fraudster captures the magnetic-stripe data, they can encode it onto another card. To a terminal that still accepts stripe transactions, the counterfeit card can look like the original.

This copying is called *skimming*. A compromised terminal, an ATM attachment, or a hidden reader can capture the stripe data. The fraudster then uses that data to create another magnetic-stripe card.

Issuer fraud systems can still look for suspicious signals, such as unusual locations, spending patterns, transaction speed, amount, or card status. But the stripe itself only identifies the card. It does not provide evidence that the genuine card is present.

EMV Chip

EMV was designed to close that gap. An EMV chip is not just an improved version of a magnetic stripe: the stripe stores data; the chip can compute.

Under the contact plate is a microprocessor with secure storage and payment applications. When the card is inserted, the terminal and chip exchange data. The chip can use transaction details, terminal data, issuer configuration, counters, and cryptographic keys stored securely on the card to produce data for that transaction.

In an online EMV authorization, the key cryptogram is the Authorization Request Cryptogram (ARQC). The chip creates it using transaction data and cryptographic material stored securely on the card. The issuer or its processor can check it during authorization.

The cryptogram is transaction-specific because it uses two changing inputs. One is the Application Transaction Counter (ATC), which increases with each transaction and can help the issuer spot suspicious gaps, repeats, or patterns.

Another is the unpredictable number from the terminal, which gives the chip new input for the calculation.

Copying chip data is not enough. A copied response from one purchase will not work for another, because variables such as amount, terminal data, counters, and unpredictable numbers change from one transaction to the next.

This model applies to both contact and contactless chip payments. A contact chip transaction occurs when the card is inserted into the terminal, and the contact plate connects to the reader. A *contactless transaction* uses the card's NFC antenna for a shorter, time-limited exchange, often with different limits and verification rules. The interface changes, but the security principle remains: the card participates in the transaction instead of merely repeating stored data.

EMV reduced counterfeit card-present fraud by making copied card data much harder to reuse at the point of sale. It did not eliminate fraud, but it pushed attackers toward weaker points: online transactions, social engineering, account takeover, merchant fraud, and terminals or markets where fallback remained available.

Magnetic Stripe Fallback

Many cards still have magnetic stripes because old acceptance paths do not disappear all at once. Some countries, terminals, and ATMs still rely on the stripe, and many issuers keep it as a backup when chip reading fails.

That backup path is called *fallback*. The terminal tries to read the chip first. If the chip transaction cannot continue, and if the transaction rules allow fallback, the terminal asks the cardholder to swipe the magnetic stripe instead. The authorization request then uses stripe data rather than chip-generated EMV data, usually with indicators showing that a fallback occurred.

Fallback keeps legitimate transactions from failing when the chip cannot be read, but it also gives fraudsters something to exploit. A fraudster may try to force a transaction back to weaker magnetic-stripe acceptance, where copied stripe data can still be useful. Issuers and networks watch fallback patterns for this reason: if a card repeatedly fails chip reading and then succeeds as a stripe transaction, that is a warning sign.

Liability Shift

Moving to EMV was as much a coordination problem as a technical one. Terminals, cards, processors, and issuer systems all needed upgrades. Someone had to pay for new terminals, issue new cards, and certify new systems. Merchants and banks do not usually make those investments just because a new standard exists.

The liability shift supplied the incentive by changing who bears the loss when fraud occurs. In EMV migrations, if a merchant accepts a stripe transaction when a chip should have been used, the merchant or acquirer bears counterfeit-fraud losses. If a bank didn't issue a chip card, it remains at risk.

Card networks often encourage change by adjusting incentives rather than only publishing technical rules. Liability shifts helped turn EMV from a technical standard into a commercial necessity.

Limits of Card-Present Security

The move from magnetic stripe to EMV was a move from stored data to transaction-specific proof. A magnetic stripe identifies the card by repeating the same values. That is also its weakness: once copied, the data can be reused. An EMV chip changes the model by producing proof for a particular transaction, using inputs that change each time.

That proof is strongest when the card is present at a terminal. Online, the chip usually disappears from the chain of evidence. The cardholder enters the card number, expiry date, and security code, or uses saved card details. The issuer then has to rely on other signals: possession of card data, device information, merchant context, fraud scoring, and, when needed, additional cardholder authentication.

EMV made physical card cloning less attractive, but it did not make stolen card data useless online. Fraud moved toward places where reusable data still had value: e-commerce, social engineering, account takeover, merchant fraud, and markets or terminals where fallback remained available.

The rest of the card system keeps adapting to the same pressure. Contactless payments preserve transaction-specific proof while shortening the terminal interaction. Mobile wallets add device-bound tokens. Online authentication adds extra evidence when the card is not physically present.

Contactless payments are the next version of this trade-off: they keep tap-and-go fast without falling back to weak, reusable card data.

Chapter 10: Contactless Payments and NFC

Contactless payments made everyday card payments faster. Instead of inserting the card or handing it to the cashier, the cardholder simply taps, hears a beep, and moves on. Often, there's no need for a signature or PIN. Whether in grocery stores, cafés, stadiums, or metro stations, even saving a second per transaction makes a difference.

A contactless payment isn't just a chip transaction without insertion. It keeps EMV's transaction-specific card data, but changes the interface: card and terminal use short-range radio instead of metal contacts. The shorter interaction changes the constraints: cardholder verification, terminal rules, issuer checks, and network limits must all work quickly enough for a tap.

In Chapter 9, we separated reusable stripe data from transaction-specific proof. Contactless keeps that distinction. The interface changes, but the need for transaction-specific proof remains.

NFC Interface

A contact chip payment begins with physical contact. The card is inserted into the terminal, the metal contact plate lines up with the terminal contacts, and the terminal powers the chip through that connection. The card stays in the reader while the terminal and chip exchange data.

Contactless payments eliminate the need for physical contact. To pay, the cardholder brings the card close to the reader – the card and terminal exchange data via NFC (near-field communication), a short-range radio technology. For payments, the working range is only a few centimeters, so the card or device has to be close to the reader.

Unlike some devices, a contactless card doesn't carry a battery. Instead, the terminal powers the card's chip by emitting a radio field for the transaction. The card activates only when in range, exchanges data, and becomes inactive as soon as it leaves the field.

Phones and watches differ from plastic cards in how they store, secure, and present payment credentials. Devices have their own power, can use wallet apps, and enable extra security features. However, at the payment terminal, both cards and devices interact using NFC: the phone or watch approaches the reader, exchanges payment data, and leaves the field.

That speed comes from the interface, not from the credential itself. Both a plastic contactless card and a mobile wallet can use NFC, but the payment data behind the tap can differ. The physical card presents data tied to the PAN; a mobile wallet can present a tokenized device credential instead. Chapter 11 explains that credential model in detail.

Contactless is fast because it shortens the physical interaction. The cardholder does not hand over the card, insert it, wait for the terminal to release it, or always enter a PIN. The card-terminal exchange is designed to finish quickly, even when the transaction still goes online to the issuer. Contactless, therefore, changes the timing budget for the whole card-terminal interaction, not just the gesture.

Cardholder Verification and Risk Controls

Cardholder verification asks whether the person using the card is allowed to use it. For contact chip transactions, the familiar answer is often PIN. Older transactions might use a signature. Some low-risk transactions may require no cardholder verification at all.

Contactless changes the balance between speed and verification. For small purchases, many markets allow no-CVM transactions: the transaction can proceed without a PIN, signature, or device-based verification when the amount and risk conditions permit.

A low-value café purchase can therefore go through without a PIN. A higher-value purchase, or even another low-value purchase after several previous contactless payments, can trigger a PIN request when cumulative limits or issuer risk rules require stronger verification.

To the cardholder, this can feel inconsistent. Yet the system uses a combination of transaction amount, terminal settings, card configuration, issuer policy, account status, merchant context, country, and recent activity to make its decisions.

No PIN Does Not Mean No Control

A no-CVM contactless transaction can still use dynamic EMV data. The terminal applies amount limits where the contactless rules require them. The card tracks counters when the product and contactless configuration use them. The issuer checks account status, merchant type, location, recent activity, and fraud signals according to its authorization rules. Network rules define when no-CVM is allowed.

No-CVM means no cardholder verification was performed at the terminal. Risk controls still apply.

Contactless became practical by moving some decisions away from the cardholder and into limits, counters, terminal configuration, and issuer authorization logic.

Mobile Device Cardholder Verification

Mobile wallets changed contactless cardholder verification because a phone or watch can do something a plastic contactless card cannot: check who is holding it before payment data is released. A plastic card can be tapped by anyone who has it, so the system manages that risk through limits, counters, issuer rules, and step-up prompts.

A phone or watch can authenticate the user before the tap reaches the terminal. The device can ask for Face ID, Touch ID, a passcode, or another unlock method. In payments, this is called *Consumer Device Cardholder Verification Method (CDCVM)*. Cardholder verification happens on the device. If the scheme, wallet, terminal, and issuer rules allow it, the terminal can accept that device check as the verification method for the transaction.

A high-value mobile-wallet tap can work without a terminal PIN because the cardholder has already verified themselves on their phone. Some of the security work has moved from the terminal to the device. That shift changes the checkout experience: relying on device verification means the terminal does not need to stop the flow to enter a PIN.

Transit and Special Flows

Transit is one of the toughest environments for accepting card payments because speed and certainty matter simultaneously. Passengers expect the gate to open immediately, even in rush hour, while the operator may not yet know the final fare. A journey can include entry and exit taps, transfers, fare caps, discounts, or daily totals. If every passenger waited for full issuer authorization at the gate, payment failures and crowding would quickly follow.

Many open-loop transit systems, therefore, separate gate access from final fare calculation. In an open-loop system, the passenger can use a contactless banking card or, where supported, a mobile wallet rather than a closed transit card issued by the transport operator. At the gate, the card or device first acts as an access credential: the system quickly decides whether to open the gate, while the final fare can be calculated later by the transit back office.

In a retail purchase, the merchant knows the amount at checkout. It is $7.50 for lunch or $38.40 for groceries. In transit, the amount depends on where the passenger exits, how many trips they take, whether they transfer, and whether a daily cap applies.

A common pattern is: tap now, calculate and charge later. The gate records the tap and checks if the card is allowed to travel. The back office collects taps, applies fare rules, adjusts fares, submits payments when known, and blocks cards that later fail payment.

The important separation is between access and payment finality. The gate does not need to finish the whole payment before opening. It needs to decide whether this card or device is allowed to start the journey. The fare calculation, payment submission, retries, and blocking decisions can happen later.

Transit risk is managed through several layers:

- fast local acceptance at the gate;
- low-value or capped exposure;
- delayed or aggregated fare calculation;
- back-office authorization and clearing logic;
- deny lists for cards with failed payments or other risk signals;
- rules for retrying failed payments.

The fastest contactless experience comes from moving complexity into the back office.

Adoption by Market

Contactless did not spread at the same pace everywhere. Markets varied: some transitioned early, while others relied on chip-and-PIN or cash for longer. The pace depended on terminal replacement, domestic-scheme readiness, regulation, merchant economics, transit habits, and consumer routines.

By the mid-2020s, contactless had become a default card-present behavior in many markets. Mastercard reported that contactless payments accounted for more than 75 percent of transactions on its network in 2025. In the United Kingdom, Barclays found that 94.6 percent of eligible in-store card transactions were contactless in 2024, a figure also cited by the FCA.

Terminal availability is usually the first constraint. Contactless cannot spread if merchants do not have compatible terminals. Replacing terminal fleets takes time, especially for small merchants, unattended devices, older POS systems, and fragmented acquiring markets.

Network and domestic-scheme support also shape adoption. A market with a strong domestic debit infrastructure may need local rules, certification, and routing decisions before contactless works broadly.

Transit can accelerate adoption by turning tapping into a daily habit. Transport for London introduced contactless bank cards on buses in December 2012 and expanded them to the Underground in September 2014. Once millions of passengers learn to tap at a gate, the same behavior feels natural at shops and cafés.

Regulation and consumer habits also shape adoption. Authentication requirements, local no-CVM limits, liability rules, and consumer-protection expectations influence the level of friction permitted. In markets where cash stayed strong, contactless adoption was slower. Where cards were common for everyday purchases, tapping felt like the next step.

Contactless adapts EMV's security model to a faster interface. The card is no longer inserted; data exchange happens more quickly, and more control shifts to terminal rules, issuer logic, limits, counters, and back-office systems.

That makes contactless fast without making it as weak as a stripe transaction. The card still participates in the transaction. The system still needs dynamic data. What changed is how much must happen while the card or device is near the reader.

Chapter 11: Mobile Wallets and Tokenized Cards

Many people say Apple Pay or Google Pay "stores the card on the phone," which is fine in everyday conversation, but technically incomplete. A mobile wallet does not simply copy the card number onto the device. If it did, every device would carry the same sensitive card number as the plastic card.

Modern mobile wallets use a different approach. When adding a card to a wallet, the real card number is replaced with a token that resembles a card number and functions within the payment system, but it is not the original number. This token is unique to a device and managed separately from the physical card.

Device Credential

In wallet tokenization, the original card number is often referred to as the *Funding PAN (FPAN)* because it is the underlying card account that funds the wallet credential.

The token created for a device is often referred to as a Device PAN (DPAN), a device account number, or a payment token. Each device receives its own DPAN, a substitute for the original FPAN, which the card payment system recognizes as belonging to that specific device.

One funding card can support multiple device tokens, each assigned to a specific device, such as a phone, a watch, or a second phone. Each token can be activated, suspended, deleted, or replaced independently, without changing the underlying card account.

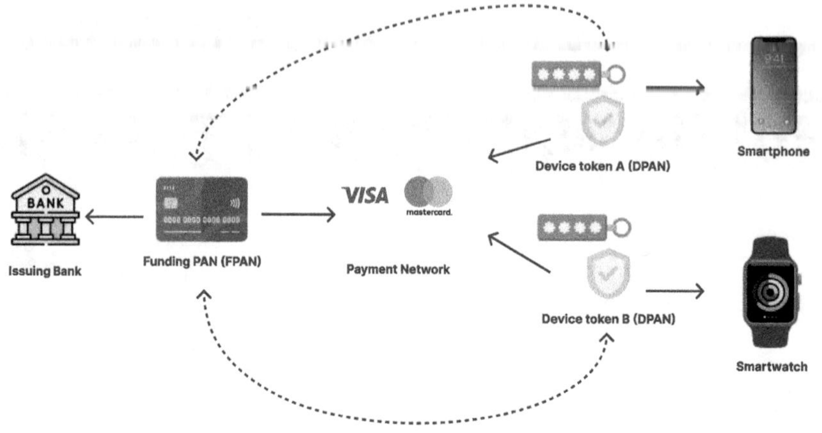

Figure 11.1: One funding card can support multiple device tokens.

Tokenization changes two things. First, the real PAN is less often exposed. A wallet transaction can use a device token instead of the same raw card number printed on the physical card. Second, each device can be managed independently. A phone token and a watch token can both point to the same funding card while remaining separate credentials within the token system.

Provisioning a Wallet Credential

Adding a card to a wallet starts with a familiar gesture: the cardholder opens the wallet app, scans the card, and waits for it to appear on the screen. In the background, the system is provisioning a new credential.

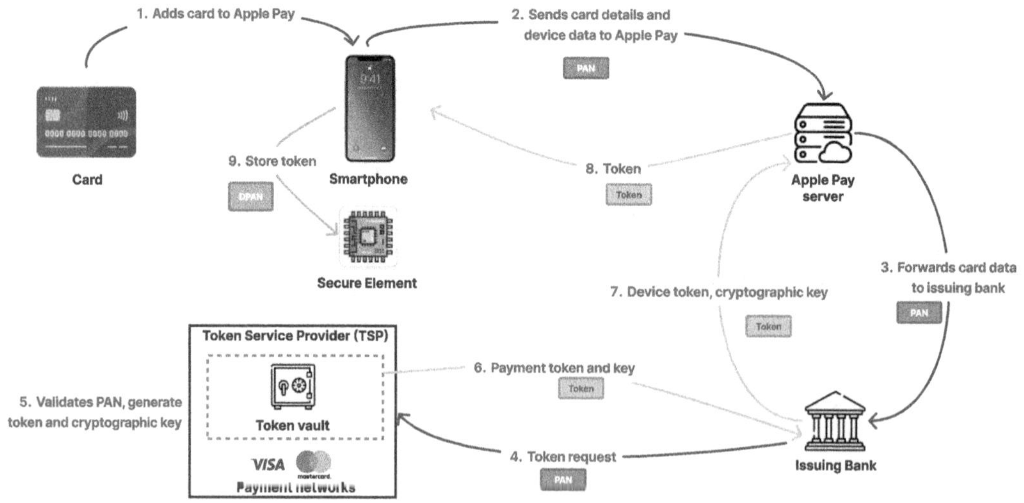

Figure 11.2: Provisioning a tokenized card credential into a mobile wallet.

Figure 11.2 traces this provisioning path. The phone captures card details, such as the PAN and expiry date. The wallet provider receives the request and submits it through the tokenization infrastructure. In Apple Pay, Apple's infrastructure is the intermediary. Other wallets use different architectures, but the core process is the same: identify the card, obtain issuer approval, and create a tokenized credential.

The BIN at the start of the card number routes the request to the right issuer. The issuer decides if the card should be allowed in this wallet on this device. It checks account status, card status, device data, fraud signals, past wallet activity, and whether extra verification is needed.

That extra verification is essential. The wallet should not create a payment credential for someone who just photographed a card. When the issuer needs stronger proof, it requires confirmation via a banking app, an SMS code, a call center, a one-time password, or another method.

If the issuer approves the request, the Token Service Provider (TSP) creates or activates the token. It manages payment tokens and keeps the mapping between a device token and the underlying funding card. Visa and Mastercard each operate token services. The token vault records that this device token represents this card account.

The TSP returns the tokenized credential and related cryptographic material through the provisioning flow. The wallet receives a tokenized credential, not a reusable copy of the plastic card. The device stores that credential using the secure storage model supported by the wallet and operating system.

After provisioning, the card shows up in the wallet. The phone now has its own unique device credential (token) linked to the funding card. Adding the card to a watch or another device creates a distinct credential for that device, not a shared copy.

> **Secure Element vs Host Card Emulation**
>
> Different wallet providers manage storage differently. Apple Pay is built around the Secure Element model: the token is stored in device hardware, and Apple is usually not involved in transactions after provisioning. Google Pay uses Host Card Emulation and cloud-backed approaches, allowing the phone to emulate a secure credential in software with Google's support.

> Both methods use tokenization and can support secure payments. The main difference is their operation: one relies on device hardware, while the other relies on software and cloud systems, enabling broader support on Android devices.

Wallet Transaction Flow

Once the card is provisioned, the wallet can be used at a terminal, in an app, or online. The cardholder experience is simple: authenticate, present the device, and receive approval. The payment data behind that action differs from typing, swiping, or tapping the physical card.

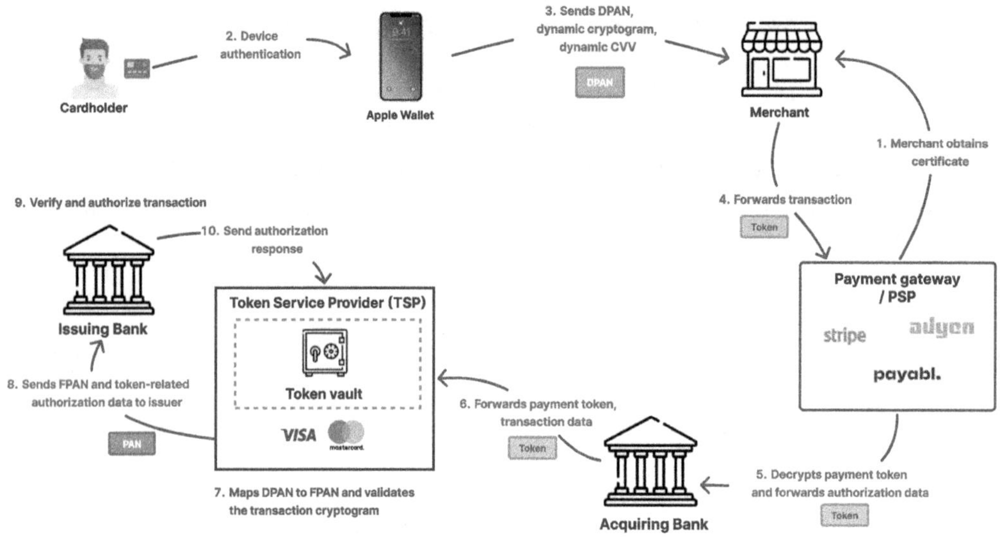

Figure 11.3: A tokenized Apple Pay in-app or web payment through the card system.

Figure 11.3 uses an Apple Pay in-app or web payment to show how a tokenized credential moves through the card system. The first step is cardholder verification on the device. The cardholder unlocks the wallet with Face ID, Touch ID, fingerprint authentication, a passcode, or another approved method. This is CDCVM in practice: the device verifies the cardholder before releasing payment data.

After verification, the wallet prepares tokenized payment data. It does not send the FPAN. It sends the DPAN and transaction-specific cryptographic data. The *DPAN* identifies the wallet credential, and cryptographic data proves that the payment originated from a legitimate device and was not reused.

For in-person payments, the device sends this data to the terminal using NFC. For in-app or online payments, the data travels through the wallet and merchant integration. Some wallet models also use merchant certificates, encryption, or gateway-side decryption to ensure that only authorized merchants or processors can receive and process payment data. Those details vary by wallet and channel, but the principle is the same: the merchant receives tokenized payment data rather than the real card number.

The merchant or payment gateway forwards the tokenized transaction through the acquiring side of the card system. From there, the transaction is routed to the payment network.

On the network side, the TSP verifies the token, maps it to the underlying account reference, and validates the associated cryptographic data. The issuer then receives the information it needs to make the account decision: available funds or credit, card status, limits, fraud rules, and token-related data.

If the issuer approves, the approval travels back through the same chain. The cardholder sees the familiar result: "Approved."

The merchant did not need the real PAN to process the wallet payment. The wallet sent a token and transaction-specific cryptographic data, and the system mapped that token back to the underlying account only where needed.

> **Apple Pay Economics**
>
> Apple does not charge merchants a separate Apple Pay acceptance fee for ordinary card acceptance. The economics can still differ for issuers. In the United States, the Department of Justice's 2024 antitrust complaint alleged that Apple charged issuing banks 15 basis points on credit-card transactions mediated by Apple Pay, while Google and Samsung did not charge US issuers in the same way. The user experience may look similar, but wallet economics can differ across platforms and markets.

Security Controls

A mobile wallet changes where sensitive data appears and how credentials are controlled.

Tokenization limits PAN exposure. The merchant receives a token, not the FPAN, so data stolen from the merchant side is less useful than a raw card number. The *token* is also narrower than the underlying card credential because it is tied to the wallet, device, merchant, or transaction context for which it was created.

Transaction-specific cryptographic data limits replay. A captured wallet transaction should not work as a new payment, since the device generates unique data for each transaction.

Device authentication changes cardholder verification. A plastic contactless card can often be tapped for low-value purchases without the cardholder being verified at the terminal. A mobile wallet usually requires the user to unlock or authenticate before releasing payment credentials. CDCVM brings the device into the cardholder-verification process.

Lifecycle management gives the issuer more precise control. A wallet token can be suspended or deleted without replacing the physical card or changing every credential linked to the account.

None of this makes a mobile wallet perfectly secure. Provisioning can be attacked by social engineering. A weak device passcode is still a risk. Account takeover, SIM-swap fraud, malware, and issuer-side weaknesses remain possible. The design is still stronger than copying a card number: the real PAN appears less often, the token is used only for limited purposes, and the device requires cardholder authentication before releasing payment data.

Token Lifecycle

A wallet token is not created once and left alone. After provisioning, it can be active, suspended, deleted, replaced, or updated. Because the token operates independently of the physical card, the issuer can manage it without changing every other credential linked to the account.

If a phone is lost, the token on that phone can be suspended. If the phone is found, the token can be reactivated. If the cardholder removes the card from the wallet, the token can be deleted. If the physical card is reissued due to expiration, the issuer and network can update the token relationship so the wallet continues to work. If the card is reported stolen, the issuer can suspend the FPAN and related tokens.

Because each token is separate, the issuer can also use tokenization to control fraud. If suspicious activity appears only on one token, the issuer can investigate or block that token. If the underlying account is compromised, the issuer can act at the FPAN level.

Tokenization gives the system more precise control than a single card number.

> **Not Every Wallet Holds Money**
>
> Apple Pay and Google Pay, when used for card payments, are not stored-value wallets. They do not hold the cardholder's funds for the transaction. They present tokenized card credentials that allow the issuer to authorize the payment against the underlying card account. Other wallet models can hold balances, but that is a different payment model.

A mobile wallet is not a copy of the card. It is a tokenized, device-specific credential with its own lifecycle, security controls, and cryptographic behavior. The cardholder sees a familiar card image on the screen. The payment system sees a token that can stand in for the real PAN without exposing it everywhere.

In the next chapter, we broaden that lifecycle view from wallet tokens to cards themselves: how cards are issued, activated, replaced, renewed, controlled, and closed.

Chapter 12: The Card Lifecycle

When a card arrives, it looks like a finished product.

It comes with a number, an expiry date, a chip, a magnetic stripe, a brand, and sometimes the cardholder's name. While some cards arrive by mail after a week, others appear instantly in a banking app. Either way, the cardholder sees a new way to pay.

The issuer sees a card with a lifecycle: setup, personalization, activation, monitoring, blocking, replacement, renewal, tokenization, and closure. Each stage changes what the card can do.

The issuer's work does not end when the card first becomes usable, since the card is a credential. To manage its lifecycle, the issuer must oversee its status, limits, PIN state, tokens, replacements, renewals, and closure. In Chapter 11, we saw this through wallet tokens. Here, we apply the same concept to the broader card relationship: one funding account can support multiple dependent credentials, not just one piece of plastic. The cardholder sees a card; the issuer's system sees a controlled credential moving through states.

Product Setup

A card's life starts before any plastic is manufactured or any virtual card appears in an app.

The issuer first defines the card product: network, BIN range, funding source, product type, allowed channels, fees, authorization rules, and card controls.

A debit card linked to a checking or current account behaves differently from a prepaid, corporate, charge, or premium credit card. The cards can look alike, but the product setup behind them is different.

Product setup answers practical questions. Can the card be used online or at ATMs? Are cash withdrawals allowed abroad? Are gambling transactions blocked? Is contactless enabled from the start? What are the daily limits? What happens if the issuer cannot be reached? Which fees apply to foreign transactions, cash withdrawals, declines, or replacements?

Some choices serve commercial objectives. Others are about risk management, compliance with regulations or network rules, or reflect the issuer's operating model.

The card profile translates these operational decisions into system behavior, setting transaction limits, allowed merchant types, country restrictions, permissions for online and offline use, PIN rules, contactless settings, cash withdrawal options, and service codes. Controls on a teen card differ from those on a corporate travel card, just as a virtual card for online subscriptions is configured unlike a physical debit card used at ATMs.

Issuing a card means creating a credential with rules attached: where it can be used, how it can be verified, which limits apply, and what happens when risk changes.

Physical and Virtual Cards

Cards take two main forms: physical and virtual.

A physical card is the familiar plastic or metal card. It can be inserted, tapped, swiped, or used at ATMs. It works without a phone, battery, or banking app. Many ATMs, older terminals, hotels, and car rental companies still expect a physical card. Physical cards must be manufactured, personalized, packaged, shipped, delivered, and activated. They often take several days to reach the cardholder.

A virtual card has the same main details as a physical card: PAN, expiry date, and CVV. The difference is that there is no plastic. It can be created in the issuer's system and shown in the banking app almost immediately after approval. It usually works for online purchases and subscriptions. For in-store contactless payments, it normally needs to be added to a mobile wallet such as Apple Pay or Google Pay. Once tokenized into the wallet, it can be used at contactless terminals.

The difference between physical and virtual cards is not product type, since debit and credit cards can both take either form. The real difference is delivery, cost, speed, and acceptance.

Physical cards offer wider acceptance and independence from a phone. Virtual cards offer faster delivery and lower issuance costs. Many issuers now combine both: a virtual credential for immediate use, followed by plastic when needed.

Why Physical Cards Remain

Virtual-first issuance has changed expectations, but physical cards remain useful. They work when the phone is dead, at ATMs, where wallet acceptance is unreliable, and in places such as hotels and car rental companies that still expect plastic in some cases. They also carry the issuer's brand in a way an app tile does not.

There is also a commercial point. For the issuer, a physical card is also a brand object. It sits in the wallet, appears at checkout, and reminds the customer which bank they use. Premium metal cards make that point even more strongly. The weight is part of the product.

That does not make physical cards better in every way. They cost money to produce and ship, can be lost or stolen, wear out, and create environmental concerns, especially when made from standard PVC. Issuers use recycled plastic, bio-sourced materials, and digital-first programs because physical card production creates both cost and waste across large portfolios.

Physical and virtual issuance solve different problems. A physical card gives reach and independence. A virtual card gives speed, lower cost, and immediate use. A tokenized mobile wallet allows in-person payments without exposing the original PAN. Modern issuers often combine all three.

Card Personalization

A blank card is not yet a payment credential. For a physical card, personalization turns a blank card into a usable credential. The PAN is printed or embossed, the cardholder's name may be added, and the expiry date appears on the card. The CVV2 (CVC2) is usually placed on the back, or, in some programs, shown only in the app. The magnetic stripe is encoded, and the EMV chip is personalized with card data, application settings, and cryptographic material.

This happens in a secure, controlled environment because personalization handles sensitive data, including PANs, chip keys, magnetic stripe data, and security codes.

The issuer's system also records how the statuses of the card, account, cardholder, product, and credential are connected. The plastic is only the visible part. The issuer's records decide what that credential is allowed to do.

PIN management is handled separately. In some programs, the issuer generates and sends the PIN in a dedicated letter; in others, the cardholder selects it in the app, at an ATM, or through another secure method. It can also be changed later. If entered incorrectly too often, PIN usage might be blocked, or the issuer might apply card restrictions.

The card and PIN are kept separate on purpose. They should not be sent together in the same envelope. If someone steals the card during delivery, they should not receive everything needed to use it at a terminal or ATM.

Virtual cards skip manufacturing and delivery, but not setup. The issuer still generates the PAN, expiry date, security code, product settings, limits, and risk controls. If the virtual card is added to a mobile wallet, it is tokenized.

Delivery and Activation

A physical card usually cannot be used immediately after it is personalized. It has to reach the cardholder, and the issuer needs some evidence that it reached the right person. That is where activation comes in.

A card can be activated in several ways: in the banking app, online, by phone, at an ATM, or through the first chip-and-PIN transaction. The method reflects the issuer's risk approach. If a card is lost in the mail, it should not be usable by anyone. Before activation, the card is usually inactive: it exists in the issuer's system, but most transactions are blocked. Some issuers allow limited use of apps or wallets after identity verification. Others block all use until activation.

Virtual cards work differently because they appear inside an authenticated digital channel. Depending on the product and risk model, the issuer treats them as active immediately or requires the cardholder to set a PIN, accept terms, or confirm activation.

Once activation occurs, the card shifts from issued but inactive to fully active.

Card Status

A card's status controls whether the issuer allows it to be used.

The simplest status is active. An active card can be used under its product rules, limits, and risk controls. The transaction can still be declined for insufficient funds, fraud risk, merchant restrictions, or technical reasons, but the card itself is usable.

An inactive card exists but is not yet fully usable. This is common before activation or during certain issuance flows.

A *frozen card* is temporarily paused, often by the cardholder in the mobile app. Freezing is useful when the cardholder believes the card may have been misplaced rather than stolen. If the card turns up under the sofa, the cardholder can unfreeze it.

A *blocked card* is more strictly restricted by the issuer. The issuer may block a card due to suspected fraud, compliance concerns, repeated incorrect PIN attempts, account issues, or operational problems. Some blocks can be removed. Others are effectively final.

The *lost or stolen status* means physical cards should no longer be trusted. The issuer blocks the card and issues a replacement. If the PAN itself is compromised, the issuer can replace it as well. Tokens tied to the card can be suspended, deleted, or migrated based on the case.

An expired card has passed its valid-through date. The account relationship may still be active, but that specific card credential should no longer authorize new transactions.

A closed card has reached the end of its life. The account may be closed, the product migrated, the customer relationship ended, or the card replaced by another credential.

Card states directly impact authorization. Whenever a transaction reaches the issuer, status is one of the initial checks performed. Normally, stolen, expired, frozen, or closed cards should be declined, while active cards proceed to risk checks.

Card Controls

Status says whether the card can be used at all. Controls define how it can be used.

A modern card can have many controls. Some are visible to the cardholder. Others work quietly inside the issuer's systems.

Cardholders might turn online payments on or off, block cash withdrawals,

define spending limits, restrict foreign transactions, suspend contactless payments, or permit only certain merchant categories. For business cards, controls can be set by employee, department, merchant category, country, time, or amount thresholds.

Issuers also apply controls that the cardholder may never see. They may block high-risk merchant categories, limit offline authorization, restrict fallback to magnetic stripe, set velocity rules, or apply different limits for ATM, e-commerce, contactless, and cross-border transactions.

MCC is one of the most important inputs. A card can be allowed at supermarkets and blocked for gambling. A corporate card can be enabled for airlines and hotels, but blocked for jewelry stores. A teen card can be restricted from adult categories. These controls depend on the MCC supplied in the transaction.

Geography changes the risk profile. Some issuers let cardholders turn off foreign transactions. Others use country-level or region-level controls internally. A transaction in the cardholder's home city and a transaction on another continent are treated differently by the fraud system, even when the card is technically active.

The channel also changes what the card can do. A card can be enabled for card-present transactions but blocked for online transactions. It can allow in-store purchases but not ATM withdrawals. A virtual card can be designed for e-commerce only until it is tokenized into a mobile wallet.

Renewal and Replacement

Cards do not last forever. The most common lifecycle event is renewal. A card reaches its expiry date, and the issuer sends a new card before the old one stops working. The new card either keeps the same PAN with a new expiry date and CVV or receives a new PAN. The choice depends on issuer policy, network rules, product migration, risk, and operational setup.

Same-PAN renewal can reduce disruption because stored credentials are easier to update. A new PAN replacement is stronger when the issuer wants to cut off compromised credentials or migrate the cardholder to a different product setup.

A lost or stolen replacement is different from an ordinary renewal. If the card may be in the wrong hands, the issuer has to decide what to invalidate. The physical card is blocked. The PAN is often replaced. Related wallet tokens may be suspended, deleted, or migrated. Card-on-file merchants may need updated credentials.

Damage and wear create another path. A card can be safe but physically unusable. The chip can fail, the magnetic stripe can wear out, or the card can crack. The issuer can send a replacement without treating the old card as stolen, often keeping the same PAN while refreshing the expiry date and CVV.

Product migration adds another scenario. A customer may move from standard to premium, from student to adult, from debit to credit, or from one network brand to another. That can require a new card profile, new card art, new fees, new limits, and sometimes a new PAN.

Replacement is a credential-management decision: what stays the same, what changes, and which dependent credentials should follow.

Account Updater Services

Card replacement is less disruptive than it used to be. If a card number changed, every merchant that stored the old card details needed new credentials. Subscription services could fail. Ride-hailing apps could decline. Streaming services could send dunning emails. Cardholders had to update the same card in many places.

Modern card systems reduce that disruption through two mechanisms: token lifecycle management and account updater services.

For mobile wallets, the issuer and network may keep or refresh the token relationship when the underlying card is renewed or replaced. If the card is stolen, the issuer may immediately suspend any associated tokens.

For participating card-on-file merchants, account updater services can provide updated credentials when a card is renewed, reissued, replaced, or closed. Visa's service is called *Visa Account Updater* (*VAU*). Mastercard's is called *Automatic Billing Updater* (*ABU*). These services help participating merchants refresh stored card details for recurring or credential-on-file payments, reducing the need for cardholders to manually update their details with every merchant.

That continuity helps cardholders and merchants until the cardholder wants the old credential to stop working everywhere. Issuers need policies for both cases: preserving legitimate recurring payments and cutting off credentials that should no longer be usable.

That is why updater services are useful but not neutral: they preserve continuity by design, and issuers need clear rules for when continuity should stop.

Closing the Card

At some point, the card reaches the end of its life. Closure can occur when the cardholder closes the account, the issuer ends the relationship, the product is withdrawn, the card is moved to a new platform, or the card is replaced with another credential. When this happens, the issuer has to close not only the visible card but also the associated credentials.

That credential cleanup includes physical card status, virtual card status, wallet tokens, card-on-file tokens, account updater participation, PIN state, limits, and outstanding authorizations. Even then, pending transactions can still clear. Refunds can still arrive. Disputes can still be opened for transactions made before closure. Closing a card does not erase its history from the system.

A card's life does not end when the cardholder cuts the plastic or deletes it from an app. The credential may become unusable immediately, but the operational record continues for reporting, disputes, compliance, fraud investigations, and reconciliation.

A card is a managed credential, not a finished object handed to a customer once and forgotten. Its life begins with product design, becomes visible during issuance and activation, and continues through statuses, controls, tokens, replacements, renewals, and closure.

Part III turns to the next question: how the system decides whether that credential, and the person or device presenting it, should be trusted.

Part III

Card Authentication

Chapter 13: Authentication in Payments

Imagine a cardholder inserts a chip card at a terminal and enters the correct PIN.

From the issuer's perspective, the evidence remains incomplete. The issuer receives data about the card, merchant, terminal, amount, time, and security values. It does not see the person standing at the terminal.

One check has passed: the cardholder knows the PIN. In a chip transaction, the chip produces cryptographic data that helps confirm the card's authenticity. In mobile wallet payments, the phone confirms that the device was unlocked via face, fingerprint, or passcode.

Those checks are authentication, but the issuer still has to decide whether to approve. It checks available funds or credit, card status, merchant eligibility, transaction limits, spending patterns, and fraud risk. A correct PIN does not change that. That decision is authorization.

The two processes often happen inside the same authorization request. The terminal, acquirer, network, issuer, and processor may pass authentication data and transaction data together. The issuer's systems may validate security values, check funds, apply risk rules, and return a single response: approved or declined. That single response blurs the distinction between authentication and authorization.

A transaction can fail authentication if the PIN is wrong, the CVV2 does not match, the chip cryptogram is invalid, the 3-D Secure challenge fails, or the wallet token is suspended.

A transaction can still be declined even after successful authentication. The cardholder can enter the correct PIN and still lack sufficient funds. The biometric check can pass while the issuer blocks the merchant. The chip can be genuine while the transaction exceeds the daily limit.

Authentication asks: does this look like the right person, card, device, or credential?

Authorization asks: should this transaction be allowed now?

The Three Authentication Factors

Most authentication methods rely on three factors: something you know, something you have, and something you are.

Something you know is a secret, such as a PIN, password, passcode, or security answer, that the cardholder is expected to remember.

Something you have means a physical or digital object, such as a payment card, a phone storing a wallet token, or printed card data. Each serves as evidence of possession, though static card data loses strength if copied.

Something you are includes unique biological traits. Everyday examples are fingerprint and face recognition. In mobile wallets, device-based biometric authentication is required before payment data is released.

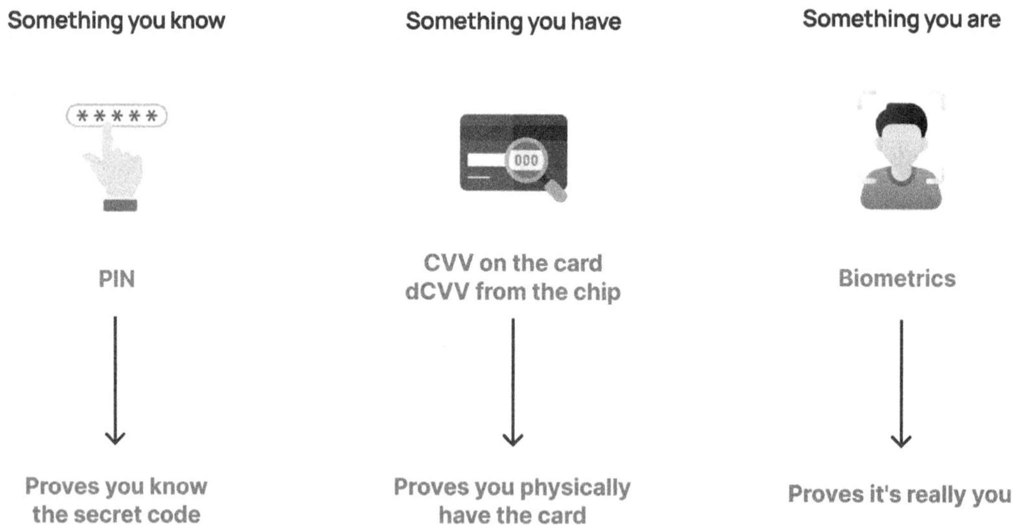

Figure 13.1: Authentication factors in card payments.

Each authentication factor has its vulnerabilities, so no single method is sufficient. That is why payment systems combine evidence. A chip-and-PIN transaction uses the card and the PIN. A mobile wallet transaction uses a device-bound credential and the device's unlock method. An online card payment may combine card data, device signals, fraud scoring, and 3-D Secure. An ATM withdrawal uses the card and PIN, then still runs authorization checks before cash is dispensed.

Attackers look for the weakest proof they can copy, steal, or bypass. Magnetic stripes made copied stripe data useful to criminals. Online commerce created demand for CVV2, fraud scoring, and 3-D Secure. Mobile wallets tied payment credentials to devices and local device authentication. Authentication keeps changing because the available evidence changes by channel.

Channels and Evidence

The same cardholder may use different authentication methods depending on where and how the card is used.

At an ATM, the cardholder normally inserts the card and enters a PIN. The system checks possession of the card and knowledge of the PIN before deciding whether to allow the withdrawal. The PIN is central because the transaction gives access to cash, and cash cannot be recovered as easily as a card purchase.

At a card-present POS terminal, authentication depends on the card, terminal, and transaction type. A chip-and-PIN transaction asks the cardholder to insert the card and enter the PIN. A contactless transaction may rely on dynamic contactless data and require no PIN below certain limits. Above a threshold, or when risk rules require it, the terminal may request a PIN or another verification method.

When the card is not present, the evidence problem changes. The merchant cannot see the card, and the terminal cannot read a chip. The cardholder enters card details on a website or in an app. CVV2 helps, but it is still a static value printed or displayed with the card. It does not prove that a genuine chip is present. Online payments, therefore, rely more heavily on fraud scoring, device signals, merchant risk controls, and 3-D Secure when additional authentication is needed.

A mobile wallet changes the card-present experience again. The cardholder authenticates on the device with face recognition, fingerprint, or passcode. The wallet then releases protected payment data. CDCVM covers this case: the phone or watch confirms that the user unlocked the device in an approved way, so the terminal does not always need a separate PIN prompt.

In recurring payments, the cardholder is not always present at all. The first setup becomes more important than a fresh cardholder action every time. The system relies on stored-credential rules, merchant risk controls, issuer decisioning, and the controls established when the cardholder first saved the credential.

Across all of these channels, the issuer is trying to answer the same authentication question, but the available evidence changes: a terminal can interact with the card, an online checkout usually cannot, ATM cash risk is high, wallets add the device, and recurring payments rely more on the original setup and stored-credential rules.

Authentication adapts, using the best methods for each channel, product, and risk situation. That is the organizing principle for the rest of this part: PINs, security codes, EMV cryptograms, 3-D Secure, Strong Customer Authentication, biometrics, and fraud systems all supply different evidence for different payment situations.

Chapter 14: PIN Verification

Most PINs have 4 digits, though some have 6. The cardholder enters the PIN at an ATM or terminal, and the system returns a simple result: correct or incorrect. To the cardholder, it feels like a simple password check.

That simple experience is misleading: a PIN should never be passed through the payment system as plain text. It should not appear in terminal logs, merchant systems, acquirer systems, network files, or bank databases. The issuer should not maintain a table listing the cardholder's PIN as 4931, and no bank employee should be able to look it up.

The PIN is a secret, and the system is designed to verify it without exposing it. The challenge is to let the cardholder enter a PIN in one place, protect it as it moves through the payment system, verify it inside a secure environment, and expose only the result.

PIN as a Knowledge Factor

The PIN is the *something you know* factor in card authentication.

The issuer may generate the PIN and deliver it separately, often through a PIN mailer, or the cardholder may choose it in an app, at an ATM, or through another issuer-controlled process.

PINs are most common at ATMs. To withdraw cash, the cardholder normally needs both the card and the PIN, because once cash is dispensed, it cannot be recovered as easily as a card purchase.

At point-of-sale terminals, the PIN serves a similar purpose. In chip-and-PIN markets, the cardholder inserts the card and enters the PIN for verification. Contactless transactions may request a PIN above certain limits, after repeated low-value taps, or when stronger verification is required.

The PIN proves knowledge of a secret linked to the card. It does not prove that funds are available, that the merchant is authorized, or that the transaction is low-risk.

Online and Offline PIN

The same PIN can be checked in two places: by the issuer or by the chip. With an online PIN, the entered PIN is protected in an encrypted PIN block and verified by the issuer or issuer processor. With an offline PIN, the terminal passes the PIN to the card, and the chip checks it locally.

The validation process looks the same to the cardholder, but the trust boundary is different. Online PIN keeps the issuer in control. Offline PIN lets the card verify the secret when the terminal cannot rely on a live issuer connection.

Online PIN

The cardholder enters the PIN at the terminal, but the terminal must not send those digits as plain text. Instead, the PIN entry device creates a PIN block: a structured value that combines the entered PIN with card data, usually derived from the PAN. The terminal then encrypts that PIN block under a terminal-side PIN key.

> **PIN Blocks**
>
> A *PIN block* is the structured, encrypted value that carries the entered PIN through the payment system. It follows formats defined in the ISO 9564 series and is encrypted under keys controlled by terminals, acquirers, networks, issuers, and HSMs.
>
> The point is to prevent the PIN from becoming an ordinary authorization message field. PIN handling stays inside controlled formats, key zones, and secure cryptographic devices.

Figure 14.1 traces the PIN block from the terminal to the issuer. In the diagram, the terminal-side key is labeled the *Terminal PIN Key* (*TPK*), and the resulting PIN block is protected within the terminal-acquirer key environment.

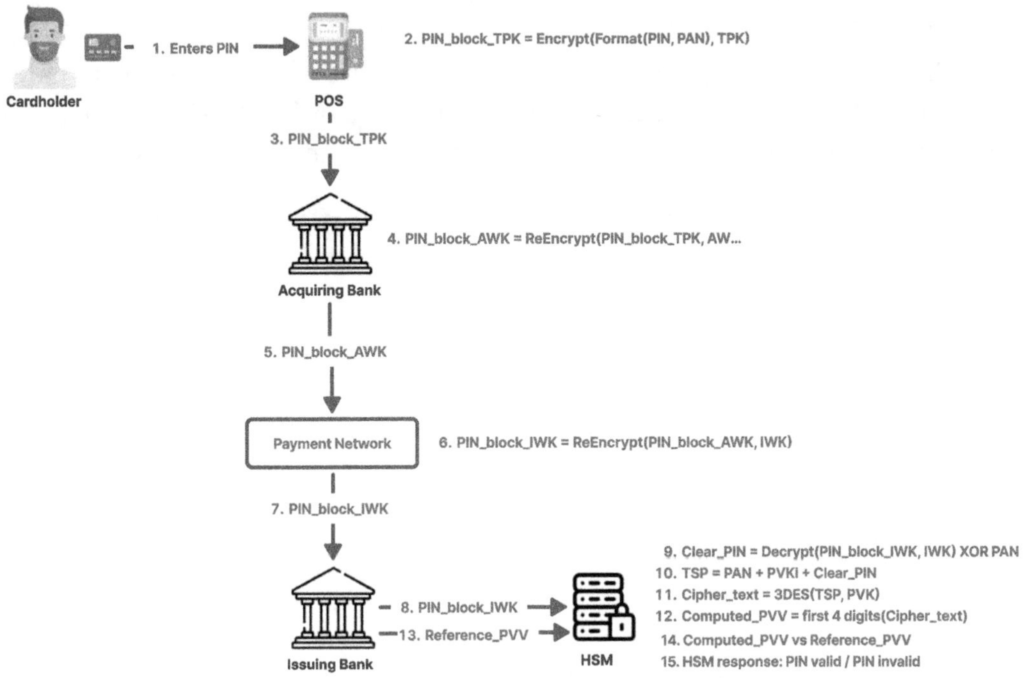

Figure 14.1: Online PIN verification.

The encrypted PIN block travels with the transaction toward the issuer. On the way, it often has to move between different key environments. The issuer does not know the terminal's PIN key, and the terminal does not know the issuer's PIN key. Each part of the system, therefore, protects the PIN block under the keys used in that part of the route.

This movement between key environments is called *PIN translation* or PIN re-encryption. The acquirer receives the PIN block encrypted under the TPK and translates it into a PIN block encrypted under an Acquirer Working Key (AWK). The payment network then re-encrypts it into a PIN block under an Issuer Working Key (IWK). The exact key names vary by implementation, but the principle is the same: the PIN block is re-encrypted as it crosses key zones.

This translation happens inside a secure cryptographic infrastructure, typically a Hardware Security Module (HSM). Ordinary merchant, acquirer, network, or issuer applications should not see the clear PIN.

On the issuer side, the PIN block is delivered to the issuer's HSM. The HSM decrypts it inside its secure boundary and verifies the PIN using issuer-controlled cryptographic keys.

One common verification method is the Visa PIN Verification Value (PVV). In a simplified PVV flow, the HSM uses the entered PIN, card data, a PIN Verification Key Index (PVKI), and the issuer's PIN Verification Key (PVK) to calculate a new PVV. The PVKI tells the HSM which key or key variant to use. The *PVK* is the issuer-controlled secret key used in the calculation.

The HSM then compares the calculated PVV with the reference PVV stored for the card. If they match, the PIN is correct.

This architecture preserves the control boundary: the issuer does not store the cardholder's PIN in plain text. It verifies the entered PIN through protected values, controlled keys, and an HSM.

Offline PIN

Offline PIN verification works differently. The PIN does not go to the issuer. The chip checks it locally.

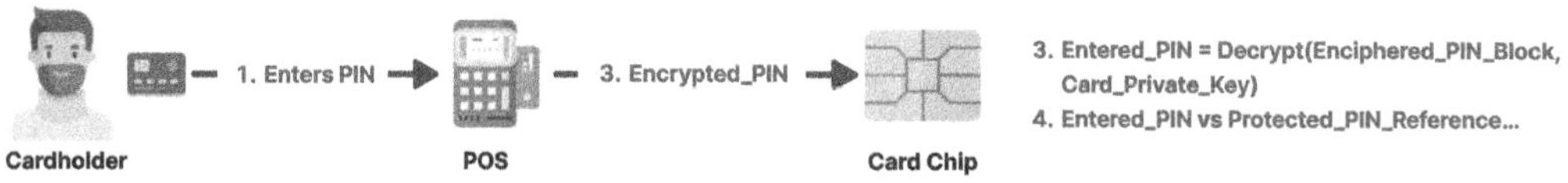

Figure 14.2: Simplified enciphered offline PIN verification.

The process starts the same way: the cardholder enters the PIN at the terminal. The terminal passes the PIN to the chip for local verification, using the offline PIN method supported by both the card and the terminal.

EMV supports two offline PIN methods: plaintext and enciphered. With a plaintext offline PIN, the PIN is sent to the chip during the local card-terminal exchange. With an enciphered offline PIN, shown in Figure 14.2, the terminal encrypts the PIN for the card, and the chip decrypts it internally before checking it.

In both cases, the PIN check happens on the card, not at the issuer. The chip compares the entered PIN with the protected PIN reference stored on the card. If it matches, the chip returns success. If not, it returns failure and updates the offline PIN retry counter.

This makes an offline PIN useful when speed or connectivity is important. A terminal on a plane may not always reach the issuer. A parking terminal does not always have a stable connection. Some unattended terminals may need the card to perform cardholder verification locally.

Changing the PIN

The difference between online and offline PIN becomes especially visible when the cardholder changes the PIN.

For online PIN, the issuer can update its own verification data. A banking app, online banking, a call center, or an ATM may be sufficient, provided the cardholder is properly authenticated.

Offline PIN has one practical complication: the card itself must know the up-to-date PIN reference. If the cardholder changes the PIN in an app, the issuer can immediately update its online PIN records. The chip, however, can still hold the old offline PIN reference until the card is used at a terminal that can update it, such as an ATM.

That is why some banks ask cardholders to use an ATM after changing a PIN. The ATM provides the issuer with a path to update the chip, so both online and offline PIN checks use the same value.

Retry Counters and Blocking

A PIN system also needs a way to stop repeated guessing. If a thief steals a card, they should not be able to try every 4-digit combination until one works. A 4-digit PIN gives only 10,000 possible values, so without rate limits, that search space is too small. Card issuers use retry counters and blocking rules to make repeated guessing impractical.

A PIN retry counter tracks how many incorrect attempts remain before PIN use is blocked. The counter may live on the chip for offline PIN, at the issuer for online PIN, or in both places.

After too many failed attempts, the card may stop accepting PINs. The issuer may decline transactions, block the card, require customer service support, or ask the cardholder to reset the PIN through an approved method. At an ATM, too many incorrect attempts may even cause the machine to retain the card.

The retry counter is one reason a PIN can be only 4 digits. Security does not come from length alone. It comes from secrecy, cryptographic protection, secure verification, and strict limits on guessing. A weak PIN is still risky – numbers like 0000, 1234, or a birth year are easier to guess – but the system is designed to block repeated attempts before brute-force attacks become practical.

To the cardholder, many PIN problems feel the same: the PIN does not work. For the issuer, a blocked retry counter and an out-of-date offline PIN reference are distinct issues that require distinct fixes.

PIN Verification Architecture

For the cardholder, the PIN is just a short code entered on a keypad. For the payment system, that entry is the start of a controlled cryptographic process.

The system has to protect the PIN at every stage: keypad, terminal, acquirer, network, issuer processor, and issuer. Online PIN does that by carrying only an encrypted PIN block through controlled key zones until the issuer's HSM verifies it. Offline PIN keeps the check inside the chip when the card and terminal support it.

Retry counters limit guessing, and PIN-change processes keep issuer-side and chip-side data aligned. The design gives the issuer or chip a verification result without exposing the cardholder's secret to ordinary payment systems.

A correct PIN is still only authentication. The issuer must still authorize the transaction.

Chapter 15: Card Security Codes

A PIN checks whether the cardholder knows a secret. A CVV verifies that the card data includes the security value expected for the way the card is being used.

There are several CVVs: magnetic-stripe transactions use one value, online purchases use another printed on the card, and chip or contactless transactions may use dynamic values that change each time.

This separation limits reuse. A code copied from a magnetic stripe should not help with an online checkout, and a printed CVV2 should not help create a valid chip or contactless transaction.

Most people call the printed code on the card *the CVV*, but that is only one member of a larger family.

Security Codes and Payment Channels

The PAN identifies the card account. The expiry date helps show whether the credential is still current. But both values are often visible, copied, transmitted, or stored in many places. If the PAN and expiry date were enough to pay, every exposure of the card number would be far more dangerous.

Visa uses the term Card Verification Value (CVV). Mastercard uses Card Validation Code (CVC). American Express and other networks have their own names and formats. The idea is similar: a value derived from card data and issuer-controlled cryptographic keys, used to check whether the transaction carries the expected security value.

The main types of codes are:

- CVV1 or CVC1, stored on the magnetic stripe.
- CVV2 or CVC2, printed on the card or shown by the issuer for online use.

- dynamic CVV or dynamic CVC, generated for a transaction rather than fixed for the life of the card.

Service Code

The service code is a 3-digit value stored on the magnetic stripe. It isn't printed on the card, but it tells terminals and issuers how the card is supposed to be used.

A service code has three positions:

Position	Controls	Example Meaning
A	Interchange and technology	International, domestic, chip-capable, test
B	Authorization and PIN rule	PIN required, PIN not required, PIN online only
C	Usage restriction	ATM only, POS only, goods only, no restriction

A service code such as 220 indicates an international chip-capable card that supports PIN handling and has no broad usage restriction. A different service code can indicate ATM-only, domestic, or POS-only use.

Terminals and issuers can use it during transaction processing. If a card's service code indicates it should be used only at POS terminals, the issuer can decline an ATM transaction because the card's usage profile does not allow it.

The service code also participates in the calculation of CVV1 and CVV2. CVV1 depends on the service code encoded on the magnetic stripe. CVV2 uses the same general family of cryptographic calculation but substitutes a fixed service-code value defined for that code type, commonly 000, rather than using the card's actual stripe service code.

Because the service code is part of the calculation, changing it changes the expected CVV1. If someone alters magnetic stripe data, for example, by changing a usage restriction, the recalculated CVV1 will no longer match. The issuer's HSM can detect the mismatch and decline the transaction.

The stripe service code therefore communicates usage controls and helps protect those controls against alteration through the CVV1 calculation.

CVV1 on the Magnetic Stripe

CVV1 is the security code used for magnetic-stripe transactions.

It is encoded in the magnetic stripe data, typically within the discretionary data on Track 2, alongside card data such as the PAN, expiry date, and service code. The cardholder doesn't see it. It's read when a card is swiped.

CVV1 was designed for a world where magnetic-stripe transactions were common. When a card was swiped, the terminal read the stripe data and sent it to the acquiring bank and payment network for transmission to the issuer. The issuer or its processor could validate whether the CVV1 matched the expected value for that card.

CVV1 is calculated from card data and issuer-controlled keys, using the PAN, expiry date, and service code, processed by a cryptographic function. The issuer recomputes and compares the value using its HSM.

The weakness is that the magnetic stripe does not change. If a criminal copies the full stripe data, CVV1 can still match because the copied card repeats the same values as the original.

CVV1 can help detect altered stripe data, but it cannot prevent copied stripe data from being reused where magnetic-stripe acceptance still applies. It belongs to a legacy security model: useful against tampering, weak against cloning.

CVV2 in Online Payments

CVV2 is the code that most cardholders recognize.

It's the 3- or 4-digit value printed on the card, usually on the back for Visa and Mastercard, and on the front for some other networks. In an online checkout, the merchant usually asks the cardholder to enter the PAN, expiry date, and CVV2.

CVV2 exists because online card payments lack the physical interaction of a card-present transaction. The merchant cannot read the chip. The terminal cannot check the magnetic stripe. The issuer can't see whether the card is physically in the buyer's hand.

The printed code gives the issuer another value to verify and allows the merchant to request card data that should not be stored after authorization.

CVV2 still has clear limits. It does not prove that the person paying actually has the card in hand. It only shows that they know a value that should be on the card, and that value can still be copied, stolen, or leaked if not handled carefully.

Figure 15.1 traces the CVV2 verification flow, which is simpler than online PIN verification.

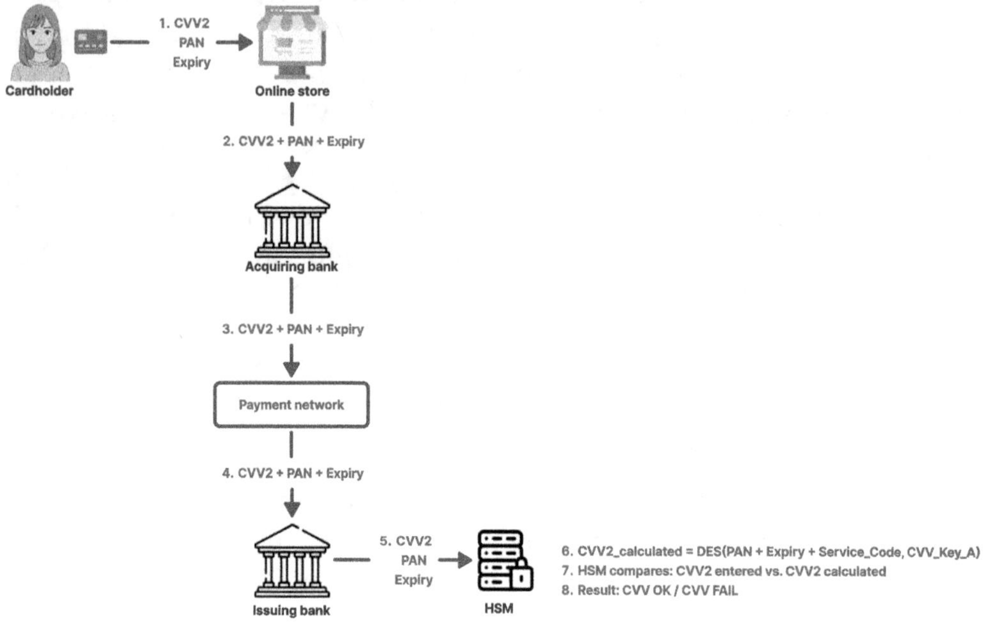

Figure 15.1: CVV2 verification.

The cardholder enters the PAN, expiry date, and CVV2 into the online store. The merchant sends those values to the acquirer as part of the authorization request. The acquirer forwards the transaction to the payment network, which then forwards it to the issuer.

CVV2 is handled differently from an online PIN. A PIN travels in a specially protected PIN block and is translated between secure key zones. CVV2 travels as part of the authorization data for the online transaction.

Because CVV2 is static, storing it after authorization would make merchant databases far more dangerous if breached. Card security rules, therefore, prohibit storing CVV2 after authorization.

When the issuer receives the authorization request, it asks its HSM to verify the received CVV2 using the PAN, expiry date, the fixed service-code input defined for CVV2, and issuer-controlled keys. The HSM recomputes the expected value and compares it with the CVV2 received in the transaction.

If the values match, the CVV2 check passes. If they do not match, the issuer can decline or apply risk rules.

CVV2 is useful precisely because it is separate from the PAN and expiry date. But because cardholders can see it and type it into websites, it is much weaker than chip-generated proof. It gives the issuer another check, but it is not strong authentication on its own.

iCVV and Chip Protection

Integrated CVV, or *iCVV*, is a chip-side security value that helps separate chip data from magnetic-stripe data.

It is conceptually similar to CVV1: both are static verification values derived from card data and issuer-controlled keys. The difference is the context. CVV1 is stored in the magnetic stripe data and calculated using the stripe service code. iCVV is stored in the chip's EMV data and uses a fixed substitution value in place of the service code, often 999 in Visa-style implementations.

That difference helps the issuer detect substitution. If fraudsters copy magnetic stripe data, they should not be able to make it appear to be valid chip data. The verification value expected for chip data differs from that for stripe data.

iCVV remains static, so it is not the primary dynamic proof in an EMV transaction. That role belongs to EMV cryptograms, especially the ARQC.

Dynamic Security Values

A *dynamic security value* is calculated for a specific transaction rather than fixed for the life of the card. Depending on the implementation, the inputs may include card data, the Application Transaction Counter (ATC), and an Unpredictable Number (UN) supplied by the terminal. The ATC is a counter that increases with every chip-based transaction. The unpredictable number is fresh terminal-provided data. Together, they help make the value unique for that transaction.

If someone captures a dynamic code, they should not be able to reuse it. The next transaction will have a different counter, a new unpredictable number, or both. Figure 15.2 traces how the dynamic value is generated and checked.

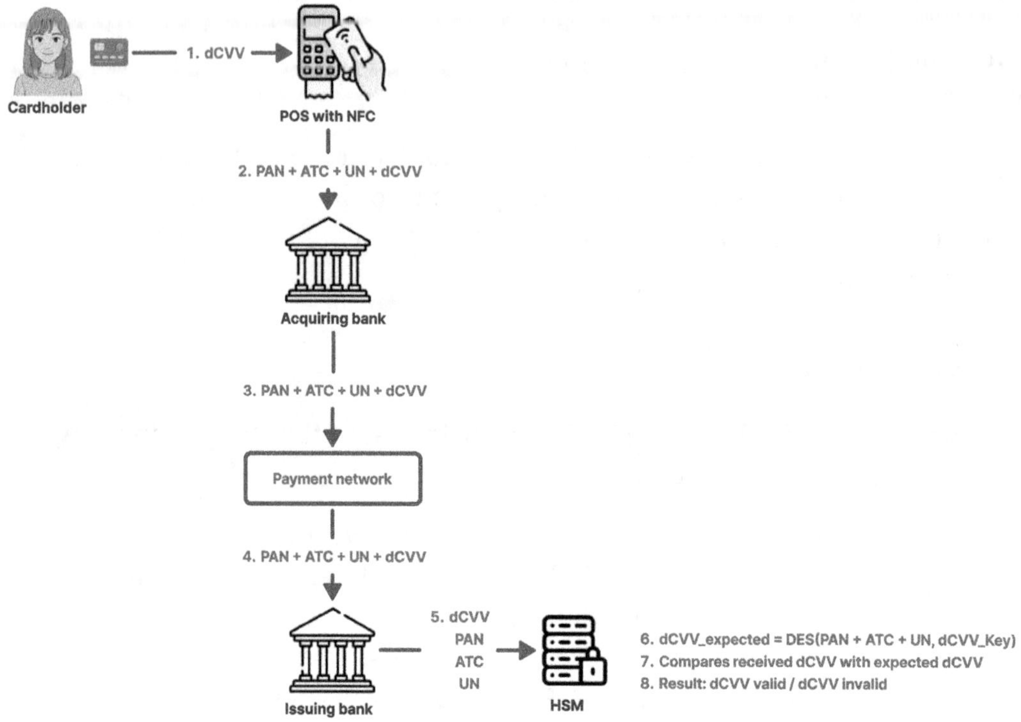

Figure 15.2: Dynamic CVV verification.

The process begins when the card or contactless credential is used for a transaction. The card, chip, or tokenized credential generates a value using transaction-specific inputs. The terminal sends the relevant data to the issuer via the acquiring bank and payment network. The issuer's HSM repeats the calculation using the same inputs and issuer-controlled keys.

If the issuer's calculated value matches the value received from the card, the check passes. If it does not match, the transaction can be declined.

The issuer is checking whether the value generated for this transaction matches its expectations. Unlike CVV2, a dynamic security value is not fixed for the life of the card.

Implementations vary by network, product, and transaction type. In some contexts, the industry may talk about dynamic CVV, dynamic CVC, a dynamic security value, or related chip-generated values. EMV cryptograms, especially ARQC, are a separate but related form of transaction-specific proof.

Security values show data integrity, not authorization. Even with matching values, the issuer must still make a decision based on account status, funds, limits, merchant rules, or fraud risk.

Security-Code Family

Each value belongs to a specific payment context:

Value	Where It Lives	What It Checks	Main Limitation
CVV1 / CVC1	Magnetic-stripe data	Whether the stripe data matches the issuer's expected value	Static; copied stripe data can still replay it
CVV2 / CVC2	Printed on the card or shown by the issuer	Whether an online or mail/phone transaction includes the expected printed security code	Static; can be copied, phished, or leaked
iCVV	EMV chip data, commonly in Track 2 Equivalent Data	Whether chip-related data is separate from magnetic-stripe data	Static; not the main EMV dynamic proof
Dynamic CVV / CVC	Generated during certain chip, contactless, or tokenized transaction contexts	Whether the transaction includes a fresh security value for that transaction	Implementation-dependent; still only one input to authorization
ARQC	Generated by the EMV chip during online authorization	Whether the chip produced transaction-specific cryptographic proof	Stronger and broader than CVV; covered in detail in Chapter 16

These values are not random numbers. They are controlled values derived from card data, transaction context, and issuer keys. They help the issuer verify that the transaction matches the payment method being used.

The strongest card-present version of this idea is EMV cryptography, where the chip produces transaction-specific proof that the issuer can verify.

Chapter 16: EMV Cryptograms

A magnetic stripe repeats stored data. A chip stores data too, but it can also generate a cryptographic response for each transaction. That response is called a *cryptogram.*

Copying the visible card number or magnetic stripe data does not grant an attacker access to the chip's secret keys. Without those keys, the attacker cannot generate valid cryptograms for new transactions. That is the security shift in EMV: the chip does more than identify; it participates in the transaction.

Authorization Request Cryptogram

The main cryptogram in an online EMV transaction is the *Authorization Request Cryptogram*, or *ARQC*. When the cardholder inserts the chip card, the terminal and chip exchange details – amount, currency, date, country, terminal type, and risk-management data. The chip combines these with stored card data and secret keys to generate the ARQC.

The ARQC travels with the authorization request through the acquirer and payment network to the issuer. On the issuer side, the issuer or its processor verifies the cryptogram inside an HSM.

A valid ARQC means the chip proof checks out, not that the transaction is automatically approved. If the issuer cannot verify the ARQC, the expected chip proof is missing, and the issuer may decline the transaction or treat it as high-risk.

ATC and Unpredictable Number

Two inputs help generate an EMV cryptogram specific to a single transaction: the card's counter and the terminal's fresh input.

The *Application Transaction Counter (ATC)* assigns each chip transaction a sequence number from the card's perspective. Each time the chip is used, the

ATC increases. The issuer receives the ATC in the authorization request and can track the sequence over time.

If the same ATC appears twice with different transaction data, something is wrong. If the counter jumps unexpectedly, moves backward, or appears out of sequence, the issuer can treat the transaction as suspicious.

The ATC is not a fraud signal on its own. Offline transactions can create gaps, and declined transactions still increase the counter. But it gives issuers something a magnetic stripe never could: a way to track the order of chip activity.

The second input is the *unpredictable number*. This is fresh data supplied by the terminal during the transaction. The chip uses it to generate the cryptogram, and the issuer uses it to check the cryptogram.

The unpredictable number helps stop pre-play attacks. Without the UN, attackers could try to collect valid cryptograms from a real card in advance and reuse them later. A strong unpredictable number makes it that much harder, because the card cannot know in advance what input a real terminal will provide.

If terminals use weak, repeated, or predictable numbers, EMV cryptograms become less secure. Cryptography relies not only on secret keys, but also on good transaction inputs and correct implementation.

Authorization Response Cryptogram

EMV also supports issuer authentication back to the chip. The issuer's response cryptogram is called the *Authorization Response Cryptogram*, or ARPC. After verifying the ARQC, the issuer generates an ARPC and sends it back through the network and acquirer to the terminal. The chip validates that response.

The ARPC allows the chip to authenticate the issuer's authorization response. Issuer scripts can be returned alongside that response to update certain card parameters, apply blocking instructions, or perform PIN-related operations, but issuer scripts are a separate mechanism and have their own integrity protection.

ARQC and ARPC work in opposite directions. The card sends the ARQC to prove itself to the issuer when requesting authorization. The issuer sends the ARPC to the card to confirm its response after authorization.

Transaction Certificates and Decline Cryptograms

ARQC is not the only cryptogram a chip can produce.

A *Transaction Certificate (TC)* indicates that the chip has completed the transaction from its perspective. In an offline approval, the TC is the card's approval cryptogram. For example, a low-value transaction at an offline-capable terminal can be completed locally if the card, terminal, and risk rules allow it. In an online transaction, the chip can generate a TC after the issuer approves and the chip completes its final checks.

An Application Authentication Cryptogram (AAC) indicates that the chip has declined the transaction. For example, the chip can generate an AAC if offline limits are exceeded, cardholder verification fails, issuer authentication fails, or the card's risk rules indicate it should not continue.

So, the three cryptograms mark three different outcomes. With an ARQC, the card sends the transaction online and waits for the issuer's decision. With a TC, the chip completes the transaction from its side. With an AAC, the chip declines the transaction.

In online transactions, the issuer usually makes the main authorization decision. But the card and terminal also apply rules before the request goes out and after the response comes back.

Processing Terms

These values are the working vocabulary of EMV: cryptograms, the counter that feeds them, the fresh terminal input that makes them transaction-specific, and the issuer instructions they protect.

Term	Role in EMV Processing
ARQC	The card requests an online authorization decision from the issuer.
ARPC	The issuer sends a cryptographic response that the card can validate.
TC	The card indicates that the transaction is approved or completed from the chip's perspective.
AAC	The card indicates that the transaction is declined.

ATC	The card's transaction counter, used as an input to cryptogram generation and replay detection.
Unpredictable number	Terminal-provided fresh data that helps make the cryptogram specific to the transaction.
Issuer script	An authenticated issuer instruction that can update certain chip parameters during an online transaction.

A chip transaction is a controlled exchange involving the card, terminal, and issuer. The chip generates transaction-specific proof, verifies responses, and completes or declines the transaction under EMV rules.

Part IV
Card Products and Business Models

Chapter 17: Debit Cards

Card products are easier to understand once you know whose funds they use.

A debit card spends money from the customer's bank account. A credit card draws on a credit line. A prepaid card uses a pre-funded balance. The checkout process can look similar, but the product logic differs.

A *debit card* is the card product closest to the customer's own funds. It does not create a loan in the standard model. It gives the cardholder access to money already held in a current account or checking account.

That simplicity hides an accounting detail. A bank deposit isn't cash stored somewhere. It's the bank's liability to the customer. When a debit card transaction posts, the bank reduces the customer's account balance and the matching liability. The cardholder sees spending; the bank sees its liability declining. That is the core logic of a debit card.

Linked Account

A debit card is linked to a transactional bank account: a checking account in the United States, a current account in the United Kingdom and many other markets, or an equivalent everyday payment account elsewhere.

The names differ by country, but the function is similar. This is the account used for salary, transfers, bills, ATM withdrawals, and day-to-day card payments. It is different from a savings account, a term deposit, an overnight deposit, or an investment account, even though all of them can fall under the broad term *deposit*.

That distinction is operational. A debit card needs an account that supports frequent debits, real-time authorization checks, holds, clearing entries, ATM withdrawals, and customer-facing balances. The card is not linked to all of the customer's money at the bank. It is attached to a specific account relationship that the issuer allows the card system to access.

When a cardholder pays with a debit card, the issuer checks the account balance, card status, limits, and risk signals. If the account can cover the transaction and the checks pass, the issuer approves the authorization request. When the transaction clears, the issuer posts the debit to the account.

Holds, Available Balance, and Posted Balance

A debit card payment does not always reduce the booked account balance when "Approved" appears on the terminal.

The reason is the split between authorization and posting. During authorization, the issuer checks the account and places a hold, reducing the available balance. This is not the final posted debit. The merchant can proceed, and the cardholder's available spending power drops, but the transaction still has to clear.

Suppose a cardholder has $500 in a checking account and uses a debit card to buy a $40 lunch.

At the time of authorization, the issuer reduces the available balance from $500 to $460. The banking app shows a pending transaction. The cardholder can't spend that $40 elsewhere, but the booked balance can still display $500 until clearing.

When the merchant submits the transaction for clearing, the issuer posts the debit. The booked balance falls, and the bank's liability drops by the transaction amount.

The difference between the available and booked balances helps explain common customer issues. Hotels often authorize more than the final bill. Fuel stations often place a temporary hold until they know the exact amount of fuel. Restaurants can authorize meals before the tip is added. If the merchant does not complete the transaction, the hold remains until it expires.

A debit card transaction, therefore, has two layers of money logic:

- Authorization reduces the available balance by reserving spendable funds.
- Clearing posts the debit to the account and reduces the bank's liability to the customer.

Overdrafts

Some debit accounts allow overdrafts, allowing the account balance to go negative up to an agreed limit. If the account has $20 and the cardholder makes a $30 purchase, the issuer can approve the transaction, leaving the account at -$10. At that moment, the bank has effectively lent the customer money.

This can make overdraft-enabled debit cards seem like credit cards, but they remain linked to checking accounts. The *overdraft* is a feature of the account, not a separate revolving credit line with billing cycles or minimum payments.

This distinction shapes classification, pricing, regulation, and customer expectations. A debit card with overdraft is still a debit product. The overdraft simply revises the rule on insufficient funds. Overdrafts prevent payment failures and declined transactions, but can be expensive with fees or interest.

Everyday Account Spending

Debit cards are simple, familiar, and broadly accessible.

The cardholder spends from the account they already use. There is no separate monthly bill, no revolving balance, and no interest for carrying card debt, unless an overdraft is used.

A debit card imposes a natural spending limit — cardholders can only spend what is in the account. This helps with budgeting and is useful for youth, students, salary accounts, or those avoiding credit.

Debit cards are easier to issue because opening a basic account is simpler than qualifying for credit. The issuer does not have to assess a credit limit before allowing the card to be used.

The main limitation is liquidity — a debit card works only if the account has enough funds. This discipline helps with budgeting, but can be restrictive in emergencies.

Fraud can also directly affect the cardholder's cash flow. With a credit card, a disputed transaction usually impacts the issuer's credit exposure during investigation. With a debit card, the disputed amount is deducted from the cardholder's available balance until the case is resolved.

A debit card stays close to the customer's funds. That is both its core advantage and its central risk.

Issuer Economics

Debit cards are not usually the highest-margin card product: credit cards generate higher interchange, interest, and fees; charge cards bring premium fees and affluent customers; and prepaid cards have their own fee economics.

Debit card economics live or die on the account relationship.

One direct revenue source is interchange. Each debit card purchase can generate a small interchange fee for the issuer, funded through the merchant side of the card system. The exact rate depends on market, network, card type, merchant category, transaction channel, and regulation. In the European Union, consumer debit interchange is capped at a low level. In the United States, large-bank debit interchange is regulated under the Durbin Amendment.

Banks also earn from account fees, ATM fees, FX markup, replacement card fees, overdraft fees, interest, and bundled account packages. Some are visible to customers; others are embedded in pricing or terms.

The larger value is the account relationship. A debit card helps make the bank the customer's main bank. If salary is deposited into the account and the debit card is used every day, the bank holds the deposits, observes spending behavior, and becomes part of the customer's routine.

A current account balance is both a liability to the customer and a funding source for the bank. The bank can use customer deposits within regulatory and liquidity constraints. A customer who keeps money in the account to support daily spending provides the bank with a lower-cost funding source than wholesale funding or high-rate deposits.

Transaction data strengthens the relationship. Card spending reveals where and how customers shop, their travel patterns, income levels, bill payment habits, and when additional products are likely to be relevant. This data aids fraud detection, credit offers, savings prompts, budgeting tools, merchant offers, and customer segmentation.

Retention is another value source. A daily debit card user finds it harder to move banks. Changing banks means moving salary, subscriptions, stored credentials, direct debits, app habits, and card controls. The debit card turns an account from passive to active.

Merchant Acceptance

For merchants, a debit card looks like any other card at the terminal. The merchant presents the transaction, receives approval or a decline, and later receives payout from the acquirer.

Debit card acceptance is cheaper for merchants than credit card acceptance in many markets, especially where debit interchange is regulated, or domestic debit networks compete with international card networks. That is why domestic debit schemes remain commercially important in countries such as Germany, France, Canada, Australia, and the United States.

Debit card acceptance is usually cheaper, but the merchant still pays for acceptance through the acquirer or PSP, often as an MDR. That price can include interchange, network fees, acquirer markup, gateway fees, and other charges.

Debit cards also create different risks for merchants who need to charge later. Car rental companies and hotels often prefer credit cards because they need a reliable way to charge for damage, fuel, deposits, or incidentals. A debit card can support a hold, but the customer can spend down the account before the final amount is submitted. If the customer empties or closes the account, the merchant has less flexibility.

Some merchants, therefore, place larger holds on debit cards, restrict their use, or require additional identification.

Market Differences

Debit cards look simple in definition, but they vary sharply by market. In some countries, they are the default card product for everyday spending. In others, credit cards dominate online purchases, rewards programs, and higher-value transactions. Transaction routing also differs. Some markets send many local debit transactions over domestic networks, while others rely mainly on Visa and Mastercard. Overdraft rules add another layer: in some countries, negative balances are a common account feature; in others, banks treat them more restrictively or separate them from everyday debit-card use.

> **PIN Debit and Network-Branded Debit**
>
> In the United States, the same debit card can often be processed through different networks.
>
> One option is a domestic debit network. This is often called PIN debit because the transaction traditionally used a PIN and was routed through a US debit network rather than through Visa or Mastercard.
>
> Another option is a Visa or Mastercard debit. In that case, the card still debits the customer's bank account, but the transaction is routed over Visa or Mastercard's rails.
>
> This routing choice affects merchants because different networks can have different costs, rules, and dispute processes. US Regulation II requires debit card issuers to enable at least two unaffiliated networks, so merchants have a choice of terminal, transaction type, and network.
>
> Outside the United States, a similar idea appears on co-badged cards. A card can carry a domestic scheme for local transactions and an international scheme, such as Visa or Mastercard, for broader acceptance.

The core product is stable, but the economics and customer experience are local. Debit cards in Germany, the United States, Brazil, India, or the United Kingdom all use a spend account, but they differ in network routing, overdraft rules, rewards, ATM fees, fraud liability, and merchant acceptance.

A debit card's business model follows from its funding source. It spends existing funds, avoids revolving debt in the standard model, and does not require credit underwriting. For the bank, it is not just a fee product; it is the operating layer of the primary account relationship, bringing deposits, transaction data, daily engagement, and retention.

Chapter 18: Prepaid Cards, Stored Value, and E-Money

A *prepaid card* is linked to a stored-value balance funded by the cardholder, an employer, a parent, a retailer, or a program sponsor. When the balance reaches zero, spending stops until more value is added.

That can make prepaid cards look similar to debit cards, but the structure is different. A debit card gives the cardholder access to their own current or checking account at a bank. A prepaid card gives access to a balance recorded in a ledger maintained by the issuer, program manager, or processor. There is not usually a separate bank account for each cardholder.

Stored-Value Balance

The key design is pooling plus internal ledgering. One cardholder has $5, another has $40, and another has $120. The issuer records those balances separately, but the money backing them is usually held together in one or more safeguarded accounts. The bank sees an account held for the issuer; the issuer's ledger shows how much of that pool belongs to each customer; and the customer sees an individual balance in an app, on a receipt, or on a website. Legally, that balance is not a bank deposit in the customer's own name. It is a claim recorded in the issuer's ledger and backed by safeguarded funds that must be kept separate from the issuer's operating funds.

In EU/UK-style e-money models, safeguarding protects customer funds, but it differs from deposit insurance. If a bank fails, eligible depositors are compensated up to the scheme limit. If an e-money issuer fails, customers rely on the safeguarding regime and the recovery process around the protected pool. These are not the same level of protection. Most customers notice the difference only when something goes wrong: the app shows a balance that looks like a bank account, but legally it is a ledger entry backed by a specific safeguarding structure.

This structure allows prepaid products to be offered through different institutional models. A bank can issue prepaid cards directly. An Electronic Money Institution, or EMI, can issue e-money products in markets that recognize that license, such as the EU and the UK, without becoming a full bank. A fintech, gift-card program, payroll provider, benefits provider, or travel-card company can offer prepaid cards by partnering with a licensed bank or EMI, as well as processors and program managers that handle card issuance, compliance operations, ledgering, and transaction processing.

Together, those arrangements create a card and a spendable balance without a full bank account behind each customer. The provider does not take deposits in the banking sense. It runs, or uses, a ledger-backed stored-value structure where customer funds are pooled, safeguarded, and separated internally by records rather than by individual bank accounts.

Authorization against Stored Value

A prepaid card transaction still goes through authorization, clearing, and settlement.

For each transaction, the merchant requests authorization. The issuer or processor checks the available prepaid balance, card status, limits, and risk rules. If sufficient stored value is available, approval normally creates a hold that reduces the available balance. The final debit is posted to the prepaid ledger when the clearing record is processed.

At clearing, the final transaction amount is posted to the prepaid ledger. Settlement moves funds through the card system to the merchant, just as with other card transactions.

The difference lies in funding. Prepaid programs are designed not to approve spending beyond the available stored balance because there is no account or credit line to draw on.

If the card holds $20 and the transaction is $25, the issuer declines. Some prepaid and gift-card environments support partial authorization: the issuer approves only the available amount, and the customer covers the rest by another method. But that process requires support from both the merchant and the terminal.

Foreign-currency transactions show why prepaid authorization is stricter. Suppose a cardholder with a dollar prepaid card pays in euros. At authorization, the issuer estimates the amount in dollars and reserves it, but the exchange rate can move before clearing. A prepaid issuer has less flexibility than a debit or credit card issuer because the prepaid card is designed to spend only the stored balance, with no overdraft protection and no credit line to cover the difference.

To avoid a negative balance, the program locks in the exchange rate at authorization, reserves slightly more than the estimated amount, or applies an additional buffer, releasing the unused portion after clearing. To the cardholder, this may appear to be an excessive hold. Operationally, it protects the prepaid balance from going below zero.

Controlled Spending

Prepaid cards solve practical problems that debit and credit cards do not always handle well.

A *gift card* is the simplest example. Someone loads a fixed amount. The recipient spends it within the program's rules — at one retailer, an online store, a mall network, or wherever an open-loop card is accepted. The giver doesn't have to choose a specific item.

The same logic works for budgeting. A traveler can set aside money for a trip before leaving. A parent can give a child spending money without giving access to the parent's main account. A company can give an employee a fixed allowance for meals, travel, or project expenses. The hard balance ceiling is the point: once the balance runs out, spending stops.

Prepaid cards can also provide basic payment access for people who do not have a full bank account. In some markets, basic prepaid products require less identity verification than bank accounts, which can help customers with limited documentation, thin credit histories, recent immigration, or limited access to mainstream banking.

That access is narrower than a bank account. Prepaid cards can carry fees, lower limits, weaker protections, no interest, and fewer features. But they still provide a way to make card payments when a full account is unavailable or unnecessary.

Prepaid cards are also useful when money needs to be kept separate. A travel card keeps a trip budget away from the main bank account. A temporary online card limits exposure for a specific purchase. A youth card separates a child's allowance from a parent's account.

Companies and public-sector bodies use prepaid for the same reason: control. Employee benefits, meal vouchers, incentive programs, expense allowances, insurance payouts, public-sector disbursements, and temporary project budgets all need money to be usable, but not unlimited. The program sponsor can define where the money can be spent, how much can be spent, and when the card expires.

The recurring pattern is controlled spending. Money is loaded for a specific person, purpose, limit, or situation.

Customer Checks and Limits

Prepaid cards are often easier to obtain than debit or credit cards, but they are still regulated.

Prepaid products carry compliance risk because they can hold value and move it through the payment system. The risk is higher when the card is anonymous, lightly verified, reloadable, cash-accessible, or usable across borders. A prepaid card with weak controls could be used to move money without clear ownership, or to split activity into smaller amounts that avoid review.

Prepaid compliance, therefore, turns into practical limits: how much money can be loaded, whether the card can be reloaded, whether cash can be withdrawn, whether the card works internationally, and how much customer identification is required.

A low-value gift card often requires little or no identity verification. A reloadable card with higher limits usually requires Know Your Customer (KYC) checks. A card that supports ATM withdrawals, international use, person-to-person transfers, or high monthly volume is subject to stricter requirements.

The closer a prepaid card gets to a bank account, the more rules it has to follow. That constraint shapes the product. Many issuers use tiered structures. A basic prepaid wallet allows small balances and limited spending with minimal information. A fully verified account allows higher balances, larger top-ups, ATM access, international transfers, and extra features. The upgrade path is part of the business model: start with limited functionality, then request more information as the customer needs more capability.

Program Economics

Prepaid programs earn revenue in several ways.

Interchange is one direct source. When a prepaid card is used at a merchant, the card network generates interchange and shares it based on the program structure. In some markets, prepaid interchange differs from debit interchange. Commercial prepaid cards, benefit cards, and specialized products can be treated differently from consumer debit cards.

Fees are another major source. Programs charge for issuance, replacement, monthly maintenance, inactivity, ATM withdrawals, foreign exchange, cash loading, or transfers. Gift-card programs charge the buyer up front. Travel cards earn from FX markup. Payroll or benefit programs often charge the sponsoring company rather than the cardholder.

Float or interest income can contribute where permitted. When cardholders load funds and do not spend them immediately, the issuer or program manager can earn income on the funds backing the balances. In tightly regulated e-money models, safeguarding rules limit how customer funds can be held or invested.

Breakage is most significant in gift cards. It is prepaid value that's never used: a lost card, a forgotten balance, a small leftover amount, or value that expires under the program rules. Once the relevant legal, accounting, and expiry rules are satisfied, the unused value can be recognized as revenue.

Prepaid also has strategic value. A prepaid program can bring customers into a financial product without full credit underwriting. It can help a fintech test demand before offering broader banking services. It can support corporate programs, public-sector disbursements, travel spending, or youth accounts. For some companies, prepaid is the main product. For others, it is the entry point into a wider account, credit, investment, or subscription relationship.

Refunds, Holds, and Operational Friction

The same controls that make prepaid useful also create friction.

Refunds are one example. If a customer pays with a prepaid card and later returns the item, the refund is normally credited back to the same prepaid balance. That is simple when the card is still active, and the customer can access it. It becomes harder when the card was a gift card, a temporary program card, or a disposable prepaid product that the customer has lost or thrown away.

The merchant may still be required to refund to the original credential, while the issuer or program manager must restore value to the correct ledger balance or customer record.

Authorization holds create a sharper problem for prepaid cards because the available balance is finite and pre-funded. A hold that would be annoying on a credit card can consume most of a prepaid balance, leaving the cardholder unable to spend money that is still technically theirs until the final amount clears or the unused hold is released.

Subscriptions create a different issue. The hard balance limit supports spending control. It can also interrupt services the customer expected to continue, because the merchant cannot collect more than the prepaid balance allows.

The design of a prepaid card defines its role: control, access, and separation. It also sets the boundaries. The card must be funded before use; legal protections differ by product and market; and the provider must manage refunds, holds, FX, and identity checks within the limits of stored value.

Chapter 19: Credit Cards

Debit cards and prepaid cards can only spend money the cardholder already has, drawing from an account or a stored balance. Credit cards work on a different clock. The issuer pays the merchant up front, the cardholder pays the issuer later, and what passes between them is a borrowing relationship rather than a transfer of funds.

A *credit card* is a payment credential tied to a revolving line of credit. The issuer sets a credit limit, the cardholder spends up to that limit, a statement arrives at the end of the cycle, and then a decision has to be made: pay the full balance or carry part of it forward.

The repayment choice is what makes the product both useful and dangerous. Paid in full, a credit card offers short-term liquidity, rewards, fraud protection, and credit history, often at no interest cost. Carried month after month, the same card becomes high-cost unsecured debt that's hard to climb out of.

Credit Line

A credit line isn't real money that the cardholder owns. It's the maximum amount the issuer is willing to lend through the card.

A $5,000 credit line doesn't put $5,000 in any account. It just means the issuer is willing to let the cardholder borrow up to that amount through purchases and other charges posted to the card, including fees, interest, and cash advances.

Three numbers describe the state of the account: the credit limit is the ceiling, the outstanding balance is the amount already borrowed and posted, and the available credit — sometimes called the available amount — is what's left after subtracting the posted balance, pending authorizations, fees, and any issuer-specific adjustments.

If the limit is $5,000 and the outstanding balance is $1,200, the available credit is roughly $3,800, with pending authorizations and fees shifting that figure in real time. A $300 payment frees up available credit again. A new $200 purchase pulls it back down.

This revolving structure distinguishes credit cards from other payment cards. The credit line can be used, repaid, and used again, with the account remaining open and available credit refilling whenever the balance drops.

Issuing a credit card is therefore an underwriting decision, not just an account-opening step. The issuer is choosing how much unsecured exposure to take on. That choice depends on income, credit history, existing debts, repayment behavior, employment, the customer's relationship with the bank, credit bureau data, internal scoring models, and local regulations.

Authorization against Available Credit

A credit-card purchase still begins with authorization, but the question the issuer asks is different. Instead of checking whether the cardholder has the funds, the issuer checks whether the cardholder has enough credit available.

The request reaches the issuer via the usual card network route, carrying the same checks: account status, available credit, authentication data, transaction limits, merchant information, and fraud signals. If everything passes, the issuer approves.

Take the same $5,000 limit and $1,200 outstanding balance from earlier. A $100 purchase reduces available credit from about $3,800 to $3,700 at the time of authorization. The transaction first appears as pending. Later, when it clears, the $100 posts to the account and is added to the outstanding balance.

No money leaves the cardholder's bank account at the moment of purchase. The issuer settles its obligation to the acquirer through the card system and records the matching obligation owed by the cardholder.

In a debit transaction, the posted amount reduces the customer's bank balance by debiting funds the customer already owns. In a credit transaction, the posted amount increases the customer's debt to the issuer, reflecting funds the issuer has lent but the customer hasn't yet repaid.

Billing Cycle

Everything on a credit card is organized around the billing cycle. The billing cycle is the period over which transactions accumulate before a statement is issued. Throughout the cycle, purchases, fees, refunds, payments, interest, and adjustments move in and out of the account, some pending and some already posted.

When the cycle closes, the issuer generates a statement with three key lines: the statement balance, the due date, and the minimum payment. The statement balance is the total amount billed for the cycle; the due date is the payment deadline; and the minimum payment is the smallest amount the cardholder must pay by that date to avoid delinquency.

The *statement* is also where the repayment choice is made. The cardholder can pay the full statement balance, pay only the minimum, or pay anywhere in between. That single choice determines whether the credit card behaves like a payment tool or a revolving loan.

Paying in Full or Revolving

The repayment choice is where one product becomes two. Paying the full statement balance by the due date keeps the card close to a pure payment tool. The cardholder borrowed the issuer's money for a few weeks and repaid them on time. In a program with a grace period, ordinary purchases do not accrue interest before the first due date.

That's why credit cards make sense even for cardholders who don't intend to borrow long-term. They offer short-term liquidity with no purchase interest attached, provided the balance is cleared under the applicable terms.

Paying only the minimum keeps the account in good standing, but it turns the card into a loan. The unpaid balance rolls into the next cycle and starts accruing interest.

Paying somewhere in between keeps the balance from clearing. Interest applies to whatever portion remains on the schedule set by the card agreement.

At that point, the economics change. The annual percentage rate, or APR, is the yearly rate used to express the cost of borrowing on the card. Credit-card APRs are typically much higher than rates on mortgages, auto loans, or secured personal loans, because credit-card debt is unsecured, flexible, and available on demand. The issuer doesn't have a house or a car to seize. It's lending purely on the strength of the cardholder's creditworthiness and repayment behavior.

The minimum payment makes the debt feel more manageable than it actually is. A cardholder with a $2,000 balance might face a required minimum of just $50, which looks easy. Paying that $50 keeps the account out of delinquency, but it does almost nothing to the underlying debt. Interest keeps building on the remaining balance, and if the cardholder keeps spending while paying only the minimum, the balance can remain steady or even grow despite monthly payments.

That's the minimum-payment trap. The cardholder isn't skipping payments. The required payment is small enough to feel survivable, while the debt itself stays expensive and hard to shake.

> **Grace Periods Depend on Paying in Full**
>
> A grace period usually protects ordinary purchases from interest only when the previous statement balance is paid in full by the due date. Once a cardholder starts revolving a balance, new purchases may lose that interest-free treatment under the card agreement. The card still works the same at checkout, but its economics have changed.

Cash Advances and Special Transaction Types

Not every credit-card transaction is treated as a purchase. A *cash advance* allows the cardholder to withdraw cash from the credit line, usually at an ATM or through a cash-equivalent transaction. Issuers price these aggressively: a cash advance fee on top of the amount, a higher interest rate than for regular purchases, and no grace period at all.

The pricing follows the economics. Merchant purchases generate interchange and fit the standard purchase model. Cash advances look more like raw, unsecured borrowing, with little merchant-side revenue and higher credit risk, so the issuer charges more to take on that risk.

Other transaction types can also fall into their own categories. Balance transfers, gambling transactions, cryptocurrency purchases, money orders, person-to-person transfers, foreign-currency transactions, and installment plans may all carry separate fees, interest rules, or restrictions, depending on issuer rules and local regulations.

The same credit card can therefore be cheap for one type of transaction and expensive for another, and the cardholder rarely sees the difference until the statement arrives.

Liquidity, Rewards, and Protection

Credit cards remain popular because they combine five functions in one product: payment, borrowing, protection, rewards, and credit history.

The liquidity benefit is the most immediate. A cardholder can pay for an unexpected repair, a hotel stay, a delayed reimbursement, or an emergency flight before the cash to cover it has arrived. If the balance gets cleared in full by the due date, that liquidity is essentially free.

Credit cards also create a buffer between a disputed transaction and the cardholder's bank account. With a debit card, fraud can drain real money from the account until the bank resolves the case. With a credit card, the disputed amount is part of the cardholder's debt to the issuer, not a hole in the checking account. Consumer protections vary by market, but the cash-flow experience is usually better: the cardholder can dispute a charge rather than trying to claw back money that's already gone.

Rewards push the credit card toward becoming the cardholder's default payment method. Cashback, points, miles, and premium benefits tend to be richer on credit cards than on debit cards, because the underlying economics can support them.

In markets where credit bureaus play a major role, responsible credit card use also builds credit history. Paying on time, keeping utilization reasonable, and keeping the account open can later help the cardholder qualify for mortgages, auto loans, rental housing, and other credit products.

Some cards offer purchase and travel protections: extended warranties, chargeback rights, travel insurance, rental car coverage, lost luggage benefits, lounge access, and emergency assistance. The exact list shifts by issuer, network, tier, and country, but for travelers and high-spend cardholders, these benefits can be worth real money.

The product looks completely different depending on how it's used. For the cardholder who pays in full, a credit card is a convenient payment tool with rewards, protections, and an interest-free grace period. For the cardholder who carries a balance, it's a loan. Under financial stress, it becomes one of the hardest forms of debt to climb out of.

Issuer Revenue

Credit cards are among the most profitable products in retail banking because they bundle payment and lending revenue in a single piece of plastic.

For many issuers, the single biggest profit pool comes from interest on revolving balances. Cardholders who don't pay in full owe interest on the amount they haven't paid off, and because credit card APRs are high, those revolving balances generate substantial interest income.

Interchange is the next major source. Credit-card interchange is typically higher than debit interchange, especially in markets without strict caps, and that revenue helps fund rewards programs, issuer operations, fraud losses, credit risk, and profit. In the European Union, consumer credit interchange is capped at a lower level than in the United States, which is one of the main reasons European rewards programs feel thinner than American ones.

Annual fees are concentrated at the premium end. A high-fee travel card bundles lounge access, insurance, statement credits, concierge services, hotel status, and elevated rewards, and the fee both funds those benefits and aims the product squarely at affluent or frequent-travel customers.

Other fees fill in the gaps: late fees, cash advance fees, balance transfer fees, foreign transaction fees, over-limit fees where regulators still permit them, replacement fees, and installment plan fees.

Rewards aren't a gift from the issuer, even when they're advertised that way. Cashback, points, and miles are customer-acquisition and engagement tools, and the issuer expects to fund them through a mix of interchange, annual fees, partner payments, and interest revenue.

Different cardholders fund the rewards in different ways. A cardholder who pays in full generates interchange and possibly an annual fee, but little interest. A cardholder who carries a balance generates interest revenue. A premium-card customer pays a high annual fee. Merchants indirectly fund part of the system through acceptance costs, and airline and hotel partners may sell points or miles to issuers while benefiting from customer loyalty on their side.

The issuer needs the rewards engine to leave room for profit after funding costs, credit losses, fraud losses, benefit costs, and operating expenses. When the math stops working, rewards quietly shrink.

Credit Risk Management

A credit card issuer is also a lender, and that single fact reshapes how it must operate. Risk management starts before the card is even issued. The issuer underwrites the applicant, decides whether to approve, sets an initial credit limit, prices the product, and determines which features or rewards tier the customer qualifies for.

The work continues for the life of the account. The issuer monitors utilization, payment behavior, missed payments, income signals (when available), fraud patterns, merchant activity, cash-advance behavior, and any changes in credit bureau data. Based on those signals, it may raise a low-risk customer's credit limit, reduce a higher-risk customer's credit limit, block a transaction in real time, reissue a card after a compromise, or close the account.

Collections is the process for handling overdue debt. When a cardholder misses payments, the issuer can send reminders, charge late fees, report the delinquency to credit bureaus, restrict spending, offer hardship programs, or hand the account over to a dedicated collections team or external agency. If the debt is unlikely to be recovered, the issuer records a charge-off, recognizing the balance as a credit loss for accounting purposes while continuing collection efforts in the background.

A debit card issuer primarily cares whether the cardholder has funds available at the time of authorization. A credit-card issuer cares whether the cardholder will repay later. That single shift in question reshapes underwriting, pricing, credit limits, rewards design, collections, capital requirements, and profitability across the entire product.

Product Logic

A credit card is a lending product dressed as a payment card.

The card lets the cardholder spend at merchants, but the credit line is what funds each purchase. The billing cycle tracks what's owed. The grace period can make full repayment interest-free, while the minimum payment lets balances stretch out and accrue interest instead. Interest charges produce revenue for the issuer, rewards pull the cardholder back to the card, and risk systems quietly decide who gets credit and how much.

That combination is why credit cards can feel like two different products. Paid in full, they're convenience, protection, rewards, and credit history, financed by short-term liquidity at no interest cost. Carried month after month, they're high-cost unsecured debt that often outlasts the things it was used to pay for.

Chapter 20: Charge Cards

A charge card looks, at first glance, like a premium credit card. It runs on the same networks, is accepted at the same merchants, and comes loaded with the same perks: travel insurance, lounge access, rewards, and concierge service. Most people call it a credit card. The term is familiar, and nothing about the checkout experience suggests otherwise.

The real difference shows up after the statement is issued. A credit card cardholder gets to choose between paying the balance in full or carrying it forward. A charge card cardholder doesn't. The full balance is due at the end of every cycle, and the product is built around that single rule.

What the charge card offers is short-term credit without the revolving debt. The issuer extends spending capacity for the month, but there's no minimum payment path quietly waiting to turn this month's bill into next year's loan.

Credit Exposure without Revolving Debt

Charge cards still involve credit. The issuer extends spending capacity before repayment, so when a cardholder runs up $3,000 in a cycle, the issuer carries that $3,000 of exposure until the invoice is paid. Merchants get their money long before the issuer gets reimbursed, just as they do with any credit card.

What changes is how long that exposure lasts. A revolving card lets the balance carry forward from month to month, accruing interest along the way. A charge card requires full repayment at the end of each billing cycle, with no rollover.

That distinction reshapes the risk profile. Credit card balances can sit on the books for years, earning interest but quietly building longer-term risk. Charge cards force a reset every cycle, so trouble surfaces fast. The moment a cardholder misses a payment, the issuer can suspend spending, apply late fees, reduce the available limit, or move the account to collections, all before the balance has a chance to grow over multiple cycles.

None of this makes charge cards risk-free. Cardholders can still overspend, businesses can still hit cash-flow gaps, and even premium customers can lose their income overnight. What charge cards prevent is the slow, quiet accumulation of revolving debt that builds month after month until it becomes hard to unwind.

Repayment and Cash Flow

The repayment schedule of a charge card looks more like a monthly payment than a loan. Transactions accumulate over the billing cycle, the issuer calculates the full balance at the statement date, and in many charge-card programs, the entire amount is automatically debited from the cardholder's bank account on or near the due date. The cardholder doesn't pick between paying the minimum, paying part, or rolling the rest forward. The balance clears when the cycle closes, by design.

That automatic mechanism is what really separates the product from a credit card. A credit cardholder can pay the minimum and carry the rest over to next month. A charge card cardholder owes the full balance, usually pulled by direct debit from an account already linked to the card. If the payment fails, the issuer can move fast: late fees, suspended spending, reduced limits, collections, or hardship arrangements under the charge-card agreement.

The structure allows the cardholder to spend before cash actually leaves the bank, without an easy on-ramp to long-term debt. It also creates pressure. A cardholder who runs up $8,000 needs to have $8,000 sitting in the account when the automatic payment hits. The product fits a predictable cash flow well and becomes unforgiving when the timing slips.

For businesses, that timing is practical. The company pays expenses throughout the month, reconciles them, and settles the full balance from the company account at the end of the cycle. The card serves as a short-term working capital bridge rather than a long-term loan.

Spending Capacity and No Preset Limit

Charge cards are known for their high spending capacity and are often described as having no preset spending limit. The phrase is technically accurate, but narrower than it sounds.

What it really means is that the issuer hasn't set a visible, fixed limit, as a traditional credit card would. Risk is still managed in the background. The issuer approves or declines individual transactions based on payment history, current balance, account age, spending patterns, merchant type, income data, and internal risk models. A cardholder who normally spends $3,000 a month is unlikely to walk into a luxury boutique and have a $60,000 charge sail through without review. Longstanding customers with a clean repayment record have more flexibility than new ones.

The feature on offer is flexible spending capacity, not unlimited spending. The model only works when the issuer trusts the cardholder to clear the balance at the end of the cycle.

Disciplined Short-Term Credit

The appeal of a *charge card* is disciplined short-term credit. The cardholder spends now and pays later, but never rolls a balance into next month. That attracts people who want the convenience, protection, and rewards of a card without the gravitational pull of long-term debt.

Most charge cards sit in the premium tier of the market, and their lists of benefits tend to be long: travel insurance, lounge access, hotel status, concierge services, purchase protection, and rewards programs aimed at heavy spenders. Those benefits make sense for travelers, business owners, and anyone funneling most of their monthly expenses through a single account.

That discipline also creates pressure. A charge card balance is due in full every month, so a delayed paycheck or an unexpected expense can turn into a real cash flow problem before the next cycle even starts.

Premium fees create another trade-off. Lounge access, travel credits, concierge service, hotel status, and insurance only earn their keep if the cardholder uses them. Someone paying a high annual fee but rarely traveling is funding benefits that never get redeemed.

Fee and Volume Economics

Charge-card economics differ from credit-card economics because the issuer can't rely on revolving interest as its primary source of revenue.

Revenue instead comes from annual fees, merchant fees, interchange, FX markup, partnerships, late fees, and the broader banking relationship in which the card sits. Payment volume becomes the main economic lever, which is why charge cards target high-spend, reliable payers in the first place.

The traditional American Express model places the same company on both sides of the transaction, with a direct relationship to both the cardholder and the merchant, making merchant fees central to the economic picture. A bank-issued Visa or Mastercard charge product works differently. The issuer relies more on interchange, annual fees, and the broader banking relationship because it doesn't own the acquiring side.

Annual fees fund the premium benefits: lounge access, insurance, concierge services, credits, hotel perks, and rewards. Heavy spending still produces revenue even without interest, because the volume itself produces interchange and partner revenue.

Late fees exist, but a healthy charge-card portfolio shouldn't depend on them. Persistent defaults are a credit problem dressed up as a revenue line. The cardholders an issuer actually wants are the ones who spend a lot and pay on time.

Charge cards also slot neatly into affluent banking and corporate expense strategies. They attract customers with high incomes, heavy travel spending, business ownership, or significant company expense flows. Those customers can later be sold deposits, loans, insurance, wealth management, business banking, or premium account packages. The card is the entry point. The wider relationship is where the money compounds.

Corporate Expense Cards

Charge cards are especially useful in the business world. Companies need employees to cover work-related expenses, and the obvious alternatives are messy. Personal cards force reimbursement cycles that frustrate everyone and mix personal credit with company spending. Revolving corporate credit cards create control problems, because balances can quietly carry from month to month.

A corporate charge card imposes a cleaner structure. Employees use the card for approved expenses, while issuers or finance teams set limits, restrict merchant categories, require receipts, push transaction data into expense software, and centralize billing. When the cycle closes, the company pays the full balance from treasury. That model works because business expenses are intended to be settled, not financed over the long term.

The accounting value often rivals the payment value. Instead of chasing cash receipts and personal statements, the finance team receives structured transaction data, including merchant, date, amount, currency, category, employee, cost center, and sometimes the invoice or receipt itself. That data flows directly into accounting, travel, and expense management systems with minimal manual cleanup.

For the issuer, corporate charge cards generate high-volume, sticky customer relationships. A company puts heavy monthly spend on the card and settles it through treasury processes, which generates payment revenue, annual or program fees, FX markup, and sometimes additional revenue from expense-management tooling.

For the company, the value is control. Visibility arrives earlier, reimbursement friction drops, policy is enforced at the point of swipe, and personal spending stays separate from corporate spending.

Charge Cards by Market

The term charge card doesn't mean the same thing in every market.

In the United States, charge cards occupy a premium niche strongly associated with American Express. The market draws a clear line between credit cards, which allow revolving balances, and charge cards, which require full repayment each cycle.

In parts of Europe, that line is much fuzzier. Plenty of products marketed locally as *credit cards* actually behave like charge cards. The cardholder spends through the month, and the full balance is automatically debited from a linked bank account once the statement is issued. Revolving credit is either unavailable, uncommon, or sold as a separate add-on feature.

Germany illustrates the point well. Many products historically marketed as Kreditkarten operate on a monthly full-repayment model. The consumer calls the product a credit card because it carries a Visa, Mastercard, or American Express logo and lets them spend before the bank account is debited. Economically, the product behaves more like a charge card, with the full balance collected at the end of each cycle.

The label is less informative than the repayment rule. If a card lets the cardholder carry a balance with a minimum payment, it behaves like a credit card, no matter what the marketing brochure says. If the full balance must be paid in full each cycle, it behaves like a charge card, even when the local market calls it something else entirely.

Chapter 21: Virtual Cards and Digital Credentials

A new customer opens an account with a digital bank on their phone. They enter their details, photograph a passport, wait while the bank verifies them, and find themselves looking at a card in the app. The card number, expiry date, and security code are displayed on the screen. The customer can use them immediately. There is no envelope arriving in a week.

Only twenty years ago, this would have looked impossible to anyone in payments: a card was something you manufactured, personalized, packed, shipped, and handed to someone. The card and the credential were effectively the same object.

Virtual cards take that equation apart. A card number can now be created for a single online purchase, locked to a single merchant, capped at a single amount, and scoped to a single employee, project, trip, or subscription. It can be added to a mobile wallet, replaced without reissuing the original, or closed the moment its purpose ends.

That shift reshapes what issuing a card actually means. Issuance is no longer only about producing and delivering a physical object. A company no longer has to give every employee the same broad credential. A cardholder no longer has to enter the same main card number on every online checkout page. Cards have become more precise and easier to manage.

From Plastic to Software

The physical card has obvious advantages. It does not need a battery. It works at ATMs. It is accepted in places that haven't caught up with phones or wallets, including the many hotel and car-rental desks where the clerk still expects something to swipe. And it carries the bank's brand into the customer's wallet, which is something issuers care about more than they tend to admit.

Those advantages come with a cost: every physical card must be manufactured, personalized, shipped, and replaced. For issuers with millions of customers, that adds up, and metal cards make digital-first issuance even cheaper.

A virtual card carries the same payment details as a plastic one: PAN, expiry date, and security code, but without the physical object. The card details are stored in a banking app, an expense management platform, or a web portal. There is no chip to encode, no magnetic stripe to write, no envelope to mail.

Virtual cards do not change the contract behind the product: a virtual debit card still draws on a bank account, and a virtual credit card still borrows from a credit line. What changes is how the credential is created, delivered, controlled, and closed.

The main benefit is speed. Traditional card issuance requires manufacturing, personalization, packing, mailing, and activation, often taking days. Virtual issuance compresses this process into minutes: the credential is created, visible in the app, and immediately usable online.

That change accelerates the start of the customer relationship: a virtual-first bank can see spending the same day, while a plastic-first model may not see transactions for a week. For cardholders, the wait disappears; for issuers, time-to-transaction drops sharply.

This is why many digital banks and fintech issuers lead with virtual cards. The physical card follows later, sometimes automatically, and sometimes only on request. But the first usable version of the card is increasingly digital.

The limit appears in the physical world, where a virtual card cannot be inserted, swiped, or tapped on its own because it has no chip, stripe, or NFC antenna. For online use, it is fine: the cardholder enters the PAN, expiry date, and security code at checkout, and the merchant sends a normal card-not-present authorization request.

For in-store use, the virtual card needs help. The standard answer is a mobile wallet: add the credential to Apple Pay, Google Pay, or another wallet, and the phone presents it at the NFC terminal. ATMs are harder. Some banks support cardless ATM withdrawals via a QR code or an app handoff, but in most of the world, a virtual card still cannot withdraw cash from an ATM on its own. Hotels, car rental companies, and merchants usually require a physical card as part of their deposit or identity verification process.

Credentials with Built-in Limits

Once a card credential is digital, the issuer can impose any rules it likes. The simplest version is a single-use card. The issuer generates a card number for one specific transaction. Once that intended use is complete, the card number is closed or made inactive. If the merchant is later breached and its database of stored card numbers leaks, the stolen numbers are useless: they cannot be charged again. Privacy.com built a consumer product around exactly this idea, generating throwaway cards on the fly for online purchases. Capital One, Citi, Discover, and many digital banks now offer their own versions to existing cardholders.

Once the issuer can close a credential after one transaction, it can also scope the credential by time or purpose. A temporary card stays active for a week, a month, or a billing cycle. A trial-subscription card is created for one merchant, used to claim a free trial, and closed before the renewal date catches up. A travel card is opened for one trip and closed when the cardholder gets home. A project card is issued to a contractor and expires when the contract does.

The security logic is the same in every case: shorten the credential's lifespan, and the stolen number becomes less useful.

What disposable cards don't solve is what comes after the purchase. Disputes can be harder to follow because the cardholder does not always recognize the credential the merchant is referring to. Recurring payments are usually a bad fit. Hotels, rental car agencies, and other merchants that charge late can find the card has expired or reached its limit before the final amount posts.

A longer-lived version of the same control is the merchant-locked card. It works at one specific merchant and nowhere else. If the credential is created for a software subscription, it can be charged by that company and declined by anyone else. If the merchant's database leaks, the credentials cannot simply be reused elsewhere.

Spend-limited cards cap the amount. A card might be capped at $500 for a single hotel booking, $1,200 for a conference trip, or $10,000 for a supplier invoice. The cap can apply per transaction, per day, per month, or over the lifetime of the credential. Other controls work the same way: merchant category, country, currency, start and end dates, transaction count, channel, and offline versus e-commerce. A procurement card can be allowed for office supplies and blocked at ATMs. A travel card can be opened for airlines and hotels and closed at casinos and jewelry stores. A contractor card can be set to expire automatically when the project ends.

Consumer Controls

For consumers, virtual and disposable cards offer three draws: faster access, better privacy, and tighter control over spending.

Online shopping is the most common use. Instead of entering the same card number everywhere, the cardholder generates a virtual card for each merchant. If a breach occurs, the virtual credential is quickly replaced without affecting the main card.

Trial subscriptions sit at the intersection of card control and consumer frustration. A streaming service offers a free trial that quietly converts to a paid subscription on day eight. The cardholder fully intends to cancel and then forgets. A merchant-locked, low-limit card can reduce the damage: the merchant can charge the trial, but an unwanted renewal can be blocked if it exceeds the card's rules. This is not a substitute for proper cancellation, since merchants may have their own collection terms, but it sets a hard limit on the damage.

Travel is another natural use. Before a trip, a cardholder can create a virtual card with a weekly budget, add it to a wallet, use it abroad, and close it after returning home.

Privacy gets less attention but does real work. Using a different virtual card for each merchant also helps with attribution. When something goes wrong, the cardholder can see which merchant-specific card was affected and narrow down where the data leaked.

Budgeting is a quieter use case that neobanks such as Revolut, N26, and Monzo have built into their products. The cardholder can create separate virtual cards for groceries, subscriptions, travel, children's allowance, or online shopping, each with its own limit. Instead of one card with one balance and one mental category, the customer ends up with several cards, each enforcing a small piece of household discipline.

A virtual card does not eliminate risk, the need to check statements, or guarantee refunds. What it offers is a disposable alternative to the main card and a clearer way to separate spending. For shopping, trials, travel, and budgeting, this is often sufficient.

Business Controls and Expense Workflows

For businesses, virtual cards solve a different problem: how to let many people spend company money without giving any of them broad access to it.

Employees need flights, hotels, meals, software subscriptions, office supplies, advertising budget, and the occasional emergency. Procurement teams need to pay vendors against specific invoices. Finance teams need approvals, receipts, reconciliation, and audit trails. Managers need budgets to hold without having to pre-approve every $14 lunch. Each purchase can be small on its own, but across a company, the process becomes a real operational drag.

The traditional answer was one of three options, all imperfect. Issue every employee a corporate card and trust them not to abuse it. Make employees pay out of pocket and reimburse them later – friction for them, float pain for the company. Or build a heavy approval workflow that drags every purchase through layers of review.

Virtual cards added a fourth option. An employee traveling to a conference receives a card limited to the trip budget, valid only during the travel dates, and blocked for use outside relevant merchant categories. A marketing team gets a card locked to one advertising platform and capped at the monthly budget. A procurement team generates a card for a single supplier invoice at the exact amount of the purchase order. A contractor receives a temporary card that expires automatically upon the engagement.

Each credential carries structured data about the purchase: the employee, the vendor, the budget, the approval, the project, and the cost center. That data feeds directly into expense management, accounting, and ERP systems. The card becomes a record of who spent what, on what, against which budget.

Companies like Ramp, Brex, Mercury, Pleo, Spendesk, and Airwallex grew into large businesses around this exact idea. The card itself is almost a delivery mechanism for software that handles approvals, receipts, categorization, policy, and reconciliation.

The fraud picture also shifts. If a card scoped to one vendor leaks, it cannot be used anywhere else. If a card created for a $4,500 invoice is charged $4,800, the charge is declined. If an employee leaves the company, all cards associated with that employee can be closed before any subsequent attempts to make transactions.

The business case is broader than security. It is visibility before the money moves, policy enforced before the transaction, and a clean, structured data trail under every charge.

Refunds, Disputes, and Recurring Charges

Narrow credentials solve some problems and create others.

Refunds are the most common friction. A merchant usually refunds to the same card that was used. If the original card was single-use, deleted, expired, or locked, the issuer or platform must map the refund to the customer's underlying account. Some platforms do it invisibly; others generate support tickets and require manual handling.

Disputes can get harder to track. The cardholder does not always recognize the card number the merchant is referring to. The merchant may show one card suffix on its records while the customer sees a different credential in their app. A business user often needs to determine which employee, vendor, or project card actually made the charge. All of this is solvable, but each step adds time that was not required when there was one card per cardholder.

Delayed charges raise another problem. Some merchants authorize first and complete the charge later, sometimes for a different amount. A virtual card that closes too soon, expires too early, or carries a limit that is too tight can fail at the moment the merchant tries to complete a legitimate transaction.

The control has to match the merchant's payment flow. A one-time card fits a one-off purchase. A merchant-locked card fits an ongoing relationship because it lets that merchant keep charging while blocking everyone else. A spend limit works when the final amount is predictable. It becomes fragile when the merchant is allowed to complete the transaction later for a different amount. A permanent virtual card is better when the cardholder wants a stable online card number that remains separate from the physical card.

Modern Card Portfolio

A modern card relationship is no longer limited to one card per account. The same customer may have a physical card for ATMs and travel, a virtual card for immediate online use, a wallet token for contactless payments, a merchant-locked card for subscriptions, and a disposable card for one-off purchases. These are not separate accounts. They are different ways to access the same underlying funding relationship.

That convenience creates operational work for the issuer. The bank or card platform has to manage card numbers, tokens, statuses, limits, expiry dates, wallet provisioning, card-on-file tokens, replacements, refunds, and closures. The cardholder sees a clean set of options in an app. Behind that interface is a system that decides which credentials can be used, where, for how long, and for how much.

This is the product logic of virtual and tokenized cards. The issuer is no longer only issuing a card. It is managing a set of scoped credentials: broad enough to be useful, narrow enough to limit damage, and simple enough for the cardholder to understand.

At checkout, they all look like card payments. Inside the system, they represent different choices about speed, control, security, and cost.

Chapter 22: Commercial, Co-Branded, and Loyalty Cards

A card product is defined not just by funding source but also by its business model. Commercial cards are issued to businesses. Co-branded cards involve partnerships between a card issuer and a retailer or service provider. Specific retailers offer private-label cards for use exclusively at their locations. Loyalty cards reward customer spending with points or benefits. All of them can use the same funding models, but what distinguishes them is the unique business relationship associated with each card type.

A commercial card helps a company manage employee spending. A co-branded airline card connects everyday purchases to miles, status, and travel loyalty. A retailer card encourages customers to return to the same merchant. A premium rewards card turns spending into points, benefits, and repeat use.

Authorization, clearing, and settlement work the same across card types. What shifts the business logic around payment is that each card product adds different rules, controls, incentives, and relationships, each aimed at a different business objective.

Commercial Spend Products

A *commercial card* is a card product designed for business spending rather than personal household use. The category includes corporate cards (general company use), small-business cards (smaller enterprises), procurement cards (supplies and services), travel and entertainment cards (trips and events), fleet cards (vehicles and fuel), and employee expense cards (individual employees). These products all solve a control problem: businesses need people to spend money on the company's behalf without losing control over how it is spent.

That problem appears in ordinary work. Employees book travel, pay for meals, subscribe to software, order supplies, buy fuel, attend conferences, and handle urgent purchases that do not fit neatly into a purchase-order process.

One approach is for employees to use personal cards and then seek reimbursement. This creates friction: employees pay upfront and wait for reimbursement, while finance must collect receipts, verify compliance with policies, approve claims, and reconcile expenses. The company may not see the expenditure for weeks.

Alternatively, a company may issue broad access to company cards. While this reduces reimbursement friction, it creates control challenges – spending becomes easier and misuse harder to prevent. Finance must still identify the purchaser, confirm approval, and allocate expenses to the correct budget.

Commercial cards offer a middle path. They give employees access to payment but impose controls. Cards can be assigned to employees, departments, projects, or cost centers; restricted by merchant category, country, or channel; or capped at specific spending limits. Some cards are broadly usable and long-lived; others, such as virtual cards, are created for individual trips, suppliers, or invoices.

The card itself addresses only part of the challenge. Just as important as the payment is the record it generates.

An effective commercial card program captures structured transaction data: employee name, merchant, amount, date, currency, merchant category, VAT or tax details, project code, department, and approval status. This data integrates with expense-management, accounting, procurement, and enterprise resource planning systems.

For companies, this data is often more valuable than the payment process itself. While card payments simplify purchasing, reconciling month-end finances remains difficult.

A procurement card can specify which supplier was paid, by whom, with whose approval, for which department, and under which budget. A travel card aggregates airfare, hotel, meals, taxis, and conference fees for a single trip.

Commercial cards also enable earlier control in the process. Companies can block specific types of spending, such as cash withdrawals, gambling, jewelry purchases, or personal entertainment. Spending categories, limits, and permissions may be tailored by role or geography.

For this reason, many commercial card products include features such as receipt capture, approval workflows, accounting exports, spend analytics, vendor controls, budget rules, and real-time notifications. The card serves as a tool within a comprehensive expense management system.

Where a consumer card centers on influencing cardholder choice at checkout, a commercial card centers on enabling controlled business spending – giving employees payment tools while keeping oversight with the company.

Corporate, Procurement, and Small-Business Cards

The commercial card category contains several different products.

A *corporate card* is usually issued to employees of a larger company for business expenses. It is common in travel-heavy roles such as consulting, sales, and management. Liability can sit with the company, the employee, or both, depending on the country and program.

A procurement card, or P-card, is used for company purchasing rather than travel and entertainment. It is often used for office supplies, equipment, subscriptions, maintenance, and lower-value purchases that would be inefficient to process through a full purchase order process.

A *small-business card* is tailored to business owners but operates similarly to consumer cards. It aims to address business needs such as working capital flexibility, separating business and personal expenses, issuing employee cards, offering category rewards, and integrating with accounting systems. Whether it is credit, charge, debit, or prepaid depends on the issuer and local market. Its main distinction is that it supports business rather than personal spending.

The operational differences between these products are largely invisible to merchants at checkout, but are significant to issuers and business customers. Merchants only see a card transaction, but for issuers and customers, controls, liability arrangements, billing procedures, reporting capabilities, and accounting integrations set each product type apart.

The common theme is control. These products turn business spending into a cleaner payment record, rather than a pile of cash advances, manual reimbursements, petty cash, and unexplained employee expenses.

Brand Partnerships

A *co-branded card* is issued by a bank in partnership with another brand to drive joint customer engagement. The partner might be an airline, hotel chain, retailer, fuel company, supermarket, sports club, marketplace, or technology platform. The card carries both the issuer's role as financial provider and the partner's relationship with the customer.

The cardholder might think of it as "my airline card" or "my hotel card," even though the credit line, account, risk decision, and regulatory obligations often sit with the issuing bank.

An airline has customers who care about travel, status, upgrades, and miles. A hotel chain has guests who care about free nights and elite benefits. A retailer has repeat shoppers and purchase data. A platform has users already engaged in its marketplace or app.

For the bank, the partnership becomes an acquisition channel. Finding cardholders directly is expensive. A co-brand partner gives the bank access to customers who already care about the brand. The card becomes a financial product distributed through an existing relationship.

For the partner, the card is a loyalty and revenue tool. A cardholder with an airline card may choose that airline to earn or redeem miles. A hotel cardholder may stay within the chain to maintain status. A retailer cardholder may return to the same store because rewards are stronger there.

The card does not force those choices, but it changes the default. If a card earns extra miles with an airline, extra points with a hotel group, or special discounts with a retailer, the cardholder has a reason to favor that brand.

Co-branded cards are valuable because they turn regular spending into ongoing engagement with the partner.

Partnership Economics

A co-branded card has more moving parts than a normal issuer card. The issuer earns interchange and can earn interest, annual fees, foreign-exchange markup, late fees, and other account revenue depending on cardholder behavior and product terms. It also carries credit risk, fraud risk, servicing costs, compliance obligations, and reward-funding costs.

The partner earns direct payments from the issuer, marketing fees, revenue-sharing, or loyalty-currency payments when the partnership agreement includes them. An airline, for example, may sell miles to the issuing bank. The bank awards those miles to cardholders. The airline receives cash up front and later provides flights, upgrades, or other redemptions under its program rules.

This is one reason airline loyalty programs can become large businesses in their own right. The airline is not only flying passengers. It's also selling loyalty currency to banks, hotels, retailers, and other partners.

Retail co-brands work differently. The retailer may see higher customer spending, better retention, higher special financing volume, increased marketing payments, or more data. The issuer gets access to customers whose spending is already connected to the partner's category.

The economics depend heavily on the contract, which determines who funds rewards, who owns the customer relationship, who pays acquisition bonuses, who handles servicing, and who bears credit losses. Those details determine how the product actually works: revenue, funding, risk, and customer control.

A co-branded card is therefore not just a card with another logo. It is a commercial agreement that has been turned into a payment product.

Private-Label Programs

A *private-label card* is issued for use exclusively at a single merchant or group of merchants. The classic example is a department store card that works only at that store. Another is a retailer-financing card that can be used only within a single retail chain. Unlike an open-loop Visa or Mastercard card, a private-label card does not work everywhere.

That limited acceptance is intentional. The retailer does not need a general-purpose payment product. It wants a financing and loyalty tool for its own customers. The card can offer store discounts, special financing, early access to sales, loyalty points, or deferred-payment plans. The customer gets benefits within that retailer's environment. The retailer gets repeat spending and more control over the customer relationship.

Private-label cards are especially powerful for retailers selling higher-ticket items: furniture, electronics, appliances, jewelry, home improvement, and fashion. A customer may not want to pay the full amount immediately. The retailer can offer promotional financing — zero interest if paid within a defined period.

The issuer or finance partner earns from interest, fees, retailer payments, and the economics of promotional financing. The retailer earns from increased conversion and larger baskets.

The risk is that private-label cards can be expensive or confusing if customers do not understand the repayment terms. Promotional financing is attractive when paid on time and costly when missed. The card may also be useful only at one merchant, which limits its everyday value.

A private-label card is not trying to be the cardholder's universal payment tool. It exists to deepen the relationship between a single merchant or merchant group and its customers.

Loyalty Programs

A loyalty program gives the cardholder a reason to reach for one card instead of another. The reason might be cashback, points, miles, discounts, status, insurance, lounge access, concierge service, merchant offers, or a mix of benefits. The format changes, but the goal is the same: make the card worth choosing at checkout.

Cashback is the simplest. Spend $100, get $1 back. The cardholder understands the value immediately. There is no conversion table, award chart, or redemption strategy.

Points give the issuer more control over reward value. The cardholder earns points that can be spent through the issuer's portal, transferred to partners, redeemed for vouchers, or applied as a statement credit. The value can vary depending on how the points are used.

Miles connect the card to travel behavior. The cardholder earns airline miles or hotel points, often through a co-branded relationship. The reward can become the promise of travel, upgrades, status, or a trip the cardholder might not otherwise pay for out of pocket.

Partner discounts shift some of the cost away from the issuer. A merchant may offer a discount to attract traffic. The cardholder gets a visible benefit. The issuer makes its card feel more useful without paying the full reward cost itself.

Premium benefits work differently. The cardholder pays an annual fee and receives services such as airport lounges, travel insurance, hotel status, concierge access, purchase protection, event access, or statement credits. The issuer is selling a bundle: payment access, credit, rewards, status, insurance, service, and brand association.

Different rewards shape different behavior. Cashback encourages general spending because the value is plain. Miles concentrate spending in travel ecosystems. Points concentrate it in the issuer's or partner's redemption channels. Premium benefits keep the cardholder loyal even when the cashback math is unclear.

A *loyalty program* is therefore more than an extra feature. It is part of the card's design.

Rewards Funding

Rewards feel like free money to the cardholder, but they aren't. They are funded through the card's economics: interchange, annual fees, partner payments, merchant-funded offers, foreign-exchange markup, interest, and sometimes breakage.

Part of the funding comes from interchange. Every time the cardholder makes a payment, the issuer receives interchange from the merchant. In markets with high interchange, issuers have more room to fund generous rewards. In markets where interchange is capped, rewards are usually more modest.

Annual fees fund rewards too. A premium card may charge hundreds of dollars or euros a year, then return value through travel credits, insurance, lounges, points, and partner benefits. The cardholder can feel they're getting more than they paid for. The issuer is counting on many cardholders never using all the benefits.

Interest income can help fund rewards, especially on credit cards. A cardholder who carries a balance can generate far more revenue than one who pays in full. The cross-subsidy works at the portfolio level, not as a direct transfer from one customer to another. The issuer designs the card around the combined economics of cardholders who pay in full, cardholders who carry balances, annual-fee customers, and people who use benefits heavily or lightly.

Partners also fund rewards in some programs: airlines sell miles, hotels sell points, merchants fund offers, retailers subsidize discounts, and networks may support promotions. The cardholder sees one reward program; behind it is a web of commercial agreements.

The issuer's cost is also reduced by breakage: rewards that are earned but never used.

Not every promised reward becomes a redeemed cost. Points can go unused, miles can expire, benefits can be forgotten, statement credits can require specific enrollment or merchants, and some travel perks are valuable only if the cardholder travels enough. The unused portion lowers the issuer's effective cost.

Rewards are designed to feel generous while remaining economically manageable. The issuer wants the cardholder to perceive high value without letting the actual cost outrun the product's revenue.

Points and Cash Value

Cashback is easy to understand because $1 is $1. Points and miles are less straightforward: a point has no universal value. It depends on how it can be redeemed, whether it expires, whether award prices change, whether partners remain available, and whether the program owner changes the rules.

Points can therefore be devalued. An airline may require more miles for the same flight next year. A hotel may move properties into higher redemption categories. An issuer may reduce transfer rates or remove a partner. The cardholder still has points, but their purchasing power has fallen.

That doesn't make the points bad. A skilled traveler may get excellent value from miles. A hotel loyalist may use points for stays they wouldn't otherwise buy. A business traveler may collect rewards on work spending and redeem them personally, depending on employer policy.

Points, however, are not cash. They are balances inside a private loyalty system, and the program owner controls the rules.

For the issuer and partner, that control is useful. Loyalty currency creates attachment. A cardholder with 80,000 airline miles has a reason to keep earning in the same ecosystem. A hotel guest close to elite status may choose the same chain again. A bank customer with unredeemed points may hesitate before canceling the card.

That attachment is part of the product. Points and miles are rewards, but they are also retention tools.

Partnership Structures

Commercial, co branded, private-label, and loyalty cards show how much can be built on top of the same payment machinery.

Cards can use the same network, authorization flow, and clearing and settlement process while serving very different business purposes. A corporate card controls employee spending. A co-branded airline card turns loyalty into everyday card usage. A retail card supports financing at the point of sale. A premium travel card fosters a deeper relationship between the bank and frequent travelers.

The payment system enables the transaction, but the business model explains the card's purpose. Some cards are defined mainly by their funding source. Others are defined by the relationship they support: employer and employee, airline and traveler, retailer and customer, bank and high-value cardholder.

Part IV has treated cards as products: what funds them, who uses them, and which business relationships they support. The next part shifts from card products to transaction processing: what happens when one of those cards is actually used.

Part V

Card Transaction Processing

Chapter 23: Authorization

Authorization starts while Emma is still waiting at the table.

She has tapped her card, but the restaurant has not yet confirmed whether the transaction can be accepted. The terminal has collected the amount, currency, merchant, terminal, and card data. Now a question travels from the restaurant's acquirer to Emma's issuer: Can this transaction be approved now?

In Chapter 1, we introduced the issuer's real-time question. Here, we slow down and examine the decision itself.

Authorization is not the payment itself, final accounting, or the point when the merchant gets paid. It is the issuer's real-time permission for a transaction to proceed, based on information available at that moment.

The decision has to be fast enough for checkout, strict enough to stop obvious fraud, flexible enough for different products and markets, and reliable enough to work across thousands of issuers, acquirers, processors, merchants, and networks.

The issuer cannot run a long investigation while the cardholder, merchant, acquirer, and network are all waiting for an answer. The authorization system has only a few seconds to make a decision.

Approved or declined: a lot of work sits behind that short response.

Real-Time Authorization Question

Authorization asks whether a specific transaction should be allowed at a specific moment. The issuer or issuer processor checks the card, account, transaction, merchant, authentication data, and risk signals. If the transaction is acceptable, the issuer approves. If not, it declines.

Authorization is, therefore, real-time permission for the transaction to proceed, not completion of the payment. That permission is conditional: the merchant still needs to capture and present the transaction later, and the final amount or hold can still change.

To make that conditional permission concrete, the issuer's decision is built from several checks:

- whether the card or token is valid;
- whether the account is open and in good standing;
- whether the card has enough available funds or credit;
- whether the transaction is within limits;
- whether the merchant, country, currency, or channel is allowed;
- whether the authentication data is valid;
- whether the transaction looks fraudulent or unusual.

The decision depends on the product: debit cards check available balance; credit cards check available credit; prepaid cards check stored value; and charge cards check spending capacity and repayment risk. Virtual cards may check merchant locks, spending limits, expiry, and channel restrictions. Wallet transactions may check token status and cryptographic data.

The product changes the checks, but not the basic question: can this credential be used for this transaction now?

Authorization Request Path

The authorization request starts at the merchant side. In a physical store, the terminal reads the card, chip, stripe, or mobile wallet. During an online checkout, the website or app collects card details, token data, wallet data, or stored credential information. Figure 23.1 follows the request to the issuer and the response back to the merchant.

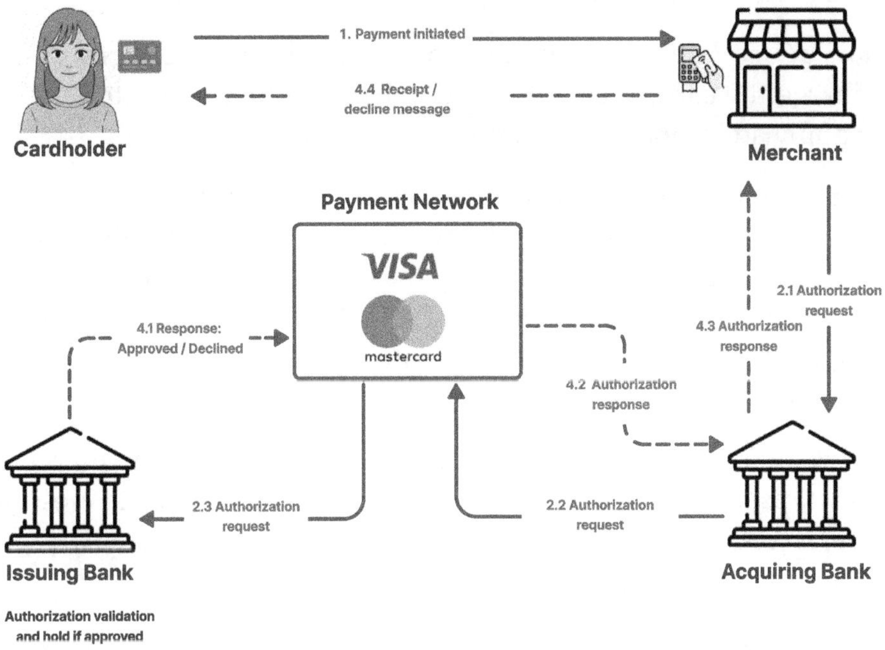

Figure 23.1: The basic card authorization flow.

Next, the merchant's system sends the transaction to the merchant's payment setup. Online, that may mean a gateway or PSP. In-store, the terminal may connect through an acquiring processor.

From there, the request reaches the acquirer or acquiring processor, where it's formatted, checked for basic validity, and sent to the right payment network.

The payment network receives the authorization request and forwards it to the issuer or its processor. The network routes the request using the card number, token range, BIN/IIN data, routing tables, and token-service information when needed.

The issuer then makes the decision, often through its processor. The response travels back the same way: issuer, network, acquirer, gateway or processor, and finally the merchant's terminal or checkout.

The cardholder sees only the result, but behind that result is a real-time chain of systems that must all be available, correctly configured, and fast.

Even a few seconds' delay can feel like an eternity at a restaurant table. A 10-second delay might prompt a cardholder to tap again, a cashier to cancel the transaction, or an online buyer to leave the checkout. Authorization is therefore built for speed under pressure.

What the Request Contains

An *authorization request* is a structured decision package, not a simple instruction to charge the card. It carries the details the issuer needs to approve, decline, or apply additional risk controls.

A typical request includes the card number or token, transaction amount, currency, merchant identifier, Merchant Category Code, terminal identifier, country, timestamp, point-of-sale entry mode, authentication data, and transaction type. Channel-specific fields add the data needed for that flow: EMV chip data, a cryptogram, CVV or CVC data, 3-D Secure results, wallet token data, recurring payment indicators, or card-on-file information.

Some fields identify the card or credential. Others identify the merchant, describe the transaction, or show how the card was used. The same message supports several jobs at once: fraud detection now, and matching, clearing, settlement, disputes, and reconciliation later.

The *Merchant Category Code* is especially important. It tells the issuer what kind of merchant is involved: supermarket, airline, hotel, gambling merchant, fuel station, restaurant, or pharmacy. Issuers use MCCs for risk rules, rewards, corporate-card controls, regulatory restrictions, and product limits.

The POS entry mode indicates how the credential was entered into the transaction. The issuer needs to know whether the chip was inserted, the card was tapped, the magnetic stripe was swiped, the details were manually entered, the transaction was e-commerce, or a wallet token was used. This field changes the issuer's view of risk.

Authentication data gives the issuer another view of whether the credential is genuine. Chip transactions include EMV data. Contactless transactions use dynamic data generated for that tap. Online transactions can include CVV2 and 3-D Secure results. Wallet transactions add token and cryptographic information. Together, these fields help the issuer judge whether the credential presented in the transaction is legitimate.

The issuer also cares about identifiers. A System Trace Audit Number (STAN), Retrieval Reference Number (RRN), terminal ID, merchant ID, and authorization code help systems find the transaction later. These values become important in clearing, reversals, disputes, and reconciliation.

Authorization is quick but not vague. The request is structured so that different institutions can interpret the transaction consistently.

Issuer Decisioning

Once the request reaches the issuer, the real decision begins with the credential. The issuer first checks whether the card, token, or account reference is valid and usable. A card can be expired, blocked, closed, reported lost or stolen, not yet activated, or restricted to certain channels. A wallet token can be active, suspended, deleted, or limited to a particular device. A virtual card can be locked to one merchant or one spending purpose.

After the credential check comes the funding check: debit cards are checked against available balance, credit cards against available credit, prepaid cards against stored value, and charge cards against spending capacity and account standing. Pending holds, recent transactions, daily limits, and product-specific rules can all affect the answer.

The issuer then applies product and cardholder controls. Card controls can block certain merchant categories. A corporate card can allow hotels and airlines, but decline jewelry stores or gambling merchants. A youth card can have lower daily limits. A virtual card can only be used with one merchant. A cardholder can turn off online payments or foreign transactions in the app.

Fraud checks run alongside these controls. The issuer uses the authorization data to determine whether the transaction aligns with the account, merchant, location, amount, channel, and recent behavior. A normal grocery purchase near home and a large online purchase from another country do not create the same risk picture.

Authentication data is validated alongside the other checks. A failed PIN, CVV2, cryptogram, token, or 3-D Secure result can push the issuer toward decline. A successful result does not guarantee approval, but it strengthens the case that the credential is legitimate.

The issuer then combines these signals into a layered decision. A transaction can fail because the card is blocked, the account is unavailable, the channel is not permitted, the authentication data is weak, the risk score is too high, or the issuer's system cannot approve it.

Approval, Authorization Codes, and Holds

When the issuer approves, it sends a response. The response includes a response code, and for approvals it usually includes an authorization code that identifies the approved transaction.

For the cardholder, approval often creates a visible balance effect.

On a debit card, the issuer places an authorization hold that reduces the available balance. If the cardholder had $300 available and the approved transaction is $40, the available balance may fall to $260. The booked balance may not change until clearing, but the customer can no longer spend the held amount elsewhere.

On a credit card, the hold reduces available credit. If the credit limit is $2,000 and $500 is already used, the available credit is $1,500 before the transaction and $1,460 after a $40 authorization.

The hold acts as a practical reservation mechanism. The merchant has approval to provide goods or services, and the issuer has reserved funds, credit, or spending capacity so the cardholder cannot use the same capacity elsewhere before clearing. But the hold is not the final transaction posted to the account: authorization gives permission, while clearing presents the transaction for posting.

Authorization and clearing do not always match perfectly. In some industries, the final amount or capture timing may differ from the original authorization. Hotels, car rentals, fuel stations, restaurants with tips, transit systems, and delayed-shipment merchants often create situations in which the approved amount, held amount, and final posted amount differ.

The authorization also has a time limit. If the merchant does not present the transaction for clearing within the network's allowed time window, the hold expires, and the reserved amount becomes available again. A merchant may also send an authorization reversal when it knows that all or part of an authorization will not be used. The issuer can then release or reduce the hold rather than wait for it to expire.

Hold expiry, reversals, captures, refunds, and corrections all begin with authorization, but their effects appear later. In Chapter 26, we explain how holds affect available and booked balances.

Decline Types and Response Codes

A decline is more than a simple no. It carries a reason, even if the cardholder sees only a short message at the terminal. Sometimes the reason is straightforward: insufficient funds, an expired card, or a blocked account. Sometimes it comes from risk rules, such as suspected fraud or an unusual transaction pattern. In other cases, the product itself blocks the transaction, for example, because the merchant category is not allowed. A decline can also be technical: the issuer may be unavailable, the message may be malformed, or one of the systems in the chain may not respond in time.

Payment systems often distinguish between soft declines and hard declines.

A *soft decline* is potentially recoverable. The transaction failed for a reason that is temporary or fixable. The cardholder may need to authenticate more strongly, retry later, use another channel, add funds, or confirm the transaction with the issuer. In online payments, a soft decline may tell the merchant to retry using 3-D Secure.

A hard decline usually means the merchant should not keep trying the same card for the same transaction without the cardholder taking action or providing a new credential. The card is stolen, blocked, expired, closed, invalid, or otherwise not usable. Repeated attempts to overturn a hard decline can create compliance, fraud, and customer experience problems.

Some declines are technical rather than financial or risk-based. A connection fails, a timeout occurs, a message is malformed, or the issuer does not respond in time. In those cases, the acquirer or network may return an error rather than a clean issuer decision.

Some response types are rare in everyday retail but still exist in the card system. A referral response may ask the merchant to contact the issuer, historically more relevant in manual or higher-risk environments. A pickup response may indicate that the card should be retained, for example, when it has been reported lost or stolen. Ordinary cardholders rarely see these distinctions, but merchants, acquirers, issuers, and networks still need them.

For the cardholder, all of this often boils down to one frustrating word: "Declined." For the merchant and issuer, the response reason determines the next steps.

The next right step depends on the reason: retry, authenticate, use another card, call the bank, stop attempting, place a hold on the order, cancel the subscription, or flag fraud.

A decline is therefore not just an error message. It is a product-and-risk decision returned in real time.

Stand-In Processing

What happens if the issuer cannot answer?

Card systems need a backup in case of certain failures. The issuer processor may be unavailable, a connection may fail, a data center may go down, or a network path may time out. The cardholder is still at the terminal, and the merchant still needs an answer.

Stand-In Processing (or STIP) allows the payment network, or another authorized party, to approve or decline certain transactions on behalf of the issuer under predefined rules.

Stand-in is not unlimited. The issuer sets parameters, and the network applies them. Stand-in can approve low-risk transactions below defined amounts, decline high-risk transactions, enforce card status files, respect limits, and apply basic risk controls. The issuer configuration defines what the network is allowed to do when the issuer is unavailable.

Without stand-in processing, every issuer outage could turn into widespread declines for that issuer's cardholders. With stand-in processing, some transactions can continue even when the issuer is temporarily unreachable.

> **Stand-In Is a Safety Valve, Not a Blank Check**
>
> Stand-in processing exists because a payment system cannot stop every time one issuer connection fails. But it is deliberately narrow. The network can operate only within rules defined by the issuer, usually with tighter limits and simpler risk logic than the issuer's own system. It preserves availability, but it cannot fully replace issuer decisioning.

The trade-off is control. During stand-in, the issuer may not have a live view of the current balance, the latest fraud alerts, or all internal controls. To manage that risk, stand-in approval is usually limited and conservative.

For debit and prepaid cards, this is especially sensitive because the available balance is the live constraint. Approving without a live balance check can create overdrafts or negative stored-value positions. For credit, the risk is additional exposure. For all products, fraud risk increases when normal issuer decisioning is unavailable.

Stand-in processing makes payment systems more resilient, but only because the rules are narrow. Approving a small, low-risk grocery transaction during a temporary issuer outage is often reasonable. Approving every transaction unquestioningly would not be.

Latency and Availability

Authorization is designed for the moment of checkout. The system cannot wait for end-of-day reconciliation, final fees, merchant payout calculations, settlement reports, or manual review. It has to decide while the cardholder is still present.

That constraint explains why authorization is narrow. It uses the data available at that moment to check the card or token, account, transaction, authentication data, and risk signals. If the issuer approves, it reserves funds, credit, or spending capacity and returns a quick response.

The later stages do the slower work. Clearing creates the formal transaction record, posting updates the account, reconciliation checks that records match, and settlement moves money. Keeping those steps separate keeps checkout fast.

The payment journey has begun, but it is not yet complete. Authorization gives the merchant permission to proceed. Clearing turns that checkout event into a record that can be posted.

Chapter 24: Clearing

Emma's receipt has been printed. From the customer's view, payment is complete, but the restaurant has not actually been paid yet.

Clearing starts in that gap between customer completion and financial completion. After the receipt prints or the online confirmation appears, the transaction still needs to be formalized as a financial record. The merchant submits it, the acquirer organizes it, the payment network sorts it, and the issuer posts it.

In Chapter 23, authorization was the real-time question: should this transaction go through now? Clearing makes it a formal record. Authorization asks whether the transaction should proceed. Clearing decides what the merchant formally presents, how it is posted and priced, and how it leads to settlement.

From Authorization to Capture

Authorization alone is usually not enough to get the merchant paid. After authorization, the transaction needs to be captured: the merchant marks it as ready for clearing. In stores, this often happens when the merchant closes out the day's sales. Online, the merchant either captures immediately after authorization or waits until the goods are shipped. Once captured, the transaction becomes a clearing instruction. The acquirer or payment service provider can then gather captured transactions from multiple merchants and prepare them for the appropriate payment networks.

The timing depends on the merchant's business model. A supermarket or restaurant usually captures quickly because the goods or services have already been provided. An online store often waits until shipping to avoid charging for items it cannot deliver. Hotels and car rental companies wait until the stay or rental is complete because the final amount can change. Marketplaces add their own timing rules because the buyer, seller, and platform each play distinct roles.

That timing gap explains why many payment systems distinguish between authorization and capture. In a simple in-store purchase, the two steps can feel almost identical. In travel, e-commerce, marketplaces, delayed shipping, and other businesses where the final amount or delivery status can change, the gap determines when the merchant can safely complete the transaction.

The merchant is balancing two risks. Capturing too early can lead to refunds, chargebacks, and customer service issues if the merchant cannot fulfill the order. Capturing too late can allow the authorization to expire, leading to declines, reauthorizations, mismatches, or customer confusion. Capture timing is therefore not just a technical choice. It reflects when the merchant knows the final amount, when it can deliver the goods or service, and how much payment risk it is willing to take.

Batches and Clearing Files

Clearing usually happens in batches. At the end of the business day, a merchant's terminal, point-of-sale system, gateway, or payment service provider collects finished transactions into a batch. This batch includes transactions from different cards and networks: some Visa, some Mastercard, and some from local or other networks.

The acquirer receives these batches and sorts them. It does not send one mixed file to all networks. Instead, it prepares clearing records in the format each network requires. Visa transactions are prepared in Visa Base II format. Mastercard transactions are prepared in the Mastercard Integrated Product Messages (IPM) format. Local networks may have their own clearing formats as well.

Figure 24.1 shows the basic process. The merchant sends captured transactions to the acquirer, who groups them by payment network. Each network receives clearing records from many acquirers, sorts them by issuer, and sends each issuer transactions for its own cards.

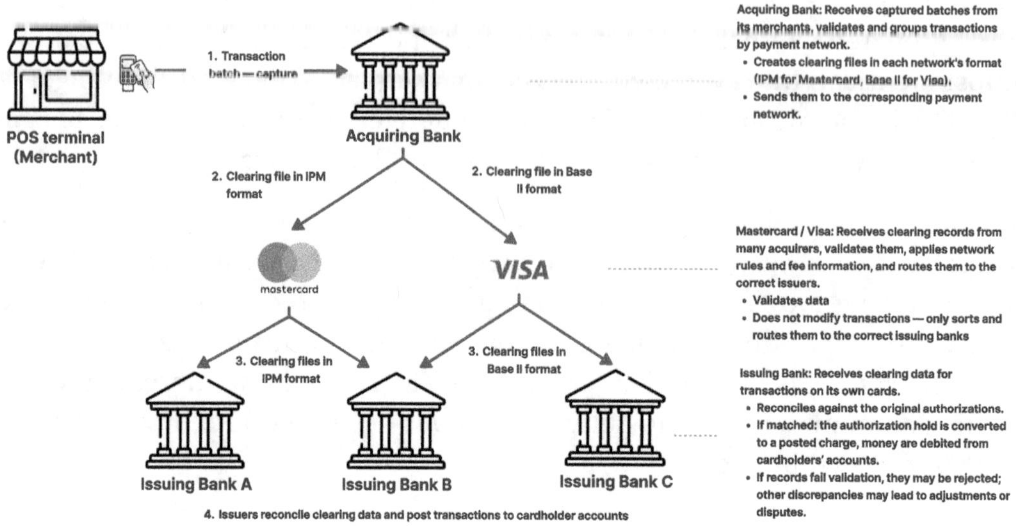

Figure 24.1: The basic clearing flow.

At scale, clearing is a process of sorting and distribution. One acquirer might handle transactions for thousands of merchants. One network can receive files from many acquirers. One issuer receives transactions from merchants around the world, groups them, and delivers them through the networks where its cards were used.

The network's role at this stage is not simply to pass data through. It checks formats, applies its rules, adds fee information, and prepares transaction records so issuers can post transactions and settlement positions can later be calculated.

Clearing has its own data layer. Authorization uses real-time messages, often based on ISO 8583 or similar formats. Clearing uses more detailed, network-specific records and files. These records carry information needed after the real-time decision: presentment data, fee indicators, interchange data, merchant details, and settlement information.

A clearing record includes more information than what the issuer needed for the quick authorization decision. Authorization must be fast, so it carries enough data for the issuer to approve or decline. Clearing needs a richer record for posting, pricing, reconciliation, settlement, reporting, and later evidence needs. That record includes fields such as the original transaction amount, final presentment amount, currency, merchant information, MCC, transaction date, clearing date, authorization code, card or token information, acquirer reference data, terminal or merchant identifiers, interchange-related data, fee indicators, and tax or service information where applicable.

The exact fields depend on the network, product, region, and transaction type. Visa Base II and Mastercard IPM are not identical. Domestic schemes have their own rules. Even within a network, different transaction types require different data.

Matching Clearing to Authorization

When the issuer receives clearing records, it tries to match them to earlier authorizations. Matching is a key part of clearing: the issuer uses the authorization code, transaction amount, card or token, merchant data, date, acquirer reference, retrieval reference number, and other identifiers to find the original authorization. If it finds a good match, it can convert the hold into a posted transaction.

A cardholder may experience clearing as the moment a hold is posted as a transaction. Operationally, it's the issuer's posting of the presented record to the cardholder's account or card balance, depending on the product type.

> **Many Clearing Problems Are Matching Problems**
>
> Many operational issues in clearing are not about whether the cardholder bought something. They are about whether two systems can recognize the same transaction. Amounts change, tips are added, hotels adjust charges, merchants batch late, and identifiers differ. Clearing converts a real-world purchase into a record that must closely match the earlier authorization to post correctly.

Debit and credit cards affect the cardholder's account differently. Still, both rely on the same clearing logic: receive the presented record, match it if possible, and post it according to the product type.

The issuer also releases or adjusts the authorization hold. If the clearing amount matches the hold, the hold is consumed. If the clearing amount is lower, the issuer releases the difference. If the clearing amount is higher, the issuer posts the higher amount when network rules allow it, or handles the difference under its own rules and risk controls.

The cardholder sees a pending transaction disappear and a posted transaction show up. When everything goes smoothly, this is simple. In unusual cases, it can be confusing.

Clearing links the earlier authorization to the final transaction record, but the final clearing amount isn't always equal to the authorized amount. The merchant often knows the final amount only after the service is complete, the goods are shipped, the currency is converted, or an adjustment is applied. These differences often reflect the gap between authorization, which is real-time permission, and clearing, which is the final transaction record. Partial capture, incremental authorization, reversals, refunds, and corrections are the mechanisms that handle those differences.

What Can Go Wrong in Clearing

Clearing is where many operational problems become visible.

One such problem is late presentment. A merchant captures the transaction after the authorization window has closed or after network rules expect presentment. The original hold may already have been released, but a valid presentment can still post. Late timing can affect fee qualification, liability, and dispute rights, so the transaction may enter exception processing.

Another problem is clearing without a matching authorization. This can occur due to offline transactions, delayed batching, technical failures, backup processing, merchant errors, or data mismatches. An unmatched clearing record is not automatically fraudulent or invalid. The issuer handles it under the applicable network and product rules, commonly by posting it and sending it to exception processing when additional review is needed. Rejection of a malformed clearing record during network validation is separate from declining an authorization request.

Duplicate presentment creates a different risk. If the merchant, payment service provider, or acquirer accidentally submits the same transaction twice, the cardholder could be charged twice, and the merchant could be overpaid. Reconciliation controls exist to catch these duplicates before they become customer problems.

Mismatches in amount and currency also create friction. The clearing amount can differ from the authorized amount due to tips, fuel adjustments, hotel deposits, partial captures, FX conversion, or delayed final amounts. Some differences are expected and allowed. Others create exceptions, customer-service issues, or disputes.

Clearing can also fail due to data issues. Merchant IDs differ, authorization codes are missing or incorrect, terminal IDs change, files arrive late, or records are rejected for not following the required format.

Clearing is therefore not routine paperwork. It is the stage at which a real-time approval is tested against the formal record the merchant presents. When that record is messy, customers see incorrect balances, merchants miss payments, issuers handle exceptions, acquirers investigate, and reconciliation teams repair the break.

Clearing Outcomes

Clearing turns the approval into a formal financial record: the merchant captures the transaction, the acquirer prepares clearing records, the network sorts and distributes them, and the issuer matches the clearing record to the earlier authorization and posts it to the cardholder's account or balance. At clearing, the transaction is posted to the cardholder's account or balance. For debit and prepaid cards, the customer's money or stored value is charged. For credit and charge cards, the customer's debt to the issuer increases.

From the cardholder's perspective, this can appear as the payment becoming final. The pending hold disappears, and a posted transaction appears on the account. But the merchant has not yet received the money.

Clearing creates the record that allows the transaction to be posted, priced, reconciled, and included in later money movement. It tells the issuer what the merchant is formally presenting and gives the system the data needed for fees, exception handling, and settlement calculations. The merchant's actual funding happens later through settlement and payout processes.

That distinction is essential. Clearing posts the transaction to the cardholder's account before the merchant's bank account is funded. The customer sees a completed purchase, and the issuer sees a posted transaction, but the merchant is still waiting for the funds to move.

Clearing takes longer than authorization because it solves a different problem. It does not have to respond to the cardholder within seconds. It has to make the transaction reliable enough for accounting, reconciliation, and later money movement.

Authorization decides whether the transaction should proceed. Clearing records what the merchant is formally presenting and posts it to the cardholder's account or balance. Settlement then uses those cleared records to move money between institutions.

Chapter 25: Settlement

By the end of clearing, the payment can look finished: the cardholder sees a posted transaction, the merchant has captured the sale, and the issuer has reduced the cardholder's balance. The missing step is interbank money movement: the issuer has not paid the acquirer, and the acquirer has not yet been funded for the merchant's sale.

Settlement is the step that moves the money — and the one part of the transaction nobody at the checkout ever sees.

Settlement turns cleared records into financial obligations between institutions and satisfies those obligations by moving money. While authorization determines whether a transaction should be allowed, clearing establishes which transactions should be posted, and settlement focuses on how obligations between issuers and acquirers are satisfied.

At settlement, the payment leaves the world of receipts, app balances, and merchant confirmations and moves to the institutional layer of the card system.

From Cleared Records to Net Positions

Once clearing has produced accepted transaction records, the network can calculate settlement positions.

Settlement works on net positions, not isolated transactions. During a settlement cycle, the network combines purchases, refunds, chargebacks, fees, currency conversion items, and adjustments. It then calculates what each participant owes or is owed.

For purchases, an issuer is generally on the paying side. For refunds or chargebacks, it can be on the receiving side. Acquirers usually receive funds for merchant sales, but refunds, chargebacks, fees, and adjustments can reduce or reverse that position.

Netting is the process of offsetting mutual obligations among participants so that only the final net amounts are settled, rather than each individual transaction. For example, a large issuer may have cardholders who make purchases at merchants served by multiple acquirers, and a large acquirer may process sales from many issuers' cards. Netting allows these numerous obligations to be combined and settled as a single net amount per participant, instead of settling each item or bank pair separately.

The payment network reduces that web into settlement positions under a common process.

For a purchase, the economic direction is simple: the issuing side funds the acquiring side. The issuer is responsible for the cardholder side of the transaction, the acquirer for the merchant side. Settlement turns that economic direction into a controlled institutional process, using the network's net positions rather than a separate money movement for each purchase.

Settlement Report

The settlement process begins with calculation and reporting: a *settlement report* is a control document for institutions, not a customer receipt.

After clearing, the network produces a report showing each participant's net position for the settlement cycle. This position is determined by cleared transactions, refunds, chargebacks, fees, currency rules, and other items as defined by network rules.

For finance and operations teams, this report becomes a reconciliation source. What the network says should settle must match the participant's internal ledger and the movement of funds through settlement accounts.

The network applies the rules, calculates positions, and tells participants what is due, maintaining alignment with prior clearing details. Participants reconcile, investigate breaks, and raise disputes or adjustments where allowed. But the daily process is standardized.

That standardization is one reason card systems scale. Thousands of issuers and acquirers can participate without maintaining separate settlement agreements with each other. They settle through the network's shared framework.

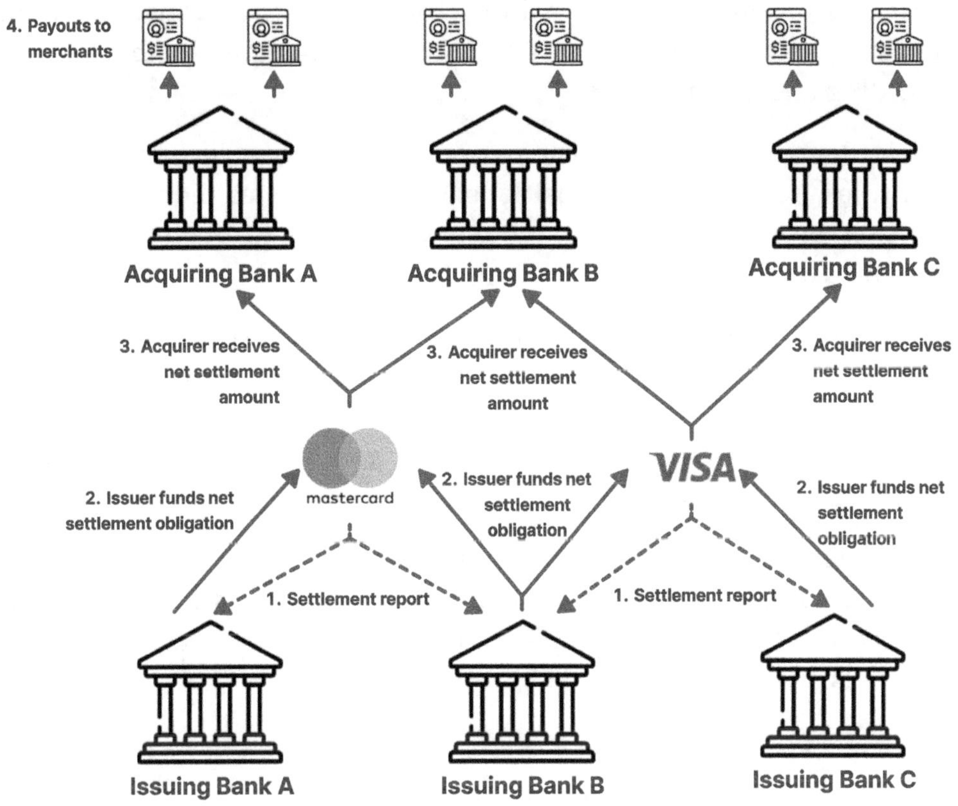

Figure 25.1: The basic settlement flow.

Figure 25.1 shows the simplified flow from settlement reporting to merchant payout. Issuers fund their obligations through the relevant settlement arrangement. Acquirers receive the funds due to them and then pay merchants under their merchant agreements.

The diagram shows the core flow, not every settlement arrangement. Actual settlement uses designated settlement banks, central bank accounts, commercial bank accounts, correspondent banks, or local clearing arrangements. The network calculates obligations and coordinates settlement instructions. It does not simply hold all funds in a single account.

Settlement Banks and Settlement Instructions

The payment network coordinates settlement, but the banking system moves the money. In many arrangements, participants settle through designated settlement banks or settlement accounts. Issuers and acquirers maintain the required accounts or banking relationships. The network calculates positions and sends settlement instructions. The banking arrangement then moves funds according to those instructions.

This gives settlement two layers. The network collects clearing data, applies settlement rules, determines net positions, and coordinates the process. The banking system provides the accounts and payment rails through which those obligations are satisfied.

Settlement structure follows the network, currency, and participant setup. Domestic arrangements can use local settlement accounts. Cross-border arrangements often rely on large commercial banks or correspondent banking relationships. Some systems settle in central bank money; others settle through commercial bank accounts.

Those arrangements differ operationally, but the boundary does not: settlement uses cleared data to satisfy interinstitutional obligations. It is separate from authorization, clearing, and merchant payout, even though merchant payout depends on it.

> **When the Issuer and Acquirer Are the Same Bank**
>
> Sometimes the issuer and acquirer are the same institution. This is an on-us transaction.
>
> Suppose a customer uses a card issued by Bank A at a merchant acquired by Bank A. The same institution is on both sides of the transaction. The payment network may still be involved for routing, rules, reporting, and the use of the network brand, depending on the setup. But interbank settlement can be reduced or eliminated because there is no separate issuer and acquirer to settle between.
>
> The transaction is not free to process. The bank still needs authorization, clearing records, merchant reporting, cardholder posting, fee calculation, dispute handling, and reconciliation. The difference is that the settlement leg becomes internal bookkeeping rather than external money movement.
>
> The cardholder and merchant may never notice. For the bank, on-

> us transactions are cheaper, faster, and strategically important, especially in domestic markets where banks, local schemes, and acquirers compete for transaction flows.

Merchant Payout

Settlement between financial institutions differs from payouts to the merchant.

The acquirer receives funds through the network settlement process, but the merchant is paid under its merchant agreement. That agreement defines payout timing, fees, reserves, refunds, chargebacks, currency, reporting, and reconciliation.

A small merchant often receives a net payout: gross card sales minus agreed fees, refunds, chargebacks, reserves, and adjustments. A larger merchant often receives its card sales gross and pays fees separately by invoice. A high-risk merchant often has a rolling reserve withheld. A marketplace often has split payout rules between the platform and sellers.

For that reason, the merchant rarely receives exactly the total of yesterday's card sales. The final payout depends on the merchant agreement and on operational items such as refunds, chargebacks, reserves, terminal or gateway fees, currency conversion, cross-border charges, and manual adjustments.

Payout timing can also differ from network settlement timing. A low-risk domestic merchant may receive funds quickly. A new, high-risk, travel, or marketplace merchant may wait longer. Some PSPs and acquirers offer faster payouts for a fee. Others delay payout or increase reserves if risk changes.

Reserves exist because merchant payout creates future exposure for the acquirer. If a merchant processes refunds, loses disputes, or fails to deliver goods after taking payment, the acquirer owes money back through the card system. If the merchant cannot cover those obligations, the acquirer absorbs the loss.

Travel is a clear example. A customer can pay today for a flight, hotel, tour, or event that takes place months later. If the merchant collapses before delivery, refunds and chargebacks may arrive long after the original settlement. The acquirer needs protection against that exposure.

That is why the merchant's view differs from the cardholder's: the cardholder sees a purchase or refund, while the merchant sees batches, fees, reserves, adjustments, and net payout. The acquirer sees a merchant balance that must be managed for risk.

Network settlement answers one question: what does the acquirer receive or owe through the card system? Merchant payout answers another: what does this merchant receive under its acquiring agreement? The two are related, but they do not always match in timing or amount.

Cross-Border and Currency

Cross-border settlement adds currency, geography, and local-rule complexity.

When a card issued in one country is used at a merchant in another, the transaction often involves different currencies, cross-border fees, foreign-exchange conversion, and additional risk controls.

The merchant wants to be paid in its settlement currency. The issuer posts the transaction in the cardholder's billing currency. The network calculates settlement in the currency defined by its rules for that region, currency pair, or participant relationship. The acquirer receives funds according to its settlement setup and pays the merchant according to the merchant agreement.

Those details vary by network rules, issuer pricing, acquirer setup, merchant agreement, and whether Dynamic Currency Conversion was used at the point of sale.

Currency conversion also creates timing and reconciliation differences: authorization can use an estimated amount, clearing carries the final transaction data and conversion details, and settlement uses the applicable settlement currency. The cardholder's posted amount includes the issuer's markup when the card product applies one.

As a result, several amounts can be correct at different points in the same transaction: merchant amount, authorization amount, clearing amount, settlement amount, and cardholder billing amount.

Settlement has to carry those differences through the process so institutions can fund, receive, post, reconcile, and report them correctly.

Settlement Outcomes

Authorization, clearing, and settlement solve different problems. Authorization is a real-time decision: should this transaction be allowed now? Clearing is the formal record: what transaction is the merchant presenting, and what should be posted? Settlement is the institutional money movement: how should the obligations created by cleared records be satisfied?

The stages are separate because each optimizes for a different constraint: authorization for speed, clearing for accuracy and reconciliation, and settlement for controlled money movement between institutions.

Without settlement, card payments would produce approvals and records, but not the money movement needed to complete the transaction between financial institutions. The issuer must fund the obligations created by its cardholders' purchases. The acquirer must receive funds for the merchant transactions it processed. The network calculates positions and coordinates instructions, enabling many institutions to settle through a shared process.

Chapter 26: Holds, Posted Balance, and Available Balance

A banking app can show several balances for the same account: posted balance, available balance, and pending card transactions. The posted balance reflects transactions that have been formally booked to the account. The available balance shows what can still be spent. Pending items show authorizations that have not yet posted.

That separation explains why a cardholder can pay for lunch and immediately see the available balance fall, even though the transaction is still marked as pending. The issuer has approved the authorization and reserved capacity for the merchant. The final account entry will come later, when the transaction is presented and posted.

The posted balance, also called the booked or current balance, reflects transactions that have formally been recorded on the account. It is the account-record view.

The available balance shows what can be spent now. It reflects the posted balance, adjusted for holds, pending transactions, overdraft lines, card limits, and other reservations applied by the issuer. It is the spending view.

Suppose a debit cardholder has a posted balance of $500 and buys dinner for $80. The issuer approves the authorization and places a hold. The posted balance is still $500 because the transaction has not cleared yet. But the available balance drops to $420 because the bank has reserved $80 for the merchant.

To the cardholder, the money can feel gone. In the bank's records, the final debit has not yet been posted.

This same structure explains many everyday payment mysteries: hotel deposits larger than the final bill, fuel-pump holds that exceed the fuel purchase, restaurant tips that appear after the first authorization, and online orders that post only when goods ship.

It also applies beyond debit cards. On credit, prepaid, and charge cards, issuers still reserve spending capacity before the final transaction posts. What changes is the kind of capacity being reserved.

What a Hold Does

An *authorization hold* is a temporary reservation created after the issuer approves an authorization request. It protects the transaction during the period between authorization and posting: the merchant receives permission to proceed, and the issuer sets aside funds, credit, stored value, or spending capacity. This prevents the cardholder from using the same capacity elsewhere before the merchant finishes the transaction.

A hold is not the same as a posted transaction, nor is it strictly the same as a pending transaction. A hold is a reservation created due to an approved authorization. Typically, a pending transaction in an app reflects an underlying authorization hold that has not yet resulted in a final posted entry.

Everyday language blurs these lines as people say they were *charged* when the available balance falls. In payment systems, however, a hold reduces the amount of spendable funds, while a posted transaction updates the account record.

If the merchant never presents the transaction, the hold should eventually be released. If the merchant presents a lower final amount, the unused part should be released. If the merchant presents a higher amount within the applicable rules, the posted transaction can exceed the original hold.

Without holds, a debit cardholder could spend the same $100 several times before the first merchant submitted its transaction. A credit cardholder could exceed the credit limit through several approved transactions that had not yet been posted. A prepaid balance could go negative because multiple merchants treated the same stored value as available.

For the cardholder, that reservation usually appears as a pending transaction.

Pending and Posted Transactions

A *pending transaction* is usually what customers see in the app when an authorization hold has been applied, but the final transaction has not yet posted. The pending status indicates a hold: the issuer has approved the transaction and set funds or capacity aside, but the entry has not been finalized.

Banks display pending transactions differently. Some apps show them in a separate section. Others blend them into the transaction list. The amount is often the original authorization amount, even if the final posted amount later changes.

Though labeling varies across apps, the usual intent is to indicate that the issuer has approved the transaction, but the final entry has not yet been recorded.

A posted transaction has been recorded in the account record. The issuer has received the clearing record and recorded the final entry.

Posting follows the product's funding model. For a debit card transaction, the customer's deposit balance is debited. For a credit card, it increases the debt owed to the issuer. For a prepaid card, it reduces stored value. For a charge card, it adds to the amount due for the billing cycle.

When the Final Amount Changes

Final transaction amounts often differ from initial authorizations for various reasons.

Restaurants are a common example in markets where tipping is added after the transaction is authorized. The terminal often authorizes the meal amount first. The customer adds a tip, and the merchant later captures the meal plus tip. The posted amount exceeds the pending amount. The extra amount is not a second charge. It is the final amount replacing the earlier hold.

Hotels create a different pattern. At check-in, the hotel often authorizes an amount sufficient to cover the room, taxes, and incidentals. The hold can exceed the final bill. At checkout, the hotel captures the actual amount. The unused hold should be released, but the release is not always immediate.

Car rentals work similarly. The rental company often authorizes a deposit because the final cost is not known at pickup. Fuel charges, late return fees, tolls, damage claims, or traffic fines can appear later, depending on the rental agreement and local rules.

Fuel pumps also authorize before the final amount is known. The pump does not know whether the customer will buy $15 or $90 of fuel until fueling is complete. The initial hold is an estimated amount, and the final posted transaction can be lower.

E-commerce adds another pattern. A merchant can authorize the full order when it is placed, then capture only the items that actually ship. If part of the order is canceled or delayed, the posted amount may be lower than the authorization. Multiple shipments can also create multiple captures.

Foreign-currency transactions can differ because authorization and posting may use different conversion timing. The authorized amount is often based on an estimate. The posted amount reflects the applicable clearing data, network or merchant-side conversion, and any issuer foreign-transaction fee or FX markup.

In these cases, authorization occurs before the final amount is known, while clearing conveys the final amount.

When a Hold Is Released

Holds are released in several ways, depending on how the transaction is completed.

The cleanest case is a matching posted transaction. The merchant presents the transaction, the issuer matches it to the authorization, and the posted transaction consumes the hold. The app often replaces the pending item with the posted item.

Another case is an authorization reversal: the merchant or acquirer sends a message telling the issuer to release or reduce the hold. This should happen when a transaction is canceled, a terminal fails after approval, a duplicate authorization is created, or an e-commerce order is not completed. Proper reversal handling makes funds available sooner.

A hold can also expire. If no clearing record or reversal arrives within the applicable time window, the issuer automatically releases the hold. Simple retail holds are released sooner than hotel or car-rental holds because lodging and rental transactions require more time for final amounts, deposits, and adjustments.

Expiry can confuse customers. When a pending transaction disappears, the cardholder assumes the merchant will not charge them. Later, the merchant presents the transaction, and the posted charge appears. This can happen when the hold expires before the clearing record arrives.

That does not necessarily mean the merchant did anything wrong. It means the authorization and clearing fell out of sync.

Duplicate-Charge Confusion

The phrase *charged twice* is one of the most common balance complaints.

Sometimes the customer is right. Duplicate presentment, duplicate authorization, merchant error, or acquirer processing problems can create real duplicates. Those cases need investigation.

More commonly, a single hold and a single posted transaction create the impression of being charged twice.

A hotel may place a $300 hold. Later, a $240 posted transaction appears. For a short period, the app can show both amounts, reducing the available balance by $540. The unused hold should be released, but if that release is delayed, the customer sees what appears to be two charges.

A failed terminal transaction creates another version. The terminal says the payment failed, but the app shows a pending hold. The cardholder pays again with another card. The first hold either expires or is reversed later. From the cardholder's perspective, the failed payment still blocked spending capacity, which feels like a charge even if it never posted.

Terminology matters here. If the transaction is pending, the better phrase is "the amount is on hold," not "the money has been taken." If the transaction is posted, it is a real account entry.

Reading Pending and Posted Transactions

Most balance confusion can be diagnosed with three questions:

- Is the transaction pending or posted?
- Is the amount reducing the available balance, the posted balance, or both?
- Could the final amount differ because of a tip, deposit, fuel purchase, foreign-exchange conversion, partial shipment, or delayed capture?

These questions do not resolve every dispute, but they place the transaction in its lifecycle. A pending hotel deposit is not the same as a posted hotel charge. A vanished hold is not the same as a refund. A lower final presentment is not a merchant discount.

Balances look confusing because banking apps expose pieces of a split process to customers who usually want one answer: how much can I spend? The answer depends on which balance the app is showing.

Chapter 27: ISO 8583 and Card Messages

A card transaction often passes through systems run by different companies: a terminal vendor, a gateway or PSP, an acquiring processor, a payment network, and an issuing processor. A transaction can span countries, currencies, and time zones and may pass through multiple technical systems before the terminal receives a response.

For that chain to work, each system must use the same language.

It is not enough to agree on the business idea of a card payment. Systems must agree on the exact message structure: what type it is, which fields are included, where the amount and card data appear, how currency is coded, how the terminal identifies itself, and where the issuer puts the approval or decline code.

ISO 8583 is the foundational model for many real-time card message formats. It provides the structure, or at least the structural pattern. Many authorization, financial, reversal, and network-management messages use this model.

It is not the network connection or the payment network itself. It is the message grammar that lets systems describe a card transaction in a way other systems can parse.

Connections and Message Formats

A payment system needs two things to exchange transaction data.

First, systems must be able to connect. A terminal or acquiring host needs a way to communicate with the next system in line. That connection might use TCP/IP sockets, private network links, leased lines, VPNs, or other setups, depending on the participants and region.

Second, the systems must agree on what the message means. A connection moves data. It does not explain what the data represents.

A phone call gives a useful analogy. The phone line lets two people hear each other, but language is what lets them understand one another. If the connection is perfect but one person speaks English, and the other speaks Japanese, they still cannot communicate.

Card systems work the same way: the transport layer establishes the path, and ISO 8583 gives structure to the transaction message that travels along it.

A socket can be open, an echo test can work, and messages can still fail. Connectivity proves only that data can move. If the message type indicator or bitmap is wrong, the amount field is malformed, or the terminal ID is in the wrong place, the receiving system may reject the transaction or process it incorrectly.

Message Structure

An ISO 8583 message is built from three core parts: the Message Type Indicator (MTI), the bitmap, and the data elements. Figure 27.1 places those parts in the order in which the receiver parses them.

Figure 27.1: ISO 8583 message structure.

The MTI comes first. It classifies the message and informs the receiver of its type: an authorization request, a response, a reversal, a network management message, or another type.

Once the receiver knows the message type, it needs to know which fields are present. That is the role of the bitmap. The bitmap serves as a field map, indicating to the receiver what data to expect before it begins reading the transaction details.

The data elements then carry the transaction facts: amount, currency, card or account credential, merchant, terminal, entry mode, timestamps, response codes, and other information needed for that message.

Together, these parts turn a card transaction into a compact statement: this is the type of message being sent, these are the fields included, and these are the transaction facts those fields carry.

That compactness comes with a trade-off. Unlike many modern API formats, an ISO 8583 message does not usually explain itself with human-readable field names. Both sides must already know what each field number means and how to parse it. The format is efficient because it is shared in advance.

This structure solves a practical problem: different types of card messages need different fields.

A contact chip authorization may carry EMV data. A magnetic-stripe fallback transaction may carry different card-reading data. A network-management message has neither a cardholder nor a merchant. A reversal needs enough information to identify the earlier transaction. A response needs fields that indicate whether the issuer approved or declined.

ISO 8583 addresses that variation by making fields optional while clearly indicating which are required.

This is what keeps ISO 8583 compact without making the receiver guess how to parse the message.

Message Type Indicator

The *Message Type Indicator* is the first part of the message. It has 4 digits. In the standard model, each digit has a purpose: version, message class, message function, and message origin. Figure 27.2 maps each digit to one of those functions.

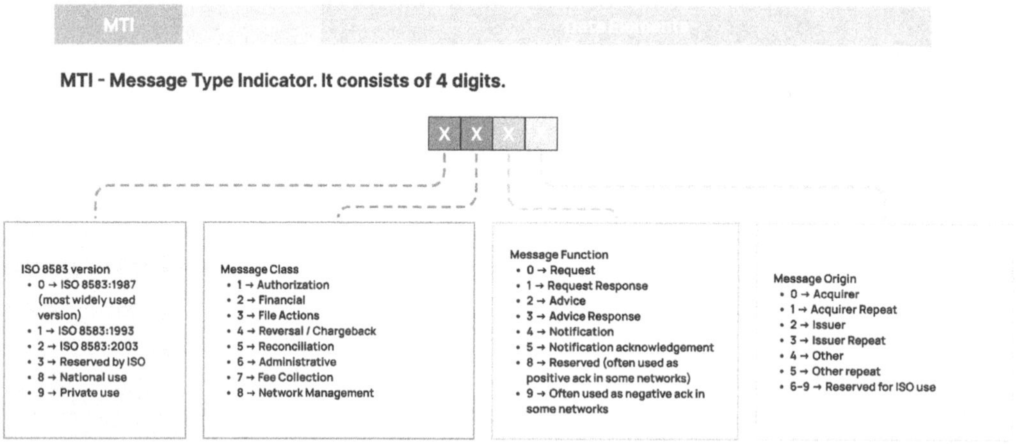

Figure 27.2: Breakdown of the MTI digits.

Take 0100.

The first digit, 0, refers to the 1987 version of ISO 8583, which is the most widely used in card systems. The second digit, 1, shows it is an authorization message. The third digit, 0, means it is a request. The fourth digit indicates that the message originated on the acquiring side.

Simply put, 0100 is the classic authorization request: the acquiring side asks the issuer whether to approve a transaction.

The matching response is usually 0110. The message is still in the authorization class, but it's now a response rather than a request. The issuer or its processor sends the result back.

The pattern becomes easier to see in common MTIs:

MTI	Common Meaning	Typical Use
0100	Authorization request	The acquiring side asks for approval
0110	Authorization response	The issuer side replies
0200	Financial request	A message used when a transaction is being completed or treated as financially effective
0420	Reversal advice	A previous transaction or authorization must be reversed or corrected
0800	Network-management request	Logon, echo test, key exchange, or connectivity check

These codes are practical shorthand. An operations analyst who sees `0100` and `0110` knows it's an authorization exchange: `0420` is a correction, and `0800` is likely an infrastructure check rather than a customer purchase.

The MTI tells the receiving system how to begin interpreting the message.

Bitmap as Field Map

The bitmap shows the receiver which data elements are included. ISO 8583 defines many fields, but no typical transaction uses all of them. The 1987 version supports up to 128 data elements; later versions can support up to 192. Each message uses the fields needed for its type and context.

The *bitmap* is a sequence of bits, with each bit matching a field. If a bit is 1, the field is present. If it's 0, the field is not included.

The first bit of the *primary bitmap* is special because it indicates whether a *secondary bitmap* is present. The primary bitmap covers fields 1–64. If there is a secondary bitmap, it extends the map to fields 65–128. Some systems go even further, but most card messages don't need that. Figure 27.3 illustrates how the bitmap marks the fields present in one message.

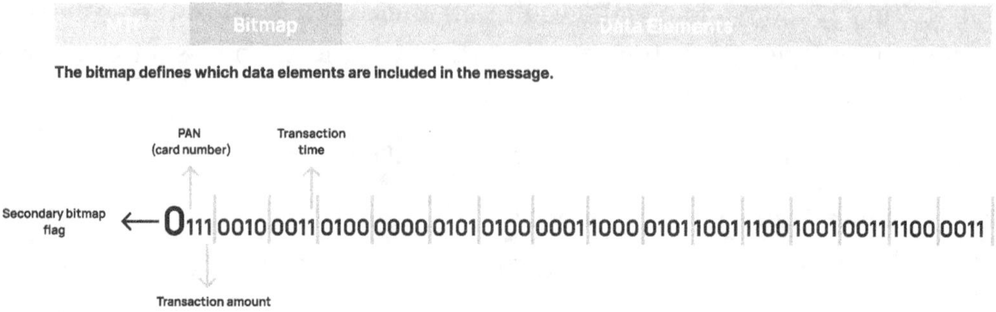

Figure 27.3: Bitmap as a field map.

The bitmap keeps the receiver from having to guess which fields are included.

If field 2 is present, the receiver expects the card number or account number field. If field 4 is present, it expects the transaction amount. If field 39 is present in a response, it expects the response code. If field 55 is present, it carries EMV chip data.

The receiver first checks the bitmap, then reads only the data elements that are present. Without that map, messages would either need to carry empty space for unused fields or rely on fragile assumptions about position and context.

That parsing dependency makes bitmap errors serious. If the bitmap says a field is present, but the field is missing, or if the bitmap omits a field that the message actually contains, the receiver can parse the rest of the message incorrectly. The problem is no longer just one bad field. The whole message can shift out of alignment.

Data Elements

The data elements hold the transaction details needed for that message. These fields identify the account credential, amount, currency, transaction type, terminal, merchant, response, and security data. Some are used during authorization, while others become important later for reversals, clearing, disputes, customer support, and reconciliation.

Some common data elements are:

Field	Name	Purpose
DE2	Primary Account Number (PAN)	Card number or account number, when present
DE3	Processing code	Type of transaction, such as purchase, refund, or cash withdrawal
DE4	Transaction amount	Amount, usually represented in minor units
DE7	Transmission date and time	When the message entered the processing path
DE11	System Trace Audit Number (STAN)	Trace number used by systems to identify the transaction
DE22	POS entry mode	How the card data entered the transaction
DE37	Retrieval Reference Number (RRN)	Reference used to locate the transaction later
DE38	Authorization code	Approval code returned by the issuer
DE39	Response code	Result of the request, such as approved or declined
DE41	Terminal ID	Identifier of the terminal
DE42	Merchant ID	Identifier of the merchant or card acceptor
DE49	Currency code	Transaction currency
DE55	EMV data	Chip-related data in many EMV transactions

Some fields have a fixed length, while others are variable. Variable-length fields use a length indicator, often called `LLVAR` or `LLLVAR`, so the receiving system knows how many characters are in that field.

Amounts are usually shown in minor units. For example, a $25.50 transaction might appear as `000000002550`. There is no decimal point, but the systems can read the amount because the field format is defined.

Currency is shown using ISO 4217 numeric codes. For example, 978 means euro and 840 means US dollar. This compact coding avoids confusion between systems and languages.

Response codes are short but important. In many systems, `00` indicates approval, and `05` indicates a general decline. The exact codes and rules depend on the network or processor.

Inside the system, a card transaction is represented as a structured set of facts: amount, currency, merchant, terminal, timestamp, entry mode, credential, authentication data, and response.

Authorization Message Example

A simplified authorization request can show how the parts fit together.

```
MTI: 0100

DE2:  4000000000000002
DE3:  000000
DE4:  000000004700
DE7:  0928173045
DE11: 123456
DE22: 051
DE41: TERM1234
DE42: MERCHANT9876543
DE49: 978
DE55: [EMV data]
```

The `MTI` shows this is an authorization request. `DE2` identifies the card or account number, though real systems might use a token or protected version. `DE3` shows the transaction type. `DE4` holds the amount. `DE7` and `DE11` help track the transaction through the system. `DE22` shows how the card data was entered, `DE41` and `DE42` identify the terminal and merchant, and `DE49` shows that the currency is the euro. `DE55` carries chip data for an EMV transaction.

A simplified response might look like this:

```
MTI: 0110

DE11: 123456
DE37: 123456789012
DE38: A1B2C3
DE39: 00
```

The response links back to the request using trace identifiers. It includes an authorization code and a response code. The terminal doesn't need to know the issuer's internal decisioning details. It needs the result and enough identifiers to store the response and connect it to later clearing or reversal steps.

The cardholder sees one word: "Approved."

The systems see a structured exchange of message type, fields, identifiers, and response codes.

Transaction Identifiers

Some ISO 8583 fields become most important after the authorization is over. Identifiers are what let different systems agree that they are talking about the same transaction.

The STAN, RRN, authorization code, terminal ID, merchant ID, transaction date, local time, and amount are the clues used to find the transaction again.

Those clues become important when the clean checkout flow breaks. If a terminal receives approval but the receipt does not print, the merchant needs to know whether the sale was completed. If an authorization hold remains after a failed checkout, the issuer must locate the original authorization. If the same transaction appears twice, the acquirer and issuer need to have matching fields to determine whether it is a duplicate. If a cardholder disputes a charge, operations teams need to link the posted transaction to the original authorization and clearing records.

Without these identifiers, later investigation becomes guesswork.

A customer might say, "I was charged twice at the supermarket last Friday." That is useful context, but it is not enough for a processor to trace the transaction. The system needs structured details: amount, date, merchant, terminal, authorization code, STAN, RRN, and other matching fields. These values help different systems determine whether they are observing the same event, a duplicate, or a separate transaction.

Network Dialects

In production, ISO 8583 is usually encountered through a network or processor dialect.

Visa, Mastercard, domestic schemes, processors, and national systems use ISO 8583 as a base, then adapt it. They define private fields, subfields, response-code behavior, EMV data handling, token indicators, security requirements, optional fields, mandatory fields, and certification rules.

ISO 8583 is the language family; the network or processor specification is the dialect.

This is why two systems can both claim to use ISO 8583 and still fail certification with each other. The shared standard gives them a family resemblance. The implementation guide defines the actual contract.

Even the field layout can change depending on the ISO 8583 version. The 1987, 1993, and 2003 versions do not treat every field the same way. In practice, most card professionals learn the version and network dialect used by their processor or scheme, rather than relying solely on the public standard.

Australia's AS 2805 is an example of a national card-message standard based on ISO 8583. Other countries and schemes have their own versions. Some modern systems use APIs, JSON, ISO 20022, or internal formats at the edges, but still translate into ISO 8583-style or scheme-specific messages deeper in the process.

The public ISO standard explains the concepts, but the scheme or processor guide defines what to build, test, certify, and operate. For real integrations, the implementation guide is the source of truth.

Modern Payment Stacks

ISO 8583 can look old compared with modern API design.

It is compact, field-based, and strict. Instead of self-describing JSON keys, it uses bitmaps. It requires exact parsing and can be unforgiving if a field is missing, malformed, or interpreted differently by two parties.

That strictness is part of its value. Real-time card processing depends on structured messages that systems can parse consistently within tight time limits.

A modern merchant usually does not use ISO 8583 directly. The merchant may connect to a PSP through a modern API and receive a simple approval response. But within the payment stack, the transaction can still be translated into a scheme-specific card message that more closely follows the ISO 8583 model than the merchant-facing API.

Real implementations vary by network, processor, region, and product. That variation is part of the payment work. But the underlying model remains recognizable: the transaction has a type, a field map, and a defined set of data elements. It is not a vague request moving through a black box.

In the next chapter, we move from real-time messages to files that carry cleared transaction data after authorization has been granted.

Chapter 28: Network Files and Clearing Formats

At the terminal, an authorization message must be compact, structured, and ready for real-time processing. The issuer needs enough information to approve, decline, or respond within seconds.

A clearing record has a different job. By the time it is created, the cardholder is usually gone, and the merchant has captured the sale. The record now needs sufficient detail to be part of the financial recordkeeping system: final amount, merchant data, authorization references, fee-relevant indicators, currency data, and fields needed for reconciliation and dispute resolution.

A real-time authorization message alone cannot do all of that.

Networks, therefore, use their own clearing formats. Visa, Mastercard, and domestic schemes each define how captured transactions must be represented for clearing. Once a transaction moves from real-time authorization to clearing, the data becomes more detailed, formal, and network-specific.

Presentment

Clearing centers on presentment.

Presentment is the merchant's formal submission of a transaction for processing via acquiring and network channels.

For a basic card-present purchase, presentment usually happens after the merchant closes a batch. In e-commerce, capture and presentment commonly happen either immediately or when goods ship. In hotels, travel, fuel, and rentals, presentment often waits until the final amount is known.

The acquiring side receives captured transactions, prepares them in the required network format, and submits them to the appropriate network.

For the issuer, presentment is the basis for posting the transaction to the cardholder's account or balance. For the network, it serves as the formal record for fee calculation, reporting, and later exception handling.

Presentment is the point at which the merchant's completed sale is entered into the card network as a formal clearing record.

Final Amounts and Fee Data

The extra detail in a clearing record usually falls into three groups: final transaction details, fee-relevant indicators, and evidence for later investigation.

Consider a restaurant transaction. The issuer authorizes $80 during the meal. Later, the merchant presents $95 after the tip is added. The clearing record must include the final amount and sufficient matching data to link the $95 presentment to the earlier $80 authorization.

Hotels need similar flexibility. The initial authorization often covers a deposit or estimated stay. The final presentment can include room rate, taxes, parking, minibar charges, or other items. The clearing record must be sufficiently clear for accurate posting and later dispute review.

Cross-border transactions add currency and conversion data. Authorization uses the amount or estimate available at the time; clearing carries the final transaction details, currency codes, conversion indicators, and fee-relevant data.

Fee calculation also depends on clearing data. Interchange and network fees can depend on product type, merchant category, region, channel, authentication method, tokenization, card-present or card-not-present status, timing, and data quality. If the clearing record lacks required fields or arrives late, the transaction can fall into a less favorable fee category.

The record must preserve what changed after authorization and what later teams will need to prove, price, or investigate about the transaction.

Visa Base II and Mastercard IPM

Two names often appear in card clearing: Visa Base II and Mastercard Integrated Product Messages (IPM).

In older VisaNet terminology, Base I refers to real-time authorization, while Base II refers to Visa's clearing and settlement side. Mastercard uses different terminology. Its clearing environment is the Global Clearing Management System (GCMS), which uses IPM for clearing messages.

These are network-specific clearing mechanisms, not generic transaction exports: a Visa transaction must be prepared for Visa's Base II process, while a Mastercard transaction must be prepared for Mastercard's GCMS/IPM process.

The same purchase can therefore appear in different technical forms across networks. A $47 restaurant transaction still needs the same business facts: amount, merchant, card or token reference, authorization reference, currency, dates, and fee-relevant indicators. But the record structure, field definitions, validation edits, reject handling, reports, and operating cycles are defined by the network.

A clearing submission is more than a list of sales. It has control structure around the transaction data: headers, transaction records, adjustment or exception records, control totals, acknowledgments, rejects, and reports. These controls let the sender, network, and receiver answer basic operational questions: what was submitted, what was accepted, what was rejected, and whether the totals reconcile.

Base II and IPM processing are cycle-based, not real-time terminal conversations. Acquirers and processors prepare network-specific clearing submissions and send them through scheduled clearing cycles. Accepted records proceed to issuer delivery, reporting, fee calculation, and, later, settlement processing. Rejected records come back as operational work.

Acquirer Clearing Records

Clearing starts on the acquiring side.

After merchants capture transactions, the acquirer or its processor turns those captured sales into network-ready clearing records. The acquiring side chooses the correct network, applies the required clearing format, adds the required identifiers and fee-related fields, and checks that each transaction is ready for presentment.

This preparation is more than formatting. The acquiring side groups records by network, merchant, currency, settlement date, region, or processing cycle. It enriches records with merchant data, acquirer identifiers, authorization references, capture amounts, POS indicators, and other fields required by the network.

Before submission, acquirers run controls such as duplicate checks, required-field validation, amount and currency checks, authorization matching, merchant-status checks, network-format validation, and cut-off controls.

These controls exist because a clearing record is not easy to fix once it has moved into network processing. A bad record can be rejected, mispriced, delayed, or difficult for the issuer to match. Merchants usually do not care which field was wrong. They care about delayed payouts, rejected transactions, or customer complaints. To merchants, a clearing failure looks like a payment failure.

The network has to prevent those failures across many acquirers.

Network Processing

The payment network receives clearing records from many acquirers. Its role is not merely to forward files. The network validates records, applies network rules, sorts transactions by issuer, prepares issuer deliveries, and generates data for fees, reports, and exception handling.

Sorting is central. A single acquirer's submission can contain transactions for cards issued by hundreds or thousands of issuers. Each issuer needs only the records for its own cards. The network performs that distribution under shared rules.

Acquirers do not need separate clearing processes with every issuer. They submit records to the network, which coordinates delivery, rule application, and downstream processing.

Cardholders do not see this coordination, but it is what lets a card from one bank be used at a merchant served by another bank, often in another country.

Issuer Processing

The issuer receives clearing records for its own cards and starts by matching them to prior authorizations.

It uses fields such as card or token data, amount, merchant, date, authorization code, RRN, STAN, acquirer reference data, terminal ID, and network-specific identifiers.

If the records match, the issuer releases the authorization hold and posts the transaction. If the final amount differs but remains within the allowed limits, the issuer posts it. If there is no clean match, the issuer follows network and internal rules for unmatched presentments.

Once the record is ready to be handled, the issuer posts the transaction to the cardholder's account or balance. The accounting effect depends on the product, but in each case, the clearing record becomes the basis for the posted account entry.

Clearing also creates control work. The issuer reconciles clearing records against authorization logs, posting records, settlement reports, and internal ledgers.

The issuer's clearing operation does more than post transactions. It protects account accuracy, customer experience, settlement accuracy, and dispute readiness.

Files and Settlement Reports

Clearing files and settlement reports are connected, but they operate at different levels: clearing files carry transaction-level records, while settlement reports summarize the net obligations that arise from cleared activity.

A clearing record says: this merchant is presenting this transaction on this card, with this authorization reference, in this currency, under this merchant category.

A settlement report says: after all cleared activity and adjustments in this cycle, this issuer owes this net amount, or this acquirer is owed this net amount.

Settlement is only as reliable as the cleared records behind it.

The approval at checkout allows the transaction to proceed. Clearing provides a durable record that lets the card system post, price, reconcile, settle, and investigate the transaction later.

Chapter 29: Accounting Basics for Payments

A card payment might appear correct in the transaction systems, but it can still be wrong in the institution's accounting records or ledgers.

Even if the authorization is approved, the clearing record arrives, the settlement amount is correct, and the merchant gets paid, the ledger entries behind these events can still be out of balance. When that happens, the institution faces a financial problem.

The reason is simple. Payments depend on messages, but banks and merchants depend on ledgers.

Messages describe what happened, such as a card being authorized, a transaction being captured, a clearing record being received, a settlement amount being calculated, or a payout being created. Ledgers, on the other hand, record the financial impact of these events, like which asset increased, which liability decreased, which receivable was created, and which payable was settled.

Two terms run through this chapter: a receivable is money expected to be received, and a payable is money expected to be paid.

To understand these records, we need a basic accounting framework. We start with the balance sheet equation and use it to examine a simple $100 debit card purchase across three ledgers: the merchant, the acquirer, and the issuer.

Money Movement and Ledger Records

A payment system operates on two levels.

The first level is money movement: funds moving between banks, settlement accounts, and merchant payout accounts. In a card transaction, settlement moves funds from the issuer to the acquirer, and merchant payout moves funds from the acquirer to the merchant.

The second level is ledger recording. Each participant keeps track of what it owns, what it owes, what others owe it, and what changed after the transaction.

Those two levels need to match, but they are not always updated simultaneously. For example, a debit card authorization can lower the available balance before the transaction is posted. Clearing can create the issuer's posting before interbank settlement is finished. The acquirer can record the amount owed to the merchant before the merchant is actually paid. The merchant can record a sale before the payout shows up in their bank account.

The main tool for keeping these records balanced is the balance sheet equation.

The Balance Sheet Equation

The basic accounting frame is the balance sheet equation:

Assets = Liabilities + Equity

Assets are things an institution owns or is owed, like cash, settlement balances, receivables, loans it has made, equipment, and other resources.

Liabilities are what the institution owes to others, such as customer deposits, merchant payables, settlement payables, borrowed funds, and other amounts it must pay or return.

Equity is what remains for the owners after subtracting liabilities from assets.

For payments, the key point is how deposits appear in a bank's records. If a customer has $1,000 in a checking account, that money is the customer's asset. But in the bank's records, it is a liability because the bank owes the customer $1,000.

Double-entry logic is fundamental in accounting. Every transaction creates two entries: a change in one account and an equal change in another. If cash increases, something else must explain why — a liability increased, a receivable was collected, revenue was recognized, or another asset decreased. If a liability goes down, the books need an equal change somewhere else.

That paired-entry system is what keeps the books balanced after every event, instead of becoming a list of unrelated transactions.

Debit, Credit, and the Bank's Liability

Debit and credit are not just other ways of saying *plus* and *minus*. They are accounting directions, and their meaning depends on the type of account.

Account Type	Debit Does This	Credit Does This	Payment Examples
Asset	Increases the account	Decreases the account	Cash, settlement balances, receivables, inventory
Liability	Decreases the account	Increases the account	Customer deposits, merchant payables, settlement payables
Equity	Decreases the account	Increases the account	Owner capital, retained earnings

This difference is why bank statements can be confusing. For the customer, a bank account is an asset. For the bank, that same account is a liability because the bank owes the customer that money.

When people say, "My money is in the bank," they might imagine the bank keeping their cash in a box labeled with their name. In accounting, it works differently. The customer has a claim on the bank, and the bank has an obligation to the customer.

If the customer deposits $1,000, the bank's cash or settlement asset increases by $1,000. At the same time, the bank's liability to the customer increases, as it now owes $1,000. The balance sheet still balances.

If the customer later spends $100 with a debit card and the transaction is posted, the bank now owes the customer $100 less. The liability goes down. The bank also records the new obligation created by the card transaction.

This is why the product is called a debit card. When a debit card purchase is posted, the issuer debits the customer's deposit account. Since that account is a liability in the issuer's books, the debit reduces what the issuer owes the customer. For the customer, this appears as a lower account balance.

One Purchase, Three Ledgers

With these rules in mind, we can apply the accounting equation to a simple $100 debit card purchase.

Figure 29.1 shows the same purchase in three separate ledgers: the merchant's, the acquirer's, and the issuer's. It doesn't show the full card payment timeline, but instead shows how each participant records the same transaction from their own perspective while keeping their books balanced.

The merchant records the value received from the sale and the value given up through the goods sold. The acquirer records an asset from settlement and a liability to the merchant. The issuer records a reduction in what it owes the cardholder and a reduction in cash or settlement assets when it funds the transaction.

The payment network coordinates transaction data and settlement calculations, but it does not keep a shared ledger for all participants. Each participant keeps their own books.

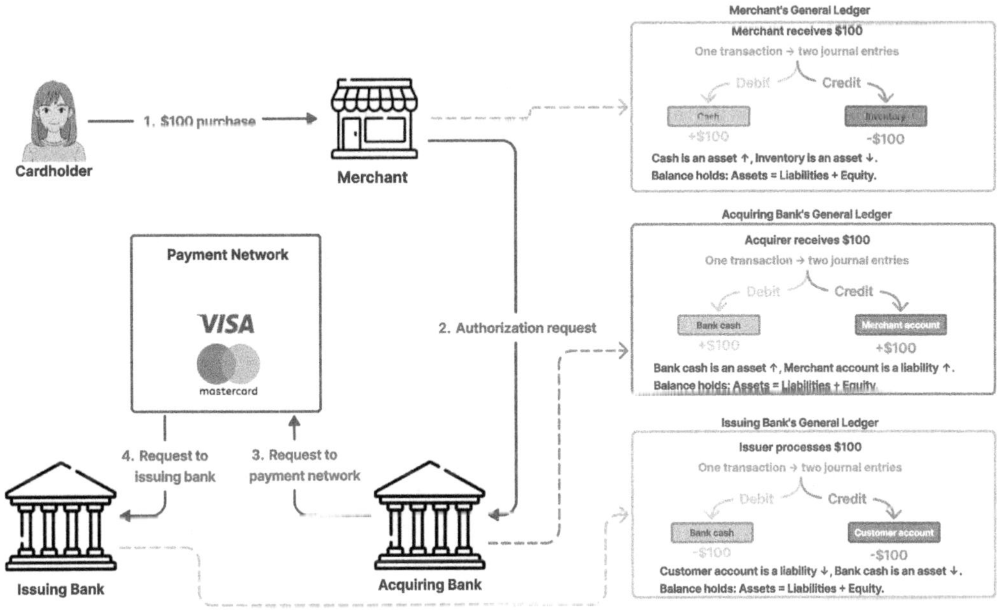

Figure 29.1: The same debit-card purchase in three separate ledgers.

The example uses $100 on each side to make the double-entry logic easy to see. Real card payments include timing differences, fees, reserves, refunds, chargebacks, foreign exchange, and more detailed internal accounts. Those details change real operations, but they don't change the basic idea: one customer payment becomes several separate accounting records.

Merchant Ledger View

In the simplified diagram, the merchant trades one form of value for another. The sale brings in $100, and the product sold is removed from inventory.

When the sale happens, the merchant records the sale and a claim to receive the payout:

Entry	Account	Amount
Debit	Receivable from acquirer or payment service provider	$100
Credit	Sales revenue	$100

When the payout arrives, the receivable turns into cash:

Entry	Account	Amount
Debit	Cash	$100
Credit	Receivable from acquirer or payment service provider	$100

If the merchant receives $97 after fees, the payout entry includes $97 in cash and a $3 payment processing expense against the $100 receivable.

What matters is the difference between sales, receivables, and cash. The merchant can earn revenue before the payout arrives. The ledger records this gap rather than pretending that cash arrived at the same time as the card payment.

The next ledger is the acquirer's. It receives the card settlement value and is obligated to pay the merchant.

Acquirer Ledger View

The acquirer sits between the card network settlement process and the merchant payout process.

In the simplified diagram, the acquirer records $100 on the asset side and a matching obligation to the merchant on the liability side:

Entry	Account	Amount
Debit	Cash or settlement account	$100
Credit	Merchant payable	$100

This keeps the balance sheet balanced. The acquirer has received, or expects to receive, value through the card system. At the same time, it owes the merchant the proceeds from the sale.

In a real card payment timeline, these effects can occur in stages. Before settlement funds arrive, the acquirer records a settlement receivable and a merchant payable:

Entry	Account	Amount
Debit	Settlement receivable	$100
Credit	Merchant payable	$100

When the settlement funds arrive, the receivable turns into cash:

Entry	Account	Amount
Debit	Cash or settlement account	$100
Credit	Settlement receivable	$100

When the merchant is paid, the merchant payable is cleared:

Entry	Account	Amount
Debit	Merchant payable	$100
Credit	Cash	$100

The acquirer's revenue is not the merchant's $100 sale. If the acquirer charges a $3 fee, the merchant gets $97, and the acquirer records the $3 as fee income. If there is a reserve, part of the merchant's payable is held back rather than paid right away.

So, the acquirer's ledger separates three things: what it expects to receive through settlement, what it owes the merchant, and what it earns as fees.

Issuer Ledger View

The issuer's ledger shows why this product is called a debit card. The customer's deposit account is a liability for the issuer, meaning the issuer owes the customer that balance. When a debit card transaction is posted, the issuer debits the customer's deposit account and reduces what it owes the customer.

In the simplified diagram, the issuer records the final balance-sheet effect of the transaction:

Entry	Account	Amount
Debit	Customer deposit liability	$100
Credit	Cash or settlement account	$100

This keeps the balance sheet balanced. The issuer's liability to the customer falls by $100, and the issuer's cash or settlement asset also falls by $100 when the transaction is funded.

In a real card payment timeline, posting and settlement can be recorded separately. When posting happens, the issuer records the reduction in the customer deposit liability and the obligation to fund settlement:

Entry	Account	Amount
Debit	Customer deposit liability	$100
Credit	Settlement payable	$100

When the settlement is funded, the issuer clears that payable:

Entry	Account	Amount
Debit	Settlement payable	$100
Credit	Cash or settlement account	$100

The simple diagram combines those entries to show the final balance-sheet effect. The staged version shows why clearing and settlement still need to be reconciled.

For a credit card purchase, the issuer doesn't reduce the deposit liability. Instead, it creates or increases a receivable from the cardholder because the cardholder now owes the issuer. The same payment network can handle both products, but the impact on the issuer's ledger differs between them.

Timing across Payment States

The accounting impact changes as the transaction moves through each step of the card process.

At authorization, the issuer can place a hold that reduces the available balance or available credit. This hold is an operational reservation, not the final posted accounting entry.

At clearing, the issuer receives the formal presentment. For a debit card, this is when the issuer posts the transaction and reduces the customer's deposit liability. The hold is then used, adjusted, or released.

At settlement, the issuer pays its net obligation, and the acquirer receives funds through the settlement arrangement. The issuer clears a settlement payable or reduces cash, while the acquirer clears a settlement receivable or increases cash.

At merchant payout, the acquirer pays the merchant under the merchant agreement. The acquirer's merchant payable decreases, and the merchant converts its receivable into cash.

These stages create a chain of expected accounting outcomes. If the issuer records a payable, it should be cleared later. If the acquirer records a receivable, incoming settlement funds should be applied to it. If the merchant records a receivable from the payment service provider, the payout should turn that receivable into cash.

From Ledger Entries to Reconciliation

The staged entries above create open ledger positions. Settlement receivables are expected to turn into cash; settlement payables need funding; merchant payables must be paid, reserved, offset, or adjusted; and merchant receivables should become cash in the merchant's bank account.

Reconciliation is the work of proving that those open positions were cleared correctly.

The *general ledger* does not simply say that a payment happened. It shows balances in accounts such as settlement receivable, settlement payable, merchant payable, reserve liability, fee income, cash, and clearing or suspense accounts. Each balance needs an explanation. If a settlement receivable still has $100 open after the settlement should have arrived, finance needs to know why. If a merchant payable has not been reduced after payout, the acquirer needs to know whether payout failed, the amount was reserved, the merchant had a negative balance, or the entry was posted incorrectly.

This is different from simply matching two transaction files. File matching asks whether two records describe the same transaction. GL reconciliation asks whether the financial positions created by those records have been cleared, paid, reserved, adjusted, or left open for a valid reason.

A simple acquirer example shows the logic. After clearing, the acquirer may record:

Entry	Account	Amount
Debit	Settlement receivable	$100
Credit	Merchant payable	$100

At that point, the acquirer expects two later events. First, settlement funds should arrive and clear the settlement receivable:

Entry	Account	Amount
Debit	Cash or settlement account	$100
Credit	Settlement receivable	$100

Second, merchant payout should reduce the merchant payable:

Entry	Account	Amount
Debit	Merchant payable	$100
Credit	Cash	$100

If both occur, the temporary accounts are reset to zero. The settlement receivable is closed because the acquirer received the funds. The merchant payable is closed because the merchant was paid. That is the clean case.

Many real cases are not that clean. If the acquirer charges a $3 fee, the merchant's payable is reduced by the fee income before payout. If the acquirer holds a $10 reserve, part of the merchant payable moves to a reserve liability instead of being paid. If a refund or chargeback arrives before payout, it reduces the amount owed to the merchant. If the settlement arrives one day later than expected, the receivable remains open until the cash arrives.

GL reconciliation explains these movements account by account. It asks:

Ledger Account	What Should Clear It
Settlement receivable	Incoming settlement funds
Settlement payable	Outgoing settlement funding
Merchant payable	Merchant payout, reserve movement, refund, chargeback, fee, or adjustment
Merchant receivable	Merchant payout received by the merchant
Reserve liability	Reserve release, offset, or agreed retention

Suspense or clearing account	Correct classification, matching entry, or manual investigation

Reconciliation does not mean forcing every account to zero immediately. Some balances are supposed to stay open for a period of time. A settlement receivable can remain open until the settlement date. A merchant payable can remain open until the payout cycle runs. A reserve liability can remain open for months. A chargeback receivable can remain open until recovery is confirmed.

The problem begins when an open balance has no valid explanation. A settlement receivable that should have cleared yesterday is a cash-control issue. A merchant payable that does not match the payout file can lead to overpayment or underpayment. A suspense account that keeps growing usually means the system is posting entries it cannot classify. A fee account that does not reconcile to pricing rules can distort revenue.

This is why reconciliation is central to payment operations. It connects transaction records to the general ledger and then to actual bank movements. Authorization logs, clearing records, settlement reports, payout files, refund records, chargeback records, and bank statements are evidence. The general ledger is where their financial effects must land.

A payment company can process messages all day and still lose control if its open ledger balances are unexplained. GL reconciliation confirms that the positions created by payment activity were collected, funded, paid, reserved, adjusted, or left open as intended.

Product Ledger Design

Accounting can seem separate from payment product design, but it shapes how payment systems behave.

A system that cannot distinguish authorization holds from posted debits will show customers confusing balances. A system that treats merchant payables as acquirer revenue will produce wrong financial statements. A system that cannot connect clearing records, settlement reports, reserves, refunds, and chargebacks will create reconciliation breaks, operational work, and incorrect merchant payouts.

Every serious payment product eventually becomes a ledger product.

Product managers and engineers don't need to become accountants, but they do need to understand the financial state their product creates. A payment event finishes when the ledgers show the correct position and all open items have been reconciled, not when an API returns a success response.

That financial state is spread across several institutions. A card payment appears to move money from the cardholder to the merchant, but underneath it creates ledger entries across parties that do not share a single balance sheet.

The issuer reduces what it owes the cardholder or records what the cardholder owes it. The acquirer records what it expects to receive and what it owes the merchant. The merchant records a sale and a claim to payout before cash arrives. The network calculates settlement obligations based on clearing data, enabling funds to move between participants.

Each party keeps its own books, and each set of books must balance. Reconciliation proves that those separate books still agree with the money that moved.

That is the accounting layer behind a card payment: not a single universal ledger, but several separate ledgers kept aligned through messages, records, settlement, payout, and reconciliation.

Part VI

Card Transaction Types and Variations

Chapter 30: Card-Present Transactions

A *card-present transaction* is defined by interaction with a terminal. When a cardholder inserts a card, taps it, or holds a phone near a reader, the payment system receives more than a card number. The terminal records how the credential was presented, applies cardholder-verification rules, and sends card-present security data to the issuer.

The term can be misleading because the payment credential does not have to be a plastic card. It can be a phone, watch, ring, or another wearable. What makes the transaction card-present is not the form of the credential, but the fact that it communicates with the merchant's point-of-sale terminal. If the same card details are entered on a website, used in an app, given over the phone, or charged later from stored credentials, the transaction is card-not-present.

That boundary affects authentication, fraud risk, liability, fees, terminal behavior, and authorization data. A terminal transaction can request that a card or device prove its authenticity. A remote transaction has to rely on different controls.

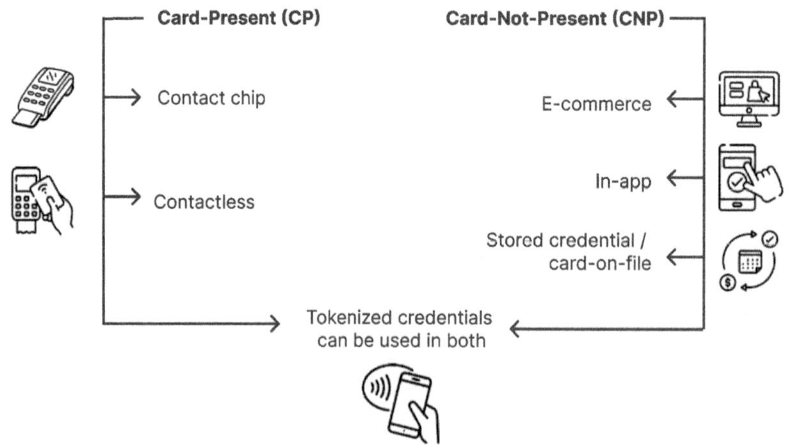

Figure 30.1: Card-present and card-not-present transactions.

The Terminal

A card-present transaction begins at the point of sale, but the terminal does more than read the card.

The terminal is the merchant device that converts a physical card or device interaction into a payment message. It reads the chip or initiates an NFC exchange, identifies the terminal and merchant, applies cardholder-verification rules, captures entry-mode data, and sends the data to the processor.

By the time the issuer receives the authorization request, the terminal has already shaped the transaction. The message can show whether the credential was inserted, tapped, keyed manually, or read from a magnetic stripe; whether cardholder verification was performed; and whether EMV or contactless data is present.

That is the main advantage of card-present payments: the physical interaction generates specific, verifiable transaction evidence that remote, card-not-present payments lack.

Chip, Contactless, and Wallet at the Terminal

Card-present transactions can begin in several ways.

A contact chip transaction begins when the card is inserted into the terminal, which reads the chip via metal contacts. Terminal and card exchange data, and the cardholder may be asked to verify identity.

The key evidence is what the chip creates during the live terminal transaction. In a typical online EMV transaction, the chip generates an ARQC — transaction-specific proof from the card delivered to the issuer. That evidence is stronger than keyed card data or purely remote card data because it changes from one transaction to the next.

A contactless transaction changes the interface. Instead of inserting the card, the cardholder brings a card, phone, watch, or wearable close to the terminal. The terminal and credential exchange payment data over NFC, usually within a few centimeters.

Contactless is designed for speed. Low-value transactions often proceed without a PIN at the terminal. When the amount or risk conditions require stronger verification, the terminal can request a PIN, decline contactless, or require contact insertion.

Mobile wallets add another variation. A phone tap at a store is still card-present because the device communicates with the terminal over NFC. The credential may be tokenized, and the cardholder may verify on the device with Face ID, Touch ID, a passcode, or another device-level method. But the transaction environment is still terminal-based.

Apple Pay at a supermarket terminal is card-present. Apple Pay inside a food delivery app is card-not-present. The brand is the same, but the transaction environment differs: one begins at a terminal, the other remotely.

Tokenization changes the credential, but it does not, by itself, change the transaction environment.

Verification and Authorization

A Cardholder Verification Method, or CVM, is how the system checks that the person using the credential is allowed to use it.

Card-present transactions can use several methods: online PIN, offline PIN, no CVM for certain low-risk transactions, CDCVM for mobile wallets, and signature in older environments. The terminal does not freely choose the method. It follows the CVM rules supported by the card and terminal and required for that transaction.

No CVM allows the transaction to proceed without checking the cardholder at the terminal. The credential is still used, terminal data is still captured, and the issuer still decides whether to approve the payment.

CDCVM works differently. The cardholder verifies themselves on a phone or wearable, and that result is sent with the payment data. This is one reason mobile wallets can be quick at checkout without shifting the transaction out of the card-present category.

CVM is therefore evidence, not the final decision. A correct PIN, successful face scan, or accepted device verification can still result in a decline for reasons outside cardholder verification: insufficient funds, suspected fraud, account status, issuer controls, or network rules.

Most modern card-present purchases then go online to the issuer. The terminal sends an authorization request through the acquirer and payment network. The issuer evaluates the account, transaction, authentication data, CVM result, and risk signals, then returns an approval or decline.

Some card-present environments also support offline logic. An offline authorization allows the card and terminal to approve certain transactions without contacting the issuer in real time. This is useful where speed or availability is critical, such as in transit, on aircraft, at remote terminals, and in some unattended environments.

Offline authorization is rule-based, not guesswork. The card and terminal follow limits, counters, and risk checks, then handle clearing later. The issuer accepts some risk to keep transactions moving when real-time issuer approval is unavailable or impractical.

The trade-off is simple: online authorization gives the issuer more real-time control; offline authorization gives the terminal more speed and availability.

Fallback and Manual Entry

Even in a card-present setting, the strength of the transaction evidence can differ.

A chip or contactless transaction gives the issuer dynamic data from the card or device. Fallback and manual entry give weaker evidence. In fallback, the terminal could not complete the preferred chip flow and instead used the magnetic stripe. In manual key entry, the cashier entered the card number manually because the card could not be read.

Both can occur at a physical checkout, but neither should be treated like a nor mal chip or contactless transaction. The terminal receives less evidence about the credential, and the issuer has fewer signals to validate.

The POS entry mode tells the issuer and network how the credential was used: chip, contactless, magstripe, fallback, manual entry, or another supported mode. This is why two purchases made in the same store can still carry different risks: one may be a chip-read transaction with dynamic data, while another may be a manually keyed transaction with much weaker proof.

Liability and Fraud Risk

Card-present transactions are generally harder to fake than card-not-present transactions.

A fraudster cannot usually succeed with card details alone. They need a physical card, a counterfeit card, a stolen device, a compromised wallet, a captured PIN, or an exploit in the terminal environment. The chip or wallet can generate dynamic data. The terminal can require a PIN or CDCVM. The issuer can see how the credential was presented.

Card-present fraud is still possible: stolen cards can be used for small contactless purchases before they are blocked; PINs can be observed; cards can be intercepted in the mail; terminals can be tampered with; fallback can be abused; and lost phones can create exposure if they are poorly protected.

When chip data and device verification reduce one type of fraud, attackers look for weaker paths: stolen cards, observed PINs, fallback, compromised terminals, or poorly protected devices.

The main difference is the attacker's starting point. In card-present fraud, the attacker usually has to overcome the physical credential or terminal environment. In card-not-present fraud, stolen credentials can be enough unless additional controls stop the transaction.

Liability rules reinforced this technology shift. During EMV migrations, networks used liability-shift rules to push chip-capable processing. The incentive was simple: when one party supported chip, and the other didn't, counterfeit-card fraud liability could shift to the party with the weaker technology.

That made running a magnetic stripe instead of a chip financially expensive. The result was a slow but steady migration from magnetic stripes to chips, and from static card data to dynamic transaction data.

Terminal Environments

A card-present transaction at a grocery store is not the same operational problem as one at a fuel pump, hotel desk, restaurant, or transit gate.

The difference is the terminal environment. It changes the transaction's risk profile and processing rules. A supermarket terminal can usually wait for an online authorization and show a clear response to the cashier. A transit gate needs speed above almost everything else. A fuel pump does not know the final amount when the card is first presented. A restaurant often needs to adjust the tip after the initial authorization. A hotel or car rental company can use the card for an initial authorization before the final bill is known. A vending machine, parking meter, or ticket kiosk operates without a cashier nearby.

The same card can behave differently across card-present settings because the terminal isn't just reading the card. It is applying rules for that specific situation. A quick café tap may need no PIN, while a higher-value purchase may ask for stronger verification. If the chip cannot be read, the transaction may fall back to the stripe. Mobile wallets change the data itself by sending a token and device-verification evidence rather than the physical card's PAN.

Calling a transaction card-present tells us that the credential interacted with a terminal. It does not tell us everything about the risk. The merchant environment, terminal capability, entry mode, and verification result complete the picture.

How Card-Present Transactions Create Evidence

A card-present transaction starts with a physical interaction: inserting a card, tapping it, holding a phone near a reader, or bringing a wearable close to a terminal.

That interaction gives the payment system evidence that a remote transaction lacks. The terminal can record how the credential was presented, which terminal and merchant were involved, whether cardholder verification took place, whether EMV or contactless data was present, and whether the transaction used a token or dynamic cryptographic data.

By the time the authorization request reaches the issuer, the message tells a richer story than a request to charge this account. A chip-read purchase, a contactless wallet tap, a magstripe fallback, and a manually keyed transaction can all happen at a physical checkout, but they do not carry the same risk.

The rest of the route is familiar: merchant to acquirer, acquirer to payment network, payment network to issuer, and back again. The difference is the evidence created at the start.

Card-present is therefore not just a channel label. It describes how the transaction began, what evidence the terminal captured, and which risk model the issuer can apply.

Chapter 31: Card-Not-Present Transactions

Card-not-present (CNP) is the label for card transactions that do not begin at the merchant's terminal.

The name *card-not-present* is misleading. The card is often very much present — physically, in the cardholder's hand — while they type its details into a checkout form. What *card-not-present* actually means is that the card isn't present at the merchant's terminal. The merchant has the number; what they don't have is the evidence that comes from a chip, a tap, or a magnetic stripe.

The common forms are familiar:

- e-commerce checkout on a website;
- in-app payment inside a mobile app;
- mail order or telephone order (MOTO);
- stored-card payments, including subscriptions and other card-on-file charges.

These transactions can use a real PAN or a token. They can also include a printed security code, 3-D Secure authentication data, device information, billing address data, merchant risk data, or stored-credential indicators.

Card-not-present does not always mean the cardholder is absent. A person can be at home, holding the physical card, typing the details into a checkout page. The card is present for the cardholder, but not for the merchant's payment terminal.

That absence changes the evidence available to the payment system. Without terminal interaction, the system cannot use chip-generated evidence, terminal PIN entry, or physical-card checks. It has to manage risk through other signals: security codes, issuer authentication, device data, stored-credential indicators, merchant data, and fraud scoring.

The familiar path remains in place: the issuer still receives an authorization request, the acquirer still sends it through the payment network, and the merchant still wants an approval. What changes is the starting evidence. Instead of asking whether a card or device interacted with a terminal, the system must determine whether the remote use of card data appears legitimate.

E-Commerce Checkout

The simplest card-not-present example is an online store. The cardholder enters the card number, expiry date, and card security code into a checkout form. The merchant's gateway or payment service provider sends the request through the acquiring side, the payment network, and the issuer. The issuer checks the account, card status, limits, fraud signals, and authentication data, then returns an approval or decline.

The route looks familiar because the underlying card infrastructure is the same. The difference is at the start. In a store, the transaction starts when the terminal reads the card or device. Online, it starts with a form, an app, a browser, a wallet button, or a stored credential.

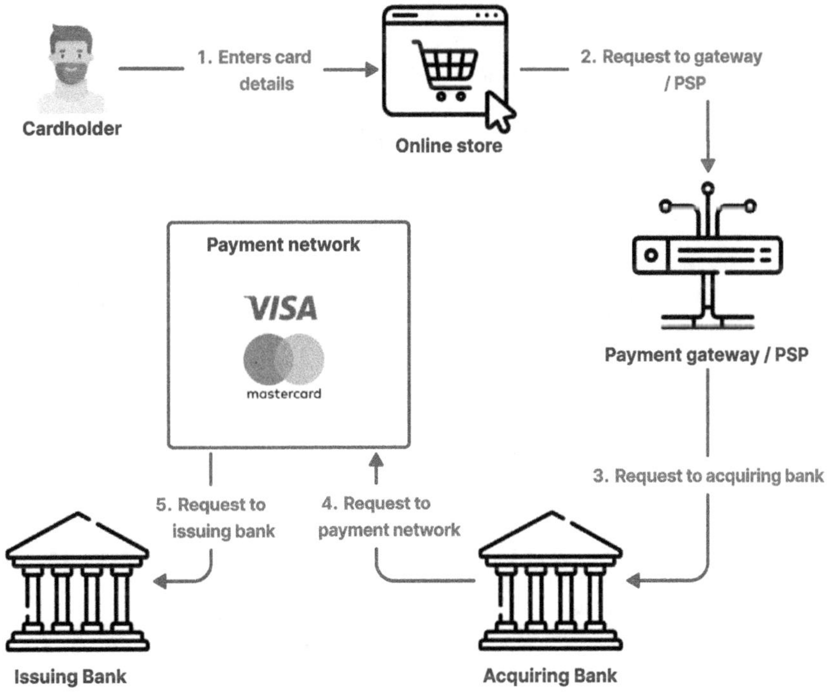

Figure 31.1: Online purchase authorization flow.

The online store must not handle card data casually. If it stores, processes, or transmits cardholder data, it must comply with the Payment Card Industry

Data Security Standard (PCI DSS). Many merchants reduce that burden by using a hosted checkout, a payment gateway, a PSP token, or a network token to keep raw PAN data out of their systems.

The printed card security code has stricter rules. The merchant can use it during authorization, but cannot store it afterward. If merchants stored it, a database breach could expose everything needed for many remote purchases.

A card-not-present transaction requires less physical proof and places greater emphasis on data security, authentication, and risk controls.

Common Environments

Card-not-present is not limited to website checkout. The same classification also covers in-app payments, MOTO transactions, and stored-card payments.

In an in-app payment, the cardholder pays inside a mobile application. The card may have been added earlier during account setup. Later, when the customer orders a ride, buys food delivery, purchases a game item, or subscribes to a service, the app submits the payment without asking for the card number again.

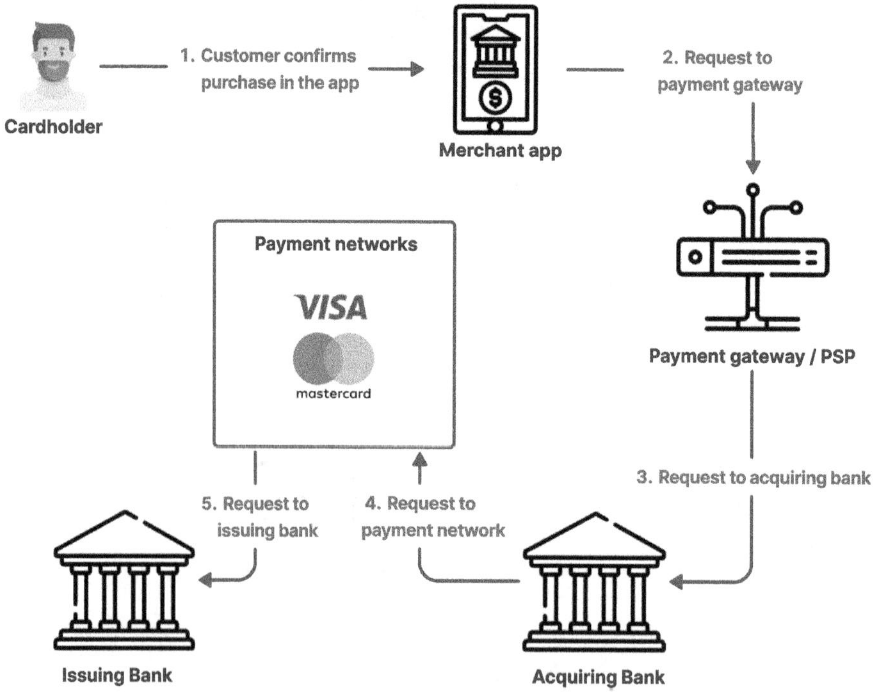

Figure 31.2: In-app payment authorization flow.

The route mirrors e-commerce: app, gateway or PSP, acquirer, payment network, issuer, then back. The difference lies in user experience and data source. The app may use a stored credential, PSP token, network token, or wallet payment data instead of a newly entered card number.

A wallet used inside an app is still card-not-present because there is no terminal interaction.

MOTO is the older CNP channel. In mail- and telephone-order transactions, the cardholder provides card details by mail, phone, or another non-terminal channel. A call center agent may enter details into a virtual terminal. These transactions can be legitimate and useful, especially in travel, hospitality, B2B ordering, and customer support environments, but they lack the browser, device, and standard 3DS signals of a modern online checkout.

Stored-card payments are another major CNP model. A cardholder provides a credential once, and later charges use that stored credential or a token. This model powers subscriptions, app stores, ride-hailing, delivery, marketplaces, hotel bookings, utility billing, and usage-based services.

A stored credential changes the convenience and risk. The cardholder does less work after setup. The merchant or PSP must correctly store, tokenize, update, retry, and cancel charges. If a forgotten subscription keeps charging a stored card, the issue can quickly escalate into a dispute.

CVV2 and the Limits of Static Proof

In a card-not-present checkout, the security code shows that the buyer had access to the printed code at the time of entry. It is not stored in the magnetic stripe, and the merchant is not allowed to retain it after authorization.

CVV2 is useful, but it is still static. If someone sees it, photographs it, phishes it, or steals it during a compromised checkout session, the value can be reused until the card is replaced or the issuer blocks it.

Having a card number and a CVV2 indicates access to card data. It does not prove that the real cardholder is making the purchase.

That is why CNP risk management adds other controls: 3-D Secure, fraud scoring, velocity rules, address checks in some markets, tokenization, device intelligence, merchant risk controls, and issuer decisioning.

3-D Secure and Issuer Authentication

The 3-D Secure protocol is the main card network protocol for authenticating cardholders in card-not-present transactions.

During checkout, the issuer can authenticate the cardholder before or during authorization. Sometimes the transaction flows with little visible interruption. In other cases, the cardholder is challenged via a banking app, a one-time code, a biometric prompt, or another issuer-approved method.

In Europe, Strong Customer Authentication under the second Payment Services Directive (PSD2) made issuer authentication central to many online card payments. In practice, this often means 3DS or a related issuer authentication flow, with exemptions and out-of-scope cases for specific transaction types.

The 3DS flow has two main effects. First, it gives the issuer a way to request stronger evidence that the person at checkout is the legitimate cardholder. Second, it can affect liability. When a transaction follows the required 3DS and network conditions, the merchant can receive better protection against certain fraud chargebacks.

A 3DS result does not guarantee approval. A transaction can pass authentication and still be declined for insufficient funds, a blocked card, issuer risk rules, merchant restrictions, or other authorization reasons.

Authentication and authorization remain separate steps.

Fraud Controls

Fraud control for card-not-present transactions uses layers because no single measure is enough.

A card-present transaction provides evidence from the chip, device, and terminal. A card-not-present transaction gets its evidence from the remote checkout environment. That evidence can still be strong, but it is not the same kind of proof.

The remote evidence is therefore more layered. CVV2 helps prove access to printed card data at the time of entry, but it is static. The 3DS protocol adds issuer-controlled authentication evidence, but it does not apply to every transaction and does not replace authorization decisioning. Tokens reduce raw PAN exposure, but they do not prove that every transaction is legitimate.

Other controls look at the remote checkout environment. Device fingerprinting and behavioral analytics can identify suspicious devices, emulators, bots, location mismatches, unusual typing patterns, or risky account behavior. Velocity controls look for repeated attempts: many cards on one account, many transactions from one device, many small authorizations, or many failures before one success.

Merchant controls add another layer: shipping restrictions, order review, account age checks, email reputation checks, delivery address analysis, IP risk analysis, purchase pattern analysis, and manual review for high-risk orders.

Issuer controls sit behind all of this. The issuer can see cardholder behavior across merchants and detect patterns that a single merchant cannot. The issuer can approve, decline, request 3DS authentication, or apply additional risk controls depending on the transaction.

Managing card-not-present risk is shared work because each participant sees only part of the situation: the merchant sees the customer session, the payment provider sees patterns across merchants, the acquirer monitors merchant risk, the network applies routing and rules, and the issuer monitors the cardholder account.

Authorization Data

A card-not-present authorization request carries different evidence from a card-present request.

It can include the PAN or token, expiry date, transaction amount, currency, merchant data, e-commerce indicator, stored-credential indicator, 3DS data, CVV2 result, billing address data where supported, device or browser data, and risk scores.

Tokens also change the credentials carried in a CNP authorization. A payment-provider token, sometimes called a PSP token, may be an internal reference used by the provider. A network token is managed through network token services and may be tied to a merchant or domain. The models differ, but the purpose is similar: reduce raw PAN exposure while still allowing the issuer to authorize the transaction. A token does not remove the need for authorization or fraud checks. It changes the credential that the system evaluates.

This data helps the issuer determine the type of remote transaction, whether the authentication evidence is sufficient, and whether the payment should proceed.

A basic MOTO transaction does not look like a 3DS-authenticated browser checkout. A wallet-based in-app purchase does not look like a manually entered card number. A recurring merchant-initiated transaction does not look like a first-time checkout.

Card-not-present is one category, but the evidence inside the authorization request can differ widely.

Remote Payment Environment

Card-not-present transactions are a major part of card payments, not a side channel.

E-commerce, app stores, subscriptions, delivery platforms, online travel, marketplaces, streaming services, software-as-a-service, and digital wallets all depend on CNP payment flows. A large share of modern card activity happens without a card touching a terminal.

That growth forced the card system to change. Static credentials were not enough, so the industry added issuer authentication, tokenization, stored-credential rules, account updater services, device intelligence, and richer risk controls.

Card-present payments rely on the moment at the terminal for evidence. Card-not-present payments use substitute evidence, such as security codes, authentication results, tokens, device signals, merchant data, customer behavior, and post-transaction proof.

Because the card is not present at the terminal, the system has to ask a different question. Not "did this card or device interact with a terminal?" but "does this remote use of card data look legitimate, authorized, and defensible?"

One especially important CNP pattern separates the checkout from later payments: the card is stored once and used repeatedly after the cardholder has left the checkout.

Chapter 32: Recurring Payments and Card-on-File

A subscription charge starts long before the cardholder sees it on a statement.

The process begins when the cardholder allows a merchant to store a payment credential for future use. During the initial checkout, the cardholder enters card details, accepts billing terms, completes any required authentication, and initiates the relationship. Later charges can then happen without a fresh checkout each time.

This separation is the core idea behind card-on-file payments. In a standard online purchase, both the cardholder's decision to pay and the authorization request occur simultaneously. With *card-on-file*, the cardholder provides a one-time permission, allowing the merchant or payment provider to use the stored credential later.

This model powers subscriptions, app stores, ride-hailing, delivery platforms, travel bookings, utility billing, marketplaces, and usage-based services.

It also introduces new responsibilities. Merchants must store credentials securely, correctly identify each transaction, handle expired or replaced cards, retry failed payments without abusing the cardholder, stop charges when permission ends, and label charges clearly enough for cardholders to recognize them.

Stored Credentials

A card-on-file transaction uses payment details saved before the payment event.

The stored payment data can include the actual card number. In practice, many merchants avoid storing raw card data. Instead, they use a token or payment reference created by a gateway, payment service provider, wallet, or network token service, allowing future payments without retaining the full PAN.

Cardholders see this model in many ordinary situations:

- saving a card for faster checkout at an online store;
- starting a monthly subscription;
- adding a card to a ride-hailing or delivery app;
- booking travel where the card can be charged later;
- using a marketplace that charges after a seller accepts or ships an order;
- paying for software, cloud services, or utilities based on later usage.

Not all card-on-file transactions are subscriptions. A key distinction is that a subscription repeats on a known schedule, whereas card-on-file arrangements involve a merchant storing a credential or token and reusing it under terms agreed with the cardholder.

A streaming service billing $12.99 every month is card-on-file. A ride-hailing app charging after the trip ends is card-on-file. A hotel charging a stored card after checkout for minibar items can be card-on-file. A marketplace charging a buyer only after an item ships can also use stored credentials.

Permission is the starting point: the cardholder authorizes the merchant to reuse payment details after their initial entry.

Initial Stored-Credential Setup

The first card-on-file transaction differs from later ones.

At the start, the cardholder is actively involved. They enter card details, choose to save the card, accept the terms, and either complete the first payment or set up the account. The merchant has to explain what the cardholder is agreeing to: one-time storage, recurring billing, future merchant charges, trial conversion, usage-based billing, or another stored-payment arrangement.

If authentication is required, setup is the natural time to perform it. In Europe, Strong Customer Authentication can apply to the initial setup when the transaction falls within scope. In other markets, issuer authentication can still be used to reduce fraud and support liability protection.

The first transaction serves two purposes.

First, it creates a payment event. That event can be a sale, an authorization, a small account check, or another setup step.

Second, it establishes the stored-credential relationship: the merchant or provider now has a credential, token, or reference that can be used later with the cardholder's permission.

After setup, later charges can be initiated under the stored-credential relationship.

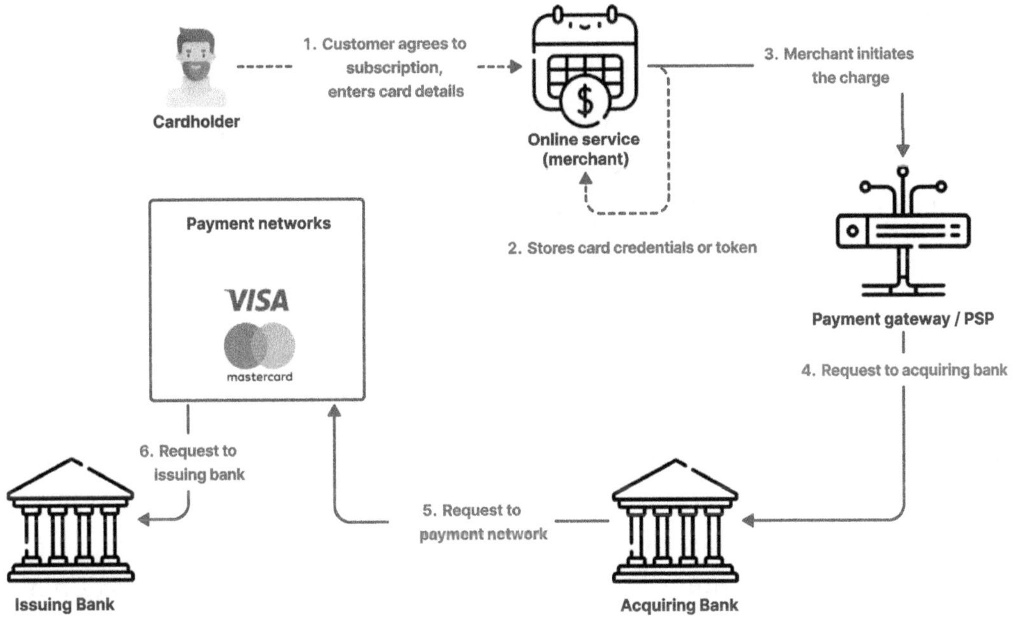

Figure 32.1: Card-on-file and recurring payment flow.

The dashed line in Figure 32.1 shows the central shift: the cardholder is active at setup, but later charges can be initiated under the stored agreement without a fresh checkout.

Cardholder-Initiated and Merchant-Initiated Transactions

Card networks distinguish between transactions initiated by the cardholder and transactions initiated by the merchant.

A Cardholder-Initiated Transaction (CIT) happens when the cardholder actively participates in the payment. The cardholder is checking out, pressing Pay, tapping a wallet button, entering card details, or otherwise confirming the payment.

A Merchant-Initiated Transaction (MIT) happens when the merchant initiates the transaction later under a prior agreement with the cardholder. The cardholder is not actively involved at the moment of payment.

This classification affects how transactions are identified, authenticated, and assessed for risk.

An initial subscription signup is typically a CIT. Later monthly renewals are usually MITs. A one-click checkout confirmed by the cardholder remains a CIT, even if the card was previously stored. A ride-hailing platform can charge the final fare after trip completion as an MIT or another stored-credential transaction, depending on how the payment flow was set up and identified.

Having a stored credential does not by itself make a transaction merchant-initiated. The initiator at the moment determines the type: if the cardholder pays now, it is a CIT; if the merchant charges later under a stored agreement, it is an MIT.

Recurring and Unscheduled Charges

Card-on-file payments can be scheduled or unscheduled.

A *recurring payment* is a specific type of card-on-file transaction that is scheduled to repeat at agreed intervals. This differs from other card-on-file uses, where timing or frequency varies. Subscriptions, such as streaming services, software, insurance premiums, and memberships, use recurring payments with billing cycles disclosed to the cardholder in advance.

The initial payment establishes the relationship: the merchant saves a credential or token and records the cardholder's consent. Thereafter, the merchant can submit charges on designated billing dates without needing the cardholder to check out again.

For cardholders, these payments often run in the background: the service continues uninterrupted while the charge appears on the statement.

For merchants, recurring payments are operationally sensitive. Subscription businesses depend on successful renewals, and even small increases in failed renewals can quickly erode revenue. Retry logic, account updater services, network tokens, clear billing descriptors, renewal notifications, and efficient cancellation – all of these affect whether the subscription business survives.

The same stored-credential model also supports unscheduled card-on-file transactions or merchant-initiated charges.

Examples include:

- ride-hailing charges after a trip ends;
- food-delivery adjustments after substitutions or tips;
- hotel charges after checkout;
- car-rental charges for fuel, tolls, or damage;
- marketplace charges after a seller accepts or ships an order;
- cloud-service charges based on monthly usage.

These payments differ from fixed subscriptions because the timing, amount, or both vary. The cardholder provides advance permission, but the merchant determines the actual charge later, under the agreed terms.

That flexibility creates more room for confusion. A cardholder is more likely to recognize a $9.99 monthly subscription than a $47.83 platform charge two days after using a service. The merchant's descriptor, receipt, notification, billing history, and terms help the cardholder connect the charge to the service. When that connection is unclear, disputes become more likely.

What Merchants Can Store

Card-on-file relies on stored credentials, but not every card data element can be stored.

The key restriction is CVV2. Merchants can request the security code during the initial transaction, but cannot keep it afterward. Therefore, later recurring or merchant-initiated transactions do not include CVV2.

Merchants and payment providers can store card numbers only under strict PCI DSS controls. Many merchants avoid this burden by letting a payment provider handle storage. The merchant keeps a token or reference, while the provider links that reference to the underlying card credential.

Several token models can appear in card-on-file payments.

A PSP token is an internal reference created by the payment provider. It lets the merchant charge the same credential again without storing the PAN.

A *network token* is issued through a payment network token service and can represent the card in a merchant or domain context. Network tokens can improve security and support credential lifecycle updates when the underlying card changes.

A device token, such as a mobile wallet token, is tied to a phone, watch, or wallet environment. It should not be confused with a merchant's stored credentials for recurring billing.

For card-on-file payments, the merchant needs a credential that it can reuse. A token or payment reference reduces the damage if the merchant's own systems are compromised.

Account Updater and Token Lifecycle

For recurring and card-on-file merchants, card replacement isn't just a lifecycle event. It is a revenue-continuity problem.

If a streaming service tries to charge an expired card, the renewal can fail. If the cardholder has to update card details manually across many merchants, some services will break. For merchants, those failed renewals create involuntary churn: customers leave because the payment failed, not because they wanted to cancel.

Account updater services reduce this problem. Visa's service is Visa Account Updater (VAU). Mastercard's service is Automatic Billing Updater (ABU). Both services allow participating merchants, payment providers, acquirers, and issuers to exchange updated card credentials for stored-payment relationships.

These services can update expiry dates, replacement card numbers, and account-status information. The merchant doesn't have to ask the cardholder to re-enter card details every time a card expires or is replaced. Instead, the stored credential can be refreshed through the network updater process when the issuer and other participants support it.

Network tokens can also help. When a merchant uses a network token, the underlying card credential can be updated without the merchant needing to know about it. The merchant can continue using the token without receiving a new PAN, as long as the issuer and network maintain the mapping.

This helps merchants keep subscriptions active. It helps cardholders avoid unnecessary service interruptions. Issuers benefit because their cards remain active in recurring and stored-payment relationships.

The same mechanism can surprise cardholders. A person might think that receiving a replacement card will stop a subscription. In many cases, it will not. If the subscription agreement remains valid and credential-update services are available, the merchant can continue charging the updated credential.

Authorization of Later Charges

A later card-on-file charge still goes through the authorization process.

The merchant sends the request through its gateway or PSP to the acquirer, payment network, and issuer. The issuer checks the account, card status, available funds or credit, limits, fraud rules, stored-credential indicators, and other controls.

The difference is the transaction context. The request can identify the payment as a recurring MIT or another stored-credential transaction. It can reference the original CIT or stored-credential agreement. It does not include CVV2. It can proceed without active cardholder authentication when properly linked to a valid prior setup and the rules permit that treatment.

The issuer can still decline the payment. The card can be blocked, the account can be closed, funds can be insufficient, the credential can be invalid, the merchant can be restricted, the request can be formatted incorrectly, or the transaction can look suspicious.

A merchant-initiated charge is not guaranteed money. It is an authorization request based on earlier permission, and the issuer still decides whether to approve it.

Declines and Retry Logic

Businesses that use recurring or card-on-file payments regularly encounter failed authorizations.

Some declines are temporary: the account balance may be too low today, a spending limit may reset tomorrow, an issuer may have a short-lived risk concern, or a network or issuer system may be unavailable. These are commonly treated as soft declines, where a later retry can succeed.

Other declines are more final. The card can be closed, reported stolen, marked as invalid or expired without an update, or blocked so the merchant cannot continue processing it. These are commonly treated as hard declines.

Retry logic is the approach merchants use to recover failed payments without creating new problems.

A subscription merchant might retry after a few hours, the next day, or after a likely payday. It might ask the cardholder to update the payment method. A ride-hailing platform might require a new card before the next ride. A software provider might keep the account active during a grace period before suspending access.

Bad retry logic is costly. Retry too little, and the merchant loses customers who still want the service. Retry too aggressively, and issuers may treat the merchant as risky, customers may complain, and network rules may be breached. Repeated retries after a hard decline can look like abuse.

A good retry system uses the decline reason, respects do-not-retry signals, uses the updater and token services when available, spreads attempts sensibly, and informs the cardholder what is happening.

A failed renewal is also a customer-retention moment: the merchant can either recover the relationship or lose the customer.

Consent, Cancellation, and Disputes

Card-on-file payments depend on clear permission.

The merchant should tell the cardholder what will happen: whether the card will be stored, when charges will occur, how much will be charged, or how the amount will be calculated, whether the payment is recurring or unscheduled, how cancellation works, and how receipts will be provided.

This is not only a legal or compliance concern. It affects disputes.

Many disputes begin because the cardholder does not recognize the charge, believes they canceled it, or did not understand that a trial would convert to a paid plan. A clear descriptor, confirmation email, renewal notice, in-app billing history, cancellation page, and receipt trail can reduce those disputes.

Trial subscriptions are especially sensitive. A free trial that converts into a paid plan can be valid under the terms and still feel unfair if the cardholder feels trapped or surprised.

The payment system can function correctly even when the customer relationship fails. If consent is unclear, cancellation is hard to find, or billing terms are buried, a technically successful recurring payment can turn into a complaint or a chargeback.

Card-on-file payments also make individual charges less visible. A cardholder who taps a card in a shop remembers the purchase. A cardholder who wakes up to a subscription renewal might not. Merchant names, billing descriptors, platform structures, and timing can make this worse. A cardholder can subscribe under one brand and see another legal entity on the statement. A marketplace can charge after an order ships, not when it was placed. A ride-hailing charge can include adjustments. A cloud service can bill based on usage rather than a fixed plan.

That confusion can turn into a dispute. The merchant then needs evidence of: original consent, stored-credential setup, billing terms, transaction history, service usage, delivery records, where relevant, cancellation status, customer communication, and authentication or authorization data.

The best way to reduce disputes is to make the payment relationship clear from the start, before chargebacks arrive.

Stored Payment Relationship

Card payments used to be single events: a card at the counter, a signature or PIN, and a receipt.

Card-on-file changed that pattern. It turned the card from a one-time checkout credential into a reusable payment relationship.

That shift made digital subscriptions, app-based services, marketplaces, recurring billing, usage-based software, one-click checkout, and many platform business models possible. It also changed the risk. The payment is no longer only about whether the cardholder approves a transaction at checkout. It is also about whether the original consent was valid, whether the credential is protected, whether later charges are identified correctly, whether declines are handled responsibly, and whether the cardholder can understand and control the relationship.

Card-on-file separates the moment of permission from the moment of payment.

Because permission and payment happen at different times, the merchant, PSP, acquirer, and issuer need clear records of consent, cancellation, transaction type, and customer communication.

Chapter 33: Pre-Authorizations, Refunds, and Transaction Corrections

A basic card payment can be broken down into authorization, capture, clearing, settlement, and payout. In the clean version, the amount is known from the start: a cardholder buys a $40 shirt, the merchant requests authorization for $40, the issuer approves, the merchant captures and presents the same $40, and the transaction posts cleanly.

However, many real transactions do not follow that path. To understand these complexities, let's examine scenarios where the basic flow changes.

Examples include a hotel that does not know the final bill at check-in, a fuel pump with an unknown final amount, a restaurant that needs to add a tip, or an online retailer that ships part of an order. Checkout failures after authorization and partial returns also differ from the clean transaction flow.

The cardholder may describe all of these as a charge. The payment system treats them as different events: an authorization hold, an incremental authorization, a capture, a partial capture, a reversal, a void, or a refund.

The main distinction is timing. Before a transaction is completed, the system usually changes, completes, or releases the authorization. After completion, the merchant usually needs a separate refund or correcting transaction to return the value.

Each event changes a different part of the payment lifecycle. The right label tells the operations team whether to look for an open hold, a completed charge, a released authorization, or a separate credit back to the cardholder.

Pre-Authorization

A *pre-authorization* is an authorization used when the merchant does not yet know the final amount or does not yet want to complete the charge.

It is still an authorization. The issuer approves an estimated or maximum amount and places a hold against the cardholder's available balance or credit. The difference is the purpose: in a normal purchase, the authorized amount is expected to become the final captured amount. In a pre-authorization, the approved amount is provisional. It reserves capacity for a later charge, which can be lower or higher, or may never be completed.

That provisional design is easiest to see in hotels. At check-in, the hotel may authorize the expected room cost plus a deposit for incidentals. The cardholder may still use the minibar, order room service, extend the stay, or check out late. The hotel does not know the final bill, but it needs assurance that funds or credit are available. When the final amount is known, the hotel completes the transaction for the actual bill. If the expected amount increases during the stay, the hotel may request an incremental authorization. If the final amount is lower than the original hold, the unused part should be released, reversed, or left to expire.

Fuel pumps use the same principle at a faster rate. The pump does not know whether the driver will buy $20 or $90 of fuel, so the merchant first sends an estimated authorization or a status-check authorization. After fueling is complete, the merchant sends a follow-up message with the final amount, and the final clearing record should reflect the fuel actually purchased.

Both examples point to the same mechanism: a pre-authorization is not a different kind of payment. It is an authorization used to reserve capacity before the final amount is known. Later messages confirm, increase, reduce, complete, or release that reserved amount.

Incremental Authorization

An incremental authorization increases the authorized amount when the original authorization is insufficient.

Hotels and car rentals often need this. Suppose a hotel initially authorizes $600 for a two-night stay and a deposit. During the stay, the guest adds restaurant charges and a late checkout fee. The expected bill rises to $780. Rather than waiting until the end and presenting a larger amount without approval, the hotel can request an incremental authorization for the additional amount.

Fuel, charging, travel, lodging, and rental scenarios may also require additional authorization as exposure grows over time.

Incremental authorization helps both the merchant and the issuer. The merchant gets approval for the higher amount, and the issuer can check available funds, limits, card status, and risk before increasing the exposure.

If the merchant does not obtain the additional authorization when required, the final transaction can become harder to clear, price, defend, or collect.

Capture

Capture is the merchant-side step that confirms the amount to be submitted for clearing.

In a simple store purchase, capture may happen automatically when the merchant closes its batch. In e-commerce, capture may happen immediately after authorization or later when the goods ship. In hotels and car rentals, capture happens when the final bill is known.

Capture tells the acquiring side the amount the merchant intends to complete. The clearing record that follows is the formal presentment through the network.

If the captured amount matches the authorization, the issuer can usually match the clearing record to the earlier hold and post the transaction cleanly. If the captured amount is lower, the issuer posts the lower amount and releases the unused hold. If the captured amount is higher, the merchant may need an incremental authorization or may face rejection, downgrade, dispute risk, or weaker protection.

A capture can be full or partial.

A partial capture happens when the merchant captures less than the authorized amount. This is common in e-commerce. A cardholder orders three items for $120, but only two items are available for immediate shipment. The merchant captures $80, and either releases the unused authorization amount or handles the remaining item through a later permitted flow.

A *partial capture* is not a refund. The cardholder was never finally charged for the uncaptured part. The unused hold is simply released rather than returned through a separate credit.

This difference changes customer support language. "We refunded $40" is not the same as "we captured $80 of a $120 authorization and released the rest of the hold." The cardholder may experience both as $40 becoming available again, but the system records different events.

Reversals and Voids

An authorization reversal cancels or reduces an authorization before it becomes a completed transaction.

This is what should happen when the merchant no longer needs all or part of the hold, such as after a checkout failure, an order cancellation before shipment, an unused hotel deposit, a fuel pump authorization exceeding the final fuel amount, or an e-commerce order that cannot be fully shipped.

The reversal tells the issuer that the merchant will not use the authorization, or will use less of it. The issuer can then release the hold and restore the cardholder's available balance or credit.

A quick reversal usually restores the cardholder's available balance sooner. If no reversal is sent, the hold remains until it expires under the issuer and network rules.

This is why a canceled sale and a released hold are not the same thing. The merchant may have canceled the order, while the issuer still has an authorization hold waiting for reversal or expiry.

A *void* is the merchant-facing term often used when a transaction is canceled before it is captured or submitted for clearing. In some systems, voiding a transaction sends an authorization reversal. In others, it prevents the transaction from being captured in the merchant batch.

Refunds

A refund is a separate transaction that sends value back after the original transaction has been completed.

Suppose a cardholder buys shoes for $100, the merchant captures the transaction, and the issuer posts the charge. Later, the cardholder returns the shoes. The merchant cannot release the original authorization because that stage is over. Instead, it sends a $100 refund transaction.

The refund is connected to the original sale, but it is not simply the original sale undone. It has its own timing, records, and reconciliation trail. A full refund returns the whole amount. A partial refund returns only part of it, such as one item from a larger order, a goodwill credit, a price adjustment, or compensation for a partial service failure.

Refund timing can frustrate cardholders. A merchant can issue a refund in its own system right away, but the cardholder does not see the credit until the issuer processes it. The merchant can truthfully say the refund was issued, while the cardholder can truthfully say the funds are not yet visible.

Refunds differ from reversals and voids by timing. A reversal or void occurs before an authorization becomes a completed charge. A refund deals with a transaction that has already been captured, posted, or otherwise completed.

That timing difference explains many support cases. If an order was canceled before capture, the cardholder is usually waiting for a hold to be released, not for a refund. If the transaction has already been posted, the merchant cannot simply release the old authorization. They need to issue a refund or another correcting transaction.

The terms direct the operations team to the right place: an open authorization, a reversal, an expired hold, a capture, a posted transaction, or a separate refund credit.

Merchant and Acquirer Responsibilities

Merchants and acquirers have to manage these flows carefully. Weak handling leads to customer complaints, reconciliation errors, and disputes.

A merchant should not leave unused authorizations open when it knows they will not be captured. It should send reversals where appropriate, capture only what it is entitled to capture, request incremental authorization when exposure increases, issue refunds promptly when a completed transaction needs to be returned, and give the cardholder receipts and descriptors that explain what happened.

The acquirer or PSP has to support these operations cleanly. It maps merchant actions into the correct payment messages, maintains references to the original authorization, handles partial capture and reversal logic, and reconciles refunds and adjustments against settlement and merchant payout.

Poor integration creates real money problems: missing reversals trap cardholder funds, incorrect captures create disputes, duplicate captures create duplicate posting, refunds without proper references create extra reconciliation work, and unsupported adjustments can be rejected or disputed.

Transaction correction is part of payment operations, not cleanup after the real payment.

These operational details are visible to cardholders through simple labels in the banking app: pending, posted, refunded, canceled, reversed, released, or declined. Those labels are useful, but they hide the actual transaction state.

That is why support teams must translate the cardholder's description into payment system terms. "Charged twice" can mean a duplicate transaction, a hotel hold plus a final charge, a failed reversal, or a delayed refund. The correct answer depends on the records behind the screen: authorization, reversal, capture, clearing, posting, refund, payout, and dispute history.

Transaction Lifecycle

The first authorization is not always the final shape of the transaction.

A merchant may need to reserve an estimated amount, increase it, capture less than expected, release an unused hold, or refund the charge after it has posted. Each action belongs to a different lifecycle stage.

The sequence determines which action is available. Before completion, the merchant is usually working with an authorization: holding it, increasing it, capturing it, or releasing it. After completion, the merchant is working with a posted charge, so the correction is usually a refund or another separate financial event.

The card system works by giving merchants controlled ways to reserve, complete, correct, release, and return funds, instead of forcing every transaction into the same flow.

The challenge is choosing the right tool for the stage the transaction has reached.

Chapter 34: Disputes and Chargebacks

A cardholder opens their banking app and sees a charge they do not recognize.

The charge could be fraud, a forgotten merchant name, a subscription the cardholder thought was canceled, an order that never arrived, a duplicate charge, or a product that did not match the description. For the cardholder, the next step is clear: contact the bank and challenge the transaction.

For the payment system, that challenge brings the network rulebook into view. In Chapter 5, we treated that rulebook as infrastructure. Here, it determines who can raise a claim, what evidence counts, how long each party has to respond, and when liability moves.

A *dispute* means the cardholder objects to a transaction. A *chargeback* is the network process the issuer uses to challenge the transaction and, at least provisionally, reverse its financial effect under network rules.

People often use *dispute* and *chargeback* interchangeably, but they do not mean the same thing. A cardholder can dispute a transaction, and the issuer may resolve it without filing a chargeback. The issuer could reject the claim, ask for more information, credit the cardholder directly, or handle the issue internally. A chargeback begins only when the issuer uses the card network's process to send the claim back through the card system.

A dispute can end without a chargeback, but every chargeback begins with a cardholder's objection.

A chargeback is also different from a refund. A refund begins when the merchant agrees to return value to the cardholder. A chargeback starts when the issuer turns the cardholder's objection into a network case. The cardholder may experience both as "getting money back," but the system treats them differently: one is a merchant-initiated return of value; the other is a rule-based claim with deadlines, reason codes, evidence rules, fees, and financial consequences.

To the merchant, a chargeback is not ordinary customer support. It is a financial claim that must be answered with evidence.

Sources of Disputes

Disputes exist because card payments separate the people who perform the transaction from the institutions that process it.

The issuer works with the cardholder. The acquirer works with the merchant. The payment network sets the rules governing interactions between its participants. When something goes wrong, the system needs a way to move the claim from the cardholder's bank to the merchant's bank and decide whether the original transaction should stand.

The common reasons are familiar:

- The cardholder says the transaction was unauthorized.
- Goods were not received.
- Services were not provided.
- The merchant processed a duplicate transaction.
- The amount was incorrect.
- The cardholder canceled a recurring payment but was charged again.
- The merchant failed before delivering the goods or service.
- The transaction was processed without valid authorization.
- The cardholder received goods or services materially different from what was described.

Some disputes involve real fraud. Others stem from merchant errors, delivery issues, customer confusion, unclear merchant names, hard-to-cancel subscriptions, slow service, or poor records. Some also involve cardholders taking advantage of the system.

The chargeback process does not begin by knowing the real cause. It starts with a claim, and then each side must provide evidence to support or challenge it.

Dispute Participants

A chargeback moves through several parties. The cardholder and merchant usually do not communicate directly during the network process.

The cardholder raises the dispute with the issuer.

The issuer reviews the claim and decides whether to file a chargeback. The cardholder often receives temporary credit while the case is under review. That credit is provisional, not always final. If the merchant later wins, the issuer may recover the funds from the cardholder.

The payment network sends messages between the issuer and acquirer and enforces the rules. During most of the chargeback process, it does not decide who is right or wrong. It provides the framework: reason codes, deadlines, evidence rules, liability rules, and escalation paths.

The acquirer receives the chargeback from the network, debits the merchant or notifies it under the merchant agreement, and then passes the case to the merchant or its payment provider.

The merchant decides whether to accept the chargeback or contest it by submitting evidence.

In many modern setups, a PSP, marketplace, or payment facilitator sits between the acquirer and the merchant. A merchant using Stripe, Adyen, PayPal, Shopify Payments, or a marketplace platform usually does not deal directly with an acquiring bank's dispute portal. The platform may collect evidence, format it, submit it, and debit the merchant's balance.

The PSP or platform may be the merchant's interface, but the underlying chargeback still flows through the issuer, network, and acquirer.

Dispute Cycle

The dispute cycle begins after the original transaction has been presented through the card system. By the time the cardholder complains, the transaction may already have been authorized, posted, settled, and paid out to the merchant. In dispute terminology, that original presentment is often called the *first presentment*.

Then the cardholder objects.

The issuer reviews the complaint. If the claim qualifies, the issuer files a chargeback and may give the cardholder provisional credit. The chargeback travels through the payment network to the acquirer, then to the merchant.

The merchant has two basic choices. It can accept the chargeback. The disputed amount is lost, the cardholder keeps the credit, and the case closes.

Or the merchant can contest the chargeback. This is called *representment* or second presentment. The merchant is re-presenting the transaction with evidence that supports its position. That evidence might include delivery confirmations, signed receipts, 3-D Secure data, accepted terms, usage logs, refund policies, cancellation records, customer messages, or other documents related to the reason code.

The acquirer sends the merchant's evidence back through the network to the issuer. The issuer reviews the case again. If the issuer accepts the evidence, the merchant wins, and the cardholder's provisional credit may be reversed. If the issuer rejects the evidence, the dispute can move to another stage.

In some cases, the next stage is *pre-arbitration*. This is another attempt to resolve the disagreement before a final network decision is made. If the parties still disagree, the case moves to arbitration. At that point, the payment network reviews the evidence and issues a binding decision. The losing side pays the disputed amount and arbitration fees.

Most cases never reach arbitration. The fees and work involved are usually too high unless the disputed amount, risk, or principle justifies escalation. Figure 34.1 brings the main dispute stages into one cycle, from the initial claim through representment and possible escalation.

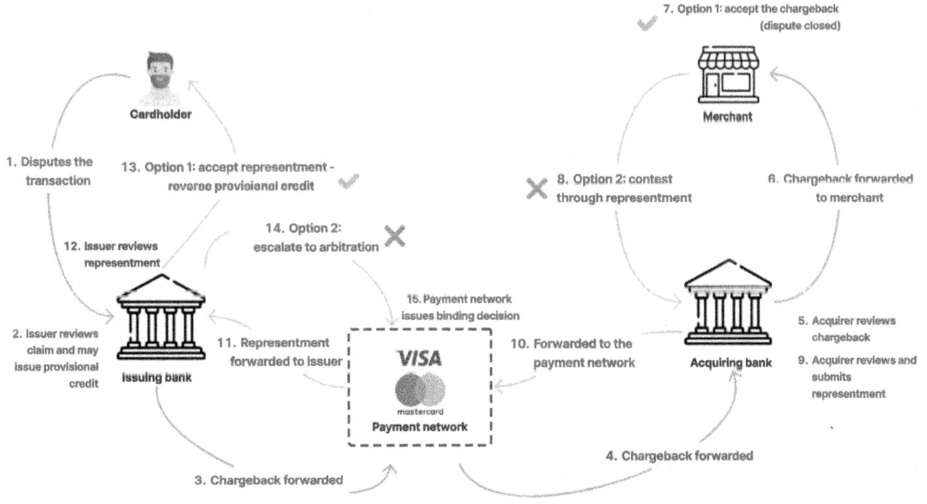

Figure 34.1: The dispute cycle.

Reason Codes

Every chargeback carries a reason code.

A reason code tells the acquirer and merchant why the issuer filed the chargeback and what kind of evidence is needed to fight it. Visa, Mastercard, and other networks use their own reason-code taxonomies, which are updated through network rule changes.

The first category is fraud. The cardholder claims they did not authorize the transaction. This is common in card-not-present environments, where stolen credentials can be used without the physical card or terminal interaction.

The second is an authorization error. The transaction was processed without proper approval, exceeded the authorized amount, or did not match a valid authorization.

The third is a processing error. These are operational mistakes: duplicate processing, incorrect amount, late presentment, currency mismatch, or messaging problems between participants.

The fourth is a consumer dispute. The cardholder participated in the transaction but claims the merchant did not fulfill the bargain. The goods did not arrive. Services were not provided. The item was materially different from what was described. A recurring payment continued after cancellation.

Two abbreviations appear often in consumer disputes. Item Not Received (INR) means the cardholder paid for goods or services, but claims they never arrived. *Significantly Not as Described* (*SNAD*) means something arrived, but the cardholder says it materially differed from what was advertised or promised.

The reason code shapes the case. A fraud dispute depends on 3-D Secure data, authentication records, device data, or proof that the cardholder participated. An item-not-received dispute depends on delivery confirmation. A duplicate-processing dispute depends on transaction identifiers and clearing records. An authorization dispute depends on authorization logs and matching fields.

A merchant does not win a chargeback by showing that it runs a good business overall. It wins by addressing the specific claim associated with the reason code.

Evidence and Representment

Evidence is how the merchant defends itself.

What counts as useful evidence depends on the reason code. A merchant fighting an item-not-received dispute needs different evidence from a merchant fighting an unauthorized-transaction dispute.

Useful evidence can include:

- proof of delivery with tracking and delivery address;
- signed receipts or signed service documents;
- 3-D Secure authentication results;
- authorization approval data;
- address-verification or card-security-code results where relevant;
- customer communication;
- refund and cancellation policy accepted by the cardholder;
- usage logs for digital goods or services;
- account login history;
- records of previous undisputed transactions;
- invoices, order records, or shipping confirmations;
- photographs, repair records, or check-in documents for travel and rental cases.

The evidence must answer the claim.

If the cardholder says the item never arrived, a signed delivery confirmation is relevant. If the cardholder says the transaction was unauthorized, delivery confirmation can help, but it is not always enough. The merchant may need proof that the cardholder authenticated, logged in, used the same device before, accepted the terms, or received the goods at a known address.

Good dispute handling starts before a dispute exists. Merchants that maintain clear order records, recognizable descriptors, proof of delivery, consent records, refund policies, cancellation logs, and customer communication are easier to defend. Merchants that rely on scattered emails, vague policies, or weak logs struggle even when their side of the story is true.

The Economics of a Chargeback

A chargeback costs more than the transaction amount.

The merchant can lose the sale amount, the goods or service already delivered, and the chargeback fee charged by its acquirer or PSP. The operational costs add up too: staff have to collect evidence, respond before deadlines, and manage the case. If dispute levels rise, the acquirer may increase pricing, hold reserves, require remediation, or apply closer oversight under network monitoring programs.

For small disputes, this creates a practical choice. Fighting may cost more than accepting. A merchant might be right and still decide not to fight if the transaction value is low, the evidence is weak, or the operational cost is not worth it.

Many merchants treat disputes as a portfolio problem. They do not fight every case. They fight the cases they can win, the cases that reveal fraud patterns, high-value cases, and cases needed to protect their dispute ratios and acquiring relationship.

Chargeback Ratios and Monitoring

Networks and acquirers monitor merchants with high dispute levels.

A chargeback ratio usually compares chargebacks with transaction volume over a defined period. Networks use these formulas, thresholds, and monitoring programs to identify merchants or acquirers with excessive disputes or fraud.

A merchant with too many chargebacks poses a risk to the acquiring bank and the network. The merchant may face higher fees, reserve requirements, mandatory remediation plans, closer review, or termination of processing.

The raw ratio can be misleading. A merchant with 10 transactions and 1 chargeback has a 10 percent chargeback rate, but the absolute count is 1. A large merchant with a lower percentage but thousands of disputes may create a bigger operational problem. Acquirers, therefore, look beyond the raw ratio: transaction count, merchant category, processing history, fraud indicators, average ticket size, seasonality, and whether the problem looks temporary or systemic.

The network formula sends a warning signal. The acquirer decides how serious the risk is and what action to take.

Preventing Disputes

The least expensive chargeback is the one that never happens.

Prevention has four practical layers.

The first layer is fraud control. For card-not-present merchants, 3-D Secure, Strong Customer Authentication, where applicable, device intelligence, velocity checks, tokenization, and fraud monitoring can prevent high-risk transactions from settling. A fraudulent transaction declined at the time of authorization cannot later become a fraud chargeback.

The second layer is clear customer communication. Many disputes begin because the cardholder is confused, not because the merchant intended anything wrong. Clear merchant names, accurate delivery dates, confirmation emails, shipment tracking, renewal notices, billing descriptors, and easy access to support can stop cardholders from going straight to the issuer.

The third layer is direct resolution. A proactive refund can be cheaper than forcing a weak case into the chargeback process. If the customer has a legitimate complaint, solving it through support may cost only a refund. Letting it become a chargeback can add fees, operational work, ratio pressure, and frustration for everyone.

Documentation is the fourth layer. Documentation does not stop the dispute, but it determines whether the merchant can defend itself. Delivery proof, signed authorizations, authentication records, accepted terms, cancellation logs, service usage records, and customer communications should be in place before the case begins.

Fraud prevention and dispute handling are related but not the same. Fraud prevention occurs before or during authorization; it aims to prevent bad transactions from being approved. Dispute handling happens after the transaction; it decides what happens when a completed transaction is challenged later.

A merchant needs both. Strong fraud tools reduce bad transactions before they settle. Clear communication, responsive support, and good records reduce the risk of legitimate transactions turning into disputes and help defend cases that still arise.

Cardholder Protection and Merchant Burden

The chargeback system provides the cardholder with a protected way to challenge a transaction with the issuer.

However, cardholders do not automatically win disputes. Merchants can win representments when they have strong evidence. The process provides card holders with a formal route to challenge fraud, merchant failures, duplicate charges, delivery problems, and other valid complaints. In many cases, the cardholder receives provisional credit while the case is reviewed.

The financial burden often falls more heavily on the merchant. The merchant pays fees, gathers evidence, and risks additional monitoring if disputes mount. The acquirer carries merchant risk and can require reserves or stop processing. The issuer manages the cardholder relationship and must balance protection with the prevention of abuse.

This protected challenge process is one reason cards are trusted for online shopping. A cardholder can buy from an unfamiliar merchant, knowing there is a process in place if something goes wrong.

That trust has a cost. Merchants, acquirers, issuers, and networks all bear that cost through dispute handling, fraud systems, monitoring, operational work, and sometimes unfair losses.

Rule-Based Reversal

A chargeback shows that settlement is not always the end of a card transaction.

Even after the merchant has been paid, the transaction can still be challenged through the network if the cardholder raises a valid claim. The issuer decides whether to act; the network supplies the rulebook; the acquirer brings the case to the merchant; and the merchant either accepts the loss or contests it with evidence.

The process can seem slow because it is solving a difficult problem across several institutions. The cardholder, merchant, issuer, acquirer, and network do not always see the same facts, and the money may already have moved.

A good payment system requires finality and a controlled process for handling fraud, errors, merchant failures, and delivery issues after the original payment is made.

The merchant's money is not fully safe until the dispute window has passed.

Chapter 35: Push-to-Card and Original Credit Transactions

Most card payments pull money from the cardholder.

For purchases like groceries, online checkouts, or renewals, the merchant initiates the payment request through the acquirer, network, and issuer. If approved, the cardholder's balance or credit line is affected, and the merchant receives funds later.

Push-to-card works in the other direction. It uses a card network infrastructure to send money to a card-linked account.

A marketplace can pay a seller. A delivery platform can pay a courier at the end of a shift. An insurer can pay a claim. A wallet can let a user cash out to a debit card. In these cases, the cardholder is not paying a merchant. The cardholder is receiving money through the card network.

The card number acts as a routing credential. It helps the network identify the card's issuer and the account relationship behind it.

Many such payments are called Original Credit Transactions (OCT). Visa Direct and Mastercard Move/Mastercard Send are key examples, but naming and supported use cases differ by network, region, and participant program. Though named differently, both send funds to card-linked accounts via the card network.

Pull Payments and Push Payments

The difference between pull and push payments is about who initiates the movement of funds.

In pull payments, the recipient, usually the merchant, initiates the debit. The cardholder provides card details, but the merchant's system sends the authorization through the acquirer. The issuer then decides if the account or credit line can be used.

That is why card purchases can feel cardholder-initiated even though they are pull payments. The cardholder gives consent. The merchant sends the request.

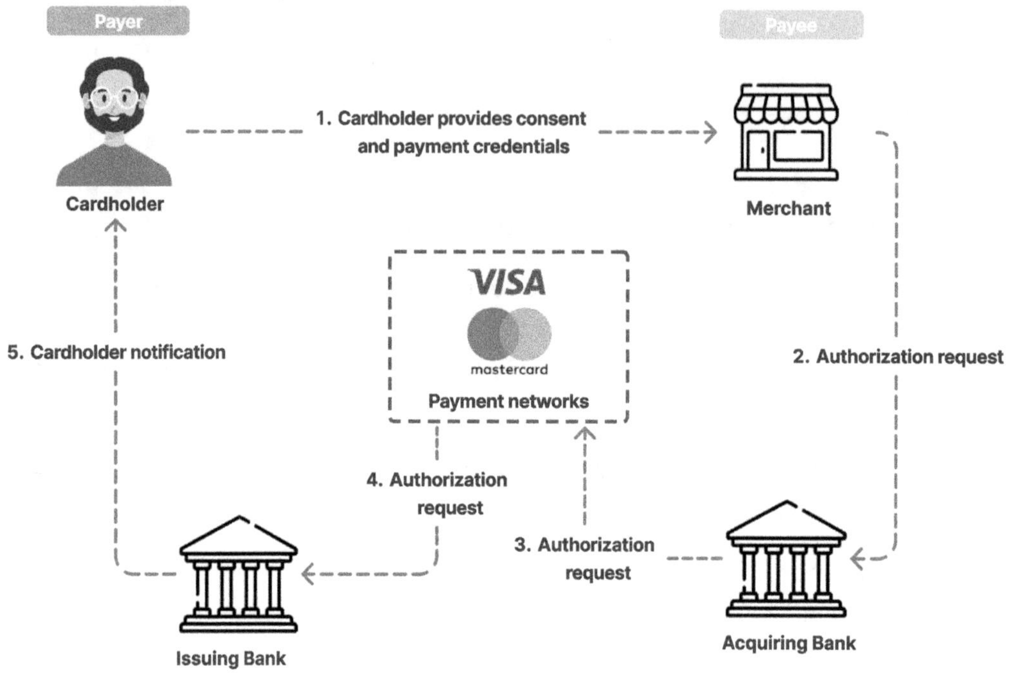

Figure 35.1: Pull card payment flow.

In push payments, the sender initiates the transfer. The recipient does not ask to debit the sender's account. Instead, the sender instructs their bank, processor, or payment provider to send funds to the recipient.

Push-to-card applies the push model to card rails. The sender does not need the recipient's full bank account details. A card credential can be enough to route the payment to the issuer and the account relationship behind the card.

Original Credit Transactions

An *OCT* is a card network transaction used to send funds to an eligible card-linked account.

Here, credit means sending money to the recipient — not credit card debt or revolving credit. Debit, prepaid, or eligible linked cards receive these if the issuer, product, country, and use case allow.

The word *original* signals that an OCT is not simply undoing a previous purchase. A refund is directly linked to an earlier sale: the cardholder paid a merchant, and the merchant returns some or all of that value. By contrast, an OCT is a new, standalone payment that doesn't rely on a previous purchase at all. For example, when a platform pays a seller, an insurer pays a claim, or a wallet pays out a balance, these are not reversals of prior purchases.

That difference changes the controls. A refund asks what value should be returned from a previous sale. An OCT asks whether the originator is authorized to send this credit to the recipient via the card network.

That makes the OCT a separate kind of card network transaction: not a purchase, not a refund, but a credit pushed to an eligible card-linked account.

Push-to-Card Flow

A push-to-card transaction starts with the originator.

The originator is the party sending money. It may be a marketplace, gig platform, wallet provider, insurer, merchant, government body, or financial institution.

The originator sends the payout request to its processor, PSP, acquirer, or bank. That party checks whether the originator is allowed to send this kind of payment, screens the transaction as required, and submits the OCT to the payment network.

The network routes the transaction to the recipient's issuer. The issuer checks whether the card is valid, whether the product is eligible for this type of credit, whether the country and account are eligible, and whether any risk or compliance rules block the transaction.

If accepted, the issuer credits the recipient's card-linked account.

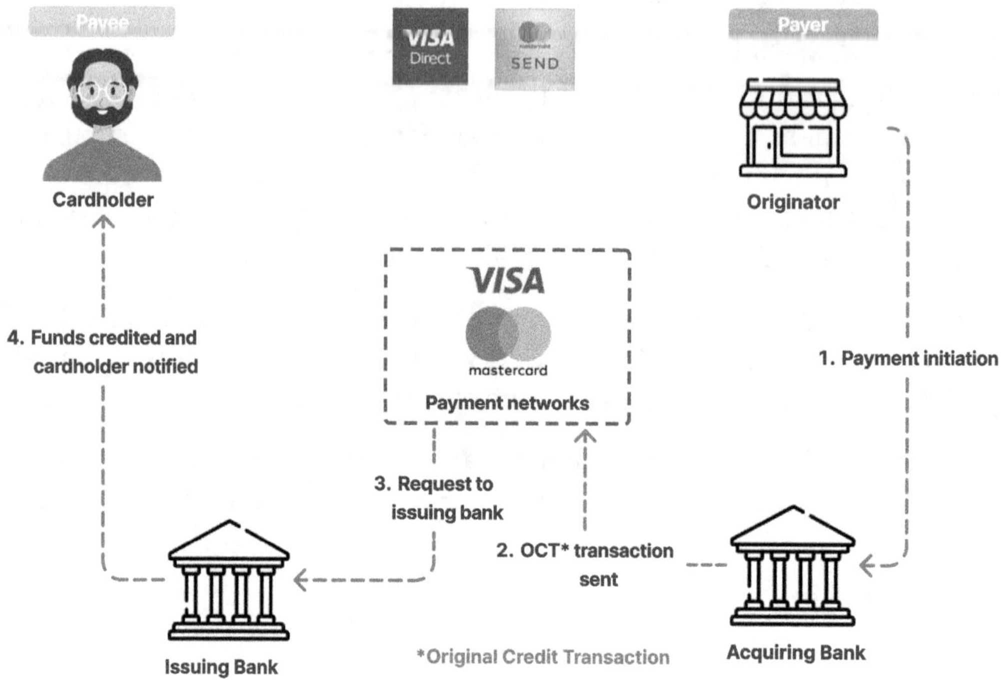

Figure 35.2: Push-to-card (OCT) flow.

Figure 35.2 looks similar to a regular card payment because it uses the same broad card network chain: the acquiring side, the payment network, and the issuer. But the business purpose is different.

In a purchase, the merchant receives money, and the cardholder pays.

In push-to-card, the cardholder receives money, and the originator pays.

This change in direction affects how the payment is used, which controls apply, and what the recipient expects.

Card Rails for Payouts

Push-to-card is useful because paying out money is often harder than accepting it.

A marketplace can accept card payments from buyers, but paying thousands of sellers is a different problem. A gig platform can collect fares from customers, but paying drivers after each shift requires a payout rail. A wallet can hold funds internally, but users eventually need a way to withdraw them.

Bank transfers can solve this, but they require bank account details, which vary by country: International Bank Account Numbers (IBANs) in much of Europe, routing and account numbers in the United States, sort codes and account numbers in the United Kingdom, and other local formats elsewhere. Cross-border payouts add more complexity.

Cards are more portable. A card number contains routing information that lets the network identify the issuer. A platform that already has a card credential does not always need to collect separate bank account details for a payout.

Push-to-card can also be faster than many traditional payout methods. In supported corridors, funds may be available in minutes rather than the next business day or later.

Speed helps, but reach is often the stronger reason. Card networks connect to many issuers across many countries. That is why push-to-card appears in payout-heavy businesses, such as gig platforms, marketplaces, wallet withdrawals, and insurance claims, where businesses need to send funds quickly to many recipients.

The core problem is the same in each case: the sender needs a payout rail that reaches the recipient without relying only on traditional bank account details.

Risk and Compliance

Push-to-card has a different risk profile from a normal purchase.

During a purchase, the issuer primarily asks whether the cardholder is authorized to spend. In a push-to-card transaction, the system must also ask why money is being sent, who is sending it, who is receiving it, and whether that payout is permitted.

That brings in payout-specific controls: Anti-Money Laundering (AML) monitoring, sanctions screening, fraud checks, program restrictions, and eligibility rules. A platform paying couriers needs to know who those couriers are. A wallet paying out to cards has to guard against stolen accounts, mule accounts, account takeover, and laundering. Gaming or gambling payouts, where allowed, bring extra licensing, age, and jurisdictional checks. Cross-border payouts can add further screening.

The originator and its financial partners need controls before sending the OCT. They may need to approve the originator's program, verify recipient identity or account status, monitor transactions, screen for sanctioned parties, apply velocity and amount limits, check country and currency eligibility, restrict use cases, and watch for account takeover or mule activity.

Eligibility is part of the same control problem. Push-to-card is not universal: the recipient's card, issuer, country, currency, and product type must support the relevant credit transaction. Some prepaid, credit, corporate, closed-loop, or restricted cards may not accept certain types of credit. Network rules may also restrict transaction types, funding sources, merchant categories, or corridors.

Limits are another control. A program often has maximum amounts per transaction, per day, per recipient, per country, or per use case. These limits are not just technical settings. They help the network, issuer, acquirer, and originator control risk.

For the recipient, the result can look simple: money arrives quickly in an account linked to their card. Behind that experience, the originator and its financial partners must ensure the payout is permitted, eligible, screened, and controlled.

Comparison with Bank Transfers

Push-to-card competes with bank transfers, but it does not replace them in every case.

A bank transfer uses account rails. It moves funds between bank accounts through local clearing systems, instant payment systems, Automated Clearing House (ACH), Single Euro Payments Area (SEPA), wire transfer, or correspondent banking, depending on the country and transaction type.

Push-to-card uses card rails to send credits to card-linked accounts via network routing.

The main differences are reach, speed, required information, cost, and availability.

A bank transfer may be cheaper in domestic markets with strong account-to-account infrastructure. It may carry richer account information or be better suited to payroll, B2B settlement, or regulated bank-to-bank transfers. It may also be required when card payouts are unsupported.

Push-to-card can be useful when the platform has a card credential but no bank details, when the recipient wants funds quickly, or when cross-border account details are hard to collect and validate.

The best payout systems often support both. They choose the rail based on recipient, country, cost, urgency, and risk.

Push-to-card does not convert every card transaction into a bank transfer, nor does it replace the ordinary card purchase model. By contrast, most card payments are still pull payments: a merchant requests funds, the issuer approves or declines the request, and the merchant is paid later.

What it changes is the role of the card credential. The same network that routes purchase requests to issuers can also route credit transactions to eligible card-linked accounts. A card can therefore be more than a way to spend. In the right program, with the right issuer support, it can also be a way to receive money.

Chapter 36: Network and Dynamic Currency Conversion

To continue the story, let's return to Emma.

Earlier in the book, we saw her traveling in Italy and paying for dinner in Tuscany with a Visa card issued by her bank in California. That transaction helped us follow the basic card payment flow: cardholder, merchant, acquirer, network, issuer, authorization, clearing, and settlement.

Now, shopping in Florence, she buys a handbag for €100. The item is priced in euros, but Emma naturally thinks in dollars.

At checkout, the terminal gives her a choice:

- Pay €100.
- Pay $118.

This option appears helpful, as it shows Emma the amount in dollars. She avoids mental exchange-rate math or waiting for her statement to reveal the conversion rate, but this is where many cardholders unintentionally select the more expensive option. Figure 36.1 contrasts the two conversion paths: network conversion after Emma pays in euros and DCC before authorization in dollars.

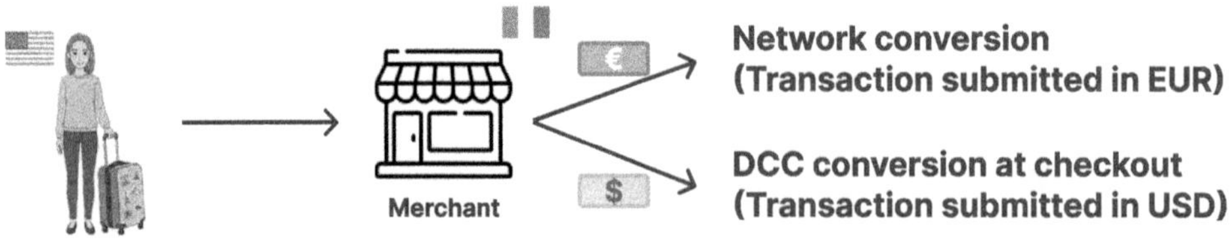

Figure 36.1: Two ways to convert a cross-border card payment.

Three Transaction Currencies

A domestic card payment usually has one currency. A German cardholder pays a German merchant in euros. The merchant prices in euros, the acquirer processes in euros, the issuer posts in euros, and settlement is also in euros.

However, when a payment crosses borders, multiple currencies may be involved.

A card transaction can involve several currencies:

- the merchant currency: the currency used to price the sale;
- the card currency, or billing currency: the currency of the cardholder's account;
- the settlement currency: the currency used between institutions under network and participant arrangements.

In Emma's case, the merchant's currency is euros because the shop is in Italy. The currency on the card is US dollars because Emma's card account is in US dollars. The settlement currency depends on the network, region, issuer, acquirer, and participant setup, but in this case, it's either dollars or euros.

Most cardholders focus on one thing: the amount on their statement.

Behind that single number, the payment system must track more details. A €100 purchase requires authorization, clearing, posting, settlement, and sometimes a refund – each step needing an amount and currency. If the card account differs from the merchant's sale currency, conversion becomes part of the process.

Network Currency Conversion

Network conversion comes into play when the cardholder chooses to pay in the merchant's local currency.

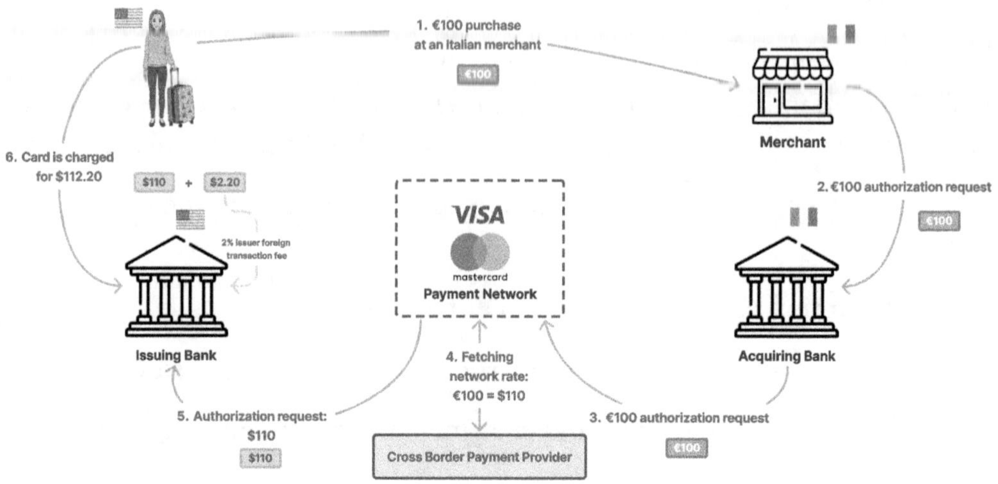

Figure 36.2: Currency conversion through the payment network.

Emma selects €100 at the terminal. The merchant submits the transaction in euros, and the acquirer sends the amount in euros to the payment network. Because Emma's card account is in US dollars, the payment network converts the euro transaction amount to US dollars using its exchange rate on the relevant processing date.

The issuer receives the transaction in the billing currency needed for Emma's account and posts it to her account.

For the merchant, the sale remains €100. The merchant is paid in the local currency. The conversion affects Emma's billing amount, not the price the merchant charged.

Network conversion can still include issuer fees. In a simplified example, if the payment network converts a €100 purchase at an exchange rate of €1 = $1.10, the converted amount is $110. If the issuer then adds a 2 percent foreign transaction fee, the fee is $2.20, and the final amount posted to the cardholder's account is $112.20.

There may also be payment network or cross-border fees in the economics between institutions, though the way these appear to the cardholder depends on market practice, issuer disclosure, and product design.

The final dollar amount is not always known at the time of authorization. In many card flows, the rate used for final posting is tied to clearing rather than the instant rate when Emma taps her card. Since clearing occurs later, the amount Emma sees in her banking app after authorization may differ slightly from the amount ultimately posted.

That uncertainty has a trade-off. Emma does not yet know the exact dollar amount at checkout, but the conversion still follows standard payment flows, using the network's exchange rate rather than a potentially less favorable point-of-sale rate.

Dynamic Currency Conversion

Dynamic Currency Conversion (DCC) follows a different path.

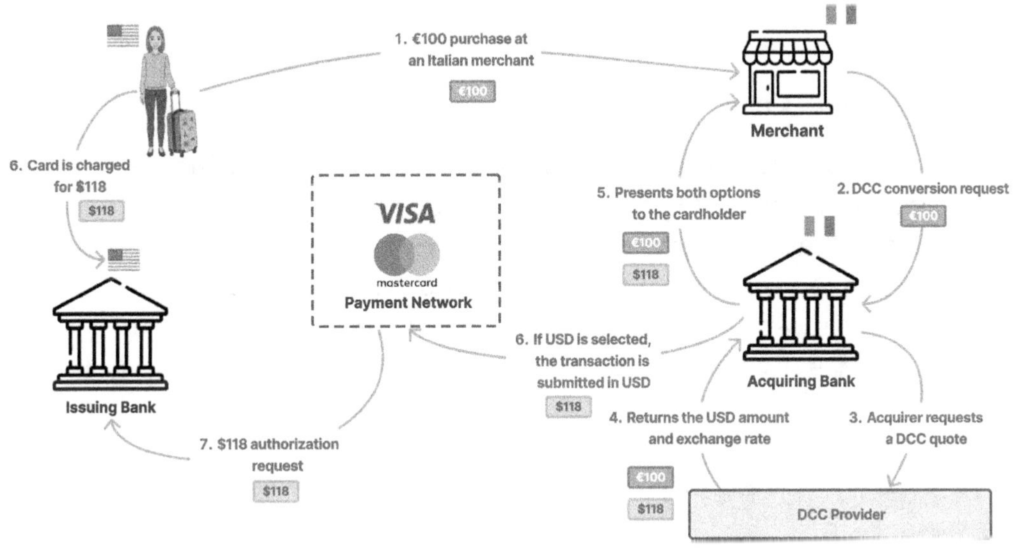

Figure 36.3: Dynamic currency conversion at the terminal.

With *DCC*, the terminal offers to convert the purchase into the cardholder's home currency at the point of sale. Instead of paying €100, Emma is offered a dollar amount immediately.

The merchant, acquirer, or specialist DCC provider detects that Emma's card is issued in another currency. The terminal asks whether she wants to pay in euros or dollars. If she chooses dollars, the conversion happens on the merchant side.

The DCC provider sets the exchange rate, almost always with a markup. This markup may appear separately, show up in the fine print, or be hidden within the rate itself.

After that conversion, the transaction continues through the regular card route in dollars. The acquirer sends a dollar transaction through the payment network, and the issuer receives a transaction already expressed in Emma's billing currency. The issuer may still apply its own product rules or fees, but the core currency conversion has already happened before the payment reaches it.

The appeal is psychological. Emma sees $118 before paying: no guessing at the exchange rate, no waiting for her banking app to update, and no surprise when the transaction posts. The amount feels final, but that certainty has a price. The markup versus the network rate is often hidden inside the exchange rate, so the visible dollar amount may cost more than letting the card network and issuer convert the transaction later.

> **DCC Usually Costs More**
>
> When a foreign terminal asks whether to pay in the cardholder's home currency, that option often includes a markup set by the DCC provider, acquirer, or merchant arrangement. DCC gives certainty at the terminal, but certainty is not the same as a better price. For most cardholders, paying in the merchant's local currency is usually the safer default.

Cross-Border and FX Fees

Cross-border pricing is not one fee. Several parties can affect the final amount the cardholder pays.

The first layer is the exchange rate. When Emma pays in euros, and her account is in dollars, the payment network converts the amount from euros to dollars using its exchange rate on the relevant processing date. This rate determines the base converted amount before any issuer fee is added.

The second layer is the issuer's pricing. The issuer may add a foreign transaction fee, often shown as a percentage of the transaction amount. This is the fee many cardholders recognize, either because it appears in the card terms or as a visible charge. Some issuers also build an FX markup into the product pricing.

The third layer is institutional pricing between participants. Payment networks charge cross-border or currency-related fees to issuers or acquirers. These are not always shown as a separate cardholder fee. One participant may absorb them, pass them through in pricing, or reflect them indirectly in the economics of the card product or merchant acquiring contract.

DCC adds a different kind of cost. If the cardholder opts for home-currency conversion at the terminal, the DCC provider sets the exchange rate before the transaction even reaches the issuer. While there might not be a separate fee, the markup can be embedded in the rate itself.

ATM and merchant-side fees are separate again. An ATM operator often charges a withdrawal fee. A merchant or acquirer arrangement may include DCC revenue. These costs sit outside the issuer's ordinary foreign transaction fee, but they still affect what the cardholder ultimately pays.

"No foreign transaction fee" does not guarantee the lowest total cost. Even without that fee, the final amount is still shaped by the exchange rate, issuer markup, network costs, DCC spread, and ATM charges.

The useful comparison is the total cost in the cardholder's own currency, not the label attached to the fee.

Authorization Rate and Clearing Rate

Currency conversion also creates a timing issue: the amount authorized may differ from the amount ultimately posted.

Authorization happens in real time. Clearing happens later. If the exchange rate used for final posting is determined later, the posted amount may differ from the pending amount shown shortly after the purchase.

Suppose Emma pays €100 and chooses network conversion. Her banking app might show an estimated dollar amount after authorization. When the transaction clears, the final rate may differ slightly. The posted dollar amount could go up or down.

The effect can be more visible in volatile currencies, over weekends, during holidays, or when clearing is delayed. It can also affect reversals and refunds because the rate applied when money is returned may differ from the rate used when the original transaction was posted.

Refunds in Foreign Currency

This mismatch can be especially frustrating when refunds are issued in foreign currency.

If Emma returns the handbag, the merchant refunds €100. The merchant is returning the same amount in euros that it charged. But Emma's card account is in dollars, so the issuer has to convert the refund into dollars.

If the exchange rate has moved, the dollar refund may not equal the dollar purchase amount. Emma may have paid $113.30 and received $112.10 back, or she may receive slightly more. Depending on issuer policy, foreign transaction fees may or may not be refunded. DCC can add another layer because the original transaction may have been processed in the cardholder's home currency.

From the merchant's point of view, the refund is correct: €100 out, €100 back.

From the cardholder's perspective, the dollar amounts do not match.

Both perspectives are correct.

Customer support teams need to distinguish the merchant refund amount from the cardholder billing amount. A merchant cannot always control the final amount the issuer posts after FX conversion.

Multi-Currency Cards

Multi-currency cards aim to reduce this friction by allowing the cardholder to hold balances in multiple currencies.

A traveler may hold euros, dollars, and pounds in the same account. If Emma has a euro balance and pays a merchant in euros, the card program debits the euro balance directly. No dollar conversion is needed for that transaction.

If the cardholder does not have sufficient balance in the merchant's currency, the provider may convert from another balance in accordance with its own rules. Some products let the cardholder pre-convert at a known rate. Others convert at the time of the transaction. Some apply weekend markups, fair-use limits, or different rates by plan.

Multi-currency cards can reduce FX friction, but they do not remove pricing decisions. They shift the conversion decision from the terminal to the card product. The cardholder needs to know which currency balance will be used, what rate will apply, and whether any markup or fee will be charged.

A multi-currency card is not automatically the cheapest choice. But if the product is well priced and the cardholder maintains the right balance, it can reduce costs. If the balance, rate, or fee structure is misunderstood, the cardholder can still face unexpected charges.

The Local-Currency Rule

For most cardholders, the practical rule is simple: when a terminal abroad offers a choice between the local and home currencies, choose the local currency.

For Emma in Italy, that means paying €100, not $118.

Paying in local currency keeps conversion on the network and issuer path. Paying in home currency at the terminal gives the DCC provider control over the exchange rate, which often includes a markup.

There are exceptions. Card products differ: some issuers charge high foreign transaction fees, while others, such as fintech or travel cards, charge little or no issuer markup. DCC disclosure also varies by market, and exchange rates can move between authorization and clearing.

Still, as a general rule, the advice is sound: choose the merchant's local currency when paying abroad.

Seeing the home currency on the terminal often means paying extra for certainty at the moment of purchase.

Chapter 37: ATM Transactions and Cash Access

An ATM withdrawal starts with a familiar sequence: insert the card, enter the PIN, choose an amount, and wait for the machine to dispense banknotes.

The payment infrastructure behind that moment is less simple.

An ATM transaction is card-present, but it is not a merchant purchase. The cardholder is not buying goods from a shop. They are using a self-service banking terminal to access cash or account services. The machine may belong to the cardholder's own bank, another bank, an independent ATM operator, or a financial institution in another country.

That difference changes the risk.

In a store purchase, authorization and later presentment are usually separate events. The issuer may first reduce the cardholder's available balance, while the final posted transaction arrives later through clearing. At an ATM, the machine is about to dispense physical cash. If the issuer approves the transaction and the machine dispenses cash, the cardholder can walk away with banknotes immediately.

Once cash leaves the machine, the transaction is harder to unwind than an ordinary purchase authorization. The evidence is no longer only a payment message. It also includes cassette counts, dispense logs, rejected notes, reversals, and physical cash reconciliation.

That cash outcome places ATM transactions in a separate category within card payments. They rely on established card infrastructure – card-present authentication, PIN verification, authorization, network routing, fees, reversals, settlement, and reconciliation – while yielding a different outcome: immediate cash disbursal. To understand the broader role of ATMs, let's examine what an ATM actually is.

ATM as a Banking Terminal

An *Automated Teller Machine* (*ATM*) is a self-service banking terminal.

Most people think of ATMs as cash machines, and cash withdrawal remains their main use. But many ATMs can also support deposits, balance inquiries, mini-statements, PIN changes, transfers, bill payments, and cardless or contactless access, depending on the bank and market.

An ATM transaction involves several parties:

- The cardholder starts the transaction by inserting a card, tapping a card or device, or using another supported access method.
- The ATM operator owns or runs the machine. This may be the cardholder's own bank, another bank, or an independent ATM operator.
- The acquirer or ATM processor connects the machine to the right routing path. The ATM operator and acquirer are closely related in many ATM programs, but they are not always the same entity.
- The issuer manages the cardholder's account or credit line.
- A payment network, local ATM network, or domestic debit network may connect the acquiring side to the issuer. The route depends on the card type, country, brand, routing rules, and participant setup.

The key difference from a purchase is the merchant's role. In a cash withdrawal, there may be no merchant sale at all. The ATM operator provides access to cash, not sells goods or services.

PIN and Card Authentication

The PIN is central to ATM security.

A cash withdrawal usually requires something the cardholder has, such as a card or token, and something the cardholder knows: the PIN. Cardless ATM access can use different steps, but the system still needs strong proof that the person using the machine is authorized to access the account.

The PIN should never travel through the system in plain text. The ATM encrypts it and sends it securely for verification. Chapter 14 covered PIN blocks and hardware security modules in more detail. The ATM-specific point is simpler: the machine should not release cash unless the cardholder has been verified.

ATM fraud is dangerous because it provides access to cash immediately. If a fraudster steals a card and captures the PIN, there is no delivery address to check, no shipping delay, and no merchant fulfillment trail. The machine can dispense value directly.

> **ATM Skimming Helped Push Chip Migration**
>
> Magnetic-stripe ATM skimming reached industrial scale in the 2000s. Criminals attached skimmers to card slots, while hidden cameras or fake keypads captured PIN entry. Networks and issuers pushed EMV not only for retail security but also because ATMs concentrate risk: the same machine can handle thousands of cards and dispense cash directly. That made ATM chip migration a major fraud-control priority.

Cash Withdrawal

A cash withdrawal starts when the cardholder chooses an amount.

The ATM reads the card or token, asks for the PIN, and prepares a transaction request. The request includes the card data, transaction type, amount, ATM identifier, ATM location, currency, and security information.

A key difference from store purchases is the transaction flow. Most merchant purchases use a dual-message process: authorization first, then a clearing/presentment message later. ATM withdrawals typically use a single-message process: authorization and the financial transaction are combined, as the machine dispenses cash immediately.

If the cardholder uses their own bank's ATM, the request stays within the bank. The bank verifies the PIN, checks the account, applies withdrawal limits, updates its internal records, and approves or declines the transaction.

If the cardholder uses another bank's ATM, the request travels from the ATM operator or acquirer through a payment network, local ATM network, or domestic debit network to the issuer. The issuer checks card status, PIN, balance or credit, withdrawal limits, daily limits, location, fraud signals, and account restrictions.

If the issuer approves, the approval travels back to the ATM. The machine dispenses the cash, records what it paid out, and the issuer normally debits the account immediately or shortly afterward.

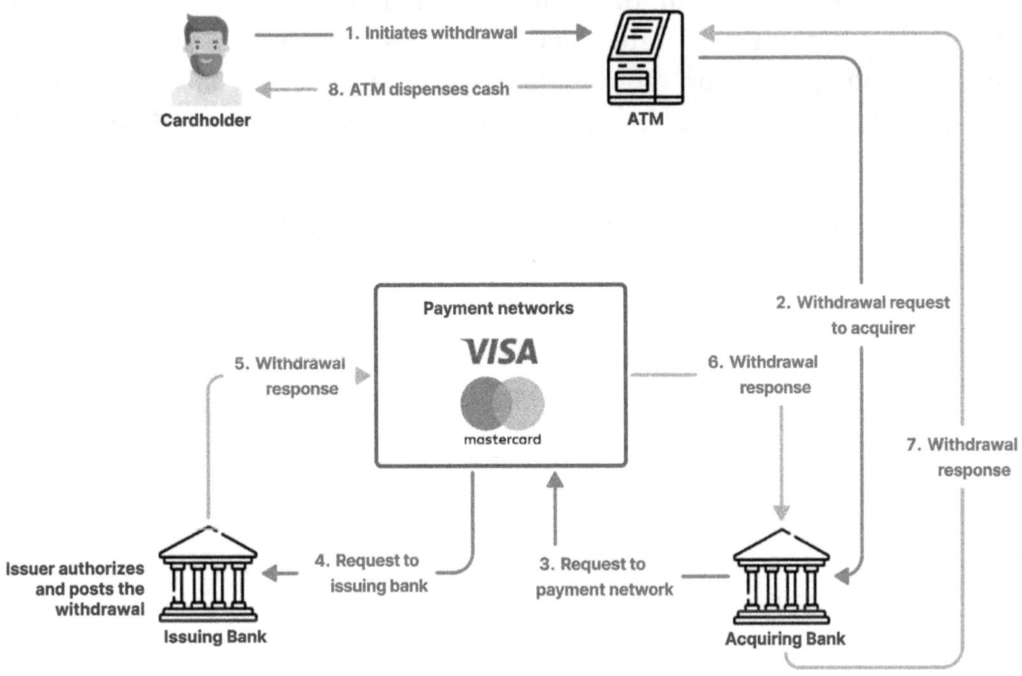

Figure 37.1: Cash withdrawal at an ATM.

This is why an ATM withdrawal feels final so quickly. In a merchant purchase, authorization and final presentment are separated. In an ATM withdrawal, the machine dispenses physical cash while the cardholder is standing there, so the transaction must be authorized, recorded, and cleared financially in a much tighter sequence.

Dispense Failure and Reversal

Cash withdrawals have one tricky physical risk: the issuer may approve the transaction, but the ATM may fail to dispense the cash.

The machine can jam, run out of cash, reject a note, lose connectivity, or fail after approval but before completion is confirmed. In that case, the cardholder may see a debit on the account even though no cash was received.

ATM systems handle these problems with reversals and reconciliation.

If the ATM knows it failed to dispense cash, it should send a reversal or failure message so the issuer can cancel the debit or return the money. If the problem is clear and the message arrives successfully, the correction may appear quickly.

If the ATM fails without sending a clean reversal, the cardholder often needs to file a claim. The ATM operator then checks the machine records: how much cash was loaded, how much should have been dispensed, how much remains, whether notes were rejected, and whether the electronic records match the physical cash.

ATM disputes differ from merchant disputes because the evidence is both digital and physical. The main question is whether the machine actually dispensed the cash recorded in its transaction logs.

Cash Deposit and Account Services

A cash deposit runs in the opposite direction: the cardholder puts cash into the machine.

The cardholder authenticates using a card or other access method, selects deposit, and inserts cash. The ATM verifies, counts, and checks the notes. If accepted, the system sends a deposit request to credit the account.

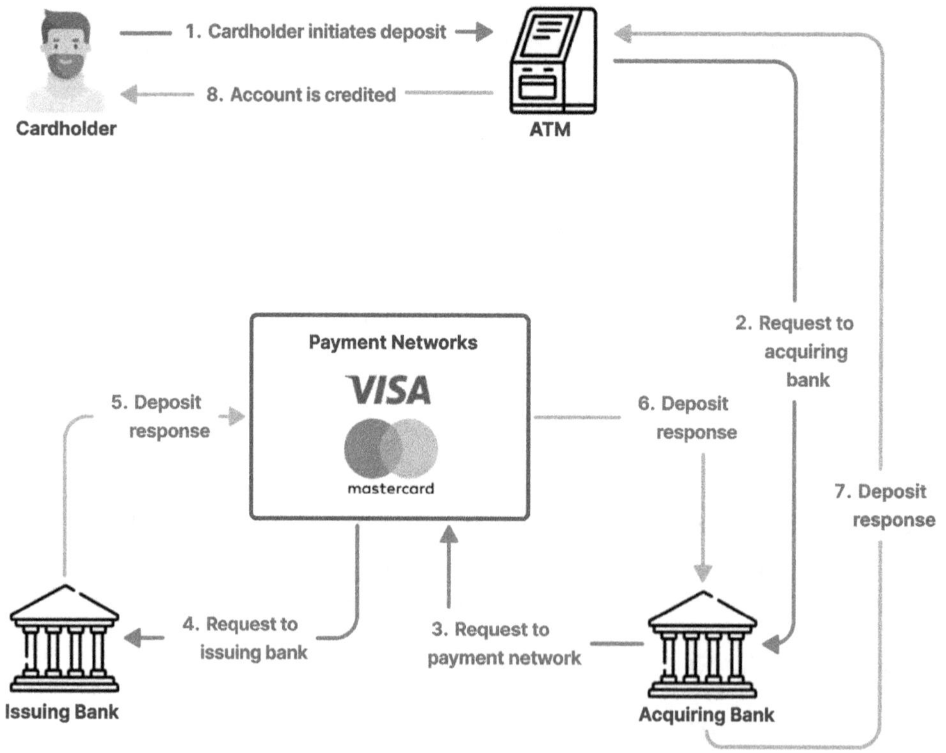

Figure 37.2: Cash deposit at an ATM.

If the cardholder uses their own bank's ATM, the deposit may become available quickly because the bank controls both the machine and the account. If another bank or independent operator is involved, availability may depend on network rules, risk checks, cash collection, and later verification.

Deposit ATMs have their own risks. The machine must detect counterfeit notes, count accurately, reject damaged bills, handle jams, and match the accepted cash to the electronic record. If there is a deposit error, the dispute turns on both the ATM logs and the physical cash count.

Not every ATM transaction moves cash. A balance inquiry requests the available balance from the issuer or the account-holding bank. A mini-statement requests recent account activity. A PIN change updates the card's EMV chip. These transactions may still be routed through networks and incur fees, even though no cash is dispensed.

An ATM is therefore more than just a cash dispenser. It is a remote banking terminal connected to card, account, and cash-management systems.

Own-Bank and Out-of-Network ATM Transactions

An on-us ATM transaction occurs when the issuer and ATM operator are the same bank.

A Bank A customer uses a Bank A ATM. The transaction does not need to route through Visa, Mastercard, or another interbank network. Bank A verifies the cardholder, checks the account, updates its own ledger, and dispenses cash from its own machine.

On-us transactions are cheaper and simpler because they remain within a single institution. There is no external issuer-acquirer relationship, no interbank ATM interchange, and often no cardholder surcharge.

The bank still needs security controls, cash reconciliation, ATM balancing, and transaction logs. The transaction is internal, but it still has to be controlled and auditable.

A foreign or out-of-network ATM transaction occurs when the cardholder uses an ATM run by another bank or provider. Foreign here does not necessarily mean international. It can simply mean out-of-network or not owned by the cardholder's bank.

The transaction now needs an interbank route. The ATM operator or acquirer sends the request through a payment network, local ATM network, or domestic debit network to the issuer. The issuer approves or declines, and the participants later settle according to network and participant rules.

For the cardholder, using their own bank's ATMs is usually cheaper because fewer external parties are paid. An out-of-network ATM adds another operator, another routing path, and often another fee layer.

ATM Fees and International Withdrawals

ATM fees can be confusing because multiple parties can charge for a single transaction.

The ATM operator often charges a surcharge for using the machine. This is usually shown on the screen before the cardholder confirms the withdrawal.

The issuer may charge an out-of-network fee, foreign ATM fee, cash access fee, currency conversion fee, or foreign transaction fee, depending on the account and card product.

The payment network or ATM network charges fees between participants. The ATM operator or acquirer may also receive compensation from the issuer through ATM interchange or similar arrangements. This differs from purchase interchange: in many purchase models, the acquirer pays interchange to the issuer; in many ATM withdrawal models, the issuer compensates the ATM side because that operator provided cash access to the issuer's customer.

International ATM withdrawals add currency conversion. A US cardholder withdrawing euros in Italy creates the same basic currency problem as a foreign purchase: the ATM dispenses local cash, while the issuer posts in the cardholder's billing currency. The transaction may be converted through the payment network and issuer path, or the ATM may offer Dynamic Currency Conversion. As with purchases, choosing the local currency is usually the safer default.

The card type also changes the cost. A debit card withdrawal uses funds from the cardholder's deposit account and is subject to balance and limits. A credit card withdrawal is usually treated as a cash advance. Cash advances typically incur fees, have higher interest rates, offer no grace period (interest starts accruing immediately), and have a separate cash advance limit.

Reconciliation and Cash Balancing

ATM operations rely on reconciliation because every cash transaction must be reconciled against two forms of evidence: the electronic record and the physical cash position.

For withdrawals, the records must explain how much cash left the machine. For deposits, they must explain how much cash the machine accepted. Later, cassette counts, rejected note records, journal logs, reversal messages, and cash-in-transit reports are compared with the transaction records.

Small operational problems become visible during this comparison. A cassette may have been loaded incorrectly. A note may have been rejected or jammed. A reversal may be missing or duplicated. A deposit may have been counted differently during later verification. A network timeout may cause one system to believe the transaction completed while another shows an incomplete result.

The operational investigation can involve the issuer, ATM acquirer, ATM operator, processor, payment network, and the cash-in-transit company that loads or collects the cash. The cardholder sees one problem: "I did not get my money," or "my deposit is wrong." The institutions have to trace messages, logs, counters, and physical cash.

ATM reconciliation is where payments become tangible. The electronic record must match the actual notes in the actual machine.

Where ATMs Still Fit

Cash use has declined in many markets, but ATMs remain important.

They provide access to cash for people who still need it: travelers, small merchants, people in emergencies, and customers in markets where digital acceptance is incomplete. They also give banks a bridge between account money and physical money.

ATM transactions show a broader pattern in card infrastructure. A transaction is not defined only by the card or network used to route it. It is defined by what the transaction is trying to do. A purchase, refund, push-to-card credit, recurring charge, and ATM withdrawal may all use card systems, but their business meanings and operational risks differ.

An ATM withdrawal is card-present, but it is not a merchant sale. The outcome is physical cash. That makes the transaction stricter on PIN verification, faster to debit, more dependent on machine logs, and different in fee economics from an ordinary purchase.

The payment message can authorize the withdrawal, but it cannot by itself prove that the correct notes left the machine. That proof comes from ATM journals, dispense records, reversals, cassette counts, and reconciliation. The electronic record must match the cash that actually left the machine or was accepted by it.

That is why ATM transactions deserve their own category. They use card infrastructure, but the result is tangible: banknotes move, and the system has to prove where they went.

Part VII

Security, Compliance, and Regulation

Chapter 38: PCI DSS and Payment Data Security

In late 2013, attackers gained access to Target's payment environment via credentials associated with a third-party vendor. They were not insiders at Visa or Mastercard. They found a path into a retailer's systems, moved toward the payment environment, and compromised payment data at scale.

The breach exposed about 40 million credit and debit card accounts and affected the personal information of many more customers. Target later reached an $18.5 million multistate settlement, and public estimates and filings put the broader breach cost at hundreds of millions once investigations, remediation, legal settlements, card reissue costs, fraud losses, and lost trust are considered.

That is the problem PCI DSS was created to reduce. Card data moves through many systems: merchant checkouts, gateways, processors, acquirers, payment networks, issuers, service providers, hosting platforms, payment applications, and support tools. Any one of those systems can become a weak point. A PAN can be stored in a database without proper controls, written into logs by mistake, exposed through a weak connection, or shown to too many employees.

A card data breach not only hurts the company that lost the data. Issuers may need to monitor accounts or reissue cards. Cardholders have to watch for suspicious transactions. Merchants may face chargebacks, forensic investigations, remediation demands, assessments, and loss of trust.

The *Payment Card Industry Data Security Standard* (*PCI DSS*) is the main industry standard for protecting payment account data. It applies to organizations that store, process, or transmit cardholder data, or that can affect its security.

PCI DSS is not a fraud engine. It does not decide whether a transaction should be approved, authenticate the cardholder, replace 3-D Secure, or settle chargebacks. Its job is narrower and more basic: reduce the chance that sensitive card data is exposed in the first place.

Security Objectives

Card payments rely on information that has to move.

A card number may pass through a checkout form, payment page, terminal, gateway, processor, acquirer, payment network, issuer, reporting system, support tool, and dispute process. Some participants need to see the card data. Others only need a token, a masked number, a transaction reference, or an authorization result.

The risk appears when card data spreads farther than it should. Before common card data security rules were established, companies handled payment data inconsistently: merchants stored full card numbers in plain text, applications kept security codes for later use, default passwords remained unchanged, flat internal networks let compromises spread into payment systems, and vendors often had broader access than their work required.

The damage from a breach is shared. The merchant may have lost the data, but issuers have to manage compromised cards, cardholders have to monitor accounts, acquirers and payment networks have to manage the incident, and other merchants may see more fraud using stolen credentials.

PCI DSS exists because card information is not ordinary business data. It is part of the payment system. If it is handled carelessly in one place, the consequences spread across many institutions.

That is why PCI DSS is an industry standard rather than only an internal security preference. It was created by the major card payment brands and is maintained through the PCI Security Standards Council. It is not a statute passed by parliament or congress, but it reaches participants through payment network rules, merchant agreements, processor contracts, and service provider obligations.

The enforcement path is therefore contractual rather than ordinary public-law inspection. A merchant usually does not comply with PCI DSS because a government inspector arrives and demands it. The obligation usually comes through the merchant agreement with the acquirer or payment processor. Payment network rules bind the acquirer, and the requirement flows down the acceptance chain. Issuers, processors, PSPs, gateways, and other service providers face PCI obligations through their own network, customer, and participant relationships.

The practical consequences can still be severe. A company that fails to comply may face remediation demands, forensic investigations, higher costs, assessments passed through to it by its acquirer, or loss of card acceptance. For a business that depends on card payments, losing the ability to process major card brands can be more damaging than a regulatory fine.

PCI DSS is not a law in the usual sense, but it is not optional for organizations that want to participate in card payments. It turns shared payment-data risk into a common security baseline.

Account Data: Cardholder Data and Sensitive Authentication Data

PCI DSS uses account data as the broader category. It includes two main groups: cardholder data and sensitive authentication data. PCI DSS separates them because the storage rules are different.

Cardholder data includes the PAN and, when stored with it, related elements such as the cardholder name, expiration date, and service code.

Sensitive authentication data is different. It includes data used to authenticate a card or cardholder, such as full magnetic-stripe track data, card security codes such as CVV2 or CVC2, and PIN or PIN block data.

That distinction drives the storage rules.

Data Category	Examples	Storage Rule
Cardholder data	PAN, cardholder name, expiration date, service code	May be stored only when there is a legitimate business need and the data is protected properly
Sensitive authentication data	Full track data, CVV2/CVC2, PIN, PIN block	Must not be stored after authorization, even if encrypted

The PAN is the main account identifier. If an organization stores PANs, it must protect them through controls such as encryption, hashing, truncation, tokenization, access control, and secure key management, depending on how the data is used.

The security code follows stricter rules. CVV2 or CVC2 may be used during authorization, but it must not be stored afterward – not in plain text, not encrypted, not hidden in logs, and not retained "temporarily" for customer support.

The reason is simple: the security code is meant to prove that the person entering the card details had access to the card at that moment. If merchants could store it, a database breach could expose both the PAN and the security code needed for many card-not-present purchases.

A PAN can sometimes be stored with strong controls in place. Sensitive authentication data must not be stored after authorization.

PCI Scope

PCI DSS applies to organizations that store, process, or transmit cardholder data. It also applies to service providers whose systems affect the security of that data.

That includes direct payment participants such as merchants, PSPs, gateways, processors, acquirers, and issuers. It also includes hosting providers, call centers, fraud vendors, software platforms, managed service providers, and vendors with access to payment environments.

The key concept is PCI scope: the systems, people, processes, and networks that store, process, transmit, or affect the security of cardholder data.

At the center is the cardholder data environment (CDE). This is the part of an organization's environment where cardholder data is stored, processed, or transmitted. But the scope extends beyond the obvious payment database or checkout page. Administrator workstations with access to the CDE, logging systems that receive full PANs, support tools that display unmasked card numbers, and connected network segments without proper separation all create a PCI scope.

PCI scope follows the participant's role. A merchant's scope includes checkout pages, terminals, PSP integrations, support tools, and third-party scripts. An issuer's scope includes card-management systems, authorization platforms, cardholder servicing tools, dispute systems, data warehouses, and vendor access. A PSP or processor operates in a broader environment because it processes payment data for many merchants.

Using a PSP can reduce a merchant's PCI scope, sometimes dramatically, but it does not remove all responsibility. The merchant's website, checkout integration, redirect flow, third party scripts, staff access, and vendor access can still affect payment security.

The practical PCI question is not just "Do we need to comply?" It is: where does card data enter, where does it go, where is it stored, and who or what can reach it?

Control Objectives and Requirements

PCI DSS is organized around 6 control objectives and 12 requirements. The requirements are detailed, but the logic is easy to follow: build secure systems, protect account data, reduce vulnerabilities, control access, monitor the environment, and maintain security governance.

1. Build and Maintain a Secure Network and Systems

The first control objective is about the technical foundation. Cardholder data should not reside in a loosely protected environment where any system, user, or network path can access it.

Requirement 1: Install and maintain network security controls. This requirement covers firewalls, network security controls, traffic restrictions, and segmentation. The organization needs to control which systems can communicate with the cardholder data environment and why. The goal is to prevent unnecessary network access to systems that store, process, or transmit cardholder data.

In practice, a web server, a database, an administrator workstation, a vendor connection, and an internal reporting tool should not have open access to one another by default. Network traffic should be allowed only where there is a business need.

Requirement 2: Apply secure configurations to all system components. This requirement focuses on hardening systems. Default passwords, default accounts, unnecessary services, insecure settings, and unmanaged configurations create easy paths for attackers. PCI DSS expects organizations to configure servers, databases, network devices, applications, cloud services, and other components securely.

A payment environment should not depend on vendor defaults. Systems should be configured deliberately, documented, reviewed, and maintained.

2. Protect Account Data

The second control objective focuses on the data itself. If cardholder data must be stored or transmitted, it must be protected with strong safeguards.

Requirement 3: Protect stored account data. This requirement covers stored PANs and related account data. Organizations should keep only the data they need, store it only for as long as needed, and protect it with strong controls such as encryption, hashing, truncation, tokenization, access restrictions, and secure key management.

The practical question is simple: if an attacker gained access to a database, log, report, backup, or support tool, would they find usable card data? Requirement 3 is designed to reduce that risk.

Requirement 4: Protect cardholder data with strong cryptography during transmission over open, public networks. Cardholder data should not travel across open or public networks in a form that can be intercepted and used. This requirement covers encryption in transit, including secure communication between browsers, merchants, PSPs, gateways, processors, and other parties.

The point is not only to encrypt the payment page. Any system that transmits cardholder data over exposed networks requires appropriate cryptographic protection.

3. Maintain a Vulnerability Management Program

The third control objective is about keeping systems secure over time. A system that is secure today can become vulnerable tomorrow if software is not patched, malware controls fail, or application code is weak.

Requirement 5: Protect all systems and networks from malicious software. This requirement covers anti-malware controls and related protections. The organization needs to detect, prevent, and respond to malicious software that can affect in-scope systems.

The exact tools depend on the environment, but the principle remains the same: systems handling cardholder data should not be left exposed to malware without detection and response controls.

Requirement 6: Develop and maintain secure systems and software. This requirement covers patching, vulnerability management, secure development, change control, and protection against common software weaknesses. Payment applications, checkout flows, APIs, and supporting systems need to be designed and maintained securely.

Many card data incidents begin with ordinary software problems: an unpatched system, an insecure plugin, vulnerable code, or a payment page script that was not controlled properly.

4. Implement Strong Access Control Measures

The fourth control objective is to limit who can access cardholder data and the systems that affect it. Most organizations do not fail because nobody had access. They fail because too many people, tools, vendors, or systems have more access than they need.

Requirement 7: Restrict access to system components and cardholder data by business need-to-know. Access should be limited to those who genuinely need it. A support agent, developer, finance analyst, database administrator, and vendor should not all have the same level of access.

This is the principle of least privilege applied to payment data. Access should be approved, limited, reviewed, and removed when no longer needed.

Requirement 8: Identify users and authenticate access to system components. Every user should have a unique identity, and access should be strongly authenticated. Shared accounts, weak passwords, missing multi-factor authentication, and unmanaged vendor credentials make it difficult to know who did what and easy for attackers to move unnoticed.

This requirement is especially important for administrator, remote, and vendor access, as well as for systems connected to the cardholder data environment.

Requirement 9: Restrict physical access to cardholder data. Security is not only digital. Physical access to systems, storage media, paper records, terminals, cardholder data, and sensitive areas must be controlled.

This can include access to data centers, offices, network equipment, backups, printed reports, payment terminals, and storage rooms. If someone can physically access systems or records containing cardholder data, they can pose a security risk.

5. Regularly Monitor and Test Networks

The fifth control objective is about visibility. It is not enough to configure controls once. Organizations need to know whether the controls are working and whether something suspicious is happening.

Requirement 10: Log and monitor all access to system components and cardholder data. Organizations need records of access and activity. Logs help show who accessed systems, what changed, what failed, and whether unusual behavior occurred.

Logging is also essential after an incident. Without logs, an organization may not know what data was accessed, how the attacker moved, or whether the incident is contained.

Requirement 11: Test the security of systems and networks regularly. Controls need testing. This requirement covers vulnerability scanning, penetration testing, detection mechanisms, and other testing activities that show whether the environment can resist or detect attacks.

Payment environments change. New systems are added, rules are modified, software is updated, vendors connect, and mistakes happen. A control that worked last year may not protect the environment today.

6. Maintain an Information Security Policy

The final control objective is governance. PCI DSS is not only a technical checklist. It also requires policies, roles, training, risk management, vendor management, and day-to-day operating discipline.

Requirement 12: Support information security with organizational policies and programs. Organizations need a security program that defines responsibilities, documents policies, trains personnel, manages third-party service providers, supports incident response, and sustains security practices after the assessment is complete.

This requirement is where PCI DSS becomes an operating model. A company can buy tools, encrypt data, and segment networks, but if nobody owns the process, manages access, reviews vendor contracts, trains staff, or responds to incidents, the environment will degrade.

The twelve requirements are therefore not twelve disconnected checklist items. Together, they answer a sequence of practical questions:

Control Area	Practical Question
Secure networks and systems	Is the environment built securely and separated from unnecessary access?
Protect account data	Is stored and transmitted cardholder data protected?

Vulnerability management	Are systems patched, maintained, and protected from malware and software weaknesses?
Access control	Can only the right people and systems access cardholder data?
Monitoring and testing	Can the organization detect problems and prove controls are working?
Security policy	Is security managed as an ongoing responsibility, not a one-time project?

How Organizations Validate Compliance

PCI DSS compliance is not validated the same way across all organizations.

The validation method depends on the organization's role, transaction volume, payment brands, acquirer requirements, and service-provider status. A large merchant may need a formal assessment by a Qualified Security Assessor (QSA) and a Report on Compliance (ROC). A smaller merchant may complete a Self-Assessment Questionnaire (SAQ) and provide an Attestation of Compliance (AOC). External vulnerability scanning may also be required, depending on the environment.

The common idea is simple: the more card data an organization handles, and the more other participants depend on it, the heavier the proof burden becomes.

A small merchant using hosted checkout may have a much simpler validation process than a large retailer that stores PANs in its own environment. A PSP, gateway, processor, issuer, hosting provider, or managed service provider may face heavier requirements because a weakness in its systems could affect many merchants, cardholders, or card accounts.

Reducing Scope: Store Less, Delegate More, Tokenize

PCI DSS does not ban all storage of cardholder data. A merchant, PSP, issuer, or processor may have a legitimate reason to keep certain data for recurring payments, refunds, reconciliation, dispute handling, reporting, cardholder servicing, or customer support.

The safer question is whether the organization needs to handle raw card data at all.

Many merchants reduce their exposure through hosted checkout, hosted fields, or PSP-controlled payment components. In these models, the customer enters card details on a page, in an iframe, via a redirect flow, or in a secure component controlled by the PSP. The PSP collects the card data and returns a token or payment result to the merchant.

This can keep raw PANs away from the merchant's servers, but it does not make security irrelevant. A compromised merchant website could still redirect customers to a fake payment page or inject a malicious script into a checkout flow. Scope is reduced, not erased.

Tokenization reduces exposure further by replacing sensitive card data with substitute values: a PSP token can represent a stored card for future payments, a network token can represent a PAN in card-on-file or wallet transactions, and a device token can represent a card inside a mobile wallet.

The security benefit is straightforward: systems that handle only tokens usually pose less risk than systems that store real PANs. A stolen token may be restricted to a merchant, device, domain, or transaction context.

That reduction is real, but tokenization is not magic. If a token can be used to initiate payments, it still needs protection. But compared with storing PANs in merchant databases, support tools, analytics systems, and logs, tokenization is a major reduction in exposure.

The easiest card data to protect is data that the organization never receives.

PA-DSS and Payment Software

Payment security also has a software dimension.

For years, the relevant standard for payment applications was the Payment Application Data Security Standard (PA-DSS). It applied to software vendors that developed payment applications used in payment environments. The goal was to prevent those applications from storing prohibited data, exposing cardholder data, or making PCI DSS compliance harder for the organizations that relied on them.

PA-DSS has been replaced by the PCI Software Security Framework. The broader message is straightforward: payment security is not only about how an organization configures its environment. It also depends on how payment software is designed, built, maintained, tested, and updated.

This applies across the card data chain. A merchant checkout application, PSP platform, gateway, processor system, issuer card-management platform, servicing tool, dispute system, reporting layer, or integration component can all create risk if it stores forbidden data, logs sensitive information, exposes PANs too widely, or is difficult to patch.

Secure software and secure operations have to work together. An organization can have disciplined internal controls and still be exposed if the software handling payment data is unsafe by design.

Compliance and Fraud Prevention

PCI DSS and fraud prevention are related, but they solve different problems.

PCI DSS protects card data. Fraud prevention evaluates transactions.

An organization can comply with PCI rules and still experience fraudulent activity. A fraudster may use card data stolen somewhere else. A cardholder may file a false dispute. A real account may be taken over. Encrypting a database does not decide whether today's order, withdrawal, or card-on-file transaction should be approved.

The reverse is also true. An organization may have strong fraud tools but poor card data security. It can block suspicious transactions while still storing PANs in logs, expose cardholder data to too many employees, or leave payment systems accessible through weak vendor access.

The consequences of weak card data security extend beyond a single fraudulent transaction. If PANs are exposed, issuers may need to monitor accounts or reissue cards. Acquirers and payment networks may require forensic investigation. Merchants or service providers may face assessments, remediation programs, chargebacks, loss of processing privileges, and reputational damage. Cardholders may lose trust even if they are reimbursed for fraudulent transactions.

Many breaches do not begin with a brilliant technical attack. They begin with ordinary weaknesses: excessive third-party access, missing multi-factor authentication, poor network separation, weak passwords, unpatched systems, card data in logs, or data retained longer than needed.

From Compliance to Operating Discipline

PCI DSS is easier to understand as an operating discipline around card data.

The central questions are simple:

- Where does card data enter the organization?
- Where does it go?
- Where is it stored?
- Who and what can reach it?
- How quickly would the organization know if something went wrong?

The safest setup is usually the simplest: avoid handling raw card data unless the business genuinely needs to. Use hosted fields or hosted checkout where possible. Tokenize stored payment methods. Mask PANs in support tools. Never store sensitive authentication data after authorization. Separate the cardholder data environment from the rest of the company. Log access, test controls, and review vendor access regularly.

PCI DSS does not make card data risk-free. It changes what is expected of every company that handles it. Merchants, PSPs, processors, acquirers, issuers, software vendors, and service providers need to treat card data as a controlled asset: know where it enters, limit where it travels, restrict who can reach it, and prove that the controls are working.

That discipline is what the standard is really about. PCI DSS turns card data security from a vague promise into a day-to-day operating responsibility.

Chapter 39: PSD2, PSD3, and Payment Regulation

A payment flow is not only a technical path from customer to bank. It is where regulation becomes visible.

When an online checkout requires strong authentication, it is not just a security choice. When a banking app shows the amount and payee before the customer confirms a payment, that is not just product design. When a fintech app connects to a bank account via an API rather than asking the customer for their online banking password, that is not just a technical integration.

Payment regulation decides when a customer must authenticate, whether a third party can access bank account data, and how quickly a provider must refund an unauthorized transaction. It also decides whether a merchant can add a card surcharge, what fees must be disclosed, and who bears the loss when a customer is tricked into sending money to a fraudster.

The European Payment Services Directive 2 (PSD2) is the clearest example. It opened regulated access to bank accounts, made Strong Customer Authentication a central requirement for many electronic payments, and strengthened consumer protection. Its successors, the Payment Services Directive 3 (PSD3) and the Payment Services Regulation (PSR), continue in the same direction: greater harmonization, stronger fraud controls, clearer open banking rules, and more consistent consumer protection.

This chapter is not a legal manual. It explains how changes in payment regulations change product architecture: authentication flows, account data access, liability, pricing, refunds, fraud controls, and the relationships among banks, fintechs, merchants, PSPs, and customers.

Regulatory Objectives

Payments are not like ordinary software.

The difference is consequence: if a music app fails, a song does not play; if a messaging app glitches, a message may be delayed. Those failures are annoying, but they usually do not move money, expose a bank account, or create a legal claim between institutions.

Payments involve all three: they move funds, create account entries, and expose personal and financial data. They can be abused for fraud, money laundering, sanctions evasion, and scams. They also sit close to the basics of economic life: salary, rent, bills, food, travel, and commerce.

Regulators, therefore, care about several things at once:

- consumer protection, so customers are not left carrying losses they cannot reasonably control;
- security, so payment credentials and accounts are not easy to abuse;
- competition, so banks cannot use exclusive control over account access to block new services;
- transparency, so fees, rights, and obligations are clear before the customer pays;
- financial crime prevention, so payment systems are not used to launder money or move funds to prohibited parties;
- operational resilience, so critical payment infrastructure remains reliable.

These goals can conflict. Stronger authentication reduces some fraud risk and introduces checkout friction, which can lower conversion when the flow is poorly designed. Open banking encourages competition, but it gives more parties access to sensitive account data. Fast refunds protect customers, but poorly designed refund rules can increase losses and abuse.

Payment regulation sets boundaries for these trade-offs. It determines which risks the market can manage on its own and which require legal rules.

From PSD1 to PSD2

The first Payment Services Directive (PSD1) was adopted in 2007. Its main purpose was to create a common legal framework for payment services in the European Union and support the development of the Single Euro Payments Area, or SEPA.

PSD1 matched the payment problems of its time. Europe needed common rules for payment institutions, credit transfers, direct debits, execution times, transparency, and basic customer rights. A payment service should not operate under completely different legal assumptions each time it crosses a national border within the EU.

PSD1 also helped create the legal category of nonbank payment institutions. That mattered because payment services were no longer only a bank activity. Nonbank providers could enter the market under a regulatory framework rather than being treated as informal outsiders.

The market then changed quickly: online shopping became mainstream, mobile banking became the norm, fintech companies began building services around bank accounts and cards, and fraud moved into digital channels. Customers began to expect payments to happen quickly and reliably, within fast, digital journeys, not through processes designed for branches and paper forms.

Another problem emerged around bank account access. Some fintech services wanted to help customers aggregate accounts, analyze spending, assess affordability, or initiate account-to-account payments. But banks fully controlled the account interface.

PSD2, adopted in 2015 and applied from 2018, responded to this new environment.

It had three broad objectives:

1. increase competition and innovation;
2. improve payment security;
3. strengthen consumer protection.

Each objective led to visible changes in payment products. Competition led to open banking and regulated third-party access. Security led to Strong Customer Authentication. Consumer protection led to stronger refund rights, clearer fee information, surcharge restrictions, and complaint-handling rules.

Open Banking and Access to Account

Before PSD2, a customer's bank account data was largely controlled through the bank's own channels.

A customer with three bank accounts often had to log into three separate banking portals. A budgeting app, accounting tool, lending product, or affordability service could not reliably access account data unless the customer manually exported files or shared their online banking credentials.

Some services used screen scraping. The customer gave login credentials to a third party, which then logged in as the customer. This worked in practice, but it created obvious problems. The bank could not easily distinguish the customer from the third-party service. The third party often received broader access than it needed. The customer had limited control over consent. Security and liability were unclear.

PSD2 introduced the Access to Account (XS2A) framework. Banks and other account-servicing institutions had to provide regulated access to payment accounts for licensed third-party providers, with the customer's consent and with authentication handled through the account-holding institution.

The account-holding provider is the *account servicing payment service provider (ASPSP)*. In ordinary language, this is usually the customer's bank or account provider.

The regulated external provider is a third-party provider (TPP), and PSD2 created two important TPP roles.

An account information service provider (AISP) can access account information in read-only form. It can aggregate balances, display transactions from multiple banks, support personal finance tools, support affordability checks, or feed credit assessment models.

A payment initiation service provider (PISP) can initiate a payment from the customer's bank account. Instead of paying a merchant by card, the customer can authorize an account-to-account payment initiated through the PISP.

Open banking is the market term for this model, although the phrase is broader than PSD2. The mechanism is straightforward: the customer gives consent, the TPP connects to the ASPSP through regulated access interfaces, and account information or payment initiation becomes available outside the bank's own app.

This did not make banks obsolete. It changed what banks could control themselves.

Before PSD2, the bank's app or online banking portal was the main gateway to account data. After PSD2, licensed third parties could build services around that data, subject to consent, security, and regulatory requirements.

That enabled multi-bank dashboards, cash-flow tools, affordability checks, account-based payments, accounting integrations, lending products, and financial management apps. It also created a new dependency: fintech products that rely on bank APIs need those APIs to be reliable, well-documented, and performant.

This became one of PSD2's weak points. The law created the access right, but API quality varied. Some interfaces worked well. Others were unreliable, inconsistent, hard to use, poorly documented, or interpreted differently by each bank.

A legal right to access account data is not much help if the interface fails in practice. This implementation gap became one of the reasons for PSD3 and PSR.

Strong Customer Authentication

PSD2 made Strong Customer Authentication (SCA) a central requirement for many electronic payments in Europe.

SCA requires authentication based on two or more independent elements from three categories:

1. Knowledge: something only the customer knows, such as a password or PIN.
2. Possession: something only the customer has, such as a registered mobile device, banking app, or hardware token or card.
3. Inherence: something the customer is, such as a fingerprint, facial recognition, or another biometric characteristic.

The factors must be independent. If one factor is compromised, it should not compromise the reliability of the other.

PSD2 also introduced dynamic linking for electronic payments. Authentication should be linked to the specific transaction amount and payee. The customer should not simply approve a generic login or vague payment action. The authentication should relate to the payment being made.

This is why banking apps often show the amount and recipient before confirmation. The customer is confirming a specific payment, not merely proving identity in the abstract.

For online card payments, 3-D Secure is one of the main mechanisms used to support SCA. The issuer can authenticate the cardholder using a banking app, a biometric prompt, a one-time code, or another supported method. In Chapter 40, we will discuss how 3DS turns that regulatory requirement into a card-specific authentication flow.

Many SCA-compliant payments create no visible challenge for the customer because exemptions, risk analysis, or out-of-scope flows apply.

Common SCA exemptions include:

- Low-value transactions: subject to cumulative limits and issuer controls.
- Transaction Risk Analysis (TRA): low-risk transactions can avoid active authentication if fraud-rate conditions are met and the issuer accepts the exemption.
- Trusted beneficiaries: a customer marks a payee as trusted through the account provider.
- Fixed-amount recurring transactions: the first transaction generally requires SCA, but subsequent transactions of the same amount may not.
- Certain corporate payment processes: use dedicated, secure corporate procedures or instruments.

Exemptions still fall under the SCA framework: the transaction is in scope, but the rules allow skipping active authentication under certain conditions.

Out-of-scope transactions follow a different logic. They are not simply exempted. They fall outside the standard customer-present SCA flow. Common examples include Mail Order/Telephone Order transactions, properly identified merchant-initiated transactions based on a prior agreement with the cardholder, and one-leg-out card transactions where either the issuer or the acquirer is outside the EEA. Authentication may still be used for risk, scheme, issuer, or merchant reasons, but these transactions are not treated as normal in-scope PSD2 SCA cases.

The operational point is simple: authentication became a regulated design issue. It affects issuer risk decisions, merchant conversion rates, PSP routing, customer experience, and liability.

Consumer Protection under PSD2

PSD2 also strengthened the customer's position.

For unauthorized transactions, the basic principle is that the customer should not bear losses they did not authorize, subject to rules on fraud, intent, and gross negligence. The payment service provider must usually refund the customer quickly after becoming aware of the unauthorized transaction, then investigate.

PSD2 also changes the evidence burden. If a customer disputes a transaction, the provider must be able to show that the payment was authenticated, properly recorded, and correctly executed. A system entry alone is not enough to prove that the customer approved it.

This changes product design. Payment providers need logs, authentication records, consent records, transaction identifiers, customer communication records, and dispute workflows. Consumer protection is not only a legal rule for the complaints team. It requires evidence throughout the payment flow.

PSD2 also required clearer fee information. Customers should know what they are being charged and under what conditions. This affects payment accounts, cards, transfers, currency conversion, ATM withdrawals, and other payment services.

It restricted surcharging for many consumer card payments in the EEA. A merchant generally cannot add an extra fee merely because the customer uses an in-scope consumer card. Commercial cards and out-of-scope transactions may be treated differently.

PSD2 also sets complaint-handling deadlines for payment-service complaints. The provider normally has to give a written response within fifteen business days. If exceptional circumstances outside the provider's control prevent a full answer within that time, it must send a holding response explaining the delay and provide a final response no later than 35 business days after receiving the complaint.

These rules change how payment products work financially. If a provider has to refund quickly, prove authorization, disclose fees clearly, and avoid certain surcharges, the product must be built with these requirements in mind from the beginning.

Pricing, Surcharging, and Interchange

PSD2 is not the only European rule that changed card economics.

The Interchange Fee Regulation (IFR) capped interchange fees for many consumer card transactions in the EU: generally 0.2 percent of the transaction value for debit cards and 0.3 percent for credit cards. The caps apply to in-scope consumer cards. Commercial cards and some other arrangements can fall outside the rule or be treated differently.

Interchange is a major revenue source for issuers and a major cost component in merchant card acceptance. Once the regulation caps it, the economics change: issuers earn less from covered consumer card transactions, merchants face lower regulated acceptance costs, and card products funded heavily by interchange need other revenue sources.

PSD2 also affects pricing through its surcharge rules. For many in-scope consumer card payments, merchants cannot simply add a separate fee because the customer chose that card. They may still recover acceptance costs through general pricing, payment-method steering where allowed, or broader commercial choices, but the cost is no longer shown as a simple card surcharge at checkout.

Currency conversion and fee disclosure follow the same logic. If a customer is offered Dynamic Currency Conversion, an ATM withdrawal, or an international transfer, the product must display the relevant fees and exchange-rate effects before the customer commits. The rule does more than push providers to charge less. It makes the cost visible early enough for the customer to make an informed choice.

Together, interchange caps, surcharge restrictions, and disclosure rules show how regulation changes the economics of payments. It not only tells providers how to secure a transaction. It also shapes who can charge, how charges are displayed, and where payment costs are applied when a direct fee is restricted.

PSD2 Gaps

PSD2 changed the market, but it left gaps.

The first gap was fraud, especially social engineering and authorized push payment fraud. A customer might be tricked into authorizing a payment to a fraudster posing as a bank employee, a government official, a supplier, or a family member. Under older rules, the provider could often argue that the customer technically authorized the payment. That left many victims in a weaker position, even though they had been deceived.

The second gap was open banking quality. PSD2 required access, but the technical experience varied widely. Fintechs often faced inconsistent APIs, downtime, different interpretations, and practical barriers to access.

The third gap was fragmentation. PSD2 is a directive, which means member states transpose it into national law. That can lead to differences in implementation and enforcement. For a market that is supposed to be single and cross-border, those differences create cost and uncertainty.

The fourth gap was the split between payment institutions and electronic money institutions. PSD2 governed payment institutions, while electronic money institutions were regulated under a separate e-money framework. In practice, many fintech business models cut across both.

PSD3 and PSR address these gaps. Their aim is not to replace PSD2's basic direction, but to make the rules more consistent, more focused on fraud, and better matched to how digital payments now work.

The Next Regulatory Package

PSD3 and PSR are designed as a package.

PSD3 is a directive. It focuses mainly on authorization, licensing, supervision, and prudential requirements for payment institutions and electronic money institutions. Because it is a directive, member states must transpose it into national law.

PSR is a regulation. It contains directly applicable operational rules for payment services across the EU. Because it is a regulation, it is intended to reduce national variation and create more uniform conduct rules.

This split is intentional. Licensing and supervision remain in a directive, while many daily conduct rules for payment services move into a regulation that applies more consistently across member states.

At the time of writing, the European Parliament and Council had reached political agreement on the PSD3/PSR package, and the Council had published final compromise texts. The package points toward stronger fraud prevention, more transparent fees, better consumer protection, improved open banking, and a more modern payment services framework.

Even before the final application date, the direction affects product planning. Banks, PSPs, fintechs, merchants, and vendors need time to prepare systems, contracts, risk processes, customer journeys, and support workflows before new rules become fully applicable.

Proposed Changes

The PSD3/PSR package translates the lessons from PSD2 into more specific operational requirements.

In fraud cases, the focus shifts from general security duties to more active prevention. Payment service providers are expected to strengthen transaction monitoring, share more fraud-related information where required, warn customers in higher-risk situations, and improve controls around impersonation fraud. The practical effect is that fraud prevention becomes part of the regulated payment process, not only an internal risk function.

For account-to-account payments, the package enhances payee verification logic. Before a customer sends a transfer, the provider may need to check whether the payee name matches the account identifier, such as an IBAN, and warn the customer if there is a mismatch. This is meant to reduce cases where a customer is tricked into sending money to an account controlled by a fraudster.

For open banking, the reform pushes banks toward more reliable access interfaces. ASPSPs are expected to provide better-performing APIs, clearer documentation, stronger availability, and fewer practical barriers for licensed TPPs. The goal is not merely to grant legal access, but to make that access usable in production.

For customer permissions, the package introduces more visible consent management. A customer should be able to see which third-party providers have access to their account and withdraw that access more easily, typically through a permissions dashboard or similar interface.

In terms of institutional structure, PSD3 brings payment institutions and electronic money institutions closer together. Instead of maintaining two separate regimes for many overlapping fintech models, the framework moves toward a more unified approach to licensing, supervision, safeguarding, and prudential requirements.

For pricing and transparency, the rules continue to push costs into the open before the customer commits. This affects currency conversion, ATM fees, transfer charges, and other payment service costs, and requires the customer to have sufficient information to understand the transaction before confirming it.

To ensure access to cash, the reform keeps physical cash on the regulatory agenda. Digital payments may continue to grow, but regulators still expect payment systems to serve people who rely on cash or need it as a backup.

In practical terms, PSD3 and PSR are not just PSD2 with more rules. They turn broad principles into more concrete products, such as API, fraud, consent, pricing, and supervision requirements.

Local Regulatory Layers

PSD2, PSD3, and PSR are European rules. They apply in a specific legal and geographic context.

Other markets have their own frameworks. The United Kingdom retained and adapted its own payment services regime after Brexit. The United States has a different mix of federal rules, state rules, card network rules, bank supervision, and consumer protection laws. India, Brazil, Singapore, Australia, and other markets have their own models for instant payments, open banking, fraud liability, and customer authentication.

Cross-border payment products have to handle these differences. A card may be issued in one country, used at a merchant in another, processed by a PSP in a third, and supported by vendors in several more. A fintech may build one user experience but operate under different regulatory obligations by market.

For that reason, any claim about liability, authentication, refund timing, surcharging, or data access must be tied to a jurisdiction.

The technology may be global. The rules usually are not.

Regulation as Product Architecture

Payment regulation changes what payment products are allowed to do, what they must prove, and who carries the loss when something goes wrong.

That is why regulation is incorporated into product design. SCA can change the checkout flow. Open banking affects bank API architecture and consent screens. Consumer protection rules shape dispute handling, refund timing, and evidence requirements. Surcharging and interchange rules alter payment economics, while fraud and data-protection rules influence monitoring, liability decisions, warnings, and the reuse of payment data.

These are not surface-level legal requirements added after the product is built. They affect screens, APIs, logs, risk controls, customer support, contracts, settlement processes, and the business model itself.

PSD1 established a common foundation for payment services across Europe. PSD2 opened that foundation to digital competition and made security a central part of the payment experience. PSD3 and PSR continue the same path: more harmonization, more fraud responsibility, more operational requirements, and less tolerance for vague implementation.

For payment companies, regulation does not come after the product is built. It sets the boundaries from the first design decision.

Chapter 40: 3-D Secure and Strong Customer Authentication

In Chapter 39, we introduced Strong Customer Authentication as a regulatory requirement: in many electronic payments, the customer must be authenticated with stronger evidence than static payment details alone.

In this chapter, we discuss the card payment mechanism that often makes that requirement visible at online checkout.

After the cardholder provides their card number, expiration date, and security code, the merchant collects these details and prepares to submit the payment. At this stage, the checkout process may pause for an additional step.

Next, a bank screen appears. This screen may prompt the cardholder to enter a one-time code, approve via a push notification in their banking app, or confirm their identity using Face ID, Touch ID, or another biometric method. This step is part of the authentication process.

The payment has not failed. The issuer is asking an additional authentication question before the payment moves to authorization: is this really the cardholder?

The 3-D Secure protocol addresses this card-not-present authentication problem through the payment network's directory infrastructure. It lets the issuer authenticate the cardholder during online checkout using a message flow that sits alongside the authorization path.

3-D Secure Objectives

Card-not-present payments have a built-in weakness. The merchant never sees the physical card, the chip cannot interact with a terminal, and the terminal cannot request a PIN in person.

For a long time, online card payments relied on static details such as the card number, expiration date, and CVV2. These details can be stolen from databases, phishing sites, malware, screenshots, hacked merchant systems, or poor storage. Once stolen, they can be used remotely.

The 3DS flow adds an issuer-controlled authentication step to the checkout process.

The merchant still collects card details and prepares the payment through its gateway and acquirer. But before authorizing the transaction, the issuer can authenticate the cardholder. If the transaction appears low-risk, the issuer quietly authenticates it. If the issuer needs more confidence, it asks the cardholder for additional proof.

The liability shift makes 3-D Secure more than a customer check. If a 3DS transaction is successfully authenticated, fraud liability shifts from the merchant to the issuer under payment network rules. This liability shift is a key reason merchants use 3DS, even in places where strong authentication is not required by law.

The Three-Domain Model and Its Components

The name 3-D Secure comes from the three-domain model used in the authentication process.

The acquirer domain contains the merchant side of the checkout: the online store, the PSP or gateway, and the 3DS Server. This is where the authentication request begins.

The issuer domain contains the issuer and its Access Control Server (ACS). The *ACS* is the issuer-side system that evaluates the authentication request, applies risk logic, authenticates the cardholder, and returns the authentication result.

The interoperability domain sits between them. It includes the Directory Server (DS), operated by the payment network. The DS identifies the correct issuer's ACS and routes 3DS messages between the acquirer and issuer domains.

Several named components appear inside those domains.

- The 3DS Requestor is the party requesting authentication. In most e-commerce transactions, this is the merchant or the merchant's digital channel.

- The 3DS Server is the component on the merchant, PSP, gateway, or acquirer side that creates and manages 3DS authentication messages. Most merchants do not build this themselves. It is usually provided by their PSP, gateway, or acquirer.
- The *Directory Server* is the payment network component that routes authentication requests to the correct issuer ACS and supports message exchange between the acquirer and the issuer.
- The Access Control Server handles issuer-side evaluation: it decides whether authentication can be completed silently or whether the cardholder should be challenged.
- In app-based flows, a 3DS SDK may collect device and application data and support the challenge experience inside the merchant's app. In browser flows, the challenge can be presented through a browser-based interface.

The cardholder sees only the visible part of this process: sometimes a regular checkout, sometimes an approval in the banking app, a one-time code, or a biometric prompt. Behind that surface, *3DS* is a protocol flow between the merchant, the payment network, and the issuer before the authorization request is sent.

Authentication Before Authorization

A 3DS checkout has two separate phases.

The first phase is authentication. The merchant side, typically using a PSP or gateway 3DS Server, sends an authentication request to the Directory Server. The Directory Server then identifies the correct issuer's ACS and routes the request. The ACS evaluates the transaction and returns an authentication result to the merchant's 3DS Server.

Only after authentication does the merchant proceed to payment authorization.

The authorization path should be familiar from earlier chapters. The merchant sends an authorization request through the gateway, the acquirer, the payment network, and the issuer. The issuer then evaluates the request using information such as account status, available balance or credit, limits, card status, fraud rules, merchant category, location, transaction velocity, and authentication data, along with other internal controls, to decide whether to approve the payment.

This separation demonstrates why a cardholder may complete a 3DS authentication challenge but still have a payment declined. Even after successful authentication, the transaction may be declined during authorization due to separate risk and account checks.

Frictionless Authentication

The ideal 3DS experience is invisible to the cardholder.

In a frictionless flow, the issuer's ACS receives the authentication request, reviews the transaction data, and returns a successful authentication result without requiring the cardholder to take any action.

The ACS may consider the checkout context, device information, browser data, IP address, transaction amount, merchant category, shipping information, account history, previous behavior, and other risk signals.

If the transaction appears normal, the ACS can silently authenticate it. The merchant receives the successful authentication result and continues with payment authorization.

For the cardholder, checkout continues as usual. For the issuer, the decision is not blind: it has received additional transaction and device context before deciding that no challenge is needed.

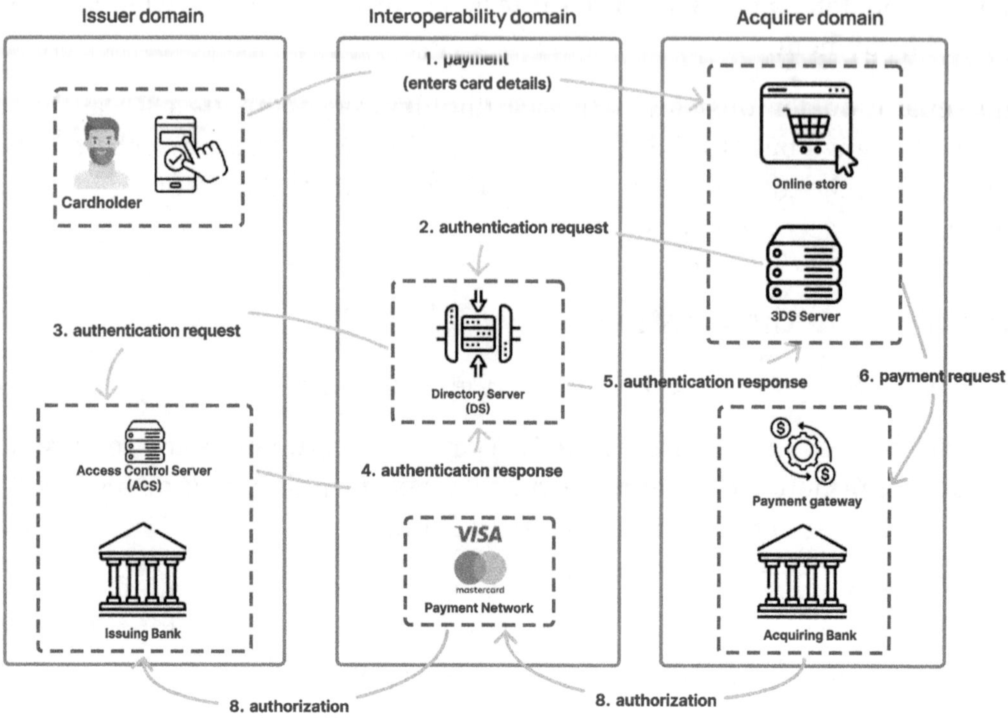

Figure 40.1: 3DS frictionless flow.

This is the main benefit of EMV 3DS. It adds authentication without challenging every low-risk transaction. The issuer gets more information than just the card number and CVV2, and the merchant avoids unnecessary checkout friction.

Challenge Authentication

A challenge flow starts like a frictionless flow, but the issuer's ACS decides that silent authentication is not enough.

The ACS returns a challenge-required response. The merchant checkout then presents the issuer's challenge flow, usually through a browser or app interface controlled by the 3DS protocol.

The challenge is between the issuer and the cardholder. The issuer may ask for a one-time code, push approval in a banking app, biometric confirmation, or another supported authentication method. After the cardholder responds, the ACS sends the final authentication result back through the Directory Server to the merchant's 3DS Server.

If authentication succeeds, the merchant can proceed to authorization. If authentication fails, the merchant usually stops the payment attempt.

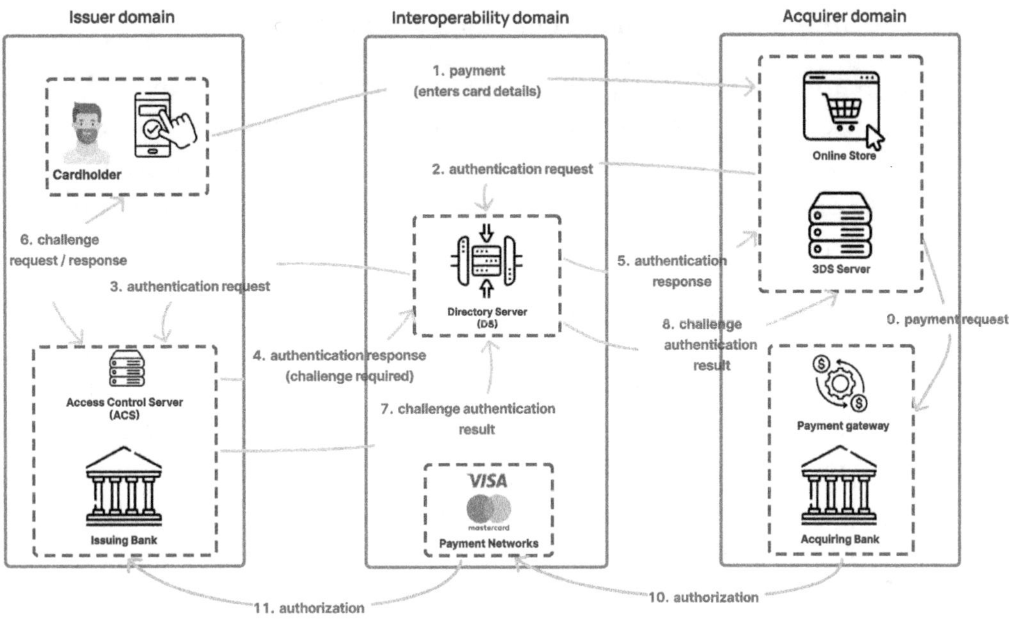

Figure 40.2: 3DS challenge flow.

Challenges improve confidence, but they add friction. A cardholder may abandon checkout, miss an SMS, fail to approve the banking app prompt, distrust the screen, or time out. A good 3DS strategy does not challenge every transaction. It gives the issuer enough data to challenge when the added confidence is worth the interruption.

3DS1 versus EMV 3DS

The frictionless and challenge flows described above are primarily the EMV 3DS world, often called 3DS2. The first version of 3DS worked differently and reflected an earlier era of online checkout.

The 3DS1 protocol was known under brand names such as Verified by Visa and Mastercard SecureCode. It often used full-page redirects, static passwords, and authentication screens that did not fit naturally into the merchant's checkout flow. It improved security by adding issuer-side authentication, while making checkout harder for many legitimate customers. Many cardholders abandoned purchases when faced with an unfamiliar bank page or a forgotten password.

EMV 3DS was designed for modern digital commerce. It supports browser and in-app checkout, richer data sharing, and risk-based authentication. Instead of challenging every cardholder, it lets the issuer review transaction data in the background and decide whether a challenge is necessary.

EMV 3DS became especially important in Europe because it provided issuers, merchants, acquirers, and PSPs with a card network mechanism to support PSD2 SCA for online card payments. The distinction between SCA and 3DS is simple: SCA specifies when strong authentication is required; 3DS is one way the card system performs it.

Inside a 3DS flow, the issuer can authenticate the cardholder using two independent elements, such as possession of a registered device plus a biometric check or passcode. The issuer can also link authentication to the specific transaction amount and merchant, thereby supporting the PSD2 idea of dynamic linking. That is why a banking app may show the merchant name and amount during confirmation: the cardholder is not only proving identity but also confirming the transaction.

Liability Shift

The 3DS flow also helps manage liability.

In many card-not-present fraud cases, merchants typically bear the risk of chargebacks. The issuer might refund the cardholder and file a chargeback, and the merchant could lose the transaction unless it has evidence to defend the case.

If 3DS authentication is successful, liability for some fraud disputes shifts from the merchant to the issuer. The exact rules depend on the network, region, transaction type, exemption, authentication result, and merchant-acquirer setup.

The logic is simple: if the issuer authenticated the cardholder, the merchant should not always be responsible for fraud losses later. The issuer had a chance to verify its customer, either silently or by challenging them.

The 3DS flow protects mainly against certain fraud liability cases, not every dispute. Goods not received, processing errors, refund disputes, and other chargeback types can still affect the merchant.

Checkout Friction

The 3DS flow helps reduce fraud risk, but poor implementation can hurt checkout conversion.

A poorly timed challenge can interrupt a purchase: a confusing issuer screen, a missing SMS, or a timed-out banking-app prompt can all push customers out of checkout, especially when they are using a foreign SIM, a new phone, or a weak connection.

Some transactions can proceed without a visible challenge because the issuer accepts a low-risk assessment, an exemption, or another valid routing outcome. The customer sees a smooth checkout, but the merchant, PSP, acquirer, payment network, and issuer still exchange the data needed to support that decision.

That trade-off is why merchants focus on their 3DS strategy. They want liability protection and regulatory compliance, but they do not want to unnecessarily challenge every good customer.

Issuers face the opposite pressure. If they let too many risky transactions go unchecked, fraud losses can increase. If they challenge too often, both customers and merchants experience more friction.

EMV 3DS helps manage this trade-off by using more data. With better transaction context, issuers can challenge suspicious payments while allowing normal ones to continue smoothly.

Authentication Decisioning

A 3DS checkout contains several decisions, made by different systems.

The merchant or PSP decides whether to initiate 3DS and what data to send. The payment network's Directory Server routes the authentication request. The issuer's ACS decides whether authentication can be frictionless or whether the cardholder must be challenged. After authentication, the issuer's authorization system decides whether to approve the payment.

These decisions happen in sequence, but they are not the same decision.

If a transaction fails before authorization, the problem may lie in authentication: a failed challenge, an unavailable ACS, a failed 3DS message flow, or a rejected authentication result. If the transaction passes 3DS but is later declined, the problem lies in authorization: funds, limits, card status, issuer risk rules, or another authorization control. If the transaction is approved and later disputed, the question moves again to reason codes, liability shift, evidence, and chargeback rules.

For anyone building or operating online card payments, this separation is the central point of 3DS. Authentication verifies that the cardholder is genuine. Authorization decides whether the payment can proceed. Fraud systems determine whether a transaction looks suspicious. Dispute rules determine what happens if the transaction is later challenged.

In the following chapter, we move from authentication to fraud: how issuers, merchants, PSPs, and networks determine whether a transaction appears suspicious, even after the customer has been authenticated.

Chapter 41: Fraud in Card Payments

Fraud systems rarely know the full story. They see signals.

Fraud rarely announces itself. It can look like a $3 test purchase online, a contactless payment abroad, an ATM withdrawal late at night, ten quick attempts at the same merchant, or a customer disputing delivery for goods they likely received.

Any of these situations could be fraud. Any of them could also be legitimate.

That uncertainty defines *fraud detection* in card payments. The system has to decide quickly, often in milliseconds, whether to allow a transaction, challenge it, block it, or send it for review. It relies on signals, history, rules, models, authentication data, merchant information, device data, and network intelligence, but it rarely has complete certainty.

Fraud in card payments is not one problem. It includes stolen cards, copied card data, compromised credentials, account takeover, fake merchants, transaction laundering, social engineering, application fraud, synthetic identity, and first-party misuse.

Authorization is the main real-time checkpoint for transaction fraud. It is the last moment when the issuer can stop a purchase before approval, but it is not the only fraud-control point in the card system. Fraud controls also appear during onboarding, authentication, wallet provisioning, merchant monitoring, clearing, payout, disputes, and portfolio review.

Fraud prevention is therefore not about rejecting everything that looks suspicious. It is about deciding which risks are acceptable, which need more checks, and which must be stopped before money, goods, or liability move further through the system.

Fraud Taxonomy

People often use the word *fraud* as if it means one thing, but in payments, it encompasses several different problems.

A stolen physical card used at a shop is different from card details used on a website. A counterfeit magstripe card is different from a phishing attack on a mobile banking account. A fake merchant laundering illegal transactions is different from a real cardholder falsely claiming that goods never arrived.

The attacker, victim, control points, and liable party can vary from case to case.

Fraud teams usually organize cases into categories:

- card-present fraud;
- card-not-present fraud;
- account takeover;
- application fraud and synthetic identity;
- merchant-side fraud;
- first-party misuse or friendly fraud;
- social engineering and scam-related fraud.

These categories often overlap. A phishing attack can lead to an account takeover, which can then be used to make card-on-file purchases. Stolen card data may be tested with small online transactions before being used for larger fraud. A merchant may start legitimately and become risky later.

Fraud moves toward the weakest point in the system.

When EMV chip cards reduced counterfeit card-present fraud, attackers moved more aggressively into online payments and fallback channels. When 3-D Secure improved online authentication, attackers invested more in social engineering, account takeover, bot attacks, and merchant abuse. When issuers tighten transaction rules, fraudsters test smaller amounts, different merchants, different devices, or different geographies.

As payment systems adapt, attackers change their methods.

Card-Present Fraud

Card-present fraud occurs when someone uses the actual card, or a fake version of it, in person.

Classic examples include lost or stolen cards. If someone finds a lost card, they may use it before it is blocked. Contactless payments can make small purchases easier, since some do not require a PIN. Limits, velocity checks, and risk rules reduce the risk, but they cannot remove it completely.

Counterfeit card fraud is another type of card-present attack. In the past, this often involved copying magnetic-stripe data from a real card onto another card. Skimming devices at ATMs or compromised terminals were used to steal this data.

The introduction of EMV chip cards changed this risk. Chip cards generate dynamic transaction data, which is much harder to copy than magnetic-stripe data. Countries that adopted EMV generally saw counterfeit card-present fraud fall, while attackers shifted toward online payments, fallback acceptance, and other weaker channels.

Magstripe fallback remains a risk where allowed. If a terminal cannot read the chip and instead uses the magnetic stripe, the transaction loses much of EMV's protection. Fraudsters target these weaker points because they are easier to exploit.

Card-present fraud can also involve PIN-related attacks. A fraudster may steal a card and obtain the PIN by watching the cardholder enter it, using hidden cameras, tampered PIN pads, or social engineering. ATM fraud often combines stealing the card, capturing the PIN, and quickly withdrawing cash before anyone notices.

Card-Not-Present Fraud

Card-not-present (CNP) fraud is the main challenge for online card payments.

Online convenience rests on weaker evidence. The merchant cannot inspect the card, and the terminal cannot request transaction-specific proof from the chip. A fraudster does not need the physical card. They need enough information to pass the checkout checks: PAN, expiry date, CVV2, billing address, device data, or a stored credential.

CNP fraud can start in many ways:

- a merchant, PSP, or processor breach exposes card data;
- a phishing site collects card details from cardholders;
- malware captures browser, device, or clipboard data;

- credential stuffing gives access to a merchant account with stored cards;
- bots test stolen card numbers against weak checkout pages;
- compromised email accounts expose receipts, addresses, and identity data.

Card testing is a common tactic. Fraudsters make small transactions to find out which cards are still active. If a card works, they use it for larger purchases or sell the information. Merchants may see these as harmless small transactions, but fraud systems can detect repeated small attempts across many cards as a warning sign.

Tools such as 3-D Secure, CVV2, address verification, device fingerprinting, velocity checks, and issuer risk scoring all help. No single tool is enough, but together they make it harder for stolen credentials to be used successfully.

Real online payments can also look unusual. A genuine customer may travel, use a VPN, change phones, ship to a new address, buy something expensive, or retry after entering the wrong CVV2. If controls are too strict, good customers are declined.

CNP fraud, therefore, requires a constant balancing act: reduce fraud without damaging legitimate approval rates.

Account Takeover

Account takeover occurs when someone gains access to a real customer's account.

For card payments, this can mean a bank account, mobile wallet, merchant account, online shopping profile, ride-hailing account, subscription account, or any app that stores payment details.

The attacker does not always need to steal the card number. Access to the stored card can be enough. If the fraudster can log in, change the email address, add a shipping address, order items, withdraw money, or make transfers, the payment method becomes a tool inside the compromised account.

Attackers often use phishing, credential stuffing, SIM swaps, malware, fake support calls, and social engineering. *Credential stuffing* is especially common because people reuse passwords. If a password is stolen from one site, attackers try it on others. If the customer reused it, the attacker can get in.

Account takeover is difficult to spot because the transaction uses a real customer profile and stored payment method. The merchant sees a familiar account, and the issuer sees a card that has been used there before. Fraud signals may appear in small details: a new device, a new IP address, an unusual shipping address, a password reset before purchase, a changed phone number, or an unusual buying pattern.

Payment fraud and identity security are closely linked. Protecting the card transaction alone is not enough if the account tied to the card has already been compromised.

Application Fraud and Synthetic Identity

Fraud can start before the first transaction.

Application fraud happens when someone opens an account, card, wallet, or credit product using fake, stolen, or manipulated information. The fraudster may want to obtain a card, raise a credit limit, pass onboarding checks, or create accounts for later laundering, mule activity, or chargeback abuse.

One type uses stolen identity data. The fraudster applies using a real person's name, sometimes combining leaked personal details with fake documents or a phone number they control.

A more durable version is synthetic identity fraud. The fraudster mixes real and fake details, such as a real national ID, a fake name, a real address, an email they control, a prepaid phone, or a manufactured credit history. Over time, this fake profile can look real enough to obtain credit or access payment systems.

This is important for card products because not all transaction fraud comes from good accounts that later go bad. Sometimes the account was fraudulent from the beginning.

Early controls, such as onboarding checks, device intelligence, document verification, phone and email reputation checks, address history checks, bureau checks, and application-velocity controls, aim to catch this before the account begins transacting. If fraud controls only begin at authorization, some losses are already built into the portfolio.

Merchant-Side Fraud

Fraud does not only come from cardholders or people using stolen cards. It can also come from merchants.

A fake merchant may sign up with an acquirer or PSP, run fraudulent transactions, get paid, and disappear before disputes or chargebacks arrive. This is a bust-out pattern. The merchant looks normal at first, then suddenly processes many high-risk transactions and vanishes.

Transaction laundering is another merchant-side risk. A merchant approved for one type of business secretly processes payments for another, often a banned or high-risk business. For example, a normal-looking website may be a front, while the real transactions involve gambling, counterfeit goods, illegal products, or other restricted activities.

There can also be collusion. A merchant and a cardholder may work together to run fraudulent transactions, withdraw funds, earn rewards, abuse refunds, or file false chargebacks.

Merchant-side fraud is mainly an acquiring-side risk. The acquirer or PSP needs to know who the merchant is, what the merchant sells, whether the website aligns with the merchant's business model, who owns the company, how delivery works, what chargeback patterns look like, and whether transactions fit the merchant's profile.

Merchant onboarding and monitoring are part of fraud prevention, not only administrative setup.

Friendly Fraud and First-Party Misuse

Friendly fraud, or first-party misuse, occurs when the real cardholder disputes a legitimate transaction.

The term friendly can be misleading. Sometimes the cardholder deliberately abuses the chargeback system. Other times, the dispute comes from confusion: a family member used the card, the merchant name is unclear, a subscription was renewed and forgotten, or delivery was late.

For the merchant, the outcome can be the same. The cardholder claims the transaction was unauthorized or that the goods did not arrive. The issuer may give the cardholder temporary credit. The merchant can lose the sale, pay a chargeback fee, and spend time collecting evidence.

First-party misuse is hard to prevent at the authorization stage because the cardholder is not an outsider. The person disputing the charge may be the same person who made the purchase. At the time of payment, the transaction can look normal.

The best controls are often operational rather than purely technical: clear merchant names, delivery proof, good customer support, easy cancellation, subscription reminders, strong record keeping, and fair refund policies. Preventing a dispute before it starts is often cheaper than fighting it later.

Fraud and disputes overlap here because they can also misuse a chargeback process designed to protect cardholders.

Social Engineering and Authorized Fraud

Not all fraud begins with stolen credentials. Some scams trick the victim into taking action themselves.

A fraudster may call a customer and pretend to be from the bank. They may claim the account is under attack and ask the customer to move money to a "safe" account. They may convince the customer to approve a push notification, share a one-time code, add a payee, or make a transfer.

The customer technically approves the action, but the approval was obtained through deception.

This kind of fraud is difficult for payment systems because authentication is real. The right device is used, the correct biometric is applied, and the customer approves the payment.

The problem is not failed authentication. The customer was tricked.

Card systems face this too, especially when fraudsters persuade cardholders to share one-time codes, approve wallet provisioning, add cards to devices, or complete 3DS challenges. Strong authentication works best when an attacker attempts to use stolen credentials. Scam fraud is different: the real customer may approve the transaction after being manipulated. That requires controls beyond authentication, including customer warnings, transaction context, payee checks, confirmation screens, cooling-off periods, and staff escalation where needed.

Authorization Controls

When the issuer receives an authorization request, it has only a short time to decide. It may evaluate:

- card status;

- available balance or credit;
- amount;
- Merchant Category Code;
- merchant identity and location;
- POS entry mode;
- country and currency;
- device or wallet data;
- previous customer behavior;
- recent failed attempts;
- transaction velocity;
- known fraud patterns;
- authentication result, including 3DS where relevant.

The issuer's fraud system assigns a risk score to the transaction. Low-risk transactions are usually approved. High-risk transactions may be declined. If risk is unclear, the system may request additional authentication, notify the customer, place a temporary block, or route the case for review.

Merchants and acquirers use similar logic from their side. Merchants may check orders before accepting them. PSPs can apply risk rules across their merchant portfolio. Acquirers monitor merchant behavior and block suspicious activity. Payment networks can provide risk alerts, scoring, and rule-based services.

Fraud prevention uses layers because no participant sees the whole picture. Merchants see the device, customer account, shopping cart, shipping address, and website behavior. Issuers see the cardholder's account history, available funds, card controls, and issuer-side authentication results. Networks see patterns across participants. Acquirers focus on merchant risk.

Many controls are simple. A daily ATM withdrawal limit reduces the risk of large cash losses. A contactless limit reduces exposure if a card is stolen. Velocity rules catch many attempts in quick succession. Merchant category blocks restrict card use in risky areas. Geography rules flag transactions from unusual locations.

These controls work because fraud often follows patterns.

A fraudster testing stolen cards may make many small purchases quickly. An account takeover may involve a password reset, a new device, a new address, and a large order within minutes. A stolen card may be used several times before the cardholder notices. A fake merchant may suddenly process much more volume than usual.

The difficult part is tuning.

A rule that blocks foreign transactions will catch some fraud and strand legitimate travelers. A rule that blocks every high-value purchase will reduce losses and frustrate good customers. A rule that blocks every new device will stop some account takeovers and punish customers who just bought a new phone.

Fraud controls should be judged by both outcomes: the fraud they prevent and the legitimate activity they interrupt.

The strongest fraud decisions use the most complete information available without slowing down normal transactions.

False Positives and Approval Rates

A *false positive* is a legitimate transaction incorrectly flagged as fraudulent.

False positives are expensive because the merchant loses a sale, the issuer frustrates a customer, the cardholder may switch cards, high-value customers may stop using the product, and support teams receive calls. The payment system looks unreliable, even though it was trying to protect the account.

Fraud prevention should not be measured solely by fraud that is stopped.

A portfolio with almost no fraud but very low approval rates is poorly managed. It is easy to reduce fraud by declining too many transactions. The harder task is to approve more good transactions while still stopping bad ones.

Payment teams watch both sides of the equation:

- fraud rate;
- chargeback rate;
- approval rate;
- false positive rate;

- manual review rate;
- customer friction;
- fraud loss by channel, merchant type, country, and product.

The right balance depends on the product. A premium credit card may tolerate more checks for suspicious luxury purchases. Transit payments need to be fast and smooth. Marketplace payouts may require stricter controls due to the rapid flow of funds. Digital wallets may focus more on account takeover signals.

There is no universal fraud setting. Each business has its own risk tolerance.

Fraud Prevention and Dispute Handling

Fraud prevention and dispute handling occur at different stages.

Fraud prevention aims to stop or challenge a transaction before it is approved. Dispute handling occurs after a transaction is approved, settled, and later questioned by the cardholder or issuer.

Sometimes the same case involves both, but the tools, evidence, and responsible teams differ.

If an issuer declines a suspicious transaction, the customer may never lose money. If the issuer approves it and the cardholder later disputes it, the case enters the chargeback process. The question changes. The system is no longer deciding whether to approve the transaction. It is deciding who should carry the loss and what evidence supports each side.

Fraud data remains useful after authorization because the same signals can become dispute evidence. Strong prevention reduces the number of disputes. Good evidence reduces losses when a disputed transaction still reaches the chargeback process.

Liability and Channel Differences

Fraud liability depends on the channel, rules, authentication, region, and product type.

In card-present transactions, EMV chip data, PIN, and contactless cryptograms reduce counterfeit fraud and can affect liability. If one party relies on weaker technology when stronger technology is available, payment network rules may shift liability.

In card-not-present transactions, merchants have historically carried more fraud risk because the physical card is not present. The 3-D Secure protocol can shift certain fraud liability to the issuer if authentication succeeds and the transaction meets the relevant conditions.

In cases of lost or stolen cards, the issuer-cardholder relationship is central. Consumer protection rules may limit the cardholder's liability, especially when the cardholder reports promptly and has not acted fraudulently or with gross negligence.

For first-party misuse, the merchant may carry the loss unless it can provide strong evidence through the dispute process.

For merchant fraud, the acquirer or PSP may carry losses if the merchant disappears, cannot cover chargebacks, or was poorly onboarded.

Fraud affects security, economics, customer trust, and operational capacity. It also determines who carries the loss. The system has to decide who could have prevented the fraud and who pays when prevention fails.

Shared Intelligence

No single participant sees the full picture of fraud.

The issuer sees activity on its own cards: spending history, account status, recent declines, customer behavior, card controls, and issuer-side authentication results. But it does not see every detail inside the merchant's checkout. It may not know whether the customer changed the shipping address, created a new merchant account five minutes ago, or failed several login attempts before placing the order.

The merchant's picture is almost the reverse. It can observe the customer account, device, basket, delivery address, login history, and website behavior. It may notice that an order looks strange for that customer or that many new accounts are trying the same promotion. But the merchant does not see the cardholder's full banking activity or how the same card is behaving across the wider network.

PSPs and acquirers see another layer. A PSP may spot patterns across its merchant portfolio, such as repeated card testing, unusual refund behavior, rising dispute volumes, suspicious merchant traffic, or clusters of transactions from the same device or IP range. An acquirer may notice that a merchant's processing volume, ticket size, product mix, or chargeback pattern no longer matches the business it originally underwrote.

Payment networks have still another vantage point. They can see activity across issuers and acquirers and may detect patterns that are invisible to a single bank or merchant. Bots may target a BIN range. A group of cards may be tested at one set of merchants and then used elsewhere. A device, merchant, or transaction pattern may appear suspicious only when viewed across many participants.

This is why fraud prevention depends partly on shared intelligence. Networks, issuers, acquirers, PSPs, fraud vendors, and industry groups exchange risk signals in many forms: compromised-card alerts, merchant risk data, device reputation data, fraud patterns, chargeback monitoring, sanctions lists, and reports on emerging attack methods.

Shared information does not replace local decision-making. The issuer still decides whether to approve its cardholder's transaction. The merchant still decides whether to accept, review, or cancel an order. The acquirer still decides how to manage merchant risk. But shared intelligence gives each participant a broader context than they could build on their own.

Fraud prevention is strongest when system-wide signals support local controls. A single transaction can look normal in isolation. Across the network, it may be part of a pattern.

Operating under Uncertainty

Fraud management is decision-making under uncertainty. The system has to act before all the facts are known: approve, decline, challenge, block, warn, review, or let the transaction through.

At authorization, the issuer may have less than a second to decide whether to approve the transaction. The merchant may better understand the customer's session and order context than the issuer. The acquirer may understand whether the merchant is behaving normally. The network may see wider patterns across participants. Each party has a partial view, so fraud control must operate as a layered system rather than a single gate.

Those layers operate at different points in the payment journey. Onboarding tries to keep bad actors out before an account or merchant relationship begins. Authentication checks whether the correct customer is present. Authorization scoring decides whether a transaction should continue. Merchant monitoring looks for acquiring-side abuse. Dispute handling determines what happened after the fact and who has evidence.

Choosing the tolerance for uncertainty is the hard part: approve too freely and losses rise; decline too aggressively and good customers leave; challenge too often and conversion falls; review too much manually and operations slow down; trust merchants too easily and fake businesses enter the system; distrust them too broadly and legitimate businesses struggle to get paid.

A mature fraud program is judged by that balance: lower fraud losses, strong approval rates, fewer false positives, controlled customer friction, and fast detection of new attack patterns.

Fraud control is therefore a continuing operating function. When one channel becomes harder to attack, fraud moves to another. The system improves, attackers adapt, and the balance has to be managed again.

Chapter 42: GDPR and Payment Data

A payment record usually contains much more than payment details.

It can show where someone was, when the transaction happened, the device they used, the merchant they paid, the card or wallet involved, the authentication result, the issuer's risk decision, the fulfillment status, and any later complaint or dispute.

That information is useful across the payment chain. Banks rely on it for fraud detection, merchants for dispute and refund processing, PSPs for routing and failure investigation, support teams for customer service, and fintech products for spending insights.

It is also personal data.

In Europe, this brings payment data under the *General Data Protection Regulation* (*GDPR*). GDPR took effect in 2018, replacing an older European data-protection framework from the 1990s. The older rules were written before smartphones, cloud platforms, behavioral advertising, modern fintech apps, and large-scale data analytics became normal. GDPR updated the European privacy framework for a world in which companies collect, combine, and reuse personal data across many systems and borders.

For payment companies, GDPR sets the rules for how personal data is collected, used, shared, protected, retained, and deleted. It does not ban payment companies from processing data. It requires them to define a lawful basis, use data for clear purposes, limit unnecessary collection, protect the data, respect individual rights, and be able to explain what they are doing.

Payment data needs careful treatment because it can reveal behavior over time. A single transaction may not say much. A month of transactions can reveal a person's employer, commute, subscriptions, medical visits, political donations, religious activity, travel habits, financial stress, and social life.

Under GDPR, not all payment data is special category data. But payment records can reveal special-category information indirectly by exposing medical visits, religious donations, political activity, trade-union payments, or other sensitive patterns.

Some payment data is obviously personal: cardholder name, email address, billing address, phone number, or identity documents collected during onboarding. Other data becomes personal because it can be linked to a person. A Primary Account Number is *personal data* when it identifies or can identify a cardholder. A token can also be personal data if it can be linked back to a customer or account. Device identifiers, IP addresses, cookie IDs, and fraud signals can also fall within GDPR when they relate to an identifiable person.

That creates the central privacy tension in payments. Payment companies need data to operate safely and legally, but the GDPR says they cannot treat that data as free to use for any purpose.

Payment Data Categories

Payment systems handle several kinds of personal data.

The first is customer identity data: name, address, phone number, email address, date of birth, documents, selfie checks, and onboarding records.

The second is payment credential data: PAN, expiration date, token, wallet identifier, account number, IBAN, masked card number, cardholder reference, and customer ID.

The third is transaction data: merchant name, Merchant Category Code, amount, currency, date, time, location, channel, terminal, checkout session, authorization result, decline reason, refund, chargeback, and settlement reference.

The fourth is authentication and risk data: 3-D Secure result, device fingerprint, IP address, geolocation, behavioral signal, fraud score, velocity pattern, login history, challenge result, and customer communication.

Support and dispute data can be sensitive, too. A support agent may see transaction history, merchant descriptors, customer explanations, delivery evidence, screenshots, identity checks, and notes from previous interactions.

Tokenization, Masking, and Pseudonymization

Security tools can help with privacy, but they do not automatically remove GDPR obligations.

Tokenization replaces a sensitive value, such as a PAN, with a substitute value. This can reduce exposure and limit the number of systems handling raw card data.

Masking hides part of a value, such as showing only the last 4 digits of a card number in a support tool.

Pseudonymization means that personal data is processed so that it cannot be attributed to a specific person without additional information being kept separately. For example, an analytics table may use customer IDs rather than names and emails.

However, these methods are not equivalent to true anonymization.

If a token, masked record, or pseudonymous ID can still be linked back to a person using data the company holds, GDPR applies. True anonymization means the person cannot be identified by any reasonably likely means. That is much harder to achieve in payments because transaction patterns themselves can be identifying. A set of transactions may identify someone even without their name attached.

Controllers and Processors

GDPR distinguishes between a controller and a processor.

A controller decides why and how personal data is processed. A processor handles that data on the controller's behalf.

In payments, this distinction can get complicated because several parties may handle the same data for different reasons.

An issuer processes cardholder data to open card accounts, authorize transactions, prevent fraud, comply with the law, and support customers. For many of those activities, the issuer is a controller.

A merchant processes customer and transaction data to sell goods, fulfill orders, handle refunds, and manage customer support. For those activities, the merchant is often a controller.

A PSP may process payment data on behalf of the merchant, but it may also process some data for its own purposes, such as fraud monitoring, regulatory compliance, dispute handling, reporting, and platform security. Depending on the activity, the PSP may be a processor, an independent controller, or a joint controller.

An acquirer, processor, fraud vendor, cloud provider, identity verification provider, and analytics vendor may each have different roles depending on the processing activity.

The role determines obligations. Controllers need a legal basis, provide privacy notices, handle data subject rights, and decide retention purposes. Processors need data processing agreements, security controls, and instructions from the controller.

A payment company cannot meet GDPR requirements by calling every vendor a processor and moving on. The actual role depends on how the company uses the data, not just what the contract says.

Legal Bases for Processing

GDPR does not say companies can process personal data only with consent. *Consent* is one legal basis, but it is not the only one, and it is often not the right one for core payment activity.

GDPR provides six lawful bases for processing personal data: consent, performance of a contract, legal obligation, vital interests, public task, and legitimate interests. Payment companies most often rely on contract, legal obligation, and legitimate interests for core payment operations, while consent is usually reserved for optional activities such as certain marketing, non-essential cookies, or optional personalization.

A payment company may process data under contract when necessary to provide the service. A card issuer needs transaction data to operate the card account. A merchant needs payment and delivery data to fulfill an order.

A company may process data under legal obligation when the law requires it. AML checks, sanctions screening, tax records, accounting records, and certain reporting duties may fall under this category.

A company may rely on legitimate interest for activities such as fraud prevention, security monitoring, some analytics, and operational improvement, provided it balances its interest against the rights and interests of the individual.

Consent may be appropriate for optional activities such as some marketing uses, non-essential cookies, or certain personalization features. But consent must be specific, informed, freely given, and easy to withdraw. A company should not pretend that core payment processing depends on consent when the real basis is contract, legal obligation, or legitimate interest.

A lawful basis is not enough by itself. The company also needs to clearly explain the processing in its privacy notice: what data is collected, why it is used, who receives it, how long it is kept, and which rights the customer has.

The legal basis affects what the company can do later. Data collected to process a payment cannot automatically be reused for unrelated marketing. A passport collected for KYC cannot be casually used as material for a growth campaign. A fraud signal collected for risk control cannot be turned into broad commercial profiling without a proper basis and notice.

GDPR does not forbid using data. It requires companies to be disciplined about why they use it.

Data Minimization

Data minimization means collecting and using only the personal data needed for the stated purpose.

This principle is important in payments because payment companies are often tempted to collect more data "just in case": device data for fraud models, transaction history for segmentation, customer data for support, and behavioral data for product analytics.

Some extra data collection may be justified. But GDPR pushes companies to ask a harder question: what do we actually need?

A merchant selling a digital product may need payment confirmation and an email address, but a full date of birth is harder to justify. A PSP can collect device and IP data for fraud prevention without giving every product team access to raw device histories. A support tool can display a masked card number and the recent payment status without revealing the full PAN or detailed fraud-model signals.

Minimization also applies inside the company. Access should be limited by role. A fraud analyst, support agent, finance user, and marketing analyst should not, by default, see the same payment data.

Good privacy design often looks like good security design: collect less, share less, keep less, and make exceptions only when necessary.

Purpose Limitation

Purpose limitation means data collected for one purpose should not be reused for another incompatible purpose.

This principle constrains the availability of a commercially attractive dataset. Payment data can show spending patterns, income timing, merchant preferences, travel, subscriptions, and life events. A company may want to use it for personalization, credit offers, targeted campaigns, product analytics, merchant insights, or risk scoring.

Some uses may be allowed. Others may require additional notice, a different legal basis, aggregation, pseudonymization, or consent. Some may be inappropriate altogether.

A customer provides identity documents to pass KYC. The company can use those documents for identity verification, AML compliance, and required retention. It cannot use the passport photo to personalize advertising or enrich marketing profiles unless there is a separate lawful basis and a clearly compatible purpose.

Payment companies should therefore maintain a clear map between data, purpose, legal basis, retention period, and access rights.

Without this clear mapping, reusing data turns into guesswork.

Fraud Controls and Privacy

Fraud prevention creates one of the hardest GDPR tensions.

A fraud team may need broad data to protect customers and the payment system: device fingerprints, IP addresses, geolocation, transaction history, account age, failed attempts, merchant risk, delivery address, behavioral patterns, chargeback history, and known fraud links.

GDPR does not prevent fraud detection. Fraud prevention is a legitimate and often necessary purpose. A payment company that refuses to use data for fraud control may expose customers, merchants, and itself to serious harm. But fraud prevention does not give companies unlimited freedom.

Fraud-related processing still needs a lawful basis, a clear explanation in the privacy notice, access limited to those who need the data, retention rules, and safeguards against reuse for unrelated purposes.

Fraud models also raise questions about GDPR fairness and accuracy. A customer may be blocked because they traveled, changed devices, share a household with someone at risk, live in an area with higher fraud rates, or behave in ways the model treats as unusual. Some of those signals may be useful, but they can still produce wrong or unfair outcomes if the data is stale, incomplete, poorly weighted, or used without review.

Automated decision-making requires particular care when it significantly affects access to a payment account, a card, a credit product, or a transaction capability. A payment company needs governance around testing, monitoring, explanation, human review, and correction, especially when the model can block transactions, restrict an account, or deny a product.

The privacy question is not whether fraud prevention should exist. It should. The question is how to build it with a clear purpose, proportionate data use, limited retention, and safeguards for customers who are wrongly flagged.

Data Retention

GDPR gives individuals rights over their data, but payment companies often cannot delete everything on request.

Payments create legal, accounting, fraud, tax, audit, dispute, and AML obligations. A transaction record may be needed to investigate a chargeback months later. A merchant payout record may be needed for reconciliation. KYC data may need to be retained after the customer relationship ends. Tax and accounting records may have statutory retention periods.

Retention is therefore more complicated than simply deleting data when a customer asks.

A company needs a retention schedule. Different data categories should have different retention periods:

- authorization and transaction records;
- clearing and settlement records;
- invoices and accounting records;
- dispute and chargeback evidence;
- KYC and AML records;
- fraud alerts and investigation notes;

- support tickets;
- marketing preferences;
- device and session logs.

Some data can be deleted quickly. Some must be retained for years. Some can be archived with restricted access. Some can be anonymized or aggregated when individual-level detail is no longer needed.

Retention needs a justified purpose. Keeping everything forever "just in case" is not a policy, it is a risk.

Customer Rights

GDPR gives individuals rights over their personal data.

The most visible is the right of access. A customer can ask a company what personal data it holds about them. In a payment company, that may include profile data, transaction records, support notes, device data, and other information, subject to legal limits and protections for other parties.

Customers may also have the right to rectification if data is incorrect, the right to erasure in certain cases, the right to restrict processing, the right to data portability, and the right to object to certain processing.

These rights become harder to apply in payment operations.

If a customer requests deletion, the company may still need to retain transaction data for legal, accounting, AML, dispute, or fraud purposes. If a customer requests all data, the company may need to exclude information that could reveal security controls, fraud-detection methods, confidential merchant data, or data belonging to another person.

These requests also have deadlines. Under the GDPR, the controller generally has to respond without undue delay, within one month. That period can be extended in more complex cases, but the customer must still be informed of the delay.

The right approach is not to automatically reject privacy requests. Companies need processes that separate data types, explain what is possible, and respond on time.

Cross-Border Transfers

Payment systems are rarely local.

A European merchant may use a US-based fraud vendor, a cloud provider with global infrastructure, a PSP operating in several regions, and a support team outside the EEA. A card transaction may involve an issuer, an acquirer, a network, a processor, a token service, and merchant systems spread across several countries.

GDPR restricts transfers of personal data outside the EEA unless an approved mechanism authorizes the transfer. This may involve adequacy decisions, standard contractual clauses, transfer impact assessments, or other safeguards, depending on the destination and arrangement.

For payments, cross-border transfers are not rare. They are a normal part of how the system works.

A company, therefore, needs to know where payment data goes, which vendors receive it, which countries are involved, and which safeguards support the transfer. This is both a legal issue and a vendor-management issue.

If the data flow map is inaccurate, the analysis of transfers will be wrong as well.

Product Analytics and Personalization

Payment data is valuable for product analytics.

A fintech may want to understand where transactions fail, how often customers use wallets, which card controls are popular, which subscriptions are common, or which users are likely to churn. These uses can improve the product, but the dataset should match the purpose. A team investigating checkout failures usually does not need raw PANs, named customer histories, or detailed fraud-model signals. Aggregated or pseudonymized data is often enough.

Personalization requires more care because it changes how data is used at the individual level. Showing a customer a spending insight inside their own app is different from using transaction history to target offers, build behavioral segments, or share merchant-level insights with third parties.

The practical distinction is between improving the service the customer is using and reusing payment data for a new commercial purpose. The further the use moves from the original payment context, the stronger the need for a clear legal basis, transparent notice, tighter access controls, and, in some cases, consent.

Support Tooling

Support teams need data to solve customer problems.

Support cases quickly become data-access requests: one customer asks why a transaction was declined, another reports a duplicate charge, another does not recognize a merchant, and another wants proof of refund. A support agent needs enough information to help.

However, support tools can create privacy and security risks if they reveal too much information.

A well-designed support tool should show the minimum useful view: masked card number, transaction amount, merchant descriptor, status, relevant timestamps, refund status, dispute state, and safe notes. It should hide or restrict sensitive data, such as full PANs, CVV2 codes, detailed fraud-model signals, unnecessary device identifiers, or unrelated transaction history.

Access should also be logged. If support agents can view customer payment histories, the company needs to know who accessed what and why.

Support tooling should therefore be designed as a controlled view rather than a general-purpose window into the customer's financial life.

GDPR, PCI DSS, and Payment Rules

GDPR, PCI DSS, and payment network rules overlap, but they answer different questions.

PCI DSS asks whether card data is protected against exposure.

GDPR requires that personal data be processed lawfully, fairly, transparently, and only as needed.

Payment network rules address card acceptance, authentication, dispute resolution, and liability.

The same data can trigger all three regimes. A PAN is cardholder data under PCI DSS. It is also personal data under GDPR. It is also needed for authorization, clearing, dispute resolution, and network reporting.

A company that encrypts PANs may satisfy one security requirement but still fail GDPR if it uses transaction history for an incompatible purpose. A company with a privacy notice may still fail PCI DSS if it stores CVV2 data. A company that follows card network rules may still need a legal basis for its data processing.

Compliance frameworks are not interchangeable. Each one addresses a different type of risk.

The privacy challenge in payments comes from having too much useful data, not too little. A payment company can often see enough to fight fraud, support customers, build analytics, personalize products, satisfy regulators, and optimize revenue. Good product design does not treat all of those uses as equally justified. It separates what the company needs to process the payment, what it needs to manage risk, what it must retain for legal or dispute reasons, and what would be merely convenient for analysis or marketing.

GDPR does not stop payment companies from using data. It forces the product and operating model to define why the data is collected, who can access it, how long it is retained, when it is anonymized or deleted, and how the customer can exercise their rights.

In a payment product, privacy is therefore not only a legal notice. It affects event logging, fraud tooling, customer support screens, analytics pipelines, data retention jobs, access controls, consent flows, and the way transaction data is reused beyond the original payment.

Chapter 43: Onboarding, KYC, AML, and Scoring

In payment businesses, the first risk decision comes before any money actually moves.

Before a bank issues a card, a fintech opens a wallet, or a PSP enables a merchant to accept cards, the institution must determine who is requesting access. A retail customer could be a genuine person with normal spending needs. But they could also be using a stolen identity, acting as a money mule, applying for credit they do not plan to repay, or opening an account for someone else.

Merchants present a similar challenge. A business might be a real online shop, but it could also be a fake storefront, a front for illegal goods, a setup for transaction laundering, or a company that processes fraudulent sales and vanishes before chargebacks come in.

This is the purpose of onboarding. It is the gate before access: a sequence of identity, compliance, fraud, credit, and product-access checks that determines whether the applicant can be served, under what conditions, and with what limits.

Onboarding Risk Selection

A payment company cannot treat every applicant the same way.

The reason is risk exposure. A low-limit debit card for a retail customer, a credit card with a $10,000 limit, a personal wallet, a merchant account, a food delivery marketplace, and a gambling merchant do not pose the same risks to the institution. Each product changes the potential loss, regulatory requirements, fraud patterns, and the controls required before access is granted.

Every product comes with its own risk profile.

Onboarding is when the company decides whether the applicant fits that risk profile. This decision depends on laws, payment network rules, internal policies, fraud data, credit models, sanctions requirements, AML rules, and business strategy.

The result is not always a simple yes or no. A customer might be approved with lower limits. A merchant could be accepted, but with a rolling reserve. A credit applicant may receive a smaller line than they requested. Suspicious cases may be sent for manual review. Prohibited businesses can be declined right away.

To the customer, onboarding can look like filling out a form, uploading documents, and taking a selfie. Within the company, these seemingly simple steps trigger a structured sequence of decisions about identity, legality, risk, eligibility, and access, laying the crucial foundation for everything that follows.

Customer Onboarding

Customer onboarding typically starts with registration.

The customer provides basic information: name, date of birth, address, phone number, email address, country of residence, and sometimes tax or national identification details. The product also often collects device data, IP address, referral source, and behavioral signals during the application.

Registration establishes the customer profile, but it does not verify that the customer is real, eligible, or low risk.

The next stages usually include:

- KYC checks: verifying that the customer is who they claim to be;
- Anti-Money Laundering (AML) checks: assessing whether the customer creates financial crime risk;
- sanctions and Politically Exposed Person (PEP) screening: checking whether the customer is prohibited, restricted, or higher risk;
- fraud screening: looking for stolen identities, synthetic identities, mule behavior, device reuse, and suspicious application patterns;
- credit or product scoring: deciding whether the customer qualifies for a credit line, overdraft, Buy Now, Pay Later (BNPL) limit, or another risk-bearing product.

These checks can run in seconds, but each one answers a different question.

KYC and Customer Verification

Know Your Customer is the identity verification layer of onboarding.

The institution needs to know that the person applying is real and that they control the identity they present. In a branch, this once meant showing a passport to a bank employee. In a fintech app, it often means scanning a document, taking a selfie, and passing automated checks.

A common digital KYC flow includes:

- document capture, such as a passport, national ID card, or residence permit;
- data extraction using OCR;
- document authenticity checks;
- selfie or video capture;
- liveness detection;
- face match between the document and the selfie;
- address verification where required;
- manual review if the automated checks are uncertain.

The goal is to connect a real person to the account being opened, using the document as evidence rather than as an end in itself.

Liveness detection addresses a specific attack: a fraudster may have a photo of the victim's passport, a stolen selfie, or a manipulated image. The system needs to know whether a live person is present during onboarding. That can involve a short video, movement prompts, passive liveness checks, or other techniques, depending on the provider.

KYC also creates an evidence record. If the account later becomes suspicious, the institution needs to know what identity was verified, which document was used, when verification happened, which provider performed the check, and whether any reviewer overrode a warning.

KYC acts as both an entry control and a record for future reference.

AML and Financial Crime Controls

KYC asks, "Who is this person?"

Anti-Money Laundering asks a different question: "Does this person or their activity create financial crime risk?"

Money laundering means making illicit funds appear legitimate. Payment institutions, banks, and fintechs are attractive targets because they provide access to accounts, cards, transfers, wallets, and payouts. Criminals look for the weakest entry point: one institution with poor onboarding, weak monitoring, or loose controls can be enough.

AML controls usually combine several checks.

The institution first builds a customer risk profile from factors such as country, occupation, expected activity, source of funds, requested product, transaction behavior, and other risk indicators.

It then screens the customer against sanctions lists and other watchlists. A true sanctions match can legally prohibit onboarding or transaction processing, so this is not just another risk score.

PEP screening is different. It applies to those whose prominent public roles, family relationships, or associations pose a higher risk of corruption or bribery. PEP status requires enhanced checks but does not imply wrongdoing.

Adverse media screening looks for credible reports of fraud, corruption, money laundering, sanctions violations, terrorism financing, or other serious misconduct.

Finally, AML continues after onboarding. A customer who appeared normal at account opening can later change behavior, be added to a new sanctions list, become a PEP, or have unusual funds deposited into a dormant account. AML, therefore, continues through transaction monitoring, rescreening, periodic reviews, investigation, and escalation throughout the customer relationship.

Source of Funds and Source of Wealth

Two phrases often appear in AML work: *source of funds* and *source of wealth.*

Source of funds refers to the origin of the funds in a specific transaction or account. Examples include salary, business revenue, property sales, inheritance, investment income, and savings. The institution may ask for payslips, bank statements, contracts, invoices, or other evidence.

The source-of-wealth question asks how the customer accumulated their wealth. This is broader. It is especially relevant for high-net-worth customers, private banking, high-risk customers, large transactions, and enhanced due diligence.

A normal retail card customer usually is not asked detailed source-of-wealth questions. A high-risk customer, a PEP, or a merchant processing large cross-border flows may be asked much more.

The key is proportionality. A student opening a low-limit debit account should not be treated the same as a company moving millions across borders. But the institution also cannot ignore suspicious facts just to keep onboarding easy.

Sanctions and PEP Screening

Sanctions screening is one of the least flexible parts of the onboarding process.

Sanctions are legal restrictions imposed by governments or international bodies, such as OFAC in the United States, the United Nations, the European Union, or national treasury authorities. They may target individuals, companies, vessels, countries, sectors, or specific activities. If a person or entity is sanctioned, a payment company may be prohibited from onboarding them, providing services to them, or processing transactions involving them.

Screening may sound simple: compare the applicant's name to a list. In practice, it is much harder.

Names can be transliterated in several ways, dates of birth may be missing, addresses may be incomplete, and common names create false matches. A customer can share a name with a sanctioned person without being that person. A company can look clean at first glance while being indirectly controlled by a sanctioned owner.

Screening usually generates alerts rather than final answers. A system might flag a possible match, and a human reviewer checks identifiers, documents, ownership, location, and context to decide whether it is a true match or a false alarm.

PEP screening works differently. A *Politically Exposed Person* is not prohibited by default. The term usually covers people who hold, or have held, prominent public functions, such as senior government officials, judges, military leaders, senior political party officials, or executives of state-owned enterprises. Depending on the rules, close family members and close associates may also be treated as higher risk.

Institutions can serve PEPs but often require senior approval, source-of-wealth checks, and enhanced monitoring.

Sanctions screening can legally block someone. PEP screening identifies a higher-risk relationship that needs extra controls.

Fraud Screening at Onboarding

Fraud screening during onboarding identifies applicants who should never reach the transaction stage.

A customer can be real and still be a fraud risk.

Fraudsters use stolen documents, manipulated selfies, synthetic identities, mule networks, or repeated applications across devices and phone numbers. They may apply for multiple accounts, test weak onboarding controls, or use a real person's identity with a controlled phone number and email address.

Common onboarding-fraud signals include repeated applications, reused documents, newly created contact details, mismatched location signals, failed liveness checks, referral abuse, and addresses linked to many unrelated applicants.

Fraud screening is different from AML. AML looks at financial crime risk, banned parties, money laundering, and suspicious funds. Fraud screening checks whether the applicant is genuine and whether the account might be misused.

The two overlap, especially with mule accounts. A money mule may be a real person who opens an account and allows criminals to use it. KYC may pass because the person is real. Fraud and AML monitoring may still need to detect that the account is being used to move someone else's money.

Credit Scoring

Not every payment product creates credit risk. A prepaid card or fully funded debit card primarily poses fraud, AML, operational, and compliance risks. A credit card, overdraft, BNPL product, or charge card creates another question: will the customer repay?

Credit scoring estimates the probability that a customer will meet their repayment obligations.

The inputs can include credit bureau data, income, employment status, existing debt, repayment history, account behavior, bank transaction data, internal history, and product-specific risk signals.

The output is not only an approve-or-decline decision. Scoring can determine:

- credit limit;
- interest rate;
- deposit requirement;
- repayment terms;
- product eligibility;
- manual review requirement;
- whether the customer starts with a restricted product and graduates later.

Two customers can both pass KYC and AML and still receive very different offers. One receives only a debit card, another receives a credit line, and a third starts with a small limit that can increase after good repayment behavior.

Merchant Onboarding and KYB

Merchant onboarding is the business version of the same gatekeeping problem, but the exposure is often larger.

A merchant does not only use a payment product. It receives money from many cardholders. If the merchant is fraudulent, insolvent, prohibited, or poorly controlled, the acquirer or PSP may face chargebacks, refunds, regulatory issues, and network penalties.

Know Your Business (KYB) is the process of verifying a business customer.

A typical KYB process includes:

- legal business name and registration number;
- registered address and operating address;
- directors and authorized representatives;

- beneficial ownership;
- tax information;
- website and product review;
- business model;
- expected transaction volume;
- countries served;
- delivery model;
- refund policy;
- Merchant Category Code;
- bank account ownership;
- sanctions, PEP, and adverse media checks on the business and key individuals.

Beneficial ownership is central. A company can look clean on paper, but the real risk depends on who owns or controls it. Regulators and acquirers need to know whether the business is controlled by sanctioned parties, criminals, hidden nominees, or high-risk individuals.

The website review provides the acquirer with evidence of what the merchant actually sells. A merchant may claim to sell clothing but actually sell counterfeit goods, adult content, gambling services, financial products, or prohibited items. The acquirer or PSP must verify whether the declared business matches the actual business.

KYB is risk underwriting. It is how the acquirer decides if a merchant should be allowed into the card system.

Ongoing Monitoring

Onboarding marks the beginning of the relationship, not the end of risk management.

Customers, merchants, ownership structures, and sanctions lists all change over time. A business that appeared low-risk at onboarding may begin processing prohibited goods, a customer who opened a normal wallet may start receiving suspicious transfers, and a merchant may suddenly process volume far above forecast.

Ongoing monitoring catches those changes.

For customers, monitoring may include transaction patterns, account activity, failed logins, device changes, unusual transfers, sanctions rescreening, and periodic KYC refresh.

For merchants, monitoring may include processing volume, average ticket size, refund rate, chargeback ratio, MCC consistency, website changes, customer complaints, negative media, and payout behavior.

Monitoring works best when the institution defines clear review triggers. A small change should not require manual review for every account. But certain changes should raise concerns: sudden volume spikes, new countries, new product categories, rising chargebacks, many refunds, suspicious counterparties, or repeated login anomalies.

Weak onboarding lets bad actors enter the system. Weak monitoring lets risk grow after a relationship has already been approved.

Onboarding as Product Design

Onboarding is often treated as a compliance step. For customers, it is one of the first product experiences.

Onboarding has to balance opposing failures: a slow process drives away good customers, a weak one lets in bad actors, a rigid one rejects legitimate cases, an unclear one creates support tickets, and poorly explained document requests erode trust.

Product teams face a difficult challenge: collecting enough information to meet risk and regulatory needs without making users feel like suspects.

A better sequence can reduce friction without weakening the control.

A low-risk wallet may start with light access and increase limits after more verification. A card product may issue a virtual card first and require more checks for credit or high limits. A merchant may start with restricted processing and earn faster payouts once it builds a stable history. A suspicious user may be escalated to additional checks, while ordinary users are processed quickly.

This approach is called risk-based onboarding. The product asks each applicant for what is needed for their level of access, not everything at once.

Approval, Limits, and Rejection

Good onboarding sometimes means refusing access: customers who cannot be identified, sanctioned parties, unsupported business types, applicants with strong fraud signals, or credit exposure the institution does not want to carry.

It also means approving carefully. A real customer may still be unsuitable for a credit line. A legitimate merchant may still need reserves. A PEP may be acceptable only with enhanced due diligence. A new business may start with lower limits until it builds a track record.

The real job of onboarding is not just collecting documents, but deciding what kind of access to give.

The payment system does not wait for the first suspicious transaction to manage risk. It starts as soon as a person or business applies to join.

With the main security, fraud, privacy, and onboarding controls in place, Part VIII shifts from card rails to bank transfer rails. Many of the same questions remain, but they appear under different message formats, settlement systems, and liability models.

Part VIII

Bank Payment Rails

Chapter 44: Bank Transfers and Card Payments

Cards and bank transfers can both move money between people and businesses, but they are built on different foundations.

A card payment begins as a request to accept a card transaction. The merchant asks the issuer for authorization; the issuer responds in real time; and later stages turn that accepted transaction into clearing records, settlement positions, and merchant payouts.

A *bank transfer* begins as an instruction to move money between accounts. One account holder tells their bank to send money to another account, or authorizes a payee to collect from the account under a mandate.

That difference changes who initiates the payment, what is checked in real time, when funds move, whether the payment is final, what protections exist, what information travels with the payment, and which use cases each system serves best.

Card Acceptance

Most card payments begin on the merchant side of the system.

The customer presents a card, phone, wallet, or card details. The merchant's system collects payment information and sends an authorization request through the system's acquiring side. In stores, this starts at the payment terminal. Online, it starts at the checkout page and moves through a gateway or PSP, an acquirer, a payment network, and the issuer.

The customer taps, inserts, or enters card details, but the merchant sends the payment request. The merchant is requesting permission to process a transaction against the customer's card account or credit line.

Card payments are often referred to as pull payments. The cardholder consents, but the merchant side initiates the request. The merchant's acquirer sends the request through the card network, and the issuer decides whether to approve it.

This setup is useful for businesses because merchants can accept cards from many issuers without having to connect directly to each bank. The payment network sets the rules, message formats, standards, dispute processes, and settlement methods.

A coffee shop does not need a direct connection to thousands of banks. It connects to its acquirer or payment service provider, and the card network handles the routing and transaction rules.

That wide acceptance across banks, countries, products, and cardholders is one of the card system's main strengths.

Bank Account Instructions

Most bank credit transfers start with the account holder sending the money. The payer opens a banking app, enters the recipient's account details or alias, chooses an amount, and confirms the payment. The sending bank validates the instruction, checks whether the account can send the money, and processes the payment through the appropriate rail.

In Europe, a typical account transfer uses SEPA Credit Transfer or SEPA Instant. In the United States, common rails include ACH Credit, Real-Time Payments (RTP), FedNow, and wire transfers. In the United Kingdom, bank transfers commonly use Faster Payments, Bacs, or CHAPS. Cross-border bank payments often use Society for Worldwide Interbank Financial Telecommunication (SWIFT) messages and correspondent banking.

Here, the bank account is central, not the card.

This leads to a different way of thinking. Card payments ask an issuer to approve a merchant's charge against a card account. Bank transfers tell one bank to send money to another account.

There may be intermediaries, clearing systems, settlement systems, and messaging networks, but the core model is still account-to-account.

Bank transfers are used for salaries, invoices, rent, taxes, supplier payments, bills, treasury movements, government payments, and sending money to other people. They were not mainly designed for retail checkout, although instant payments and open banking are starting to change that.

Push, Pull, and the Direct Debit Exception

Most bank credit transfers are push payments. The sender starts the transfer and pushes funds to the recipient.

This is how salary payments, supplier payments, transfers to friends, and instant account-to-account payments usually work. The sender's bank receives the instruction and sends the money through the relevant rail.

Direct debit is the main exception to bank transfers.

With *direct debit*, the payee starts the process. A utility company, insurer, gym, subscription service, or lender collects money from the payer's bank account with prior authorization. The payer does not approve each payment as it happens. They agreed in advance through a mandate.

This makes direct debit resemble the card pull model, but it is still not a card payment. It uses bank accounts and mandates instead of card credentials, and it has its own rules for returns, refunds, timing, and customer protection.

The distinction can be summarized this way:

- Most credit transfers are payer-initiated pushes.
- Card purchases are merchant-initiated acceptance requests based on cardholder consent.
- Direct debits are payee-initiated bank account pulls authorized by a mandate.

Clearing and Settlement Patterns

Cards and bank transfers both use the terms *clearing* and *settlement*, but their operational meanings differ.

In cards, the merchant receives an immediate authorization response, while later stages produce clearing records, settlement positions, and merchant payout. The details vary by network and region, but the broad lifecycle is familiar by now: authorization first, clearing later, and settlement afterward.

Bank transfers are less uniform. Once the sending bank accepts the payment instruction, the rail determines the next steps. ACH-style systems process payments in batches. Real-time gross settlement (RTGS) systems such as Fedwire and CHAPS settle individual high-value payments in central bank money. SEPA Credit Transfer moves through the European clearing and settlement infrastructure, while SEPA Instant provides near-real-time availability. RTP and FedNow are instant payment rails. SWIFT is different again: it carries payment messages, while settlement happens through correspondent accounts and local systems.

That is why the same words can be misleading. Clearing in a card system does not follow the same operational process as clearing in ACH, SEPA, CHIPS, or another bank payment system. Settlement within a card network does not look like settlement in a central bank RTGS system. Batch processing in ACH is different from batch card clearing.

Finality, Reversibility, and Customer Protection

Finality refers to the point at which a payment is considered settled and cannot normally be reversed through the payment system itself. It is one of the clearest differences between card payments and bank transfers.

A card payment is not final in the same way as a wire, RTGS payment, or instant credit transfer. Card networks have dispute and chargeback rules that allow a cardholder to challenge a transaction after the sale, but the payment is not freely reversible at the cardholder's request. If the cardholder does not recognize a transaction, did not receive goods, was charged twice, or was billed incorrectly, the issuer can raise a dispute through the network. The merchant can respond with evidence, and the acquirer represents the merchant's side of the process. The result is a formal post-transaction process with evidence requirements, time limits, and network rules, not an automatic undo button.

Many bank transfers become harder to unwind once settled. A wire transfer, high-value RTGS payment, or instant credit transfer cannot usually be reversed through the ordinary payment flow unless the recipient agrees or a specific recovery process applies. If a customer sends money to the wrong person, the bank may try to recover the funds, but the result depends on the payment system, country, bank policy, and whether the recipient cooperates.

The difference becomes especially visible in merchant disputes. If a customer pays a merchant by bank transfer and does not receive the goods, the issue may become legal, fraud-related, or a bank support issue. It is not usually handled like a card chargeback because the bank transfer rail was not built around merchant acceptance and network-dispute rights.

Direct debit differs in that the payee collects funds from the payer's account under a mandate. Direct debit schemes, therefore, usually include the right to return or obtain a refund. In SEPA Direct Debit, for example, the payer has strong refund protections, especially under the core scheme. These protections come from the direct-debit mandate and scheme rules, not from chargebacks on card networks.

This is one reason cards remain popular for online shopping. They offer not only a way to pay but also a well-established system for acceptance and disputes. Bank transfers can be cheaper and faster in some cases, but their protection model is different.

The fraud consequence is clear. With an instant credit push, there is often little time to intervene once the payment has been approved and settled.

Payment Data Differences

Card payments and bank transfers carry different types of information.

A card authorization message is designed for quick decisions. It includes card number or token, amount, merchant ID, merchant category, terminal type, country, currency, authentication details, and transaction IDs. The issuer needs this information to quickly approve, decline, or challenge the payment.

A bank transfer message focuses on the accounts and parties involved. It may include sender and receiver details, account numbers, bank identifiers, payment notes, purpose, references, addresses, and regulatory information.

For business payments, the important fields are often not only the amount but also the remittance information: invoice number, customer reference, purpose code, structured creditor reference, or another identifier that allows the recipient to match the incoming payment to the correct obligation.

These differences reflect how each system is used.

Cards need quick approval at checkout. Bank transfers often need to support reconciliation, accounting, invoice matching, compliance checks, and tracking funds between accounts.

Many modern bank payment systems use ISO 20022 messages because they can carry richer, more structured data than older formats. That richer data helps companies match payments to invoices, helps banks check names and parties, and reduces manual repair when payment details are incomplete or ambiguous.

Cards and Bank Transfers in the Payment Mix

If bank transfers can move money directly, why do we still use cards?

Because direct account movement is only one part of what a payment system must do.

Merchants want broad acceptance, quick checkout responses, fraud controls, dispute rules, reliable funding, easy integration with PSPs and acquirers, and the ability to sell to customers across many banks and countries. Cards were built around those needs.

Payroll departments, governments, businesses, and consumers often need something different: low-cost account movement, reconciliation references, direct settlement between bank accounts, and rails suited to salaries, invoices, taxes, rent, treasury movements, and person-to-person transfers.

The boundary is not fixed. Instant payments, QR codes, open banking, request-to-pay, and account-to-account checkout are pushing bank transfers into retail and online commerce. Card networks are also expanding beyond purchases through push-to-card payouts, tokenization, wallets, and additional services. Even so, the underlying models remain different.

Person-to-person payments follow the same naming trap. P2P describes who is paying whom, not the rail underneath. A transfer between two people can run over a bank rail, a card network push payment service, or an internal wallet ledger. We saw push-to-card in Chapter 35, and Chapters 50 and 51 return to wallet-ledger and open-banking payments. For now, the key point is that the user experience does not always reveal the underlying payment system.

No single system is best for every situation. Cards are strong where acceptance, authorization, and buyer protection are central. Bank transfers are strong where direct account movement, lower cost, richer payment data, or final settlement are more important.

Chapter 45: ACH and US Bank Rails

There is no single US bank transfer rail.

US bank transfers use several systems for distinct needs. ACH manages high-volume batch payments like payroll, bills, tax refunds, and business transfers. Fedwire handles high-value transfers with final settlement. RTP and FedNow offer instant account-to-account payments. *Zelle* lets consumers send P2P payments easily, but it isn't a base settlement rail.

The US payment landscape becomes easier to read once these systems are separated by speed, finality, cost, direction, and use case.

ACH Network

With this landscape in mind, let's turn first to ACH, which underpins many familiar payment types in the US.

It was built in the 1970s to replace the manual processing of paper checks. Before electronic clearing, checks had to be physically transported, sorted, presented, and settled between banks. ACH kept the interbank-payment idea behind checks but replaced physical presentment with electronic files and batch processing.

ACH is not flashy. It does not process payments instantly or provide customers with the immediate feedback they get when tapping a card or seeing a real-time confirmation. But its scale is enormous: in 2025, Nacha reported that the ACH Network processed 35.2 billion payments totaling $93 trillion.

ACH carries payroll, bill payments, business transfers, taxes, benefits, account funding, subscriptions, and other account-to-account flows.

ACH supports two basic directions:

- ACH Credit: the sender pushes funds to the receiver.
- ACH Debit: the receiver pulls funds from the sender's account under

prior authorization.

A salary payment is typically an ACH Credit. The employer sends money to the employee.

A utility bill or mortgage payment is often an ACH Debit. The biller withdraws funds from the customer's account after the customer has authorized recurring collections.

This push-and-pull idea follows the distinction introduced in the previous chapter. A credit entry sends money out, while a debit entry collects money in.

ACH Credit

Payroll best illustrates ACH Credit.

An employer needs to pay hundreds or thousands of employees. Each employee may have an account at a different bank. The employer does not want to send individual wires. It wants one low-cost file that can be processed across the banking system.

ACH is designed for exactly this.

Figure 45.1 traces the payroll file through the employer's bank, the ACH operator, and each employee's bank. The employer, called the originator, prepares payroll instructions. Often, a payroll processor such as ADP, Gusto, or another provider prepares the file on the employer's behalf. The employer's bank is the Originating Depository Financial Institution (ODFI). The employee's bank is the Receiving Depository Financial Institution (RDFI).

The ACH operators sit between them. There are two: FedACH, operated by the Federal Reserve, and the Electronic Payments Network (EPN), operated by The Clearing House. They are interoperable, so a payment can enter through one operator and reach a bank connected through the other.

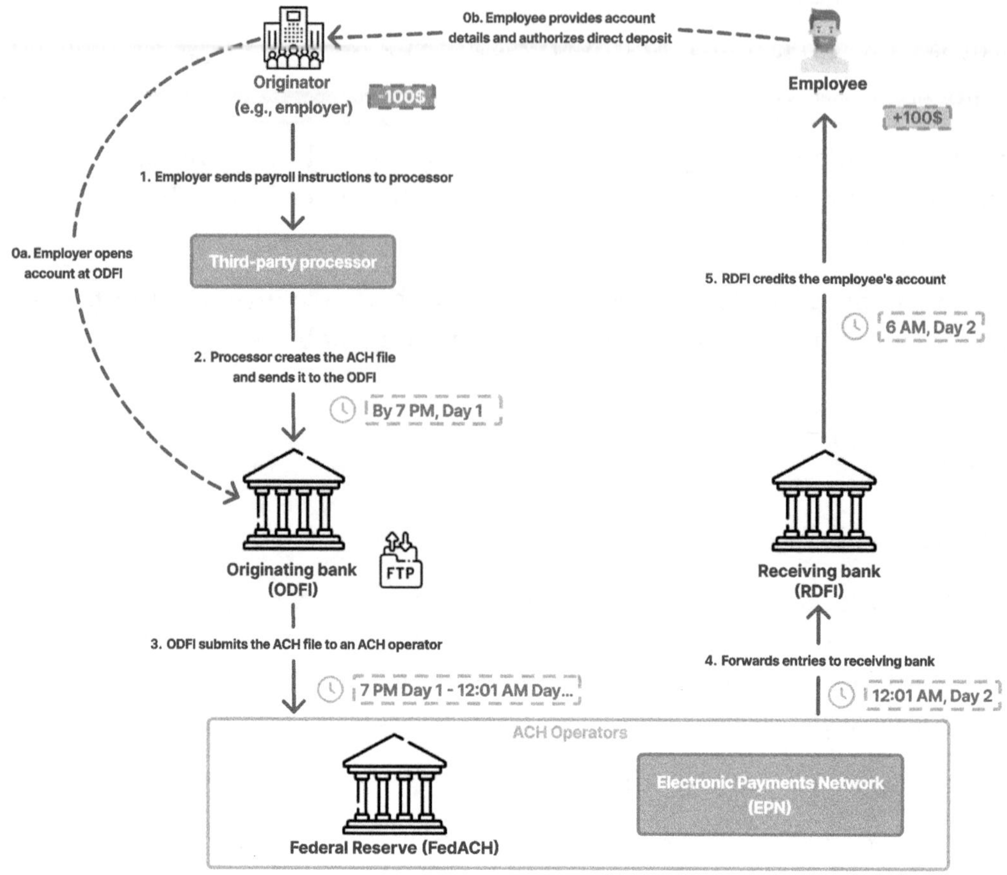

Figure 45.1: ACH payroll flow.

The flow is simple in concept:

1. The employer compiles payroll payments.
2. The payroll processor creates an ACH file and sends it to the ODFI.
3. The ODFI submits the file to an ACH operator.
4. The ACH operator sorts and forwards entries to the relevant RDFIs.
5. Each RDFI credits its customer's account.

The employee sees the result: salary arrives in the account.

A file-based network ensures smooth processing of large payment volumes.

The ODFI/RDFI structure exists because the originator and receiver usually do not bank at the same institution.

An employer might bank with JPMorgan Chase, while employees use Bank of America, a credit union, or a small community bank. The employer does not need separate connections to each receiving bank. It sends payroll through its own bank, the ODFI. The ACH operator sorts the entries and delivers them to the correct RDFIs.

If both parties used the same bank, ACH would not be needed for that payment. The bank could move funds internally. ACH exists because the US banking system is large, fragmented, and made up of thousands of institutions that need a standardized way to exchange payment entries.

ACH Debit

ACH Debit operates in the opposite direction.

The receiver of funds initiates the collection. A utility company, lender, insurer, subscription service, or gym requests to withdraw funds from the customer's account. The customer must first authorize the debit, usually through an online agreement, form, or account setup process.

Once authorization is in place, the biller can submit debit entries through its ODFI. The ACH operator routes the debit to the customer's RDFI. The customer's bank posts the debit to the account, unless the transaction is returned.

ACH Debit is used for recurring payments: mortgage collections, rent, insurance premiums, utilities, subscriptions, and loan repayments.

ACH Debit comes with different risks than ACH Credit. Since the payee starts the debit, the system needs rules for authorization and returns. Customers can dispute unauthorized debits, and banks can return payments for insufficient funds, closed or invalid accounts, unauthorized debits, or stop payments.

ACH return codes specify why an entry was returned, such as insufficient funds, closed or invalid accounts, stop payments, or unauthorized debits.

Standard ACH Batch Processing

ACH is a batch system. Payments are grouped into files, sent at specific processing times, sorted by an ACH operator, and then delivered to the correct banks. Settlement happens on a set schedule, not instantly when someone sends a payment.

This setup keeps ACH affordable and capable of handling large volumes of routine payments that do not require immediate settlement.

Payroll is the classic example. A company knows the payroll date in advance. It can prepare the file in advance. The employee does not need each salary entry to be a real-time payment. The money just needs to arrive reliably on payday.

Many bills, subscriptions, government benefits, and business payments follow this pattern.

The main drawback is timing. ACH processes on banking schedules, so weekends, holidays, and cut-off times affect when payments are delivered and settled. A payment sent after the cut-off may not arrive until the next cycle.

ACH is therefore not designed for situations in which both parties need immediate confirmation that the payment is final.

Same Day ACH

Same Day ACH is an enhancement to ACH, not a separate instant rail.

It allows eligible ACH payments to settle on the same business day if they are submitted within the required processing windows. This is useful for time-sensitive payroll corrections, insurance payments, account funding, tax payments, and business disbursements.

Same Day ACH improves the timing of ordinary ACH without changing its basic design. A payment submitted early enough can settle later the same business day, which is fast enough for many payroll, funding, and disbursement use cases.

That improvement has a clear limit: same-day settlement is still not real-time settlement. Same Day ACH remains batch-based, uses business-day processing windows, and does not operate continuously. RTP and FedNow are different because they process individual payments in real time, around the clock.

Same Day ACH has a per-payment limit of $1 million. Nacha has approved an increase to $10 million effective September 17, 2027. That future increase expands Same Day ACH's usefulness for larger business payments, but it does not change the rail's batch-based design.

Fedwire: High-Value Real-Time Settlement

ACH is designed to handle large volumes of routine payments. Fedwire is designed for high-value payments where final settlement is more important than low cost.

Fedwire is the Federal Reserve's real-time gross settlement system for US dollar payments. It is used for high-value and time-critical transfers between banks, financial institutions, corporations, and government entities.

The phrase real-time gross settlement describes the core design.

Fedwire is a real-time gross settlement system: payments are processed continuously during operating hours, settle one by one rather than in net batches, and move balances between participating banks' accounts at the Federal Reserve.

Once a Fedwire payment is settled, it is final in the payment system. Recovering funds after that point requires a separate legal, operational, or recipient-cooperation process rather than an ordinary reversal of the payment.

That makes Fedwire suitable for large-value payments where certainty is more valuable than low cost: interbank transfers, securities settlement funding, corporate treasury movements, real estate closings, and other high-value transactions.

Fedwire is not used for ordinary utility bills or routine payroll. It is too costly and operationally heavy for everyday low-value payments. ACH suits better for those.

RTP: Private-Sector Instant Payments

RTP stands for Real-Time Payments.

It is an instant payment network operated by The Clearing House. It launched in 2017 and was the first new core US payment rail in decades. RTP supports credit-push payments that settle in seconds and operate 24/7/365.

RTP is not ACH, a card network, or Zelle. It is an instant account-to-account payment system.

A sender initiates an RTP payment through a participating financial institution. The payment is sent to the receiver's financial institution in real time. The receiver's account is credited immediately. Both sides receive confirmation.

RTP also supports features such as payment requests, in which a biller or merchant can send a request, and the payer can approve a credit push. This keeps payments a push model from the payer while giving businesses a way to prompt payment.

RTP is useful for:

- instant account-to-account transfers;
- wallet funding and withdrawals;
- earned wage access;
- insurance payouts;
- marketplace disbursements;
- bill payments;
- business payments that require immediate confirmation.

The RTP network supports transactions up to $10 million. Bank-level limits and customer availability can still differ.

RTP changes what customers and businesses can expect from account-to-account payments: confirmation in seconds and funds available right away.

FedNow: Federal Reserve Instant Payments

FedNow is the Federal Reserve's instant payment service.

It went live on July 20, 2023, and, like RTP, supports real-time account-to-account credit-push payments. It operates 24/7/365 and settles payments in central bank money through Federal Reserve infrastructure.

FedNow exists alongside RTP. It does not replace RTP, and RTP does not replace FedNow. The United States has two major instant payment rails: one operated by The Clearing House and one operated by the Federal Reserve.

By late 2025, both RTP and FedNow had raised their network transaction limits to $10 million. Bank-level limits, availability of participating institutions, customer eligibility, and product configuration can still differ.

FedNow provides another path to instant payments for institutions that already maintain relationships with the Federal Reserve. But adoption takes time. A payment system only works well when both the sender's and receiver's banks are connected or can access the service.

FedNow and RTP do not replace ACH. ACH remains cheaper and widely used for regular batch payments. Instant payment systems are better when speed, confirmation, and immediate availability of funds are more important than cost.

Zelle as a P2P Overlay

Zelle is a bank-based person-to-person payment network. Its value is the user experience: a customer sends money using a phone number or email address instead of entering routing and account numbers. The service is integrated into many US banking apps, which makes it feel like a native bank transfer.

Zelle's bank-integrated model became even clearer after the standalone Zelle app stopped supporting payments in 2025, pushing users toward participating banks and credit unions. The service is primarily experienced inside bank and credit union apps.

Zelle is not a core settlement system like ACH or Fedwire.

Instead, Zelle is a layer that connects banks via a directory and a user-facing messaging experience. The way money actually moves depends on the banks involved and their systems.

Zelle feels instant, simple, and bank-native, but its risk profile often resembles that of authorized push payment fraud. The customer initiates the transfer, so the issue is not usually a stolen credential or an unauthorized card transaction. The issue is manipulation: the customer was deceived into approving the payment.

That is different from a stolen-card transaction. In card fraud, the customer usually says, "I did not make this payment." In many Zelle scams, the customer did make the payment but was manipulated into doing so.

Instant and near-instant bank P2P systems, therefore, need protections against scams: recipient verification, clear warnings, customer education, transaction monitoring, and recovery workflows where available. Speed is useful, but it leaves less time to stop a bad payment.

Comparing the Main US Rails

The simplest way to understand the different US payment systems is to look at what each one was designed to do.

Rail	Basic Model	Speed	Direction	Typical Use Cases	Finality / Reversibility
ACH	Batch clearing	Next business day or same business day	Credit and debit	Payroll, bills, benefits, subscriptions, account funding, B2B	Returns possible under ACH rules
Fedwire	Real-time gross settlement	Real-time during operating hours	Credit push	High-value bank and corporate payments	Final once settled
RTP	Instant account-to-account rail	Seconds, 24/7/365	Credit push	Instant transfers, disbursements, bill pay, wallet movement, business payments	Immediate; recovery is limited after acceptance
FedNow	Federal Reserve instant rail	Seconds, 24/7/365	Credit push	Instant transfers, disbursements, bill pay, wallet movement, business payments	Immediate; recovery is limited after acceptance
Zelle	Bank-based P2P overlay	Near-real-time from the user's perspective	Credit push	P2P payments through bank apps	Recovery depends on rules, bank policy, and circumstances

US Payment Rail Mix

The US payment system can seem complicated because it is layered rather than unified.

ACH came from check replacement and batch processing. Fedwire serves high-value final settlement. RTP and FedNow provide instant account-to-account transfers. Zelle gives consumers a bank-app P2P experience across participating institutions.

Despite the newer rails, ACH remains important because not every payment needs instant settlement. Payroll files, recurring bills, government payments, subscription collections, account funding, and many business transfers can be scheduled, batched, and processed at low cost. Instant rails are better when timing, confirmation, and immediate availability of funds are central. ACH is still well-suited to routine payments where predictability and broad reach are more useful than speed.

Banks, fintechs, payroll providers, lenders, merchants, and corporates therefore do not choose a generic bank transfer. They choose a rail based on cost, timing, finality, reach, reversibility, risk controls, and customer experience.

No single rail fits every use case. ACH, Same Day ACH, Fedwire, RTP, FedNow, Zelle, and card payments each solve a different combination of speed, cost, finality, reach, and reversal risk.

Chapter 46: SEPA and European Bank Rails

In an account-to-account payment, the starting point is a bank account. The payer sends an instruction, or the creditor collects under a mandate. Banks exchange payment messages, and settlement happens through the banking infrastructure rather than a card network.

In Europe, the Single Euro Payments Area (SEPA) is the shared framework for euro account-to-account payments across participating countries. It was created so that euro transfers between countries such as Germany and France, or Spain and Italy, could follow the same basic rules, formats, and expectations as domestic transfers.

SEPA is a family of euro bank payment schemes, not a single payment method. Its main instruments are:

- SEPA Credit Transfer (SCT), for standard euro push payments;
- SEPA Instant Credit Transfer (SCT Inst), for euro push payments processed within seconds;
- SEPA Direct Debit (SDD), for pull payments based on a customer mandate.

Together, these schemes make account-to-account payments a normal part of European financial life: salaries, invoices, rent, subscriptions, merchant payments, open banking flows, and personal transfers can all start from bank accounts rather than card credentials.

European Payment Standardization

Before SEPA, a cross-border euro payment within Europe behaved like an international wire transfer.

For example, a business in Germany paying a supplier in France used to deal with different forms, bank identifiers, fees, and processing times compared with domestic payments. Even though the money remained within Europe, the banking systems did not act as a single market.

SEPA changed what people expect from cross-border euro payments.

Now, euro payments within the SEPA zone are standardized. The sender uses an IBAN, banks use ISO 20022 message formats, and common rules apply to credit transfers and direct debits. Cross-border euro payments in SEPA should no longer feel like special international transactions.

SEPA provides a common foundation for euro account-to-account payments, while banks still differ in limits, pricing, interfaces, fraud controls, customer experience, and local habits.

For businesses and consumers, the practical change was simple: a euro transfer across participating countries became closer to a domestic bank transfer than to an international wire.

IBAN and Bank Identifier Codes

Every SEPA payment requires an account identifier to be credited.

The main identifier is the International Bank Account Number (IBAN). An IBAN is a structured code that includes a country code, check digits, and a national account identifier. That national part usually contains bank and account information, but the exact structure varies by country.

A German IBAN looks like this: DE 44 1001 0010 1234 5678 95.

Part	Example	Meaning
Country code	DE	Germany
Check digits	44	Validation digits
Bank identifier	1001 0010	Identifies the bank
Account number	1234 5678 95	Identifies the account

The check digits help catch errors. If someone enters an IBAN incorrectly, the system can often spot the mistake before sending the payment.

The other key identifier is the Bank Identifier Code (BIC), also known as a SWIFT code. The *BIC* identifies the bank itself, not the customer's account.

A BIC for Deutsche Bank in Frankfurt looks like this: DEUTDEFF500.

Part	Example	Meaning
Bank code	DEUT	Deutsche Bank
Country code	DE	Germany
Location code	FF	Frankfurt
Branch code	500	Optional branch identifier

For most SEPA transfers, customers only need to enter the IBAN. The bank can derive the routing information from it. BICs remain important for international payments outside SEPA and for SWIFT transactions, but regular SEPA payments are built around the IBAN.

SEPA Credit Transfer

SEPA Credit Transfer, or SCT, is the standard euro push payment.

The payer initiates the transfer by instructing their bank to send a specified amount to a specific IBAN with a reference. For example, a customer in Berlin might send €200 to a friend in Paris by entering the recipient's IBAN, the amount, and a payment reference in their banking app.

That is the visible part of the payment. Underneath, several systems and messages carry the transfer from the sender's bank to the recipient's bank.

The flow starts when the payer submits the payment instruction. The sender's bank receives it and performs its own checks: whether the payer is allowed to make the transfer, whether the IBAN format is valid, whether the account has sufficient funds, and whether fraud, sanctions, or compliance rules block the payment.

If the checks pass, the sender's bank prepares the payment for the SEPA infrastructure. In ISO 20022 terms, the customer-to-bank instruction is commonly represented by a `pain.001` message, the customer payment initiation message. The details of ISO 20022, which is a global standard for financial messaging, belong in a later chapter. The relevant point here is that SEPA transfers use structured bank payment messages rather than card authorization messages.

The sender's bank then submits the interbank credit transfer into the SEPA clearing infrastructure. That interbank transfer is commonly carried out as a `pacs.008` message, which is an Interbank Credit Transfer message in the ISO 20022 messaging standard. It tells the receiving side which account should be credited, for what amount, in which currency, and with what payment reference.

The payment is routed through the relevant clearing and settlement arrangements to the recipient's bank. The recipient's bank receives the incoming credit transfer, applies its own checks, and posts the funds to the recipient's account.

After posting, the recipient sees the credit on their account. The bank may also generate account reporting or notification messages, such as `camt.053` for account statements or `camt.054` for debit or credit notifications.

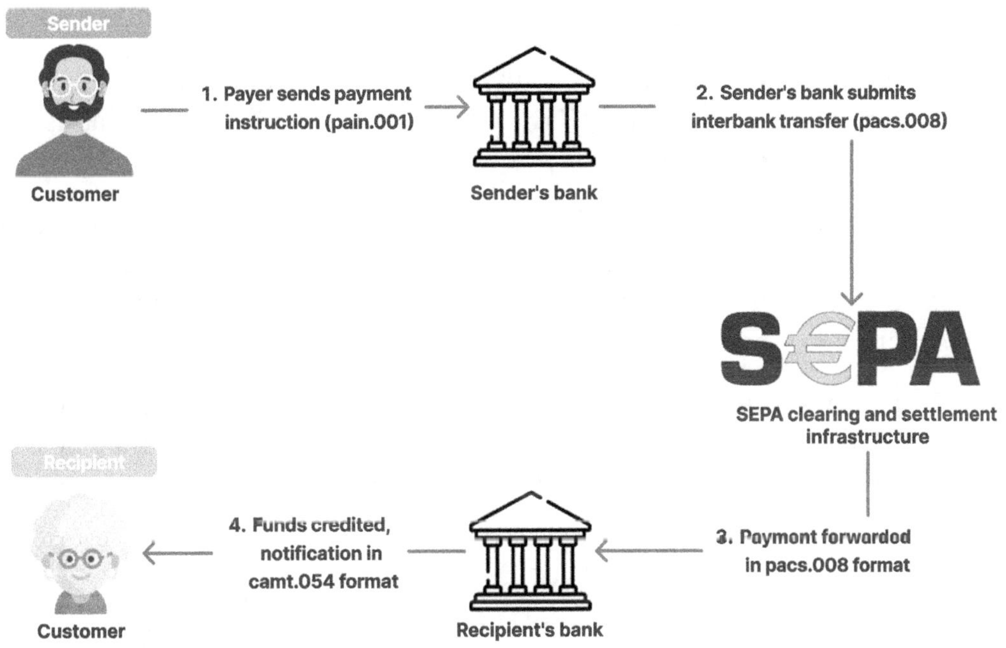

Figure 46.1: SEPA Credit Transfer flow.

The important distinction from cards is that there is no merchant authorization request and no card network approval. *SCT* is a payer-initiated account transfer. The sender's bank validates the instruction, the banks exchange structured payment messages, and the recipient's bank credits the account.

SCT is reliable and low-cost, but it is not instant. It follows normal processing cycles, so cut-off times, weekends, and holidays can affect when the recipient gets the money.

This makes SCT a good fit for supplier payments, invoices, regular personal transfers, and other payments where next-day processing is acceptable. It is less suitable when both parties need confirmation within seconds.

SEPA Instant Credit Transfer

SEPA Instant Credit Transfer, also known as *SCT Inst*, removes the normal waiting period.

It has the same basic purpose as a regular SEPA Credit Transfer: the payer sends euro funds from one account to another. The difference is timing and confirmation. Instead of waiting for a normal processing cycle, the payment is sent to an instant payment infrastructure, such as RT1 operated by EBA Clearing or TIPS, the Eurosystem's TARGET Instant Payment Settlement service.

SCT Inst is designed to make funds available to the payee within seconds, around the clock, including weekends and public holidays.

The sequence begins in the payer's banking app or another customer channel. The payer enters the recipient's IBAN, or selects a saved recipient, adds the amount, and confirms the transfer.

The sender's bank then validates the instruction before releasing it into the instant rail. It checks whether the account can send the payment, whether the destination data is usable, whether limits allow the transfer, and whether fraud, sanctions, or compliance rules block it.

If the checks pass, the sender's bank submits the payment to the instant payment infrastructure. In ISO 20022 terms, the customer instruction may be represented by a `pain.001` message, while the interbank credit transfer is carried as a `pacs.008` message.

The instant infrastructure forwards the payment to the recipient's bank, which has to respond quickly. The recipient's bank checks whether the account can receive the payment and, if it accepts the transfer, credits the recipient's account.

The response then travels back through the instant infrastructure. In ISO 20022 terms, this status is commonly carried using a `pacs.002` message. Once the sender's bank receives the confirmation, it can show the payer whether the payment succeeded or failed. The recipient can see the incoming credit almost immediately.

Later account reporting or notification may use `camt` messages, such as `camt.054`.

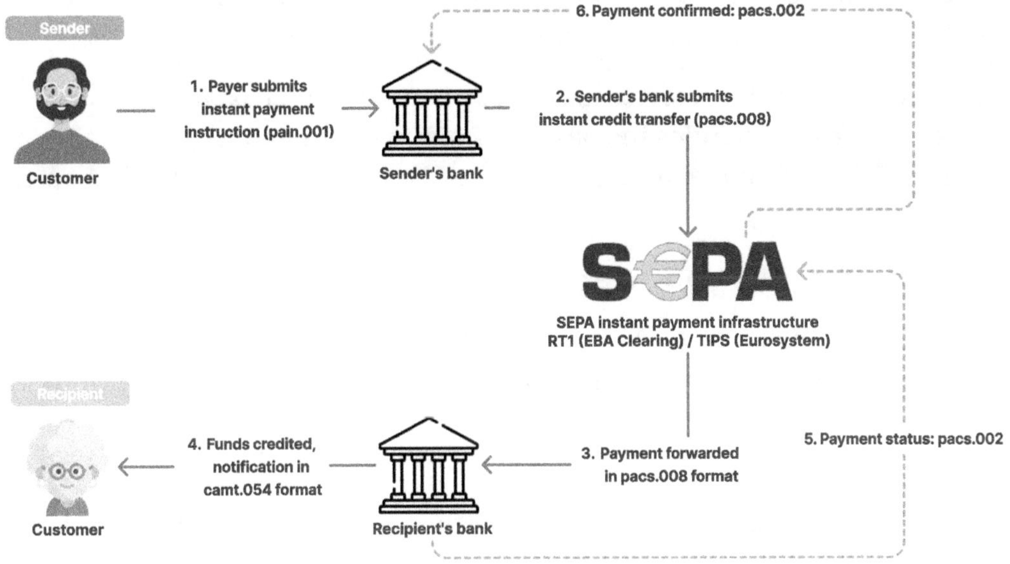

Figure 46.2: SEPA Instant Credit Transfer flow.

For customers, SCT Inst feels more like an instant app transfer than a traditional bank payment. Both the sender and recipient see results quickly, and the bank does not wait until the next processing cycle.

That speed changes both use cases and risk controls. SCT Inst is useful for urgent personal transfers, account funding, merchant payments, emergency payouts, small business payments, and any situation where the recipient needs confirmation right away.

With slower systems, there is more time to spot problems before the payment is final. In instant systems, fraud checks, sanctions screening, recipient verification, and scam warnings must occur quickly because payments move within seconds.

SEPA Direct Debit

SEPA Direct Debit, or SDD, works the other way around.

A *credit transfer* is a push payment: the payer initiates the payment. A direct debit is a pull payment: the creditor collects funds from the payer's account.

This makes SDD useful for recurring and bill payments, such as utilities, insurance, rent, subscriptions, telecom bills, memberships, and loan repayments. The customer doesn't have to send money each month. The creditor starts the collection themselves.

The creditor cannot simply take money from the customer's account. The customer must first permit a SEPA mandate.

The mandate allows the creditor to collect money from the payer's account under agreed terms. It includes the payer's IBAN, creditor details, and a mandate reference. The mandate can be paper-based or electronic, depending on the setup.

Once the mandate is in place, the collection flow can begin.

The customer signs or accepts the SEPA mandate and provides their IBAN to the creditor. This creates the permission record that allows the creditor to initiate collections.

When a payment is due, the creditor prepares a direct debit request and sends it to its bank. In ISO 20022 terms, the creditor-to-bank initiation is commonly represented by a `pain.008` message.

The creditor's bank then forwards the collection into the SEPA infrastructure as an interbank direct debit message, typically a `pacs.003` message. This message tells the payer's side which account should be debited, for what amount, and under which mandate reference.

The SEPA infrastructure routes the debit request to the payer's bank. The payer's bank receives the request, checks the account and relevant scheme conditions, and either processes the debit or returns it.

The processing result travels back through the system. In ISO 20022 terms, this status is carried using a `pacs.002` message. The creditor receives the result through its bank, and later account reporting or debit and credit notifications use `camt` messages, such as `camt.054`.

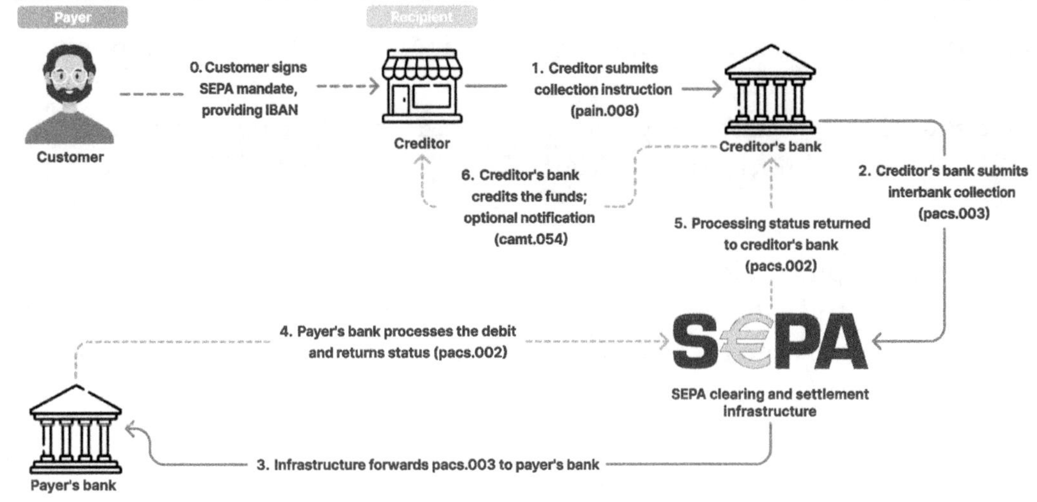

Figure 46.3: SEPA Direct Debit flow.

SDD offers strong protections for payers. For authorized collections under the SEPA Core Direct Debit scheme, the payer can request a refund within eight weeks. If the collection was unauthorized because no valid mandate existed, the refund period extends to thirteen months.

The SEPA B2B Direct Debit scheme works differently. It is designed for business payers and does not provide the same no-questions-asked refund right as the Core scheme.

The protections exist because SDD gives the creditor control over the collection. The payer does not send money each month. The creditor starts the debit. The mandate grants permission, and the refund rules prevent that permission from becoming unchecked power.

Credit Transfers versus Direct Debits

The main difference between SCT and SDD is not speed, but control.

Feature	SEPA Credit Transfer	SEPA Direct Debit
Direction	Push	Pull
Initiator	Payer	Creditor
Authorization	Payer initiates each transfer	Payer signs a mandate in advance
Common uses	Supplier payments, personal transfers, invoices	Utilities, subscriptions, insurance, memberships
Customer action	Yes	No, if mandate remains valid

each time		
Main risk	Sending to the wrong or fraudulent recipient	Unauthorized or incorrect collection
Protection logic	Bank and payment rules; limited reversal after execution	Refund rights and mandate controls

Cards also use pull logic in many purchase scenarios. The merchant requests authorization and later presents the transaction for clearing. But card-pull payments are governed by card network rules, chargebacks, authorizations, clearing, and settlement.

T2, TARGET Services, and TIPS

SEPA schemes define how euro credit transfers and direct debits should work. They do not, by themselves, settle every payment.

Settlement sits inside the Eurosystem's broader TARGET Services and related clearing arrangements.

T2 is the Eurosystem's real-time gross settlement system for large-value euro payments and for settling obligations between participating institutions in central bank money.

TIPS, or TARGET Instant Payment Settlement, is the Eurosystem service for instant payment settlement. It supports instant payments by enabling settlement in central bank money around the clock.

A simplified view looks like this:

Layer	Role
SEPA schemes	Define rules for credit transfers, instant credit transfers, and direct debits
Clearing mechanisms	Exchange and process payment messages between banks
T2	Settles high-value euro payments and settlement obligations in central bank money
TIPS	Supports instant euro settlement
Bank systems	Provide customer interfaces, account posting, risk checks, and reporting

Customers do not see these layers. They open a banking app, enter an IBAN, and confirm. Behind that simple action are scheme rules, message formats, clearing mechanisms, settlement accounts, bank ledgers, and account-posting processes.

This layered setup is common in payments. The customer sees a single action, but the system breaks it down into rules, messages, risk checks, clearing, settlement, and account posting.

Domestic European Rails

SEPA is central to euro account-to-account payments, but Europe is not a single-rail market.

Several countries also have domestic rails that serve local needs. The United Kingdom is the clearest example because it sits outside the euro area and has long-standing sterling payment systems.

The main UK rails are:

- Faster Payments: near-real-time retail account-to-account payments;
- Bacs: batch payments, especially payroll and direct debit;
- CHAPS: high-value same-day sterling payments with final settlement.

The useful comparison is functional, not structural. For standard account transfers, SEPA Credit Transfer plays the euro role, while Bacs covers many scheduled sterling batch payments in the UK. For faster retail transfers, SEPA Instant is the euro instant-payment scheme, while Faster Payments serves a similar everyday role in sterling. For pull payments, SEPA Direct Debit and Bacs Direct Debit both support mandate-based collections, though their rules and refund models are not identical. For high-value payments, T2 provides euro central-bank settlement, while CHAPS provides high-value same-day sterling payments.

These systems are not interchangeable. They are governed differently, settle differently, and operate in different currencies and legal environments. The comparison simply helps group them by purpose: standard transfers, instant transfers, recurring collections, and high-value settlements.

The European Payment Rail Mix

European bank payment systems are easier to understand when grouped by purpose.

SEPA Credit Transfer handles standard euro push payments. SEPA Instant handles euro push payments that require funds to be available within seconds. SEPA Direct Debit handles mandate-based collections. T2 provides high-value euro settlement in central bank money, and TIPS supports instant euro settlement. Domestic systems such as Faster Payments, Bacs, and CHAPS serve national needs outside the eurozone or alongside SEPA.

This rail mix affects product design. A supplier invoice does not need the same system as an emergency transfer. A monthly utility bill is different from a high-value bank settlement. A real-time account-to-account checkout works differently from a card payment, even when the customer sees the same result: money leaving one account and arriving in another.

That is why Europe has a strong account-based alternative to cards. SEPA standardized euro transfers. SCT Inst made instant euro transfers possible. SDD made recurring collections easier. PSD2 and open banking were then built on this account infrastructure, allowing licensed third parties to access account data and initiate payments with customer consent.

A payment initiation service can ask a customer to approve an account-to-account transfer. Instant payment infrastructure can move money quickly. Merchants can avoid some card costs, and consumers can pay directly from their bank account without entering card details.

Cards still have major advantages: global acceptance, established dispute rules, cardholder protections, credit features, offline use, and a mature merchant network. But Europe also has a robust account-to-account payment layer, which is not the case everywhere.

SEPA is the shared euro payment layer, but it is not the whole European payment system. The European rail mix includes standard transfers, instant transfers, recurring collections, high-value settlement, domestic clearing, and account-based payment products built on top of those rails.

Chapter 47: SWIFT and Correspondent Banking

A German company can pay a supplier in France using SEPA. In the United States, an employer can use ACH to pay salaries. In Brazil, customers can send money instantly with Pix.

These systems work well because payments stay inside a country, a currency area, or a domestic payment network. The participating banks share rules, message formats, clearing arrangements, and settlement infrastructure.

Cross-border bank payments are more difficult because there is no single, shared system for all banks, countries, and currencies. There is no global account where every bank holds every currency, and no worldwide clearing house that links every bank directly.

Currencies add another layer. Dollar payments require access to dollar settlement systems, euro payments require euro settlement, and pound sterling payments require sterling settlement. Even if a payment starts in one country, it usually has to be settled through the banking system of the currency being used.

Regulation adds more complexity. Banks have to check cross-border payments for sanctions, money laundering, terrorist financing, fraud, and missing or inconsistent details. Domestic transfers can also require checks, but international payments face more scrutiny because they cross legal systems.

International payments often pass through several banks before reaching the beneficiary. The chain is not just extra paperwork. It is a practical solution for a world where banks are not all directly connected.

Correspondent banking solves the challenge of accessing different markets and currencies for fund transfers. SWIFT addresses the distinct problem of secure communication and standardized messaging between banks.

SWIFT provides a secure, standardized messaging network for banks to send payment instructions. By contrast, correspondent banking enables the actual movement of funds between banks in different currencies and markets through specific account relationships. SWIFT communicates what should be done. Correspondent accounts and settlement systems are how funds move.

Understanding the clear distinction between SWIFT's communication role and the account-based role of correspondent banking is essential to the rest of this chapter.

SWIFT Messaging Network

SWIFT stands for Society for Worldwide Interbank Financial Telecommunication. It began in 1973 to replace telex-based bank messaging with a secure, standardized means of communication for banks.

Before SWIFT, banks sent international payment instructions by hand or with partly manual systems. Messages were often slow, inconsistent, and prone to mistakes. Missing codes, unclear names, or incorrect formats could delay payments for days.

SWIFT standardized the language. It provides a secure network for sending financial messages. A message can instruct another bank to credit a customer, move funds between correspondent accounts, confirm a trade, report account activity, or investigate a payment.

SWIFT is not a settlement system. It does not hold customer money or maintain the accounts where dollars, euros, yen, or pesos are stored. It carries the instruction; the funds move through bank accounts, correspondent relationships, and settlement systems.

That is why the phrase "the money went through SWIFT" is imprecise. The payment instruction went through SWIFT. The money moved somewhere else.

Correspondent Banking

A *correspondent bank* is a bank that offers services to another bank, usually in a country or currency where the other bank cannot operate directly.

For example, if a Japanese bank needs to make payments in US dollars, it might not be part of the US dollar clearing system. Instead, it works with a US bank that can handle dollar transactions. The US bank is its correspondent.

The relationship between the two banks is described with two classic terms: nostro and vostro.

A *nostro account* means "our account with your bank." For the Japanese bank, its dollar account at the US correspondent is a nostro account.

A *vostro account* means "your bank's account with us." From the US bank's perspective, that same account is a vostro account, holding the Japanese bank's funds on its books.

It is the same account, but the name changes depending on which bank is looking at it.

These terms may sound old-fashioned, and they are, but the idea is still important. International payments rely on banks holding accounts with other banks in the currencies they need.

A bank does not need a direct relationship with every bank worldwide. It needs correspondent relationships that give it reach into the currencies and markets its customers use.

Cross-Border Payment Flow

Imagine a Japanese car manufacturer that needs to pay a Mexican auto parts supplier in US dollars.

The buyer is in Japan, the supplier is in Mexico, and the payment currency is US dollars. The Japanese bank and the Mexican bank do not necessarily have a direct account relationship, so the payment moves through correspondent banks that can handle dollars.

The flow starts with the car manufacturer instructing its Japanese bank to make the payment. The bank checks the customer, the amount, the beneficiary details, the payment purpose, sanctions, and internal risk rules.

The Japanese bank then sends a SWIFT payment message. The message tells the next bank in the chain what payment should be made, who should receive it, and which accounts or correspondent relationships should be used.

On the money side, the Japanese bank's US correspondent debits the Japanese bank's dollar nostro account. If the Mexican bank uses a different US correspondent, the dollar position has to move between those correspondents. That movement may involve US dollar clearing and settlement systems such as CHIPS or Fedwire, depending on the banks and the route.

CHIPS, operated by The Clearing House, is a private-sector US dollar clearing system for large-value payments. It uses a netting design to reduce liquidity needs between participants.

Fedwire, operated by the Federal Reserve, is a real-time gross settlement system that settles payments in central bank money. Depending on the route, a dollar leg in a correspondent payment may involve one or both types of infrastructure.

Once the receiving correspondent has the funds, it passes the payment information to the Mexican bank. The Mexican bank uses those payment details to credit the supplier's account.

The supplier sees a credit on its account. Behind that simple credit is a chain of messages, correspondent accounts, compliance checks, clearing, settlement, and bank ledger entries.

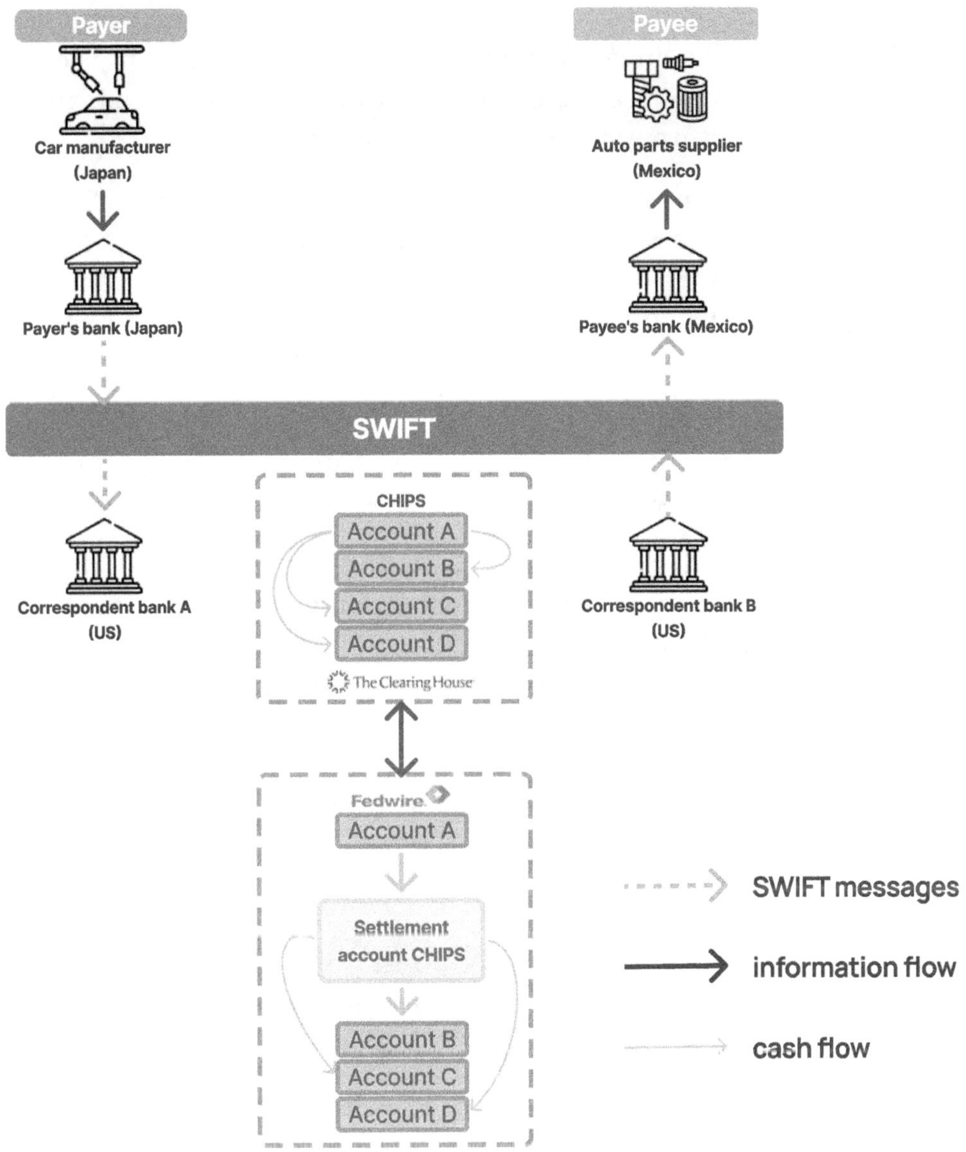

Figure 47.1: SWIFT and correspondent banking flow.

Figure 47.1 separates three things that are often blurred together. The SWIFT message path carries instructions and status-related information between banks. The correspondent-banking path shows the operational links between correspondent banks and the US dollar clearing or settlement infrastructure. The cash-flow path shows balances moving between correspondent accounts and settlement systems.

This is the most useful way to read a cross-border bank payment. The message flow tells banks what should happen: who is paying, who should be credited, the amount, the currency, the account, the reference, and the purpose. The money flow is where balances actually move: one bank's account is debited, another bank's account is credited, net obligations may be cleared, and final settlement may occur through a central bank system.

A SWIFT message can be sent before the final settlement happens. A payment can be delayed even after a message has gone through. A message can be repaired, investigated, or rejected if information is missing or sanctions screening finds a problem. The instruction is necessary, but it is not enough on its own.

This is one reason cross-border payments have often been slower than domestic payments. The delay comes from correspondent chains, cut-off times, currency settlement windows, compliance checks, missing data, beneficiary-bank processing, or time zones.

SWIFT improved tracking and transparency through gpi and related tracking services, giving banks and their customers better visibility into payment status along the chain. Its broader modernization also includes ISO 20022 and Transaction Manager, which aim to preserve richer payment data and make cross-border processing more consistent. But even with better tracking, the underlying architecture remains the same: instructions move through SWIFT. Funds move through bank accounts and payment systems.

Fees, Deductions, and FX

Cross-border payments can be expensive because multiple parties may be involved in the transaction.

The sending bank may charge an outgoing transfer fee. An intermediary bank may deduct its own fee from the amount in transit. The receiving bank may charge a landing fee before crediting the beneficiary. If currency conversion is involved, one of the banks may apply an FX spread.

The recipient may therefore receive less than the sender expected.

International wire transfers often use three charging options:

Charge Option	Meaning	Practical Effect
OUR	Sender pays the fees	Recipient is intended to receive the full amount
SHA	Fees are shared	Sender pays sending-bank fees; recipient bears intermediary or receiving-bank fees
BEN	Beneficiary pays the fees	Fees are deducted from the amount received

The labels can still produce messy outcomes. Some intermediary charges are not always fully visible upfront. FX spreads can be embedded in the exchange rate. A receiving bank may also apply its own local fees.

Compliance, Repair, and Better Messages

Cross-border payments are heavily screened.

Banks check names, countries, banks, addresses, industries, and payment purposes against sanctions lists and internal risk rules. A payment involving a sanctioned party, a restricted country, a high-risk sector, or a suspicious purpose may be stopped.

Sometimes the problem is not criminality but poor data.

A beneficiary name may not match the account. An address may be incomplete. A purpose code may be missing. The beneficiary bank may need additional information before crediting the funds. In those cases, the payment can be directed to repair or investigation.

Repair is the less glamorous part of international payments. It means people or semi-automated systems have to fix, clarify, or add to the payment instruction before the payment can proceed. Each repair step adds delay, cost, and uncertainty. The sender may believe the payment has been sent, while the beneficiary has not yet received usable funds.

Clean message data reduces repairs, delays, costs, and uncertainty in correspondent banking.

For decades, SWIFT cross-border payments used MT messages, such as MT103 for customer credit transfers and MT202 for bank-to-bank transfers. These formats became globally familiar, but they were compact and carried limited structured data. Important details could be squeezed into free-text fields or formatted inconsistently across banks.

The industry is moving toward ISO 20022 because richer, more structured messages can carry clearer debtor and creditor information, addresses, remittance references, purpose codes, and ultimate-party information. A better structure helps banks screen payments, automate reconciliation, reduce repair work, and provide businesses with clearer information about each payment.

That improvement is still about messaging, not settlement. ISO 20022 does not move money. It improves the instruction. The correspondent banking chain still needs accounts, clearing, settlement, compliance checks, and bank processing. In Chapter 48, we examine ISO 20022 directly. Here, the key point is simpler: better payment data reduces friction in a system where every missing or ambiguous field can slow payments.

Correspondent Banking Use Cases

It is tempting to call correspondent banking outdated. That criticism is partly fair. Compared with modern domestic instant payment systems, correspondent banking can be slow, expensive, and hard to trace. But it exists because the global banking system is fragmented.

Thousands of banks operate across different countries, currencies, and legal regimes. They cannot all hold direct settlement accounts with each other. They cannot all connect directly to every domestic payment system. Correspondent banking creates reach through relationships: one bank can serve customers in currencies and markets where it does not operate directly.

The trade-off is complexity.

A domestic payment can often be processed within a single shared system. A cross-border bank payment may need a chain. Each extra bank adds cost, screening requirements, cut-off times, liquidity constraints, and operational risk.

Fintechs and networks have attacked this problem in different ways. Wise reduces its reliance on correspondent banking by holding local accounts in many countries and paying out domestically on both sides. Visa Direct and Mastercard Send use the card network rails to push funds to eligible cards. Instant payment linkage projects try to connect domestic account-to-account systems across borders.

These models address specific corridors while leaving the underlying architecture intact for large-value, multi-currency, multi-legal-system flows. Correspondent banking persists not because it is good, but because the global banking system was not designed with a single alternative in mind.

Chapter 48: ISO 20022 and the Modernization of Bank Messaging

In banking, the message tells the system what to do: send €100 from one account to another, debit a company under a mandate, return a payment, notify a customer, or report account activity.

Earlier, in the card-message chapter, we saw how fields and codes discipline card authorization. The same idea appears in bank transfers. Fields and codes are not paperwork around the payment. They are how banks, clearing systems, compliance tools, and accounting systems understand the payment.

For years, major payment systems used different message formats. SWIFT used MT messages; ACH in the United States used NACHA files; domestic clearing systems had their own formats; card networks used ISO 8583; and SEPA adopted ISO 20022. Each format worked inside its own environment, but connecting them required translation, shortening, mapping, repair, and manual checks.

ISO 20022 reduces fragmentation at the messaging layer. *ISO 20022* is a message standard, not a payment rail, network, or settlement system. It gives financial institutions a shared way to describe messages using a common data model, richer structure, and more precise fields.

The standard covers a wide range of financial services, including payments, cash management, securities, foreign exchange, trade services, and cards. This chapter focuses on bank payments.

In payment messages, ISO 20022 provides three practical advantages.

First, each important fact has its own designated place. ISO 20022 uses named elements — debtor, creditor, account information, references, and payment details — enabling reliable machine processing.

Second, the message contains richer data about parties, references, and payment purposes. This supports reconciliation, compliance, fraud monitoring, and customer support.

Third, ISO 20022 provides a more consistent vocabulary across systems. When two systems both use the standard well, they need less translation between them. Integration is not automatic, but there is a lower risk of data loss or misinterpretation.

ISO 20022 creates space for better data, but it does not force every bank, company, or payment provider to fill every field correctly. A richer message format only helps if the data inside it is clean and usable.

Limits of Legacy Payment Messages

Older payment formats were built to fit the limits of their era.

They had to work with limited network capacity and older banking systems. These formats often used fixed fields, short character limits, and compact codes. That made sense when the main goal was to move instructions reliably between banks.

Modern payments require more from each message.

A corporate treasurer wants a payment to reconcile automatically against an invoice. A bank's compliance system wants clean names and addresses for sanctions screening. A fraud system wants context. A support team wants to see why a payment failed without opening a manual investigation. A customer expects a useful reference on their statement, not a cryptic line of truncated text.

Sparse messages make all these tasks harder.

When data is missing or unstructured, payment operations teams have to clean it up. A beneficiary name may be cut short. An invoice reference may be buried in free text. A field may mean one thing in one country and another thing elsewhere. A payment may be stopped for compliance review because the screening system cannot determine whether a name is a person, a company, or an address fragment.

The impact is not just technical. Poor data leads to delays, false positives, failed payments, customer complaints, and extra manual work.

ISO 20022 does not fix all these problems on its own, but it provides the industry with a better message format.

Richer Payment Data

A simple payment involves more than just an amount and an account number. Even a basic bank transfer can include several parties and references.

At a minimum, the message needs a debtor, a creditor, their accounts, the amount, and the currency. But modern payments may also require:

- the ultimate debtor, if the party funding the payment is different from the account holder;
- the ultimate creditor, if the final beneficiary is different from the account owner;
- structured remittance information, such as invoice numbers;
- a payment purpose code;
- a category purpose, such as salary, pension, supplier payment, or tax;
- charge information;
- status and return information;
- references that survive across the payment chain.

This structure is especially helpful for businesses. A company that receives thousands of payments does not want staff to manually match each credit to an invoice. It wants each payment to include a clear reference that the accounting system can read automatically.

It also helps with compliance. A sanctions engine performs better when it receives clearly separated name, address, country, and account number fields rather than a single block of free text.

Banks also benefit, as cleaner data means fewer repairs, exceptions, and more efficient straight-through processing.

Straight-through processing means a payment can go from start to finish without anyone needing to step in. In payments, that is often the real test of operational quality.

Message Families

ISO 20022 includes many message families. The names can seem technical at first, but the pattern is simple: each family has a short prefix and a message number. The prefixes are usually written in lowercase followed by a message number, such as `pain.001` or `pacs.008`.

For bank payments, three families do most of the work:

Family	Full Name	What It Is Used For	Common Examples
pain.*	Payment Initiation	Messages between a customer or company and its bank	pain.001 credit transfer initiation; pain.008 direct debit initiation; pain.002 payment status report
pacs.*	Payments Clearing and Settlement	Interbank messages between banks and payment infrastructures	pacs.008 credit transfer; pacs.002 payment status report; pacs.004 payment return
camt.*	Cash Management	Account reports, statements, and notifications	camt.052 intraday report; camt.053 end-of-day statement; camt.054 debit or credit notification

A few other families appear outside day-to-day payment flows:

Family	Full Name	What It Is Used For
acmt.*	Account Management	Account opening, changes, and closure
semt.*	Securities Management	Securities transactions and reporting
fxtr.*	Foreign Exchange Trade	Foreign exchange transaction messages

The naming convention helps show where the message fits in the payment chain.

A `pain.001` is a customer-to-bank instruction. A company sends it to its bank when it wants to initiate a credit transfer, such as a payroll file or supplier payment batch.

A `pacs.008` is an interbank credit transfer message. Once the sending bank has accepted the instruction, the payment moves between banks and clearing systems using `pacs` messages.

A `camt.054` is a notification. It tells an account holder that a debit or credit has been posted.

Payment Message Example

Consider a €100 payment from John Doe in Germany to Maria Rossi in Italy.

In a SEPA Credit Transfer, John or John's company may initiate the payment through a `pain.001` message. That message includes a group header, the debtor, the debtor account, the amount, the creditor, and the creditor account.

A simplified example looks like this:

```
<Document xmlns="urn:iso:std:iso:20022:tech:xsd:pain.001.001.03">
  <CstmrCdtTrfInitn>
    <GrpHdr>
      <MsgId>PAYMNT12345</MsgId>
      <CreDtTm>2025-09-02T12:00:00</CreDtTm>
      <NbOfTxs>1</NbOfTxs>
    </GrpHdr>
    <PmtInf>
      <Dbtr>
        <Nm>John Doe</Nm>
      </Dbtr>
      <DbtrAcct>
        <IBAN>DE89370400440532013000</IBAN>
      </DbtrAcct>
      <CdtTrfTxInf>
        <Amt>
          <InstdAmt Ccy="EUR">100.00</InstdAmt>
        </Amt>
        <Cdtr>
          <Nm>Maria Rossi</Nm>
        </Cdtr>
        <CdtrAcct>
          <IBAN>IT60X0542811101000000123456</IBAN>
        </CdtrAcct>
      </CdtTrfTxInf>
    </PmtInf>
  </CstmrCdtTrfInitn>
</Document>
```

This simplified example shows that every piece of data has its own place.

The debtor name is in the `<Dbtr>` element. The debtor account is inside `<DbtrAcct>`. The instructed amount is in `<InstdAmt>`, with the currency set to `Ccy="EUR"`. The creditor name is inside `<Cdtr>`. The creditor account is inside `<CdtrAcct>`.

That structure is the key. A German bank, an Italian bank, a clearing system, a compliance engine, and an accounting system can all read the same message and find the same information in the same place.

Adoption Contexts

SEPA has used ISO 20022 since its launch. The `pain.001`, `pacs.008`, `pacs.002`, and `camt.054` messages from the SEPA chapter all belong to the ISO 20022 family.

SWIFT has also moved cross-border payments and reporting toward ISO 20022. For in-scope SWIFT cross-border payment instruction messages, the coexistence period between MT and ISO 20022 messages ended on November 22, 2025. Some reporting and non-instruction message timelines extend beyond that. In that context, ISO 20022 messages, such as `pacs.008` and `pacs.009`, are the standard successors to legacy customer and bank payment messages, such as MT103 and MT202.

Several modern US rails also use ISO 20022. FedNow uses ISO 20022 messages. RTP, operated by The Clearing House, uses ISO 20022-based messaging, including `pacs.008` for credit transfers. The Fedwire Funds Service completed its migration to ISO 20022 in July 2025.

ACH is the main exception in the United States. It still uses the Nacha file format, which is based on fixed-width records. This format is old, efficient, and deeply rooted in payroll, bill payments, benefits, and account funding. It works, but it does not carry the same rich, structured data as ISO 20022.

The United States, therefore, has a mixed landscape of bank payment messaging. Newer instant and high-value payment rails use ISO 20022, while ACH, the large batch system, still uses its older file format.

ISO 20022 versus ISO 8583

The name ISO 20022 might make it seem like it replaces ISO 8583, but that is not the right way to think about it.

ISO 8583 handles card authorization messages between POS terminals, acquirers, payment networks, processors, and issuers when a card transaction needs a real-time approval or decline. It is compact, fast, and built for request-response processing. A card authorization message does not need to carry a full invoice reference, structured remittance data, ultimate debtor, or rich account reporting fields. It needs to ask a narrow real-time question: should this transaction be approved?

In the bank transfer context, ISO 20022 is used for payment initiation, interbank clearing and settlement, status, returns, and account reporting. It is built for a world where richer data helps banks, clearing systems, corporates, compliance tools, and reporting systems interpret payments more precisely.

Dimension	ISO 8583	ISO 20022
Primary use	Card payments, POS authorization, ATM transactions	Bank transfers, clearing, settlement, instant payments, reporting
Format	Fixed fields, bitmap, compact data elements	Structured named elements, commonly exchanged as XML
Main strength	Speed and compact real-time authorization	Rich data, extensibility, interoperability
Exchange mode	Mostly real-time request and response	Batch files and real-time messages
Typical examples	Card authorization at POS; ATM authorization	SEPA Credit Transfer; SWIFT CBPR+; FedNow; RTP; Fedwire
Core question	Should this card transaction be approved?	What payment, status, return, or report is being exchanged?

A modern payments company needs both standards. The card processing system uses ISO 8583, while the bank transfer system uses ISO 20022. The accounting and reconciliation tools may need to handle both.

Migration beyond Message Format

ISO 20022 migration can look like a technical file-format change: replace the old message, map a few fields, update the interface, and close the project.

In reality, migrations are much harder.

A bank has to change message schemas, validation rules, screening systems, repair queues, customer channels, reporting tools, archives, and operational procedures. It has to decide how old data maps to new fields. It has to test with market infrastructures, correspondent banks, corporate clients, vendors, and internal systems.

The hardest part is often ensuring the data within the ISO 20022 message is sufficient to make the migration worthwhile.

If a bank fills a rich ISO 20022 field with the same messy free text as before, the message is modern in format but poor in practice. The payment might still need manual repair, reconciliation could still fail, and the compliance engine may still get unclear data.

That is the main limitation of ISO 20022: it standardizes the container but not the quality of the data it contains.

Product Consequences of Richer Data

For product teams, ISO 20022 is not just a backend infrastructure topic. It changes what bank-payment products can show, automate, and control.

Richer payment data gives product teams more useful fields to build on. A business banking product can display structured remittance details rather than a vague payment reference. A treasury tool can match incoming payments to invoices with fewer manual checks. Compliance systems can screen payer and payee data more cleanly. Support teams can see where a payment stands instead of guessing from a generic failure message.

If the user interface gives the customer one unstructured text box labeled *Reference*, much of the benefit is lost before the message leaves the first system.

ISO 20022 does not make payments instant, settle money, remove correspondent banking, or eliminate fraud and sanctions checks. Its value is narrower and more practical: it provides payment instructions, statuses, and returns, and uses a richer language.

That richer language helps because payments involve more than balances moving between accounts. They also carry messages between institutions, systems, and legal entities. The more precise the message, the easier it is to automate, reconcile, screen, investigate, and explain.

Chapter 49: Instant Payment Systems

Historically, bank transfers were not designed with immediate customer feedback in mind. Payments were collected into files, processed in batches, and settled at set times. A transfer that missed a cut-off could wait until the next cycle, with weekends and holidays adding more delay.

That timing worked for salaries, bills, supplier invoices, government benefits, and internal transfers. These payments needed reliability more than immediacy.

Customer expectations changed. Instant messaging, delivery tracking, card approvals, and real-time app balances made a one-day bank transfer feel slow, even when the system was working correctly.

Instant payment systems were created to close that gap. They allow money to move directly between bank accounts within seconds, with immediate confirmation and funds available to the recipient.

These systems have expanded account-to-account payments. Bank transfers are no longer only for payroll, invoices, and bills. In many markets, they are front-end payment methods for people, merchants, wallets, apps, and businesses.

Instant Payment Criteria

An instant payment system usually combines four features: speed, availability, confirmation, and push-based movement.

Confirmation means both sides quickly know whether the payment succeeded or failed, rather than waiting while the payment remains in a vague processing status.

Most instant payment systems are credit-push systems. The payer sends money to the recipient. The recipient does not pull funds from the payer's account as in a direct debit.

That design changes the risk model. The payer's bank checks the account, fraud risk, limits, and payment details before sending the payment. Once the recipient's bank accepts and credits the funds, the payment is usually hard to unwind through the ordinary payment flow.

Instant payments, therefore, differ from card payments. A card purchase begins with authorization, and the funds are moved later through clearing and settlement. In an instant account-to-account payment, the money movement and confirmation are much closer to the payment event itself. Fraud controls and refund processes may exist, but the protection model is not the card network chargeback model.

Basic Flow

A simple instant payment begins when the payer initiates a transfer in a banking app, a wallet, or a merchant's checkout. The payer selects a recipient, enters an amount, reviews the details, and confirms.

The payer's bank then checks whether the account can send the payment. It looks at available funds, limits, fraud risk, sanctions screening, recipient details, and any scheme-specific controls. If the payment passes those checks, the bank sends it into the instant payment infrastructure.

The infrastructure routes the payment message to the recipient's bank. The recipient's bank checks whether the account can receive the funds and, if so, credits it. A confirmation then travels back through the system so the sender's bank, the recipient's bank, the payer, and the recipient know the outcome.

In a well-designed system, this sequence takes seconds.

For instant payments to work smoothly, two things must happen at the same time: the message must move quickly, and the funds must become available asap. Older systems could show a pending balance before final settlement. Instant payment systems are designed to deliver usable funds to recipients almost immediately.

Settlement design varies. Some systems settle each payment individually in central bank money. Others use prefunded accounts, deferred settlement, or hybrid models. Customers do not always see these differences, but banks do. Settlement design affects liquidity, operating hours, risk, and cost.

Everyday and Business Use Cases

Instant payments make account-to-account transfers usable in situations where batch payments are too slow.

For person-to-person payments, they remove the awkward delay: the recipient can see the money immediately. For bills, they let customers pay close to the deadline and still receive confirmation. For disbursements, they make emergency benefits, insurance payouts, marketplace payouts, and wage advances more practical. For account funding, they reduce the waiting time between bank accounts, wallets, brokerage accounts, and fintech apps.

At checkout, instant payments offer a bank account alternative to cards. A customer approves a transfer directly from their account, often via a QR code, a payment request, or a banking app confirmation. Where the scheme supports real-time confirmation, the merchant gets faster payment certainty and lower acceptance costs than many card flows.

The broader change is that bank transfers can align with the customer experience, not just back-office needs.

Common Design Features

Instant payment systems differ by country, but the successful ones often solve the same practical problems: how to identify the recipient, how to make merchant payments easy, how to let a recipient request money, and how to reduce mistakes before funds leave the sender's account.

Aliases and Proxies

Most people do not want to enter a long account number when paying at a store or sending money to a friend.

Many instant systems solve this with aliases. A phone number, email address, national ID, tax ID, or virtual payment address can point to a bank account. The user enters the alias, and the system resolves it to the underlying account inside the operating model.

Pix in Brazil uses keys such as phone numbers, email addresses, tax identifiers, and random keys. In India, UPI uses virtual payment addresses. Other systems use phone numbers, email addresses, or domestic identifiers.

Aliases make payments simpler by replacing account numbers with phone numbers, email addresses, or other familiar identifiers. They also create fraud and privacy questions, because the alias can reveal information about the person or business behind the account. Showing the recipient's name before payment can help prevent mistakes and impersonation. Showing too much information can reveal personal data. Each system has to balance usability, safety, and privacy.

QR Codes

QR codes are one reason instant payments can compete at the point of sale.

A merchant can show a static QR code printed near the till or a dynamic QR code generated for a specific transaction. The customer scans it, reviews the recipient and amount, and confirms the payment in their app.

Dynamic QR codes are usually safer and simpler because they include the amount and payment details. Static QR codes cost less and are easier for small merchants to use, but customers often need to enter the amount themselves.

In both cases, the QR code does not move the money. It captures the payment details so the transfer can happen through the instant payment system.

Request to Pay

Some systems support request to pay. Instead of the payer manually creating a transfer, the recipient sends a payment request. The payer reviews it and approves or rejects it.

This feature is useful for bills, online shopping, subscriptions, and merchant payments. It preserves the push nature of the payment while making the experience feel closer to a merchant-initiated checkout.

It also creates risk. A fake request can trick someone into sending money to the wrong party. Clear recipient confirmation, readable screens, and strong fraud warnings help reduce that risk.

Confirmation of Payee

A simple but powerful control is showing the payer who will receive the money before they confirm.

If the payer enters an account number or alias and the app shows "Maria Rossi," the payer can spot a mismatch before sending. This does not stop all fraud, but it reduces misdirected payments and some impersonation scams.

Instant payments need these controls because there is little time to stop a payment once it has been accepted.

Examples around the World

The phrase *instant payment system* covers different market designs. Some systems are public infrastructure, some are privately operated rails, and some have become broad consumer and merchant payment platforms.

System	Market	Basic Model	Notable Features
UPI	India	Account-to-account instant payment platform	Virtual payment addresses, QR codes, P2P and merchant payments, broad app ecosystem
Pix	Brazil	Account-to-account instant payment system	Pix keys, QR codes, 24/7 availability, strong consumer and merchant adoption
RTP	United States	Private-sector instant payment rail	Credit push, 24/7 operation, request for payment
FedNow	United States	Federal Reserve instant payment rail	24/7 instant payments, ISO 20022 messaging, immediate funds availability
Faster Payments	United Kingdom	Domestic faster payment rail	Near-real-time transfers, broad bank coverage, major base for UK account-to-account payments
SEPA Instant Credit Transfer	SEPA area	Euro instant credit transfer scheme	Funds available within seconds across participating payment service providers

UPI and Pix have moved beyond being bank transfer utilities and have become everyday payment habits. They support P2P transfers, merchant payments, QR-based payments, and embedded payment experiences inside apps.

RTP and FedNow show a different pattern. The United States has strong card usage, an entrenched ACH system, and a fragmented banking market. The adoption of instant payment is therefore more gradual. The infrastructure exists, but broad consumer and merchant behavior takes longer to change.

SEPA Instant sits somewhere else again. Europe already had a strong account-to-account infrastructure, but adoption depended on bank participation, reachability, pricing, regulation, and customer experience. Recent EU rules are pushing instant euro transfers toward broader reachability and pricing closer to standard SEPA transfers. That regulatory pressure should make instant euro payments more common, although adoption still depends on bank implementation, customer experience, and merchant use cases.

A system succeeds when rules, bank involvement, user experience, fraud controls, merchant support, and pricing fit together.

Finality and Customer Protection

Finality is one of the most important differences between instant payments and many other retail payment methods.

In many instant payment systems, once the payment is accepted and credited, it is final from the system's perspective. The sender's bank cannot simply pull the money back through the ordinary payment flow. Recovery may still be possible, but it usually requires a separate process, cooperation from the receiving bank, or action by the recipient.

That finality is useful for recipients. A merchant wants certainty that a payment has been received. A freelancer wants to know that a payout will not casually disappear. A supplier wants confidence before releasing goods or services.

The same finality creates a hard consumer-protection problem when the payer was deceived. Rules for scam reimbursement, bank liability, and recovery vary by country and are still evolving in many markets.

The policy challenge is to keep instant payments fast and reliable without leaving scam victims entirely exposed.

Fraud Problem

The strength of instant payments is also their weakness: money moves quickly, leaving little time to detect, stop, or recover a bad transfer.

The central risk is authorized push payment fraud, often shortened to APP fraud. The customer is tricked into sending the money themselves. A fraudster may impersonate a bank employee, a government agency, a delivery company, a romantic partner, a supplier, or a family member. The payment is technically authorized, but the authorization was manipulated.

That makes the problem different from many card-fraud cases. The issue is not always a stolen credential or an unauthorized merchant transaction. The issue is that the genuine customer was deceived into approving a real-time account transfer.

Instant systems also increase the value of mule accounts. Fraudsters need accounts that can receive funds and move them onward before banks can intervene. Onboarding, KYC, behavioral monitoring, device signals, transaction analytics, and interbank cooperation all become more important.

Instant payments are not inherently unsafe, but their controls need to keep pace with their speed. Recipient verification, scam warnings, mule detection, transaction monitoring, and fast recovery workflows are not optional add-ons. They are part of making instant payments usable at scale.

Cross-Border Instant Payments

It is difficult to make instant payments work within one country. Making them work across borders is even harder.

A domestic system can rely on a single currency, legal framework, central bank, settlement model, and set of participation rules. A cross-border payment has to deal with currencies, FX rates, sanctions screening, AML checks, different data standards, different operating hours, and different liability rules.

There are several ways to approach the problem.

One approach is to connect domestic instant payment systems together. Project Nexus, developed by the BIS Innovation Hub, is an example of this direction. The idea is to let participating instant payment systems interoperate so that a payer in one country can reach a recipient in another without every bank having to build separate bilateral integrations.

Another approach is to use card network push payment products such as Visa Direct and Mastercard Send. These use the card network reach to push funds to eligible cards or accounts.

A third approach is the fintech treasury model used by companies like Wise. Instead of moving every payment across borders via correspondent banking, the provider uses local accounts and local payouts in each country, with internal treasury and FX operations connecting the two.

All three methods aim at the same expectation: people want cross-border payments to feel as fast and reliable as domestic ones. The industry is still working toward that goal.

Adoption by Country

Instant payment adoption is not only a technical question.

A country may have excellent instant payment infrastructure and still see slow adoption if customers are happy with cards, banks price instant transfers poorly, merchants have no reason to change, or fraud controls are weak.

Adoption tends to accelerate when several conditions are present:

- broad bank participation;
- simple customer identifiers, such as phone numbers, aliases, or QR codes;
- low or no consumer fees;
- clear merchant acceptance tools;
- strong fraud controls and recipient verification;
- regulation or central bank pressure;
- good developer access for fintechs and payment providers.

Brazil's Pix and India's UPI show how quickly behavior can change when the system is easy, cheap, widely accepted, and supported by strong public or quasi-public infrastructure. The United States shows the opposite challenge: existing systems already work well enough for many use cases, so new rails must fight for distribution and habit. Europe has a strong bank transfer culture, but widespread adoption of instant payments depends on reachability, pricing, and consistent implementation across countries.

Place in the Payment Stack

Instant payments are one of the most important shifts in modern payment infrastructure because they bring bank accounts closer to the moment of interaction.

They are well-suited to P2P transfers, domestic merchant payments, bill payments, disbursements, wallet funding, and some business payments. They are less naturally suited to transactions that need card-style dispute rights, credit, rewards, offline acceptance, or global merchant reach.

Cards remain powerful where acceptance, credit, fraud rules, and consumer protection are central. ACH and other batch systems remain useful where cost and scale are more useful than speed. SWIFT and correspondent banking remain relevant where cross-border complexity cannot be avoided. Instant systems fill the gap for account-to-account payments that need to be fast, always available, and easy to use.

Each rail reflects a different trade-off between speed, cost, reach, and finality. Instant payments are the latest layer in that stack, not the last.

Part IX
Alternative Payment Methods

Chapter 50: Digital Wallets beyond Cards

When someone pays with a phone, the payment may run over very different systems.

With Apple Pay, the transaction is still a card payment. The wallet changes the interface and credentials, but the issuer, network, acquirer, authorization, clearing, and settlement logic still follow the card model.

With PayPal, the wallet funds the purchase using a linked card, bank account, PayPal balance, or a credit product. The merchant is paid directly by PayPal, often without seeing the customer's card or bank details.

With Alipay or WeChat Pay, the payment stays within the wallet's ecosystem. The customer spends from a wallet balance or linked funding source, and the merchant gets paid through the same platform. In that model, a card network is not involved in the wallet payment itself.

All of these are called digital wallets, which is why the term is both useful and misleading. It describes the customer interface, not the underlying payment mechanism.

A *digital wallet* is an app or service that stores payment credentials, initiates payments, or holds value for the user. That definition is broad because wallets do not all work the same way. A wallet may store a tokenized card, connect to a bank account, hold a prepaid balance, apply loyalty value, support QR payments, enable person-to-person transfers, or operate a closed-loop merchant network.

The app may show the same basic action — authenticate, confirm, pay — while the underlying payment can be a card transaction, a bank account instruction, a wallet balance transfer, or an internal platform transfer.

For customers, these differences are often invisible. Merchants, banks, regulators, and wallet providers determine who holds funds, who sees payment data, who charges the merchant, who manages disputes, who carries the fraud risk, and which rules apply.

Three Wallet Models

The three main wallet models are: pass-through, staged, and stored-value. Each model has specific features and payment flows.

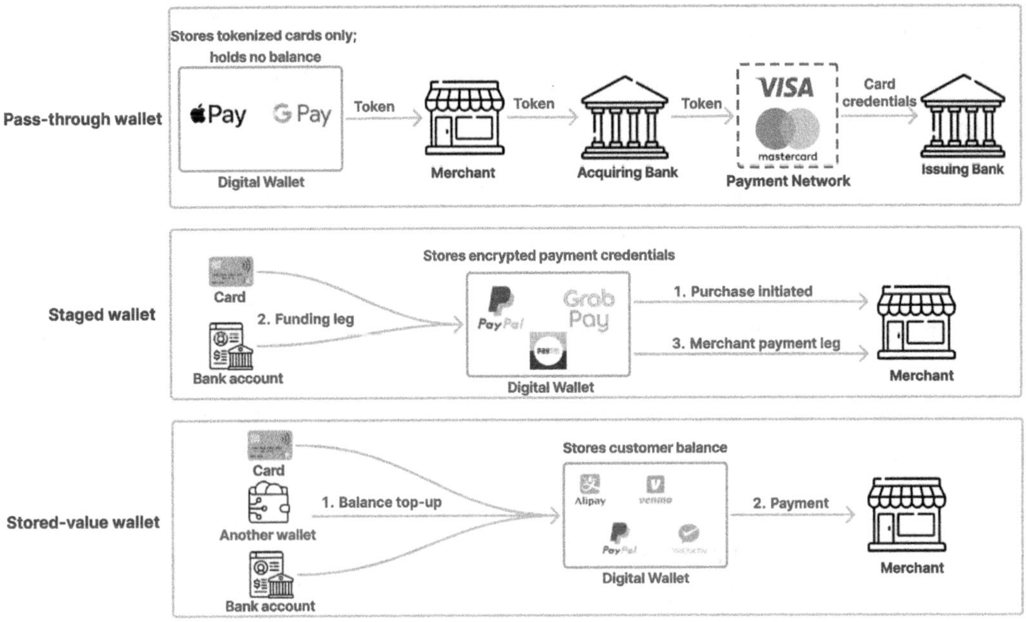

Figure 50.1: Three digital wallet models.

Figure 50.1 places the three wallet models side by side. A pass-through wallet sends a protected credential into another rail, usually the card system. A staged wallet serves as a bridge between the customer's funding source and the merchant. A stored-value wallet holds a balance and can move value inside its own ledger. The customer can see the same action on screen, but the payment underneath can be completely different.

Pass-Through Wallets

A pass-through wallet does not hold the customer's money or replace the underlying payment rail. It presents a protected payment credential and allows the transaction to run on another system, most commonly the card system.

Apple Pay and Google Pay clearly show that distinction. When a customer pays with a tokenized card in one of these wallets, the wallet changes the interface and the credentials. The transaction still follows the card model: issuer authorization, card network routing, clearing, settlement, fraud rules, disputes, and merchant acceptance economics.

The same idea applies to a merchant wallet or browser wallet that stores a tokenized card for later use. The wallet improves convenience and credential security, but the underlying payment method remains card-based.

Pass-through wallets may appear to be new payment methods, but they rely on existing ones.

Staged Wallets

A staged wallet serves as a bridge between the customer's funding source and the merchant. It separates the customer-funding leg from the merchant-payment leg.

The customer chooses the wallet at checkout. The wallet funds the purchase from a linked card, bank account, stored balance, or credit product. The merchant is paid by the wallet provider under the wallet's merchant acceptance arrangement.

PayPal is the classic example. Wallets such as GrabPay and Paytm also illustrate how staged wallet models can integrate stored balances, cards, bank accounts, and local payment methods.

This model gives the wallet provider greater control over the checkout process: it can keep card details away from the merchant, manage buyer and seller protection, handle cross-border checkout, and build its own merchant relationship.

The trade-off is complexity. A staged wallet may involve two linked events: one between the customer and the wallet, and another between the wallet and the merchant. Fees, refunds, chargebacks, buyer protection, seller protection, and fraud liability depend on the wallet's rules and the funding source used.

For the merchant, the important relationship is often with the wallet provider, not directly with the customer's bank or card issuer. That simplification gives the wallet provider more control over the transaction experience, data, and dispute process. The merchant gains reach, but accepts a more powerful intermediary between itself and the customer.

Stored-Value Wallets

A stored-value wallet holds a customer's balance. The customer loads funds into the wallet in advance or receives funds from another wallet user, then spends from that balance.

Alipay, WeChat Pay, Venmo, GrabPay, and many other mobile money systems offer stored-value wallet features. In some markets, this is one of the main ways people pay for everyday purchases.

The customer tops up the wallet from a bank account, a card, a cash agent, another wallet, an incoming P2P transfer, or another funding source. The wallet records that value as the customer's balance. When the customer pays a merchant, the wallet debits the customer's wallet balance and either credits the merchant's wallet account or settles funds to the merchant's bank account later.

If both the customer and the merchant are within the same wallet ecosystem, the payment can be largely an internal ledger transfer. The wallet lowers the customer's balance and raises the merchant's balance. No card network needs to authorize the transaction, and no external bank transfer is required at that moment.

Wallet-to-wallet P2P uses the same internal ledger logic. The sender opens the app, chooses a recipient by phone number, email address, or wallet handle, enters the amount, and taps send. From the user's perspective, the money moves immediately. Inside the wallet provider's system, the transfer is simply two ledger entries: debit one wallet's balance and credit another.

The total value inside the wallet system does not change. External rails come into play at boundaries: when users fund the wallet with a card or bank account, when merchants withdraw funds to a bank account, or when the operator settles with external partners. Transfers within the wallet are fast because the operator updates balances in its own ledger by design.

This is what makes a closed-loop stored-value system powerful. The wallet operator controls the customer account, merchant relationship, ledger, user interface, risk controls, and often the dispute process. It can make internal transfers feel instant because it does not need external settlement for every transaction. It can price merchant acceptance differently because card network economics do not apply.

> **Stored-Value Wallets and Float Income**
>
> Suppose a wallet has ten million users, and each user keeps an average balance of $20. The wallet operator is now holding $200 million of customer funds, even before anyone makes a payment.
>
> Those funds are not revenue. They belong to customers and are usually safeguarded under local rules. But while the money sits in pooled safeguarding accounts, it may generate interest or other income for the operator, depending on the regulatory regime.
>
> This is called *float income*. It can make stored-value wallets economically attractive when balances are large and interest rates are meaningful. But regulation can limit or remove that benefit. If customer funds must be segregated, protected, or held in low-yield accounts, the wallet may earn little or no float income.
>
> That is why stored-value wallets are not just payment interfaces. The way customer balances are legally held can shape the entire business model.

Stored value also brings regulatory weight. If a company holds customer funds, it may be issuing e-money or operating a regulated stored-value facility, depending on the jurisdiction. It may require safeguarding arrangements, customer verification, transaction monitoring, redemption rules, and customer fund protection.

Multi-Model Wallets

Most successful wallets do not fit neatly into only one model.

A customer may hold a PayPal balance, pay from a linked card when the balance is empty, receive funds from another PayPal user, and withdraw to a bank account. Depending on the transaction, PayPal may act as a stored-value wallet, a staged wallet, or a checkout intermediary.

Revolut can hold balances, support card payments, enable P2P transfers, issue cards, and connect to bank rails. GrabPay may hold a wallet balance, support merchant QR payments, and link to cards or bank accounts. Alipay and WeChat Pay combine stored value, QR acceptance, P2P, merchant services, credit, wealth products, and mini-apps.

The label *wallet* does not tell you much by itself.

The better question is where the money for the payment comes from:

Wallet Funding Source	What It Means
Card credential	The wallet is using the card system behind the interface.
Linked bank account	The wallet pulls from or pushes to a bank account.
Stored balance	The wallet debits value already held inside the wallet.
Credit line	The wallet or partner lender finances the purchase.
Rewards or loyalty balance	The wallet applies noncash value toward the purchase.
Another wallet transfer	Value arrives from another user inside the same ecosystem.

The user may see a single button, but the system behind it can support multiple payment methods.

Closed Loops

The most successful wallet companies often become closed-loop systems, not merely payment tools.

In an open card network, no single party controls the whole journey — the issuer, acquirer, network, processor, merchant, and cardholder each see only their part. A closed-loop wallet changes that. The customer has a wallet account. The merchant has a wallet acceptance relationship. The wallet provider manages the ledger, user interface, merchant tools, risk controls, and often the data layer.

In a card payment, the merchant pays for access to the card system through its acquiring arrangement. In a closed-loop wallet payment, fewer external parties sit between the wallet provider and the merchant. The wallet provider can keep more of the merchant fee, price the service aggressively to grow acceptance, or bundle payments with other merchant services.

A wallet ecosystem may also see both sides of the transaction: the customer, the merchant, the basket, the location, the promotion, the refund, and future engagement. That data can support fraud detection, merchant lending, advertising, loyalty, rewards, and other financial services.

External rails still carry money into and out of the wallet. Inside the ecosystem, however, the wallet provider can control much more of the payment experience than a normal card interface can.

Wallet Economics

Wallets make money in different ways depending on the model.

A pass-through wallet may not charge customers directly. It can create value by making the device, operating system, bank account, or platform more useful. It may also earn revenue through commercial arrangements with issuers, networks, or partners.

A staged wallet earns merchant fees, cross-border fees, FX spread, withdrawal fees, seller fees, or revenue from value-added services. It can also reduce checkout friction and increase merchant conversion, which helps justify its cost.

A stored-value wallet earns from merchant acceptance, withdrawals, FX, lending, advertising, loyalty, or other services built around payments. Where allowed, it may also benefit from income on customer balances.

For merchants, the practical question is whether the wallet improves the business: does it bring in customers they would not otherwise reach, lift checkout conversion rates, reduce fraud losses, lower acceptance costs, or serve customers who already prefer that wallet?

For wallet providers, each payment keeps the user inside the wallet environment. The business model often comes from what the wallet can build around that repeated contact: merchant services, credit, FX, advertising, loyalty, subscriptions, or financial products.

Regulation and Stored Value

Regulation depends heavily on what the wallet actually does.

A pass-through wallet that only stores tokenized card credentials is treated very differently from a wallet that holds customer funds. The first is closer to a technical payment interface. The second may be a regulated financial product.

If a wallet holds customer balances, several questions arise:

- Are the funds customer money or the wallet provider's money?
- Must the funds be safeguarded in a separate account?
- Can the wallet provider earn interest on pooled balances?
- What happens if the wallet provider becomes insolvent?
- What customer checks are required before a user can hold or transfer value?
- What monitoring applies to wallet-to-wallet transfers?
- Can the balance be redeemed into bank money at par?

In the EU and UK, many stored-value wallet models fall under e-money or payment institution frameworks. In other markets, regulators focus on the same fund-holding function: if a company holds users' funds and allows those funds to be transferred, it is considered financial infrastructure.

This is especially important for superapp wallets and mobile money systems. Once users treat a wallet balance like money, the wallet provider becomes part of the financial system, even if it started as a technology company.

Wallets, Cards, and Bank Accounts

Wallets are often described as replacements for cards or bank accounts. In practice, they usually depend on them.

Pass-through, staged, and stored-value wallets all depend on other rails in different ways: a pass-through wallet needs the card, a staged wallet may need a card or bank account for funding, and a stored-value wallet may need bank rails for top-ups and withdrawals. Even a closed-loop wallet needs external settlement when money enters or leaves the ecosystem.

The wallet changes how payments look and feel. It may hide the card number, make authentication easier, add loyalty rewards, simplify P2P transfers, or keep money inside an app. Underneath, there is still a funding source, a transaction record, and a way to settle value.

The customer interface does not reveal how the payment actually works.

A tap with Apple Pay is a card transaction. A QR payment in WeChat Pay is a wallet ledger movement. A PayPal checkout is a staged transaction funded by a card or bank account. A Venmo payment is an internal balance transfer until the funds are withdrawn.

The word *wallet* describes the container. To understand the payment, look inside: card credential, bank account, stored balance, credit line, reward value, or internal ledger entry. The same checkout button can hide very different claims and rails.

Chapter 51: Buy Now, Pay Later

A customer reaches checkout with a $100 pair of headphones in the basket. Next to the card and wallet buttons, another option appears: pay $25 today, then three more payments over the next six weeks.

The button looks like just another payment method, which is part of its appeal. But BNPL is a credit loan built into the checkout process, not simply a new way to move money.

The promise is simple: the customer gets the product now and pays in equal installments over time, often every two weeks, with the first payment taken immediately. The remaining payments are collected automatically from the customer's linked card, bank account, or wallet.

The merchant is paid, usually after a fee is deducted. The repayment risk then lies with the BNPL provider, issuer, or merchant, which collects the payment from the customer later. Many short-term plans are marketed as interest-free if the customer pays on time, because the merchant covers the financing costs through a fee deducted from the settlement amount.

BNPL still uses familiar payment systems: an installment might be charged to a card, a merchant payout might arrive by bank transfer, and a wallet may appear in the checkout interface. What changes is when the customer pays, who funds the purchase, and who carries the risk until repayment.

This is why BNPL grew quickly in online retail. It appears when the customer has already chosen the product and is deciding whether to complete the purchase. A smaller first payment can make the order feel easier to accept.

BNPL brings three views into one checkout button: for customers, a cash-flow tool; for merchants, a conversion and basket-size tool; for providers, a credit-risk business.

Product Types

BNPL is a family of checkout financing models. The name covers several product types.

Pay in 3 or Pay in 4 is the best-known model. The purchase is divided into equal installments, usually over a few weeks. The first payment is taken immediately, and the remaining installments are collected automatically. For customers who pay on time, these plans are often marketed as interest-free. The provider earns mainly from merchant fees.

Pay in thirty days delays the whole payment instead of splitting it. The customer receives the goods immediately and pays the full amount later. This format fits fashion and retail especially well. A customer can order several sizes, try them at home, return what does not fit, and pay only for what they keep.

Long-term installments stretch repayment over months or years. At this point, BNPL starts to resemble traditional consumer credit. The product may include interest, fixed fees, or promotional 0 percent financing. It is common for larger purchases such as electronics, furniture, travel, or medical services.

Short-term BNPL is often free for on-time customers because the merchant covers the cost. Longer-term options are closer to loans, where the customer may pay interest or fees.

Funding Models

The product type explains how the customer pays. The funding model explains who provides the capital and who takes the loss if the customer does not repay.

BNPL economics usually fall into three models: provider-funded, issuer-funded, and merchant-funded.

Question	Provider-Funded BNPL	Issuer-Funded Installments	Merchant-Funded Financing
Source of funds	BNPL provider	Card-issuing bank	Merchant or financing partner
When the merchant gets paid	Usually soon after purchase, minus provider fee	Through standard card acquiring	Over time, or upfront through a partner arrangement
Main risk owner	BNPL provider	Issuer	Merchant or financing partner

Revenue source	Merchant fee, interest, funding income, portfolio sale, or servicing revenue, depending on product	Interest or installment fees charged by the issuer	Sales growth, customer retention, or subsidized financing economics
How it looks to the customer	New checkout credit arrangement with automatic repayments	Installment plan on an existing card	"0% financing" or store financing from the merchant

In a provider-funded model, the BNPL company serves as an intermediary between the customer and the merchant. It approves the customer, pays the merchant, and collects installments later. Klarna, Afterpay, and Affirm are common examples, though each provider has its own product structure and funding arrangements.

In an issuer-funded model, the customer's existing card issuer turns a purchase into installments. The merchant is paid through standard card acquiring. The customer repays the issuer over time. Visa Installments and American Express Plan It follow this logic. To the customer, it feels like a feature of an existing card rather than a separate BNPL account.

In a merchant-funded model, the retailer either carries the receivables itself or subsidizes financing provided by a partner. This is the classic store-financing model: "0 percent financing for twelve months," often used for furniture, electronics, travel, or other high value purchases.

All three models can look similar at checkout. The real difference lies in who provides the money, who collects from the customer, and who bears the loss if the customer does not pay.

Provider-Funded Flow

Most people think of provider-funded BNPL when they hear the term. This model shows why BNPL is more than a payment button.

Take a $100 purchase and split it into four payments of $25 each.

Before or during checkout, the customer confirms their identity with the BNPL provider and links a repayment method, such as a card or bank account. The provider securely stores the repayment method, typically as tokens rather than raw card or account data. It may run a soft credit check and use device, behavioral, account, and repayment-history signals to assess risk.

At checkout, the customer selects BNPL. The merchant's integration sends the provider the transaction amount, merchant details, basket information, and fraud signals. The provider makes a real-time decision: approve or decline.

If approved, the provider funds the purchase. The merchant might receive $96 on a $100 sale. The $4 difference is the provider's fee. From the merchant's perspective, the sale is effectively complete. The merchant has been paid, minus the fee, and can ship the order.

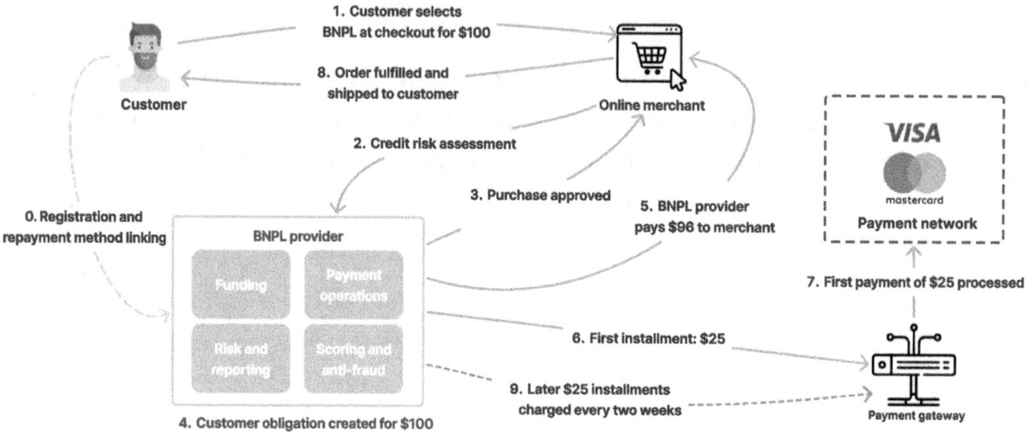

Figure 51.1: Provider-funded BNPL transaction flow.

The customer now owes the provider $100. The first installment may be charged immediately. If the customer linked a card, that first $25 charge is a normal card transaction. It travels through a payment gateway, the payment network, and the issuing bank for authorization. For that installment charge, the BNPL provider is effectively acting as the merchant.

The remaining installments are collected later, usually from the stored repayment method. If that method is a card, the later charges are typically card-on-file transactions initiated by the provider under the repayment agreement. The customer does not have to approve each installment again at checkout.

The provider follows the schedule, retries failed payments, sends reminders, and may charge late fees where permitted. If the customer stops paying, the provider may restrict the account, hand the debt to collections, sell the receivable, or write it off.

The core trade is simple: the merchant gets paid now, the customer pays over time, and the BNPL provider earns a fee for bridging the gap.

The Economics of BNPL

Merchants usually do not offer BNPL because it is cheaper than card payments. They add it because it can help increase sales.

The checkout effect is the point. A $100 purchase can be paid in $25 installments today and three more $25 payments later. That smaller initial payment can make the purchase feel more manageable, improve conversion rates, and encourage higher-value baskets. For some merchants, that sales lift justifies a higher cost of acceptance.

BNPL fees are often higher than standard card-acquiring fees because the provider is doing more than processing a transaction. It underwrites the customer, funds the merchant, carries repayment risk, handles collections, and provides a checkout experience designed to reduce hesitation. BNPL is therefore closer to a sales and financing tool than a simple payment processing tool.

That same structure changes the customer experience. Used carefully, short-term interest-free BNPL can help manage cash flow without revolving credit card debt. The customer receives the goods now and repays over a defined schedule, often without interest if payments are made on time.

The risk is that the debt can become fragmented. With a credit card, the customer has one balance with one issuer. With BNPL, the customer may have separate plans with Klarna, PayPal, Afterpay, a store's own financing program, and a card issuer installment feature. Each plan can look small on its own, while the combined repayment burden becomes harder to track.

Missed payments can trigger late fees, blocked access to future BNPL purchases, collection activity, or negative credit reporting. The consequences depend on the contract, provider policy, and local rules. BNPL can feel lighter than a credit card because the checkout is quick and the repayment schedule looks simple, but the customer is still receiving value now and promising to pay later. That makes it credit, even when it is presented as a payment option.

For the provider, the business depends on approving enough profitable transactions while avoiding customers and orders that are unlikely to repay. That decision has to happen at checkout, often in milliseconds, using signals from the customer, merchant, basket, device, repayment history, fraud checks, and affordability assessment.

The trade-off is tight. If the provider is too strict, merchants lose potential sales. If it is too lenient, more customers fail to pay. Too many checks make checkout harder, but too few checks increase credit losses and fraud.

In short-term BNPL, the provider earns mainly from merchant fees. In longer-term products, it may also earn interest or fixed charges from the customer. Some providers also sell receivables or installment portfolios to banks or institutional investors.

BNPL companies, therefore, play several roles at once: payment partner for the merchant, lender for the customer, fraud detector at checkout, and collector after the sale. The product works only when those roles stay in balance: enough lift for the merchant, enough clarity for the customer, and enough repayment performance for the provider.

BNPL versus Credit Cards

People often compare BNPL to credit cards because both let customers buy now and pay later. The comparison is useful, but only up to a point.

A credit card gives the customer a revolving line of credit before the purchase. The issuer approves a limit during the card application process. At checkout, the issuer authorizes the transaction against that existing limit. The customer can later pay the full balance, pay a minimum amount, or carry debt and pay interest.

With BNPL, approval often happens at checkout and can depend on the specific purchase. A provider might approve a $60 clothing order but decline a $900 electronics order from the same customer. The repayment schedule is usually fixed in advance, especially for short-term plans.

Dimension	BNPL	Credit Card
Credit decision	Often made instantly at checkout	Limit approved in advance by issuer
Repayment	Fixed installment schedule	Flexible monthly repayment, subject to minimum payments
Customer cost	Often zero interest for short-term plans if paid on time	Interest applies to carried balances
Merchant cost	Usually higher merchant fee	Standard acquiring cost
Risk owner	Provider, issuer, or merchant depending on model	Issuing bank
Regulation	Tightening and jurisdiction-specific	Long-established credit regulation

BNPL can also overlap with card installments. In issuer-funded models, the customer's own bank splits a card purchase into installments. That can look like BNPL in the app, but the underlying relationship is different. The merchant receives a normal card payment. The issuer manages the installment plan afterward.

Card-linked installment offers show why the label is less useful than the funding model. The checkout interface may sit inside a wallet or banking app, but the credit can still be provided by a bank, card issuer, BNPL provider, or merchant-finance partner.

Regulation and Credit Classification

BNPL became popular partly because it did not neatly fit into existing categories. It looked like a payment method, acted like short-term credit, and in some places avoided rules that applied to credit cards and traditional loans.

That ambiguity is becoming harder to maintain. Regulators are converging on the same concern: a checkout button can still be a credit agreement. Once BNPL gives the customer goods now and collects payment later, familiar credit questions appear. Was the cost shown clearly? Was repayment affordable? What happens after missed payments? How are complaints handled? How is credit information reported?

The UK has moved toward bringing deferred payment credit, including BNPL, under FCA regulation. Australia has brought BNPL providers into its credit-licensing framework. The EU's revised Consumer Credit Directive expands consumer credit rules to cover smaller and shorter-term credit products, including BNPL-style arrangements. In the United States, federal treatment has been less settled: the CFPB issued a 2024 interpretive rule applying certain credit card protections to BNPL, then withdrew it in 2025. Even there, the underlying concerns remain visible in supervision, enforcement, state law, and provider practices.

Across markets, BNPL is increasingly treated less as a lightweight checkout feature and more as a credit product with disclosure, affordability, complaints, refunds, reporting, and customer-protection implications.

Chapter 52: QR Payments

A QR code does not move money, authorize a transaction, or settle funds. It is a machine-readable container for data: a way to pass information from one device or screen to another.

In payments, that data can include the merchant ID, payment account, amount, currency, order reference, expiry time, and other transaction details. The customer's app uses that information to prepare the payment.

What happens next depends on the system behind the scan. The payment may run through a card network, a bank transfer system, an instant payment rail, a digital wallet, or a closed-loop platform. Scanning the code might start a bank transfer, open a wallet for checkout, or pass card payment data to a network such as Visa, Mastercard, UnionPay, or a local card scheme.

In Chapter 50, we separated wallet interfaces from the underlying payment mechanisms. QR is also an interaction layer: it initiates the payment, but the underlying system determines the cost, speed, settlement timing, dispute process, and fraud risk.

A coffee shop in Brazil, a street vendor in China, an online store in India, and a small merchant using a card network QR code may all display similar-looking codes, even though the underlying payment processes can differ widely.

Two Ways to Classify QR Payments

The simplest way to classify QR payments is to look at two questions: first, is the code static or dynamic; second, who presents the code, the merchant or the customer?

A static QR code is created once and reused. It usually identifies the merchant or payment account. The customer scans it and, in many implementations, enters the amount themselves. This is cheap and easy to deploy: a merchant can print a sticker and start accepting payments without buying a terminal. The trade-off is weaker control. Static codes can create problems with amount entry, order matching, and tampering.

A dynamic QR code is created for a specific transaction. It can encode transaction-specific data such as amount, currency, merchant, order ID, expiry time, and more. When the customer scans it, their payment app receives all these details. This allows the payment process to be tightly matched to the transaction, supporting better order reconciliation and reduced tampering. However, this approach requires software to generate a unique code for each transaction and to associate each code with the correct payment.

In a merchant-presented QR flow, the merchant shows the code, and the customer scans it. This is common in small shops, restaurants, market stalls, donation points, online checkouts, invoices, and payment links. The code might appear on a printed sticker, a POS screen, a receipt, a website, or a checkout page.

In a customer-presented QR flow, the customer shows the code, and the merchant scans it. This is common in wallet-heavy environments where the customer opens an app, displays a payment code, and lets the merchant's scanner or POS device read it.

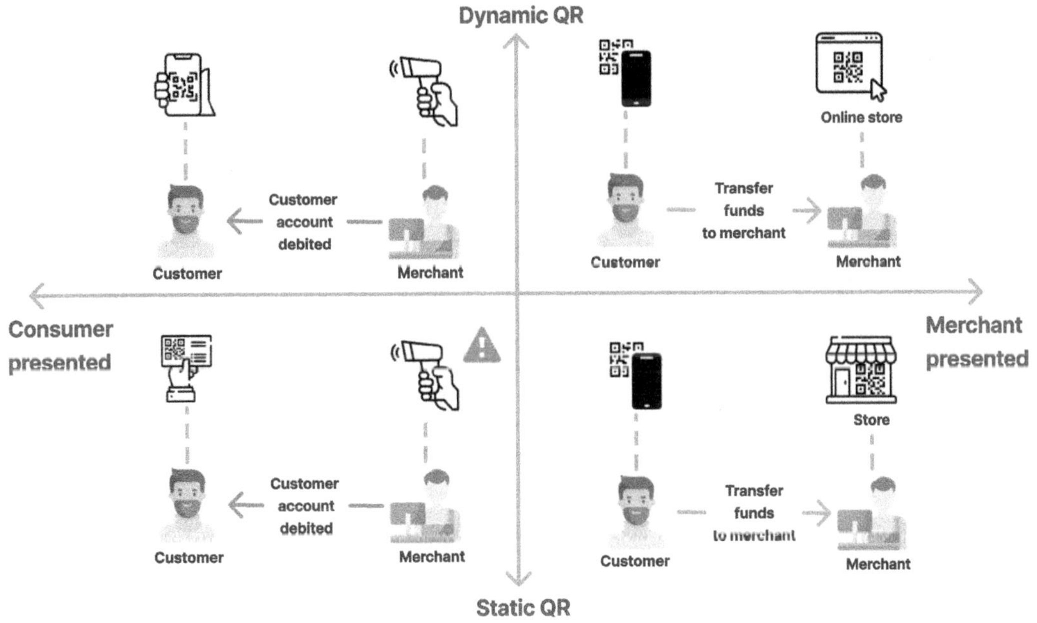

Figure 52.1: Classification of QR payment flows.

Figure 52.1 combines the two questions into four scenarios:

Type	Who Shows the Code	What the Code Contains	Typical Use
Customer-presented dynamic QR	Customer	A fresh payment code generated by the customer's wallet or banking app	Wallet payments at staffed checkouts
Customer-presented static QR	Customer	A reusable customer identifier or payment credential	Rare or limited closed-loop use cases
Merchant-presented dynamic QR	Merchant	Amount, merchant, currency, order reference, and transaction data	Retail checkouts, online payments, invoices
Merchant-presented static QR	Merchant	Merchant identifier or account details	Small merchants, donations, market stalls

This classification describes the interaction. It still does not tell us which payment rail moves the money.

Static QR Codes

Static QR codes became popular because they make digital acceptance cheap. The merchant does not need a payment terminal. A printed sign is enough. This is useful for small merchants, taxis, market stalls, street-food vendors, charities, and informal sellers. It lets them accept both digital and cash payments with little or no dedicated hardware.

That simplicity creates three practical problems.

The first is amount entry. If the static code only identifies the merchant, the customer usually needs to enter the amount. They can mistype it. The merchant often needs to manually check the confirmation. At a busy checkout, this slows the transaction.

The second is reconciliation. If many customers scan the same code and send different amounts, the merchant needs a way to match incoming payments to orders. Without a transaction reference, that matching can become messy.

The third is tampering. A printed code can be covered with another printed code. The customer thinks they are paying the merchant, but the payment instruction points to someone else. This is a low-tech attack, which is exactly why it can work.

Static QR codes are useful thanks to their low cost, but harder to control because of their simplicity.

Dynamic QR Codes

Dynamic QR codes address many of the weaknesses of static QR codes.

When the merchant generates a new code for each transaction, the amount can be locked to that code, the customer does not need to type it manually, the order ID can be included, the code can expire, and the merchant can automatically match the incoming payment to a specific sale.

This makes dynamic QR better suited to restaurants, supermarkets, online checkouts, invoices, and any environment where the merchant needs to link a payment to an order.

Dynamic QR also gives the customer a clearer confirmation screen. Instead of scanning a generic code and entering the amount, the app can display the merchant's name, amount, currency, and reference before the customer approves the transaction.

The trade-off is software. Dynamic QR requires a POS system, checkout page, invoice system, or merchant app that can generate new codes, link them to orders, receive payment confirmations, and close transactions. A printed sticker cannot do that on its own.

The choice is practical: static QR keeps setup costs low; dynamic QR gives better control, cleaner reconciliation, and stronger protection against common errors.

Merchant-Presented QR

Merchant-presented QR codes are the most common form of QR acceptance. The merchant shows the code, the customer scans it with a phone, the app displays the merchant and payment details, and the customer confirms.

The same scan-and-confirm gesture can use several underlying payment models.

The main models are card-based QR, account-to-account QR, and wallet-based

QR. Here, wallet-based means a wallet or super-app model, not a network-tokenized card wallet such as Apple Pay or Google Pay.

Model	What the Customer Does	Underlying Rail	Merchant Economics	Settlement Pattern
Card-based QR	Scans a QR code and pays with a card credential inside an app	Card network	Similar to card acquiring	Follows card-processing timelines
Account-to-account QR	Scans and approves a bank transfer	Domestic instant or bank transfer rail	Often lower than card acceptance	Often near-real-time, depending on the rail
Wallet-based QR	Pays from wallet balance or linked funding source	Wallet ledger, card, bank account, or local rail	Depends on wallet rules	Internal wallet transfer or external settlement

The customer usually sees the same action: scan, confirm, and wait for a success message. The merchant may also see only that the payment was completed. Underneath, however, each model carries different economics, settlement timing, fraud exposure, and refund handling.

Card-Based QR

In a card-based QR payment, the QR code replaces the physical interaction with the card and terminal. The customer does not insert a card, tap an NFC card, or type a card number. Instead, the customer's app reads the QR code and starts a payment using a card credential, often a tokenized one.

The interface changes, but the merchant economics, participant roles, and post-transaction handling still follow the card-acceptance model rather than the QR interface. The transaction may still involve an acquirer, payment network, issuer, authorization, clearing, settlement, fraud rules, disputes, and card-based merchant pricing.

This model can be useful where card acceptance is desirable but terminal infrastructure is expensive, unavailable, or operationally difficult. A merchant can display a code instead of installing full terminal hardware. The customer's phone and banking app become the payment interface.

The QR code changes the entry point. It does not necessarily change the rail.

Account-to-Account QR

In an account-to-account QR payment, the customer scans the code and approves a transfer from their bank account to the merchant's. No card network is required.

This model is common in markets with strong instant-payment infrastructure and broad adoption of mobile apps. The QR code provides the customer's app with the information it needs to initiate the transfer: the merchant identifier, amount, reference, and, sometimes, additional payment metadata.

For merchants, the appeal is direct. Account-to-account QR can lower acceptance costs, move funds quickly, and remove the need for a card terminal. For small merchants, that can change the economics of accepting digital payments: a printed code or generated checkout code can replace hardware that might otherwise be too expensive.

The risk profile differs from cards. Account-to-account QR payments are often push payments, so the customer authorizes the transfer in their own app. That can reduce classic card-chargeback exposure for merchants, but it creates different problems around scams and authorized push payment fraud. If a customer is tricked into approving the transfer, recovery can be harder than in a card-dispute model.

The QR code carries the instruction. The bank transfer system decides what happens next.

Wallet-Based QR

In a wallet-based QR payment, the customer pays through a digital wallet or super app. The funding source for the wallet may include a wallet balance, a linked card, a bank account, a credit line, a reward balance, or an internal wallet transfer. The wallet system manages initiation, money movement, and settlement.

This is different from using a card wallet at an NFC terminal. In wallet-based QR, the wallet can be the customer interface, merchant network, ledger, risk engine, and acceptance layer. Large super-app wallets can combine merchant payments, P2P transfers, loyalty and rewards, messaging, mini-apps, credit products, and merchant tools into a single environment.

A wallet-based QR payment may be kept entirely within the wallet provider's system. If both parties use the same wallet, the provider can debit and credit the relevant wallet balances internally. In this scenario, no external bank or card network is used for that transaction.

Alternatively, the wallet may fund the payment using a linked card or bank account. The QR experience can look identical to the customer, while the underlying money movement is completely different.

Online Checkout

QR payments are not limited to physical stores.

In an online checkout, the merchant can display a dynamic QR code on the screen. The customer scans it with a phone and confirms the payment in a banking app or wallet. This avoids entering card details on the website and works especially well when the customer starts checkout on a desktop computer but has the payment app on their phone.

The QR code serves as a bridge between the website and the app that authorizes the payment: the website shows the code, the phone reads it, the banking app or wallet prepares the transaction, the customer confirms, and the merchant receives confirmation and completes the order.

This is another example of QR as an interaction layer. It connects the checkout page to the app that can actually start and confirm the payment.

Adoption and Reach

QR payments became powerful because they solved an acceptance problem.

Card terminals require hardware, connectivity, certification, maintenance, and merchant onboarding. Large retailers can absorb those costs and processes. A small food stall, a taxi driver, an independent seller, or an informal merchant may not.

A QR code lowers the barrier. The merchant can show a printed code, a phone screen, a tablet, or a checkout page. The customer already has the scanner: a smartphone camera in a banking, wallet, or payment app.

This made QR especially useful in markets where card acceptance was not universal, small merchants were underserved, and consumers were already using mobile apps. Instead of waiting for every merchant to install a terminal, the market could move toward phone-based payment acceptance.

QR also fits naturally with account-to-account payment systems. A domestic instant-payment rail can move funds quickly. The QR code tells the customer's app where to send the money and how to label the payment.

> **Why QR Won in Parts of Asia Before Europe**
>
> QR payments became dominant in China, India, and parts of Southeast Asia because the local conditions favored them. Card acceptance was less universal, terminals were expensive for small merchants, and large platforms or public payment rails had strong incentives to expand QR code acceptance quickly.
>
> In much of Europe and the United States, cards and contactless terminals were already widespread by the time mobile QR payments became viable at scale. QR codes are still useful in some niches, especially in wallets, invoices, restaurants, P2P, and online checkout, but they don't need to replace ordinary card-present checkout.

A full payment system sat behind the QR scan. Without the wallet, the bank rail, the merchant account, and the risk controls, a QR code is only a square pattern.

Risks

QR payments come with their own risks.

The most obvious is code tampering. Someone can replace a merchant's printed code with a fake one. The customer thinks they are paying the merchant, but the money goes somewhere else.

Another risk is misdirection. A fake website, invoice, parking notice, delivery message, or support email may include a QR code that points to the wrong destination. QR codes can look legitimate because customers cannot see the destination from the pattern alone.

Static QR codes can also create honest mistakes. If the customer enters the amount, they might pay too much or too little. The merchant might not notice immediately. Matching incoming payments to orders also becomes harder when transfers are not linked to a specific sale.

Account-to-account QR payments introduce push-payment scam risk. If a customer is tricked into approving a transfer, recovery can be difficult because the customer authorized the payment, even if they were deceived.

Good QR systems reduce these risks through dynamic codes, merchant name display, amount confirmation, transaction references, expiry times, app-based authentication, and fraud monitoring. The customer still has a simple job: check the merchant name and amount before approving the payment.

Chapter 53: Local Payment Methods

A card network can work worldwide and still fall short in a local market.

When a merchant expands into a new country, offering Visa and Mastercard is not always enough. Customers may abandon checkout not because of price or technical issues, but because the payment options do not match how they typically pay.

In the Netherlands, many customers expect iDEAL. In Poland, BLIK is widely used. In Brazil, Pix and Boleto serve different payment needs. In Mexico, OXXO enables online shoppers to pay in cash at convenience stores. In China, Alipay and WeChat Pay dominate everyday transactions. In Kenya, M-Pesa grew through mobile money and agent networks instead of cards.

These are usually called *local payment methods*, or *LPMs*. Payment service providers may also refer to them as *alternative payment methods (APMs)*. The word *alternative* can be misleading. In some markets, the local method is the default way customers expect to pay.

Local payment methods reflect payment habits shaped by local banking systems, regulations, merchant needs, and consumer trust.

Local Payment Method Scope

A local payment method is a payment method widely used within a specific country or region. It aligns with customers' payment preferences and behaviors in that location, typically reflecting what they trust, recognize, or expect when making purchases.

It is not defined by one technical rail. An LPM might use a bank transfer, wallet balance, cash voucher, domestic card scheme, QR code, direct debit, mobile money account, or an instant payment system. The checkout button is only the visible part.

That variety sets LPMs apart from categories such as card payments. A card payment has a recognizable model: issuer, acquirer, network, authorization, clearing, and settlement. Local payment methods are a commercial grouping, not a single technical architecture.

A few examples show the range:

Local Method	Market	Basic Model
iDEAL	Netherlands	Bank account payment for online checkout
BLIK	Poland	Banking-app code used for checkout, ATM, and P2P flows
Pix	Brazil	Instant account-to-account payments
Boleto	Brazil	Payment slip that can be paid through bank, app, ATM, or cash location
OXXO	Mexico	Cash payment for online purchases through convenience stores
Alipay / WeChat Pay	China	Wallet and super-app payment ecosystems
M-Pesa	Kenya and other markets	Mobile-money system using telecom and agent infrastructure
Bancontact	Belgium	Domestic card and mobile payment scheme

These systems are different, but each solved a local problem better than international cards could. For a global merchant, that is the practical point. A checkout page with only card options may work well in one country and underperform in another.

Local Market Conditions

Local payment methods usually grow from a few recurring conditions.

First, domestic banking habits may already be strong. If customers are used to paying directly from a bank account, a bank transfer method can feel more natural than entering card details. This explains why bank-based checkout methods became powerful in parts of Europe.

Second, regulation or public infrastructure may push the market toward a specific model. Instant-payment schemes spread quickly when central banks, regulators, or industry bodies create common rules, encourage participation, or make the service attractive for banks and merchants.

Third, card penetration may be low. If many consumers do not have cards, a card-only checkout excludes them. Cash voucher methods and mobile money systems often expand in these environments.

Fourth, consumer trust may differ by market. In some countries, customers trust bank authentication more than card entry on a merchant website. In others, they trust a familiar wallet brand more than an unknown online store.

Fifth, merchant economics may favor the local method. A merchant may accept cards for reach but prefer account-to-account payments because they settle faster, cost less, or carry fewer card-style dispute risks.

These forces often overlap. Pix in Brazil reflects central bank design, broad bank participation, low consumer cost, and a market ready for a faster alternative to cash, cards, and older bank methods. Alipay grew from a trust problem in Chinese e-commerce and expanded into a broader financial and commercial platform.

The strongest local methods do not win because they are local, but because they solve a local problem better than alternatives.

Bank-Transfer-Based Methods

Some local payment methods use bank accounts.

In these flows, the customer does not enter card details. Instead, the payment is initiated from the customer's bank account, usually with authentication inside the bank's own interface or app. The merchant receives a confirmation that the payment has been initiated, accepted, or completed, depending on the scheme and provider.

A simplified online flow looks like this:

1. The customer selects the local bank transfer method at checkout.
2. The customer chooses their bank, or the bank is selected automatically.
3. The customer authenticates with the bank.
4. The bank initiates the transfer.

5. The merchant receives payment confirmation.
6. Settlement follows the rules of the payment system in use.

This model appears in different forms across Europe. iDEAL in the Netherlands is the clearest example. The customer selects iDEAL, chooses their bank, authenticates in the bank environment, and confirms the transfer. The merchant receives confirmation and can continue with the order.

Sofort and Trustly built related propositions around bank account payments, though their technical and regulatory models differ across markets and over time.

Open banking overlaps with this category, but it is not identical to it. A local bank transfer method may predate open banking regulations. Open banking creates a regulated API framework for account access and payment initiation. The product at checkout can look similar, but the legal and technical foundation can differ. In Chapter 54, we examine that distinction directly: how open banking enables licensed third parties to initiate payments or access account data via bank APIs, and why that changes the relationships among banks, merchants, and fintech products.

For merchants, the attraction is commercial rather than definitional. Bank transfer methods cost less than card payments because they use a different pricing and risk model. They may also reduce card chargeback exposure by requiring customers to authenticate with their bank. But they are not frictionless by default. Redirects, bank selection screens, inconsistent authentication flows, and slower settlement can all hurt conversion.

A bank transfer option is not automatically better than a card option. It works best when customers recognize it, trust it, and expect to use it.

Cash and Voucher Methods

Some local payment methods exist because not every customer wants, trusts, or has access to fully digital payments.

A cash voucher method allows a customer to start a purchase online and complete payment offline. The merchant's payment provider generates a reference, barcode, or payment slip. The customer takes that reference to a cash location, bank branch, convenience store, ATM, or mobile app and pays later.

Boleto in Brazil is a classic example. OXXO in Mexico follows a similar logic through convenience stores. Konbini payments in Japan let customers pay for online purchases at convenience stores.

The flow is different from a card transaction:

1. The customer chooses the cash or voucher method at checkout.
2. The system generates a payment reference.
3. The customer pays through an approved offline or semi-offline channel.
4. The payment method provider confirms the payment.
5. The merchant releases or ships the order.

This approach solves a real access issue. Some customers want to shop online but do not have a card, do not trust entering card details, or prefer to use cash. Cash voucher methods allow these customers to buy online without a traditional card.

The downside is timing. Cash voucher payments can stay pending until the customer pays, and sometimes the customer never completes the payment. This can complicate operations for merchants, who may need to reserve inventory, handle expired orders, and carefully match payment references.

For merchants, these methods can open access to customers who would otherwise be excluded. Mechanically, they behave more like delayed payment instructions than real-time card authorizations.

Domestic Wallets and Super-App Payments

Wallets can also become local payment methods.

In some markets, the wallet has become the main consumer payment interface rather than a place to store card credentials. Alipay and WeChat Pay in China are the strongest examples. A customer can pay merchants, transfer money to friends, use mini-apps, pay bills, shop, access promotions, and use financial services within the same environment.

For the customer, the payment is familiar and fast. They open the app they already use, scan a QR code or choose the wallet online, and confirm. For merchants, accepting the wallet can mean access to customers, promotions, loyalty tools, and platform traffic, not just payment acceptance.

M-Pesa shows another version of the same principle. It did not start with card acceptance or bank account payments. It grew out of telecom infrastructure and agent networks in markets where access to bank branches was limited. Customers could deposit cash with an agent, send value through a mobile phone, and cash out elsewhere. The agent network substituted for bank branches.

These examples are different. Alipay, WeChat Pay, and M-Pesa come from distinct systems and address different local problems. Still, they show that successful local payment methods often grow out of tools people already use daily.

Direct Debit and Mandate-Based Methods

Some local methods rely on pull payments from a bank account.

A direct debit allows a merchant or service provider to collect money from a customer's account with prior authorization. In Europe, SEPA Direct Debit is the standard example. In other markets, domestic direct debit schemes play similar roles.

This is especially useful for recurring bills and subscriptions. The customer does not need to initiate every payment. The merchant collects under the mandate.

The mechanism is different from card-on-file. With card-on-file, a stored card credential is charged through the card system. With direct debit, collections run through bank account rails and mandate rules.

This difference changes the risk profile.

Direct debit can be reliable for recurring billing because bank accounts do not expire like cards. There is no card replacement cycle, no expiry date, and no card network token update problem. But direct debit usually has stronger refund or return rights than merchants expect. A consumer can reverse an authorized direct debit within the window specified by the scheme rules. Unauthorized collections may carry an even longer dispute period.

Direct debit works well for merchants when payments are regular and predictable. It is less useful when they need payments to be final right away.

Domestic Card Schemes

Not every card payment is processed by Visa or Mastercard.

Many countries have domestic card schemes that route local transactions through national infrastructure. Examples include Cartes Bancaires in France, Girocard in Germany, mada in Saudi Arabia, KNET in Kuwait, and Bancontact in Belgium.

Some of these schemes are co-badged with international networks. A card may route domestically through the local scheme and internationally through Visa or Mastercard. To the cardholder, it may look like a single card. In terms of infrastructure, routing depends on where and how the card is used.

Domestic card schemes often exist due to costs, local regulations, national oversight, or the way the market has developed over time. They give banks and regulators more control over payments and can be cheaper to process than international networks.

For international merchants, domestic schemes raise a practical question: is accepting cards enough, or does the checkout need to explicitly support the local scheme? In some markets, local debit methods carry more reach or trust than international credit cards.

Merchant Decision

For merchants, adding a local payment method is not just about adding another logo to the checkout page. It changes how customers complete purchases, how much the merchant pays, when funds arrive, how refunds work, how disputes are handled, and how cleanly payments can be reconciled.

A merchant, therefore, has to evaluate a local method on several dimensions: reach, conversion, cost, settlement, reversibility, and reconciliation. These metrics determine whether the method will help the business or create new operational problems.

Reach comes first. If customers in a market expect iDEAL, BLIK, or Pix, not supporting it can cost sales before price or product quality enters the picture.

Conversion is the next test. A familiar local method can make checkout feel safer and easier. An unfamiliar redirect, confusing bank-selection screen, or poorly localized flow can have the opposite effect. The same payment method can perform differently across countries, devices, and customer segments.

Cost is only one part of the decision. Some local methods are cheaper than cards, especially account-to-account methods that avoid card interchange. Others, including wallets, cash vouchers, and BNPL-style methods, can carry meaningful fees. The useful comparison is total acceptance cost: transaction fees, provider markup, refunds, disputes, failed payments, operational work, and support costs.

Settlement also changes the economics. A method that confirms instantly may still settle later. Funds may arrive gross or net of fees, per transaction or in batches, in local currency or another settlement currency. For a merchant operating across markets, those details affect cash flow, treasury operations, and reporting.

Reversibility and reconciliation are just as important. Some methods have card-like disputes. Some have bank-return windows. Some are difficult to reverse once the customer has pushed the payment. A method also needs stable references: order ID, payer reference, settlement reference, and refund link. A payment method that converts well but reconciles poorly can lead to costly back-office work.

A local payment method should be evaluated by how it performs in operations, not just whether customers recognize its logo.

Integration Complexity

PSPs often package local payment methods behind a single API and multiple payment buttons. That packaging is useful, but it can hide important operational differences.

Each method has its own lifecycle. A card transaction, a bank transfer, a voucher, and a wallet payment all create different statuses, refund paths, settlement reports, and reconciliation needs. A voucher may sit in pending status until the customer pays or the reference expires. A wallet may confirm instantly inside its own system, but settle with the merchant later.

The data model varies as well. One method may provide a clean payer name, an order reference, a settlement reference, and a refund link. Another may provide only a transaction ID and amount. Refund support can also differ: a method may allow partial refunds, only full refunds, or no direct refund at all, without a separate payout. Disputes follow the same pattern. Some methods have a defined scheme or bank processes; others leave the merchant and PSP to resolve the case manually.

Adding local payment methods is operationally harder than adding more checkout buttons. The real work involves handling statuses, managing expiries, reporting settlements, communicating with customers, processing refunds, and reconciling payments.

A merchant adding local methods should ask practical questions before launch:

Question	Consequence
When is the payment final?	Determines when the merchant can ship or deliver.
When does the merchant receive funds?	Affects cash flow and settlement reporting.
Can the customer reverse the payment?	Determines dispute and refund exposure.
What references are included?	Affects reconciliation and customer support.
Are partial refunds supported?	Important for returns, cancellations, and split orders.
What happens if the payment expires?	Critical for voucher and delayed-payment methods.
Who handles customer complaints?	Determines operational ownership.

These details determine whether the payment method will work in the real world.

Scale

Local payment methods are often underestimated because many are not global brands. For a merchant entering a new country, that assumption can be expensive.

A local method can be more important in its home market than any international network. The choice is not between a global method and a niche local option. It may be between a checkout that feels familiar and one that loses customers before they complete the purchase.

That is why global acceptance cannot mean offering the same payment methods everywhere. Merchants have to decide, market by market, how customers prefer to pay, which methods they trust, how quickly funds settle, how disputes are handled, and what operational work each method creates.

Cards remain central to global commerce. They are hard to match for cross-border reach, online acceptance, and consistent operating rules. But local payment methods show the other side of the system. Payments are also shaped by domestic banks, public infrastructure, mobile platforms, cash access, regulation, and local trust.

Payment habits do not form in isolation. They grow around the infrastructure people can access, the brands they trust, the protections they expect, and the tools merchants can afford to accept. Local payment methods keep winning when they better fit those conditions than the global default.

Chapter 54: Open Banking Payments

A customer reaches checkout and chooses Pay by Bank.

The customer does not provide card details or use a wallet balance. Instead, the checkout sends them to their bank, where they log in, review the payment, approve it, and return to the merchant. Behind the scenes, a regulated third party initiates a bank transfer from the customer's account.

Open banking payments allow customers to pay directly from their accounts via regulated APIs, with built-in consent and authentication. The customer doesn't copy account details, enter references, or share credentials with the merchant.

Open banking does not replace banks. The bank still holds the account, authenticates the customer, checks the instruction, and sends the payment into the relevant bank rail. The change is that a licensed third party can connect the merchant experience to the customer's bank account through a controlled interface.

That makes open banking payments sit at the intersection of several worlds. They look like checkout methods, use bank transfer rails, depend on APIs, and are shaped by regulation. In some markets, they compete with cards, wallets, and local bank transfer methods. In others, they remain a specialist option used for account funding, invoices, bills, or financial apps.

From Closed Banking to Account Access

Before open banking, third-party access to bank accounts was fragile. It depended on direct bank integrations, manual exports, or screen scraping.

Screen scraping enabled early financial apps, but it was a weak foundation for a payment system. Customers had to share sensitive login details, banks couldn't always distinguish between customer and service usage, site changes could break access, and both consent management and liability were unclear when things went wrong.

Open banking was created to replace that fragile workaround with secure, permissioned API access.

The bank holding the account is the account servicing payment service provider (ASPSP). The external regulated provider is the third-party provider (TPP). Two types of TPP are especially important:

Type	Full Name	What It Can Do
AISP	Account Information Service Provider	Access account information in read-only mode, with the customer's consent
PISP	Payment Initiation Service Provider	Initiate payments from the customer's account, with the customer's consent

AISPs are responsible for accessing and reading account information. PISPs are responsible for initiating payments from the customer's bank account.

A budgeting app that shows balances across several banks uses account information access, while a checkout provider enabling bank account payments uses payment initiation.

Account Information Services

Account information services were the first open banking use case that many customers experienced.

A customer connects several bank accounts to one app. The app shows balances, transactions, spending categories, cash-flow patterns, and alerts. Instead of logging into three banks separately, the customer sees a consolidated financial picture.

This can support personal finance apps, affordability checks, accounting tools, lending applications, and financial dashboards.

A lender may ask the customer to link a bank account to verify income and spending patterns. A small-business accounting tool may pull transactions from several banks and match payments to invoices. A consumer finance app may categorize spending and identify subscriptions.

The purpose here is not to make a payment. It is to use the account data.

That makes account information services valuable to fintech products, but they are different from open banking payments.

Payment Initiation Services and Pay by Bank

A payment initiation service allows a licensed third party to initiate a bank transfer on the customer's behalf.

The customer does not share their bank password with the third party; instead, they agree to the payment, authenticate with the bank, and approve the payment details. The payment initiation service provider (PISP) submits the payment request via an API, and the bank executes the transfer.

At checkout, this usually appears as Pay by Bank. Instead of asking for card details, the merchant offers a bank payment option. The customer approves the payment through their bank, and the merchant receives a status update that allows them to continue the order.

A typical flow looks like this:

1. The customer selects Pay by Bank at checkout.
2. The merchant's checkout provider passes the payment request to a PISP.
3. The customer selects their bank, or the checkout routes them automatically.
4. The bank displays the payment details.
5. The customer authenticates and approves.
6. The bank initiates the transfer.
7. The PISP returns payment status to the merchant or checkout provider.
8. The merchant confirms the order under its risk policy.

The customer experience can resemble a wallet redirect or a 3-D Secure challenge: the customer leaves checkout, authenticates elsewhere, and returns to the merchant. The payment underneath is different. The customer is not presenting a card credential or spending a wallet balance. They are approving a bank account payment.

Open banking provides the access layer. The underlying payment rail moves the funds. In the euro area, the transfer might use SEPA Credit Transfer or

SEPA Instant. In the UK, it might use Faster Payments. Other markets have their own domestic rails. That rail determines settlement timing, refund handling, and operational risk.

For merchants, Pay by Bank can cost less than cards because it avoids card networks and interchange fees, and may reduce exposure to chargebacks. Funds may arrive faster using instant rails. The customer also skips manual bank transfer steps, such as entering details, and hopes the payment is matched to their order.

A good Pay by Bank product does more than initiate the transfer. It helps the merchant match payments to orders, track status, handle failed or expired payments, support refunds, and reconcile settlement reports. That is where a strong PISP or checkout provider adds value.

Regulatory Framework

Open banking is not only a technology trend. In many markets, it is a regulated access model.

In Europe, PSD2 laid the foundation for AISPs and PISPs, introduced Strong Customer Authentication requirements, and granted licensed third parties access to payment accounts with the customer's consent. In the UK, open banking developed through a dedicated implementation framework and technical standards. Other markets have followed different paths, including broader consumer-data frameworks, market-led standards, bank partnerships, and commercial API access.

Regulation created a formal access model, but it did not make every connection equally good. API quality, uptime, documentation, error handling, authentication design, and payment status reporting can vary widely across banks and markets.

That is why the next phase of regulation and standard-setting focuses less on access itself and more on making it reliable, secure, and usable. European reforms under PSD3 and the Payment Services Regulation package continue that direction, with attention to API performance, fraud controls, permissions, consumer protection, and consistency across payment services. Open banking is also expanding toward open finance, where access may extend beyond payment accounts to savings, investments, pensions, insurance, and other financial products.

Adoption

Open banking payments can be attractive on paper. They use bank accounts directly, rely on strong bank authentication, reduce dependence on card networks, and can be cheaper for merchants.

Adoption has still been uneven.

The first constraint is API quality. If bank APIs are slow, unreliable, inconsistent, or difficult to integrate with, customers experience failed checkouts and merchants lose confidence.

Coverage is another constraint. Pay by Bank works well only when enough banks are supported. If the customer's bank is missing, the payment option feels incomplete.

User experience can also limit adoption. A smooth bank redirect can feel simple. A clumsy flow can feel worse than a card payment: select a bank, leave checkout, authenticate, approve, wait, return, and hope the merchant receives confirmation. Each extra step increases the risk of customer drop-off.

Trust is harder to build than technical access. Customers understand cards and may be familiar with PayPal or a wallet. They may not immediately understand what it means for a third party to initiate a payment from their bank account, even when the process is regulated and secure.

Consumer protection also shapes behavior. Cardholders are used to disputes, chargebacks, refunds, rewards, and sometimes credit. Open banking payments handle these issues differently. That difference may be acceptable for bills, account funding, invoices, and some domestic checkouts. It may be less attractive when customers expect card-style protection or rewards.

Habit is the hardest constraint. Payment behavior doesn't change just because a new option appears – it changes when the new option is clearly easier, cheaper, faster, or trusted enough that the old habit no longer makes sense.

Open banking payments can be technically available and still underused. Infrastructure creates the possibility. Adoption depends on coverage, reliability, user experience, trust, pricing, and habit.

Fraud and Scam Risk

Open banking payments reduce some risks and introduce others.

Customers don't need to share card details with merchants. The bank handles authentication. Payment details can be prefilled, reducing errors. The flow can also avoid some card-not-present fraud because there is no card number or security code to steal.

That removes some card data risk, but it leaves manipulation risk. If a scammer tricks a customer into approving a payment, the bank may still see it as a valid instruction because the customer authenticated and confirmed it. The problem is not that authentication failed. The problem is that the customer was deceived.

This is the same broad issue seen in instant payments: authorized push payment fraud, often shortened to APP fraud. The payment is authorized, but the authorization was obtained through social engineering.

Open banking payment products, therefore, need clear confirmation screens, recognizable recipient names, scam warnings, transaction monitoring, behavioral checks, and controls against mule accounts. Authentication proves that the customer approved the payment. It does not prove that the customer understood the situation correctly.

Fraud also looks different for merchants. Pay by Bank reduces some card-specific fraud, but merchants still need to handle account takeovers, fake confirmation screens, refund abuse, and rail-specific disputes.

A different rail creates a different risk model.

Refunds, Returns, and Disputes

The post-payment experience is one of the biggest differences from cards.

Open banking payments typically do not include a card-style chargeback framework. If the customer requests a refund, the merchant or provider often must issue a separate payment. If there is a dispute, handling depends on local law, provider rules, bank obligations, and the merchant's terms.

That can help merchants in some cases. Fewer card-style chargebacks can mean fewer operational disputes. Customers may still experience friction, especially when they expect refunds to work as easily as card refunds.

For product teams, refunds need to be designed, not assumed. A good Pay by Bank product needs clear refund paths, stable references, status updates, customer notifications, and support tooling. The merchant should be able to link the original payment, the refund, the settlement entry, and the customer order without manual detective work.

Making the sale is only the first part of the payment lifecycle.

Product Design

Open banking changes what product teams can build around bank accounts.

Once a third party can access account data or initiate payments with consent, the bank account can be used inside many different products: merchant checkouts can offer direct account payments, lending apps can verify income from bank transaction data, personal finance apps can aggregate accounts, accounting products can reconcile incoming payments, wallets can fund themselves from bank accounts, and marketplaces can build collection and payout flows with better bank connectivity.

All of these products depend on the same fragile point: the customer has to understand what they are approving. That might be a one-time payment, recurring access, account data sharing, a specific account, a specific amount, or a specific recipient. It also includes the less visible terms, such as how long the consent lasts and how the customer can revoke it.

That makes consent design part of the product, not just a compliance screen. If customers feel tricked into sharing account access, they may not use the product again. If they see clear payment details, a familiar bank login, a recognizable recipient, and a reliable confirmation, they are more likely to trust the flow.

The old model was closed banking. The workaround was screen scraping. Open banking replaces that workaround with permissioned access: the customer consents, the bank authenticates, the third party initiates a payment or reads account data only within the approved scope, and the money still moves through existing bank rails.

That is the real change. The bank account becomes something regulated third parties can connect to, not something only the bank can present. The bank stays in the system, but it is no longer the only interface to the account.

Part X

Fintech Infrastructure, Digital Money, and AI

Chapter 55: Neobanks and Digital Banking

A bank branch makes an impression the moment the customer walks in. There is a counter, a waiting area, staff, forms, back-office rooms, and usually a sense that banking is local, physical, and formal.

A neobank changes that first impression: the branch becomes an app, the card may be virtual, and a customer can open an account from the sofa, receive spending notifications seconds after a purchase, freeze a card from the phone, and see foreign exchange costs before paying rather than discovering them later on a statement.

The product feels lighter because the visible experience is simpler. But the deeper machinery has not disappeared. As we saw across the chapters on issuing, bank transfers, compliance, fraud, disputes, and settlement, those obligations still apply. A neobank changes how banking is delivered more than it changes the obligations behind it.

A neobank can remove branches, paper forms, and slow sign-up journeys. It still needs licensing, customer checks, payment networks, processors, ledgers, fraud controls, dispute handling, settlement, safeguarding or deposit protection, customer support, and sound economics.

Neobanks made banking feel modern. They did not make banking infrastructure optional.

Operating Models

A neobank is a digital-first financial institution or banking app that provides banking services without relying on traditional branches.

That definition is useful, but it hides an important distinction. The app the customer uses is not always the regulated institution that holds the customer's money. Some neobanks are fully licensed banks. Others are electronic money institutions. Some operate through partner banks. Some are front-end platforms assembled from licensed banks, processors, compliance vendors, card issuers, and infrastructure providers.

For this chapter, the most useful definition is practical rather than legal: a neobank offers a digital-first banking experience built on licensed financial infrastructure.

This usually means a current account or wallet, a debit card, money transfers, spending insights, foreign exchange, instant notifications, card controls, and customer support in the app. Some neobanks also offer lending, subscriptions, investments, crypto, insurance, business accounts, or marketplace services.

The customer sees one brand, one app, and one account-like experience. Underneath, several regulated and technical layers may be doing the work. Customer funds may be held as bank deposits, safeguarded as e-money, or held through a partner bank. These balances can look similar on screen, but they are protected and regulated differently.

The chapter follows that distinction. Neobanks compete on customer experience, but their business models depend on who holds the license, who owns the customer relationship, and who assumes the regulatory responsibilities.

Banking through a New Interface

Traditional banks relied on branches because customers needed a place to open accounts, deposit cash, sign paperwork, talk to staff, and resolve issues. That model worked for a long time, but it was expensive, slow to adapt, and ill-suited to mobile-first customers.

Neobanks started by changing delivery. Instead of visiting a branch with documents, customers could download an app, scan their ID, take a selfie, pass checks, and gain access within minutes or hours. The exact timing still depends on local rules and risk checks, but the customer's expectations have changed: opening an account should feel as simple as starting any other digital service.

Card issuance became faster as well. A virtual card can be created immediately and added to a mobile wallet before the physical card arrives. The customer can start paying before a piece of plastic is printed, personalized, shipped, and activated.

Day-to-day money management also changed. Push notifications show transactions as they happen. Spending can be grouped by merchant or category. Foreign exchange costs can be shown more clearly. Customers can freeze and unfreeze a card, set limits, view a PIN, replace a card, or contact support from the app.

Pricing changed too, especially in the early wave. Many neobanks offered free accounts, low-cost foreign exchange, and simple subscription tiers. Over time, some free services became limited or moved into paid plans. As a result, *neobank* does not automatically mean *cheap*. It means digital-first, and the economics still have to work.

These changes improved the customer experience, but they did not remove the underlying financial system.

The card program, for example, still has to behave like a card program. There must be an issuer, a BIN range, a connection to a payment network such as Visa or Mastercard or to a domestic card scheme where relevant, and a process for authorization, clearing, settlement, fraud, disputes, and chargebacks. A clean mobile app does not make card operations disappear.

The account layer has its own requirements. Customer balances need a ledger. Incoming and outgoing transfers need reconciliation. Fees, reversals, refunds, interest, holds, and adjustments need to post correctly. The app can make the account feel simple, but the records behind it must remain accurate.

The same is true for compliance. Customer onboarding still requires identity verification, sanctions screening, suspicious-activity monitoring, politically exposed person checks where required, and regulatory recordkeeping. Faster onboarding does not remove the duty to know who the customer is and how the account is being used.

Customer funds need a legal home. Bank deposits, e-money balances, and partner-held funds can look the same in the app but differ in protection, regulation, and insolvency treatment.

Neobanks did not remove the core systems. They repackaged them into a better customer interface and a different operating model.

Licensing Models

The term *neobank* covers several infrastructure models. The key question is: who holds the license, and who is legally responsible for the financial product?

Fully Licensed Bank

Some neobanks hold a full banking license. This allows them to take deposits, lend from their own balance sheet, issue cards, connect more directly to payment systems, and own the regulated customer relationship.

This model gives the company more control. It can offer more products, capture more economics, and rely less on a sponsor bank. It also carries the heaviest regulatory burden. The company must meet capital requirements, manage liquidity, comply with governance and risk rules, undergo audits, report to regulators, protect deposits, and be subject to close supervision.

A licensed neobank is a bank delivered through a digital interface. The app may be new, but the regulatory responsibility is real.

Electronic Money Institution

In Europe and some other markets, a neobank may operate as an electronic money institution, or EMI. An EMI can issue electronic money and provide payment services, but it is not the same as a bank. It generally cannot accept deposits in the banking sense or lend customers' funds the way a bank can.

Customer money must usually be safeguarded. That can mean keeping customer funds separate from the company's own money, often in segregated bank accounts or other permitted safeguarding arrangements. This is not the same as deposit insurance. If a bank fails, insured deposits may be protected up to a legal limit. If an EMI fails, customers rely on safeguarding rules and the insolvency process, not the same deposit guarantee framework.

To the customer, an e-money balance may appear to be a regular account balance. Legally, it is different.

Partner Bank or Sponsor Bank Model

Some neobanks do not hold the main banking license themselves. They operate through a licensed partner bank. The neobank owns the brand, app, customer experience, and parts of the product design. The partner bank holds the regulated account, issues cards, provides access to payment rails, or performs other licensed functions.

This model makes it easier to launch. A fintech can reach the market without becoming a bank first. But the dependency is real. The partner bank controls risk appetite, compliance requirements, product boundaries, and operational constraints. If the partner bank changes its terms, stops onboarding, tightens controls, or ends the relationship, the neobank's business can be directly affected.

The neobank can use a partner's infrastructure, but cannot avoid regulatory responsibility. The partner still has obligations, and the fintech must operate within those.

Processor-Led and BaaS Infrastructure Models

A fourth model sits close to Banking-as-a-Service, which we discuss in Chapter 56. A fintech may rely on an issuing processor, program manager, BIN sponsor, ledger provider, KYC vendor, fraud tool, and compliance partners to assemble the product.

The customer sees one card and account experience. The operating model may involve many specialized providers.

This setup scales by dividing the work across specialized companies. The same division creates coordination risk: outages, reconciliation issues, fraud losses, dispute handling, settlement errors, and unclear responsibility can involve several companies at once.

Model	Who Holds the Main License?	What the Neobank Controls	Main Advantage	Main Constraint
Fully licensed bank	The neobank	Product, balance sheet, deposits, lending, customer relationship	Maximum control and economics	Heavy regulation and capital requirements
EMI	The neobank as an e-money institution	Wallet or account experience, payments, cards, safeguarding model	Faster than becoming a bank; strong payments focus	Not a bank deposit; limited lending model
Partner bank model	Sponsor or partner bank	Brand, app, customer experience, distribution	Faster launch and lower regulatory entry barrier	Dependency on partner-bank risk appetite and compliance

Processor-led / BaaS model	Licensed institution and infrastructure partners	Product packaging and customer journey	Modular and scalable	Many dependencies; complex accountability

Revenue Models

Early neobank marketing often emphasized what customers would not have to pay: no branch fees, no hidden charges, no expensive foreign exchange, and no slow paperwork. That message was powerful, but a business cannot survive only by removing fees. It still needs revenue.

Neobanks usually earn money from several sources.

The first is interchange: the issuer-side revenue generated when customers use their cards. If the neobank is the issuer or shares economics with the issuing bank, it receives a portion of that revenue. This works best when customers use the card frequently. In markets where debit interchange is capped, interchange alone is rarely enough to support a full banking business.

The second source is subscriptions. Many neobanks offer paid plans with benefits such as travel insurance, higher foreign exchange allowances, metal cards, lounge access, cashback, purchase protection, priority support, or higher withdrawal limits. Subscriptions turn the relationship from occasional transaction revenue into recurring income.

The third source is foreign exchange. A neobank may offer better rates than traditional banks while still earning a spread or charging fees beyond a free monthly allowance. Travel and cross-border spending were early strengths for several neobanks because customers could see the difference immediately.

The fourth source is lending. Once a neobank has customer balances, transaction data, and frequent engagement, lending becomes attractive: overdrafts, personal loans, credit cards, BNPL, salary advances, or business credit. Lending changes the business from payment activity to credit exposure. The margins can be stronger than payments, but credit losses can quickly erase years of interchange revenue.

The fifth source is wealth, crypto, insurance, and partner products. Trading commissions, custody fees, referral fees, insurance distribution, cashback partnerships, and merchant-funded offers can all add revenue. These products move the neobank toward a broader marketplace model: one account, many services.

None of these revenue streams is guaranteed. A customer who opens an account for a free card, uses it twice, and keeps their salary elsewhere does not create much value. The business performs better when the neobank serves as the customer's primary financial account.

Unit Economics

Neobanks often look cheaper to run than traditional banks, and in many ways, they are. They do not carry the same branch-network costs. Digital onboarding reduces manual work. Cloud infrastructure can scale more flexibly than legacy systems. Product teams can ship faster.

Lower visible costs do not automatically create profitability.

Customer acquisition can be expensive. Paid marketing, referral bonuses, free cards, and promotional pricing can bring users quickly, but users are not the same as profitable customers. A dormant account still incurs costs: compliance monitoring, infrastructure, customer support, card production (if a physical card was issued), and regulatory reporting.

Support costs are easy to underestimate. Even with a digital app, customers still need help when a transfer fails, a card is stolen, a dispute appears, a refund is missing, or an account is blocked for review. Chat support changes the support channel. It does not remove the need for support.

Fraud and compliance costs grow with scale. Fast onboarding attracts the customers a neobank wants and the fraudsters it has to keep out. Account-opening fraud, mule accounts, card testing, APP scams, chargebacks, synthetic identities, sanctions screening, and manual reviews all become operating costs.

Interchange may be too thin to carry the business. In capped markets, each debit card transaction generates only a small amount of revenue. If customers mostly use the account for low-value purchases and do not buy paid products, the neobank needs a very large active customer base to cover its costs.

Deposit economics also depend on licensing and interest rates. A fully licensed bank may earn net interest margin from deposits and lending. An EMI or partner-bank model may not capture the same economics. The app may look similar, but the income statement differs.

This explains why some neobanks grew quickly and still struggled to make money. They learned how to acquire users before they proved that those users could become profitable customers.

Super-App Ambition

Once a neobank becomes part of a customer's daily financial life, the next goal is to offer more services.

A customer who opens the app to check spending can also be offered travel insurance, an investment account, a savings vault, a loan, a crypto trade, a hotel booking, a business account, or merchant services. Each additional product creates another revenue line and another reason to keep using the account.

This is the super-app logic. The app stops being only a bank account and becomes a financial marketplace, and sometimes more than financial. In parts of Asia, super-apps grew around messaging, commerce, mobility, and payments. In Europe and the United States, the model has been harder to copy because financial services are more tightly regulated, licensed, and shaped by different consumer expectations.

The strategy is still understandable. More services can create more engagement. More engagement can produce more data, which can support better risk decisions, more relevant offers, and stronger customer retention.

The risk is loss of focus. If a neobank adds too many features too quickly, the app that once felt simple can become crowded with unrelated products. The trust built on clarity can fade if customers feel they are constantly being sold something.

A neobank should expand only if the main account continues to work reliably.

Success and Failure Modes

Neobanks run into trouble when their apps are better designed than their businesses.

A polished interface can attract attention, but it cannot compensate for weak economics, poor risk controls, or low customer trust. Free accounts work only if they lead to profitable use. Fast sign-ups become dangerous if fraud controls are weak. Cheap foreign exchange may attract customers who use only that feature. Paid subscriptions only work if customers continue to see value. Lending works only if the neobank can manage credit risk through good and bad economic conditions.

Successful neobanks usually do one or more of four things well.

First, they become the primary account. This is the hardest and most valuable outcome. Salary comes in, bills go out, the card is used daily, and the customer treats the account as their financial home. Primary relationships create stable balances, more transactions, more data, and more opportunities to offer useful products.

Second, they focus on a strong niche. Some neobanks serve travelers, freelancers, small businesses, migrants, students, teenagers, creators, or underbanked customers. Serving a specific group can be more effective than offering a generic account, especially where traditional banks underserve that group.

Third, they build profitable layers beyond payments. Subscriptions, lending, business accounts, acquiring, wealth, and foreign exchange can turn a low-margin account into a broader financial relationship.

Fourth, they take risk management seriously. Good onboarding, fraud checks, sanctions screening, dispute handling, customer support, complaint management, and strong operations make the institution work.

Trust sits underneath all of this. Traditional banks may be slow and expensive, but customers often trust them with salaries, mortgages, and savings. Neobanks have to earn that trust over time. Outages, frozen accounts, poor support, unclear checks, or sudden fee changes can quickly damage the relationship.

The weak neobank story is: "We have a better app."

The stronger story is: "We have a better distribution model, a clear license structure, disciplined risk controls, and economics that improve as the relationship deepens."

Packaging and Distribution

Neobanks show a pattern that appears throughout modern fintech: the customer experience can change dramatically while the underlying financial machinery changes much more slowly.

The familiar infrastructure is still there. Card payments run through card networks or domestic schemes. Transfers move through bank rails. Customer onboarding depends on identity checks and monitoring. Balances need a ledger, customer funds need a legal home, disputes need evidence, fees need to cover costs, and growth still depends on trust.

The innovation is real, but it is not magic. Neobanks used the components described throughout this book to deliver a better customer experience.

That is why they are best understood as a new way to package banking, not as a replacement for banking infrastructure. Branches became less central because many regulated products could be delivered through a better interface. The rules still applied, but the customer no longer had to walk into the building.

Chapter 56: Banking-as-a-Service and Embedded Finance

A customer orders food through a delivery app. After completing a shift, the courier sees the payout reflected in the same app. A marketplace seller uses a branded debit card for business expenses. A small business software platform provides financing based on invoice history. A travel site offers insurance during checkout.

None of these companies resembles a bank, and customers may never see a bank logo. Still, every product relies on regulated financial infrastructure: a licensed institution, a ledger, a processor, compliance checks, payment rails, and settlement.

Embedded finance integrates financial products into non-financial experiences. The bank, payment institution, or other regulated provider remains present, but operates behind the platform's interface.

Banking-as-a-Service (*BaaS*) gives platforms API access to banking functions: accounts, cards, payments, customer checks, ledgers, reporting, and, sometimes, lending or e-money services. The platform owns the visible product. Banks and BaaS providers carry the regulated and operational layers.

This is the next step after neobanks. A neobank turns banking into an app. Embedded finance puts banking inside an app that was never meant to be about banking.

Banking as Infrastructure

For most of modern banking, the bank was the place where financial services lived. To open an account, apply for a loan, send a transfer, or get a card, the customer went to the bank's branch, website, or mobile app.

Embedded finance changes where financial services are offered.

Customers no longer need to start in a bank channel. Financial services appear where needed: a merchant checkout offers installment payments, a marketplace offers seller financing, a gig platform offers instant payouts, a payroll provider offers earned wage access, and an accounting platform offers a business account.

Financial services, regulation, and money movement are all still real. The main change is how the customer reaches them.

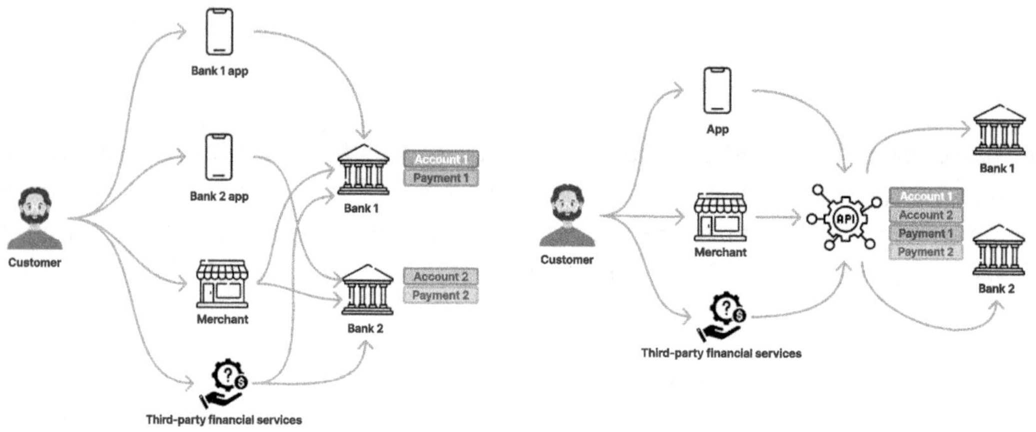

Figure 56.1: From a bank channel to embedded finance.

This is different from a bank improving its own mobile app. A better banking app still makes the bank the main destination. Embedded finance embeds financial services within another product.

That shift changes who manages the customer relationship. In traditional banking, the bank controls the interface. In embedded finance, the platform typically controls the interface, while the bank or regulated provider provides the financial capability within the operating model.

BaaS Capabilities

People often describe BaaS as *banking through APIs,* which is not wrong but incomplete. APIs are only the access layer. The real value is access to regulated financial capabilities without having to rebuild every regulated system from scratch.

A BaaS provider may support account creation, card issuing, onboarding and screening, payment initiation and transfers, ledgering and balance management, and reporting and reconciliation.

The exact model depends on the jurisdiction and on the provider's license. In one market, the BaaS provider may be a licensed bank. In another, it may be an e-money institution. In another, it may be a technology company sitting between a sponsor bank and a platform.

Platforms typically do not want to become banks: a marketplace has no interest in building a core banking system, a payroll platform does not want to join card networks directly, and a software company does not want to build regulated monitoring and reporting from scratch.

BaaS exists to bridge that gap. It bundles these capabilities so platforms can offer financial products faster. But using another's infrastructure does not remove responsibility. It shifts where responsibility sits and how it is supervised.

Main Participants

A typical embedded-finance program splits work among the platform, the sponsor bank, the BaaS provider, the processor, the ledger provider, and the compliance vendors.

The platform is the customer-facing participant, such as a marketplace, app, SaaS product, retailer, employer platform, or mobility provider. The platform is responsible for the user experience, deciding where the financial service appears, its description, and integration within the customer journey.

Behind the platform, the BaaS provider provides regulated financial services via APIs. The BaaS provider coordinates various operations, including accounts, cards, ledgers, onboarding workflows, transaction monitoring, reporting, and reconciliation. They act as the bridge between the platform and regulated financial entities.

The licensed institution is the regulated entity, such as a sponsor bank, e-money institution, or payment institution. It holds the necessary licenses to provide deposit-taking, e-money issuance, payment services, lending, or card issuing. This institution is responsible for regulatory compliance and must oversee the entire program's activities.

Processors handle transaction operations. In card programs, the processor manages card accounts, authorization logic, transaction routing, clearing files, card lifecycle events, and connections to payment networks. For account-to-account products, processors handle domestic payment rails. For wallet products, they connect to e-money infrastructure and banks for funding and withdrawals.

Risk and compliance providers support regulatory safeguards. These include identity verification vendors, sanctions screening tools, fraud engines, device intelligence services, chargeback systems, and case-management tools that protect the program against risks and help ensure compliance.

While the customer interacts with only one app, the service is delivered by a coordinated chain of platforms, BaaS providers, licensed institutions, processors, and compliance solution providers, each with a clear role.

Platform Incentives

Platforms pursue embedded finance for four main reasons.

The first is retention. A platform that only helps a seller list goods can be replaced. A platform that also manages payouts, working capital, cards, and business spending becomes harder to leave.

The second is monetization. Financial services can generate new revenue streams, including interchange, account fees, foreign exchange spreads, lending margins, subscription plans, insurance commissions, and payment processing revenue.

The third is data. A platform often knows more about its users' real activity than a bank does: marketplaces see sales volume, payroll providers see income, delivery apps see working patterns, and accounting platforms see invoices and cash flow. This data can support better underwriting, better fraud detection, and more relevant offers.

The fourth is payment control. Platforms that control payouts improve user liquidity – a marketplace pays sellers faster, a gig platform offers daily earnings, and a SaaS platform unifies invoicing, payments, and reconciliation.

These benefits explain why platforms pursue embedded finance. They do not simplify financial operations.

Bank Incentives

From the bank's perspective, embedded finance is a distribution strategy.

A sponsor bank does not always have the brand, product design, or customer acquisition engine to reach a specific segment directly. A platform may already own that relationship. By partnering with the platform, the bank can reach customers it would otherwise struggle to acquire.

The bank may earn program fees, deposit revenue, interchange share, lending income, or payment volume. It may also gain access to specialized verticals, such as freelancers, sellers, creators, gig workers, small businesses, logistics companies, or property managers.

The API model does not remove the bank's regulatory risk. If the platform onboards poor-quality customers, fails to detect suspicious activity, misleads users, mishandles complaints, or fails to implement strong controls, the bank cannot simply say, "That was our partner." Regulators usually look up the chain and ask which licensed institution authorized the activity.

This is the central tension in BaaS: platforms want speed and flexibility, while banks need control and accountability.

Regulated Capability Ownership

Embedded-finance programs can look similar on-screen while being built on very different regulatory foundations. The important question is not only what the customer sees, but who is allowed to provide the financial service behind it.

Sometimes the platform holds the license itself. It can be a bank, an e-money institution, or a payment institution, with the license matching the products it offers. More control brings more regulated obligations: capital, safeguarding, compliance, governance, reporting, and supervision.

In other cases, the platform works through a sponsor bank or regulated provider. The platform owns the customer experience, while the licensed institution provides the account, card, payment, lending, or e-money capability. A BaaS provider may sit between them, handling APIs, processing, onboarding workflows, ledgers, reporting, or program operations.

The trade-off is control versus speed. Owning a license gives greater product and economic control, but is slower and more expensive. Using a regulated partner enables speed but introduces dependencies, oversight risks, and shared risk.

BaaS is a matter of regulated responsibility before it is a technical integration: who is allowed to offer the product, who controls the customer journey, and who is responsible when something goes wrong.

Embedded Cards

Cards are among the most common forms of embedded finance because they naturally fit into platform workflows.

A company may give employees expense cards, allow creators to spend against platform earnings, offer marketplace sellers a business debit card, issue fleet cards to drivers, create virtual cards for travel bookings, or link a debit card to a wallet balance. In each case, the card appears to the customer as part of the platform rather than as a separate bank product.

That is the distribution change. The platform already owns the customer relationship and understands the workflow around the card: seller payouts, employee expenses, driver fuel purchases, travel bookings, wallet spending, or business procurement. The card becomes useful because it is placed where the need to spend already exists.

Underneath, however, the product is still an issuing program. The same building blocks apply: BIN sponsorship, card personalization, tokenization, authorization, clearing, settlement, fraud monitoring, disputes, and network rules. The customer may view the card as a platform feature, but the infrastructure must treat it as a regulated payment product.

The economics are split across the companies that make the program work. Card revenue and costs may be shared among the sponsor bank, the BaaS provider, the processor, and the platform. Interchange, program fees, processor fees, network fees, fraud losses, and dispute costs must all be allocated somewhere.

Embedded Lending

Embedded lending also uses distribution through a nonbank platform, but the risk is different.

Credit works best when it appears at the moment of need. A seller looking at marketplace cash flow may need working capital. A buyer at checkout may want to split the purchase into installments. A worker may want access to earned wages before payday. A business using accounting software may need financing against unpaid invoices. A traveler booking a trip may want to spread the cost over time.

The platform's advantage is context. A traditional lender often has to request statements, tax records, and financial projections before it can understand the borrower. A platform already has live signals such as sales, refunds, ratings, seasonality, invoices, expenses, bank feed data, or earned income. Used carefully, that information can speed up underwriting and make it more relevant to the customer's actual activity.

But lending is still a regulated credit decision, not a checkout decoration. The offer needs funding, credit assessment where required, ownership of default risk, collections, complaint handling, and compliance with consumer credit or commercial lending rules.

Embedded lending can make credit feel immediate and useful. It also brings credit risk, funding needs, collections, complaints, and regulatory obligations into the platform's operating model.

Embedded Payments and Payouts

Payments are the most common embedded-finance use case because platforms already sit at the center of transaction flows.

A marketplace has to collect money from buyers and pay sellers. Gig-work, creator, property, and SaaS platforms face the same basic problem in different forms: they need to accept funds, allocate them correctly, deduct fees, and send money to the right party at the right time.

The payment product can use cards, bank transfers, wallets, local payment methods, or instant rails. The platform then works through the structure that fits the model: a PayFac, PSP, BaaS provider, or licensed payment institution.

The hard part is keeping the money movement, ledgers, settlement files, customer balances, and partner reports aligned. The platform needs to know who paid, which invoice or order the payment belongs to, whether the seller has been paid, whether a fee was deducted, whether a refund or payout reversal occurred, which balance should change, and which ledger entry proves it.

Embedded payments turn payment systems into part of the product itself. If the money does not move correctly, the whole product fails.

Ledger Problem

Every embedded-finance product eventually needs a ledger. A platform can create an attractive card, wallet, or payout screen, but if it cannot track balances accurately, the product becomes risky.

The ledger has to answer basic questions in real time. How much does the customer have available, and how much of that is pending? Which funds are reserved for card authorizations, and which entries have actually posted? Which fees have been charged, and which balances belong to the platform, the customer, the merchant, or the bank? Which entries reconcile to bank statements, network files, or settlement reports?

This is where many embedded-finance projects become harder than expected. Building the customer interface is usually easier than making the ledger, reconciliation, exception handling, and audit trail work safely.

If the ledger is weak, every operational problem can become a financial risk.

BaaS Operational Risk

BaaS sounds simple when presented as infrastructure. In practice, it is difficult because financial services are not inherently low-risk just because they are exposed via APIs.

Responsibility is the first difficulty. The more a platform appears to offer banking, payments, cards, or lending, the more regulators will ask who is accountable for the activity. A platform can own the customer interface, but a licensed institution still has to understand the program, approve the controls, monitor the risk, and intervene when something goes wrong.

That responsibility is spread across several parties. The platform, BaaS provider, sponsor bank, processor, and compliance vendors all depend on one another. A weak onboarding process, a processor outage, a reconciliation failure, or a fraud-control gap can damage the whole program. Embedded finance can look like a single product to the customer, but operationally it is a chain.

The economics can also be thinner than the pitch suggests. Transaction revenue may be capped or shared among several parties, while onboarding checks, fraud prevention, support, compliance, reporting, and dispute handling all create real costs. Fraud losses can wipe out the revenue from many good customers.

Resilience is another constraint. If an ordinary SaaS feature fails, customers may be frustrated. If a BaaS integration fails, customers may lose access to accounts, cards, payouts, or wallet balances. Downtime can stop people from spending or receiving money, so reliability becomes part of the financial product itself.

Scale makes all of this harder. Launching a card, account, or payout program is only the first step. Running it across millions of users, thousands of exceptions, multiple partners, regulatory reviews, and daily settlement cycles is a different operating challenge.

BaaS makes it easier to launch financial products. It does not make them easy to run.

Open Banking and BaaS

Open banking and BaaS are often grouped because both rely on APIs and shift banking capabilities outside traditional bank channels. But they solve different problems.

Open banking exposes existing bank accounts to licensed third parties. With customer consent, a third party can read account data or initiate a payment from the customer's bank account.

BaaS enables a platform to offer its own financial products, typically by using regulated infrastructure from a bank or specialist provider.

The key difference is who owns the financial product.

If a budgeting app shows balances from several existing bank accounts, that is open banking. If a marketplace offers sellers a new account and card under its own brand, that is BaaS and embedded finance. If an e-commerce checkout allows a customer to pay directly from their bank account via a PISP, that is an open banking payment initiation. If the same e-commerce platform offers a stored-value wallet for sellers, that is closer to embedded finance.

Open banking provides access to existing bank accounts. BaaS helps platforms create new financial products inside their own customer experience.

They can be used together, but they are not the same thing.

Product Effects

Embedded finance changes distribution more than it changes the underlying laws of finance.

The customer may see a payout button, a platform card, an instant loan offer, a wallet balance, or an insurance option at checkout. Underneath that feature, someone still has to hold the license, run the ledger, move the money, screen the customer, monitor transactions, reconcile settlements, handle complaints, and absorb or allocate losses.

That is why embedded finance is powerful and easy to misunderstand. It makes financial services appear in the right place at the right moment, inside the software the customer already uses. But the feature only works if the underlying infrastructure is sound.

Embedded finance works when both sides are designed together: the product journey that makes the service feel natural, and the financial machinery that makes it reliable, compliant, and economically viable.

Chapter 57: Cryptocurrencies and Blockchain Payments

In 2009, new software made it possible to send value without using a bank, a card network, a payment processor, or a central operator. The system was Bitcoin. The whitepaper was signed by Satoshi Nakamoto, though the real identity behind that name is still unknown.

Bitcoin was not designed to improve card payments. It did not solve merchant acceptance, disputes, chargebacks, refunds, or consumer protection. It solved a different problem: how to maintain a shared record of ownership without relying on a single trusted institution to keep the ledger.

Cryptocurrency systems are built around that ledger problem.

Traditional payments rely on institutions and account ledgers: card payments use issuers, acquirers, networks, rules, and later money movement, while bank transfers use bank account ledgers and the payment systems that connect them.

A cryptocurrency transaction works differently. It relies on a shared ledger maintained by a network. The ledger says which addresses control which assets. A transaction is a signed instruction to move value from one address to another. The network checks the signature, validates the transaction, and records it.

There is no bank to approve the payment, no card network to route the authorization, no acquirer to support the merchant, and no issuer to reverse the transaction.

Crypto payments remove institutional approval from the transfer, but they also remove the institutional services that card and bank rails normally provide.

Blockchain as a Shared Ledger

A *blockchain* is a shared ledger. It is a record of transactions that many computers keep together.

A normal bank ledger has one official keeper: the bank. If Alice has $100 and sends $20 to Bob, the bank updates its records. Alice's balance goes down, Bob's balance goes up, and the bank's ledger is the source of truth.

A public blockchain uses a different model: instead of a single bank maintaining the official record, many computers in the network keep copies of the ledger. When a new transaction appears, the network checks whether it follows the rules. If the transaction is valid, it can be added to the shared record.

The ledger is updated in batches called blocks. Each block contains a group of transactions. When the network accepts a new block, it links it to the previous block. The next block links to that one, and so on. This is where the word blockchain comes from: blocks of transactions linked into a chain.

The link between blocks is created with cryptography. Each block includes a kind of digital fingerprint of the previous block. If someone changes an old transaction, the fingerprint of that block changes too. That would break the link to the next block, then the next one, and so on through the rest of the chain.

So, rewriting history is not as simple as editing a single database row. An attacker would have to change the old block, rebuild the later blocks, and convince the network to accept the altered version instead of the version everyone else already has.

Attacks are still possible. The design goal is to make rewriting the past difficult, expensive, and visible to the network.

The ledger does not usually contain real names. It contains addresses.

A typical blockchain transaction says, in effect:

> Address A transfers this amount of value to Address B.

The person, company, or software behind each address is usually not shown on the ledger. Still, on many public blockchains, anyone can view the transaction record. That makes most public cryptocurrencies pseudonymous, not anonymous.

A bank ledger is private but identity-based. The bank knows the customer, and outsiders do not have access to the full ledger.

A public blockchain ledger is visible but address-based. Everyone can see the movement of funds, but the real-world identity behind an address may only become clear when that address touches an exchange, merchant, wallet provider, or other service that performs identity checks.

Crypto is often described as a privacy technology, but many crypto transactions create a permanent public record.

Cryptocurrency as a Network Asset

A *cryptocurrency* is a digital asset recorded on a blockchain or similar distributed ledger. It can be transferred between addresses according to rules enforced by software.

The word *cryptocurrency* is often used as if it describes one kind of thing. It does not. The term encompasses several structures, and the differences matter because they serve distinct purposes and carry distinct risks.

The first category is payment cryptocurrencies. These are the closest to digital cash: assets designed for direct transfer between users without a bank or card network in the middle. Bitcoin is the best-known example. It runs on its own blockchain, has its own asset, and uses its own rules to determine which transactions are included in the ledger. Litecoin and many other cryptocurrencies follow a similar model. The main trade-off is volatility. The market price can fluctuate sharply, making these assets difficult to use as everyday money.

The second category is tokens. Tokens do not usually have their own blockchain. They are issued on top of an existing one, most commonly Ethereum. A token is not necessarily a currency. It is a programmable digital instrument that can represent access to a service, voting rights in a decentralized organization, a claim on an asset, a stablecoin balance, or a unique digital asset such as an NFT. Ethereum is the infrastructure layer on which many tokens and applications run. Ether is the network's native asset, used to pay transaction fees and secure Ethereum through proof of stake.

The third category is stablecoins. These were created to reduce volatility. A *stablecoin* is designed to track the value of another asset, usually a fiat currency such as the US dollar. USDT and USDC are common examples. Stablecoins are used inside crypto markets as a relatively stable unit of account and store of value, and they are increasingly relevant for cross-border transfers. Their risk profile differs from that of bitcoin or ether: reserves, redemption, issuer trust, operational controls, and regulation become central. In Chapter 58, we look at stablecoins in detail.

The fourth category is central bank digital currency, or CBDC. A *CBDC* is fundamentally different from the others. It is issued by a central bank and represents official money in digital form. It is not a decentralized cryptocurrency in the usual sense, nor is it independent of the financial system. China's e-CNY is one of the most advanced large-scale retail CBDC projects. The European Central Bank is developing a digital euro. We will discuss CBDCs in Chapter 59 as public digital money rather than private crypto assets.

The key distinction is who stands behind the asset. Payment cryptocurrencies and many tokens are not issued as claims on a bank, company, or government. Stablecoins are issued by private companies and are supposed to be backed by reserves or other stabilization mechanisms. CBDCs are issued by central banks. Similar technical language can hide very different structures, risks, and legal claims.

Wallets, Addresses, and Private Keys

A crypto wallet doesn't hold coins in the way a leather wallet holds cash. The assets stay on the blockchain, not in the wallet. The wallet stores, manages, or provides access to the cryptographic keys that control those assets.

A public address is a destination for receiving funds. It can be shared.

A *private key* is the secret that allows the holder to sign a transaction and move funds from that address. It must be protected.

Many wallets also use a seed phrase, usually a set of 12 or 24 words that can be used to recover the private keys. Losing the seed phrase can permanently mean losing access. Anyone who obtains it can usually move the funds.

This is very different from the normal banking experience.

If a customer forgets a bank password, the bank can reset it. If a card is stolen, the card issuer can block it and issue a replacement. If a transaction is unauthorized, a dispute process is usually available.

With a crypto wallet, there may be no institution to call. A lost private key makes the funds inaccessible forever. A stolen key allows an attacker to move the funds, and the confirmed transaction is final.

When people say crypto gives users control, this is what they mean. Control shifts to the user. But so does responsibility for managing keys, protecting the wallet, and avoiding irreversible mistakes.

Custody: Who Controls the Keys?

Crypto wallets fall into two broad custody models.

A *custodial wallet* is controlled by a third party, such as an exchange or crypto platform. The user logs into an account. The platform stores the user's private keys, manages security, and executes withdrawals on the user's behalf.

This feels familiar. It works much like an online bank or brokerage account. The user can reset a password, contact support, and rely on the platform's security systems.

The trade-off is platform exposure. If the platform freezes withdrawals, is hacked, mismanages customer assets, or fails, the customer does not have direct control over the funds. The blockchain may continue to run perfectly, while the customer's practical access depends on the custodian.

A non-custodial wallet gives the user direct control of the private keys. Browser wallets, mobile wallets, and hardware wallets are common examples. The user can transact without asking a platform for permission. No exchange can freeze the wallet simply because it dislikes the transaction.

That control comes with a major trade-off. Lost keys are usually unrecoverable. A user tricked into signing a bad transaction has no chargeback, no help desk, and no institution able to reverse the transfer.

Custody is not a technical detail. It determines who controls the asset, who can block access, who can fix mistakes, and who takes the risk.

Hot Wallets and Cold Wallets

Wallets are also described as hot or cold.

A *hot wallet* is connected to the internet. It could be an exchange account, a mobile app, or a browser extension. Hot wallets are convenient for frequent transactions, but being online makes them vulnerable to malware, phishing, compromised browser extensions, and fake websites.

A cold wallet keeps private keys offline. A hardware wallet stores the key on a physical device and signs transactions without exposing the key to an internet-connected computer. Cold wallets are less convenient, but they are usually safer for large or long-term holdings.

These categories overlap with custody.

Wallet Type	Custodial	Non-Custodial
Hot	Exchange account, hosted wallet	Browser wallet, mobile wallet
Cold	Exchange cold storage, institutional custody	Hardware wallet, paper seed phrase backup

A browser wallet is usually hot and non-custodial. It is connected to the internet and lets the user sign transactions directly, but the user controls the keys. A mobile wallet can work the same way.

An exchange account is usually hot and custodial from the user's perspective. The user logs in to the exchange, not directly to the blockchain. The exchange may keep most customer assets in internal offline storage, but the customer still depends on the exchange to approve withdrawals and maintain access.

A hardware wallet is cold and non-custodial. The private key stays on a physical device, and the user signs transactions without exposing the key to an internet-connected computer. For long-term holdings, this is safer only when the user protects both the device and the seed phrase.

A large exchange often uses cold custodial storage internally. In that case, the assets are offline, but they remain under the exchange's control. The exchange handles much of the security operations, and the customer accepts the platform's risk in return.

The best wallet model depends on the use case. A trader may want quick access and be willing to accept greater platform dependency. Someone holding assets for the long term may prefer a hardware wallet and direct control. A business accepting crypto may need approval workflows, accounting records, segregation of duties, treasury controls, and clear responsibility for key management.

The phrase "not your keys, not your coins" captures an important truth, but it does not tell the whole story for businesses. Holding keys directly is not automatically safer if a person or company cannot manage them securely.

Crypto Transaction Flow

A cryptocurrency transaction begins when the holder of a private key signs an instruction.

Suppose Alice wants to send Bitcoin to Bob. Her wallet creates a transaction that identifies the source of funds (Bob's address), the amount, and the network fee. Alice signs it with her private key. The signature proves that the person in control of the relevant key authorized the transfer.

The transaction is broadcast to the network. Nodes check whether it follows the rules. They verify the signature, confirm that the funds are available, check that the same value has not already been spent, and reject malformed transactions.

A valid transaction then waits to be included in a block. Miners or validators assemble transactions into blocks and propose them to the network. Once a block is accepted, the transaction becomes part of the ledger.

The card model separates approval, record exchange, and institutional money movement. Bitcoin collapses those stages into a ledger update that gains confidence through confirmations.

Finality varies by network. Bitcoin users often wait for several confirmations for larger transactions. Some newer networks finalize transactions faster. But the principle is the same: confidence increases as the transaction becomes deeper in the accepted chain or reaches finality under the network's consensus rules.

Consensus and Network Agreement

A blockchain needs a way to determine which transactions are valid and which ledger version is authoritative. That process is called consensus.

The two best-known consensus models are proof-of-work and proof-of-stake.

In proof-of-work systems, miners compete to solve computational puzzles. The winning miner proposes the next block and receives a reward. Bitcoin uses proof of work. The model is expensive by design: attacking the network requires enormous computing power and energy.

In proof-of-stake, validators lock up, or stake, the network's native asset and participate in block creation and validation. If they behave dishonestly, they can lose part of their stake. Ethereum moved from proof-of-work to proof-of-stake in 2022.

The technical details get complicated because the core problem is hard: the network needs a way to agree on the ledger without a central authority.

That need for distributed agreement is what sets crypto apart from conventional payment infrastructure. Visa does not require a consensus protocol to determine whether its own records are valid. A bank does not need thousands of strangers to agree on its account ledger. The institution is the authority.

A public blockchain tries to replace institutional authority with economic incentives, cryptography, and shared rules.

Smart Contracts and Programmable Assets

Bitcoin proved that a decentralized network could maintain a ledger for a digital asset. Ethereum extended the idea: what if the ledger could also run programs?

A *smart contract* is code deployed on a blockchain. It can hold assets, enforce rules, and execute transactions automatically when conditions are met.

For example, a smart contract can run a token exchange. A user sends Token A to the contract, and the contract returns Token B under its pricing rules. No broker approves the trade. No exchange operator manually matches the order. The code performs the operation.

Smart contracts enable decentralized finance (DeFi). Lending protocols, decentralized exchanges, stablecoin systems, liquidity pools, and on-chain governance all depend on code that holds and moves assets.

That automation creates a new kind of risk. If the code contains a bug, an attacker may exploit it. If the contract is poorly designed, users may lose funds even though the system behaves exactly as written. In traditional finance, a mistaken process can sometimes be corrected by an institution. In smart contract systems, the code may execute the error at full speed.

The saying "code is law" sounds clean until the code has a mistake.

Comparison with Card Payments

Crypto payments and card payments solve different problems.

A card payment is designed for merchant acceptance. It comes with a commercial operating framework that includes rules, risk allocation, dispute processes, economics, and consumer protections.

A crypto transfer is designed to move control of a digital asset from one address to another. It is global, always available, and independent of card networks or bank rails. But it does not automatically include merchant acquiring, refunds, chargebacks, buyer protection, tax reporting, or customer service.

A customer might scan a QR code, confirm in an app, and see a message that says "Paid," while the legal and operational setup differs beneath the surface.

Feature	Card Payment	Crypto Transfer
Core object	Card credential linked to an account	Digital asset controlled by private key
Main participants	Cardholder, merchant, acquirer, payment network, issuer	Sender, recipient, wallet, blockchain network, possibly exchange or custodian
Authorization	Issuer approves or declines in real time	Network validates signed transaction
Finality	Staged card-processing model	On-chain confirmation or finality
Reversibility	Disputes and chargebacks may apply	Usually irreversible once confirmed
Consumer protection	Built into regulation and network rules	Depends on wallet, platform, merchant, and jurisdiction
Main strength	Acceptance, rules, protection, operating model	Direct transfer, 24/7 availability, programmability
Main weakness	Cost and intermediary complexity	Key management, scams, volatility, limited protection

The card system moves data, allocates liability, establishes dispute rights, and coordinates settlements among regulated institutions. It is a governed acceptance system.

A blockchain is a ledger with a consensus mechanism, ownership rules, and a shared record that participants can verify without a central operator. It is not a merchant acceptance system by default.

Both can be used in payments, but one cannot simply replace the other.

Payment and Treasury Use Cases

Crypto rails are strongest where the existing system is slow, expensive, inaccessible, or fragmented.

Cross-border transfer is the obvious example. A crypto asset can move from one wallet to another outside banking hours and across borders. In practice, this is most useful when the asset has a relatively stable value, which is why stablecoins dominate many payment use cases.

Crypto can also be useful when programmable settlement is required. Smart contracts can release funds when conditions are met, split payments automatically, or interact with digital assets without manual reconciliation.

In places where banking is hard to access, crypto wallets can let people transfer value digitally without a bank account. Other constraints persist: internet and smartphone access, exchange liquidity, local regulations, fraud risk, and the ability to convert crypto into local currency.

For merchants, crypto acceptance can make sense in specific niches: digital goods, cross-border customers, crypto-native communities, high-risk sectors that struggle with card acquiring, or businesses that want blockchain-based settlement. For ordinary retail, cards and local payment methods still better meet merchants' daily needs.

The practical test is whether crypto solves a real payment problem better than current systems, once regulation, price movements, conversions, taxes, support, and fraud risk are factored in.

The honest answer depends on whether the payment problem is genuinely cross-border, genuinely time-sensitive, or genuinely underserved by banks and cards. Most retail payments are none of those things. Some cross-border and crypto-native ones are all three.

Risks: Volatility, Scams, and Lost Keys

Crypto payments carry risks that are less common, or at least differently allocated, in traditional payment systems.

Volatility is the most obvious. Bitcoin, ether, and many other crypto assets can move sharply in price. A merchant paid in a volatile asset may lose value before converting it. A customer may hesitate to spend an asset they believe will appreciate in value. Stablecoins reduce this risk, but they introduce issuer, reserve, and redemption risks.

Irreversibility changes the consumer-risk model. Once a transaction is confirmed, it usually cannot be recalled. Irreversibility creates certainty of settlement for the recipient and risk for the sender. A user who is scammed, misled, or careless with an address may turn a mistaken transfer into a permanent loss.

Key management adds another risk. Users must protect private keys, seed phrases, wallet devices, and signing workflows. A bank customer can usually recover from a forgotten password. A crypto user who loses a seed phrase is often unable to recover at all.

Many users also face platform risk because they do not interact directly with blockchains. They use exchanges, brokers, custodians, and wallet providers. Those institutions can be hacked, mismanaged, sanctioned, insolvent, or subject to regulatory restrictions.

The regulatory and tax treatment can be difficult as well. Crypto assets are treated differently across jurisdictions. A payment may create a taxable event. Businesses accepting crypto need accounting, valuation, sanctions screening, source-of-funds controls, and reporting processes.

Consumer protection is often weaker or more fragmented than in traditional rails. In card payments, a cardholder may have dispute rights. In bank payments, certain protections may exist depending on the rail and jurisdiction. In crypto, protection depends heavily on the intermediary used, if any. A non-custodial on-chain transaction may lack a practical dispute process.

Crypto and Existing Payment Rails

Crypto advocates sometimes say blockchain payments remove unnecessary intermediaries. That is partly true, but incomplete.

Intermediaries also perform work. Banks run customer checks, conduct sanctions screening, implement fraud controls, handle account recovery, provide reporting, and offer support. Card networks provide acceptance rules, dispute processes, tokenization frameworks, global interoperability, and operating standards. Acquirers onboard merchants, monitor risk, handle settlement, and support chargeback processes. Processors connect merchants and financial institutions to the rails.

When crypto removes intermediaries, it also removes many of the functions they perform. Some of those functions can be rebuilt in crypto-native ways. Others are pushed to wallets, exchanges, custodians, analytics providers, stablecoin issuers, or regulated payment companies.

Practical crypto payment systems often reintroduce intermediaries. A merchant accepting crypto uses a payment processor that converts to fiat, screens transactions, handles refunds, and provides reporting. A consumer uses a custodial wallet because self-custody is too risky. A business relies on a regulated exchange because direct on-chain treasury management is operationally complex.

The technology changes how the ledger and settlement work. It does not remove the need for regulation, fraud prevention, tax treatment, accounting, customer support, or trust.

Crypto as Ledger-Based Infrastructure

A cryptocurrency system is best understood first as a ledger.

That sounds simple, but it changes the starting point. In card payments and bank transfers, the ledger is maintained within an institution. The bank, issuer, acquirer, processor, or payment system maintains records and operates under rules that define who can participate, how errors are handled, and what happens when something goes wrong.

Crypto begins from the opposite direction. The ledger is shared across a network, and the system is designed to allow participants to verify the record without trusting a single central operator. That makes direct transfer possible in a way traditional account systems do not. It also enables programmable assets and smart contracts because the ledger can do more than store balances; it can enforce rules written in code.

This is powerful, but it is not the same as being a complete payment system.

A merchant does not only need proof that value moved. The merchant also needs acceptance tools, pricing, reconciliation, refund handling, fraud controls, tax records, customer support, and a way to convert value into the currency used to pay suppliers, employees, and taxes. A consumer needs stability, recovery, protection against mistakes, and confidence that their payment will be accepted wherever they want to spend.

That wider requirement is why crypto has not simply replaced cards or bank transfers. It solves one layer of the problem differently: how ownership is recorded and transferred. Sometimes that layer is the real constraint, especially in cross-border transfer, programmable settlement, or crypto-native markets. In ordinary commerce, the harder problems are often elsewhere: acceptance, price stability, regulation, customer protection, and trust.

Crypto is not magic internet money, and it is not a scam by default. It is a different way to record and move value. It is strongest when a shared ledger, direct control, programmability, or cross-border transfer solves a real problem. It is weaker when users need the surrounding machinery that traditional payment systems have built over decades.

Chapter 58: Stablecoins and Digital Money

Bitcoin showed that value could move without a bank or card network, but its price changes too much for everyday payments. Ether can run smart contracts, but it is also volatile. A merchant cannot easily price a product in a token whose value may change significantly before the merchant converts it into regular currency. A freelancer may not want to be paid in an asset that could lose value before rent is due.

Payments work best with a stable unit of account. People budget in dollars, euros, pounds, pesos, rupees, or naira. Businesses issue invoices in national currencies. Salaries, taxes, rent, bills, and accounting records are usually tied to ordinary money.

Stablecoins were created to bring that familiar unit of value into blockchain environments.

A stablecoin is a digital token designed to maintain a stable value relative to another asset, usually a national currency. In the common dollar-backed version, the promise is simple: one token should be worth $1.

That promise makes stablecoins useful. In crypto markets, traders can move from bitcoin or ether into a dollar-like token without leaving an exchange. In decentralized finance, stablecoins serve as a unit of account for lending, borrowing, liquidity pools, derivatives, and trading pairs. For payments and treasury operations, a dollar-like token can cross borders and bypass bank cut-off times.

The stablecoin is therefore not interesting only because it is crypto. It is interesting because it connects a familiar unit of value with a new settlement environment.

A fiat-backed stablecoin is like a transferable claim ticket. The token moves on-chain, but its credibility still depends on the issuer and the off-chain assets backing it.

Design Goal

The basic stablecoin promise is: This token should be worth the same as the reference asset.

Not all stablecoins maintain value the same way. A fiat-backed stablecoin relies on an issuer and reserves. A crypto-collateralized one uses overcollateralization, smart contracts, liquidations, and market prices. An algorithmic stablecoin depends on incentives and confidence. A commodity-backed stablecoin relies on custody, valuation, and redemption of the underlying asset.

To users, these products may all appear as a token balance in a wallet. Behind that balance, the stability mechanism can vary widely.

Stablecoin Model	How It Tries to Stay Stable	Main Risk
Fiat-backed	Issuer holds cash or cash-like assets and issues tokens against reserves	Reserve quality, issuer failure, redemption risk
Crypto-collateralized	Users lock crypto collateral in smart contracts to generate stablecoins	Collateral volatility, liquidation failure, oracle risk
Algorithmic	Protocol uses incentives and supply changes to defend the peg	Confidence collapse, reflexive death spiral
Commodity-backed	Issuer claims backing by assets such as gold	Custody, valuation, redemption, audit risk

Fiat-Backed Models

The most important model for payments is the fiat-backed stablecoin.

USDC and USDT are leading examples. Both are designed to trade near $1, but the token itself is not a dollar bill or bank deposit. Its credibility depends on the issuer, reserve assets, redemption process, custody, and regulatory framework.

Suppose a large customer sends $1 million to a stablecoin issuer or its banking partner. After the fiat money is received, the issuer mints one million stablecoin tokens and sends them to the customer's wallet. Those tokens can then move on-chain between wallets, exchanges, trading firms, payment companies, or other users.

Redemption runs in reverse. The customer sends one million tokens back to the issuer. The issuer burns the tokens, removing them from circulation, and returns $1 million through the banking system, subject to the issuer's rules, compliance checks, banking cut-off times, and redemption eligibility.

The reserve is what makes the promise believable. If there are ten billion tokens in circulation, holders expect the issuer to have roughly $10 billion in cash or highly liquid assets available to support redemptions.

Reserve quality depends on concrete details. A reserve made mostly of cash and short-term government securities is easier to understand and liquidate than one made of commercial paper, secured loans, crypto assets, or harder-to-value instruments. Custody also changes the protection model. Assets held with regulated custodians and clearly separated from the issuer's own funds provide holders with stronger protection than assets held through unclear or complex arrangements.

Redemption rights are just as important as reserve composition. A professional trading firm can redeem directly with the issuer when the stablecoin program permits direct redemption. An ordinary user who bought stablecoins on an exchange often has to sell them back through that exchange instead. In calm markets, both users may experience the token as worth $1. Under stress, the difference becomes important: direct redemption, exchange liquidity, banking access, and compliance reviews can determine whether the user really exists at par.

A stablecoin can trade close to $1 in normal times and still be fragile under pressure. If many holders try to redeem at once, the quality, liquidity, custody, and legal structure of the reserves become the difference between a stable claim and a broken promise.

Minting: From Fiat to Token

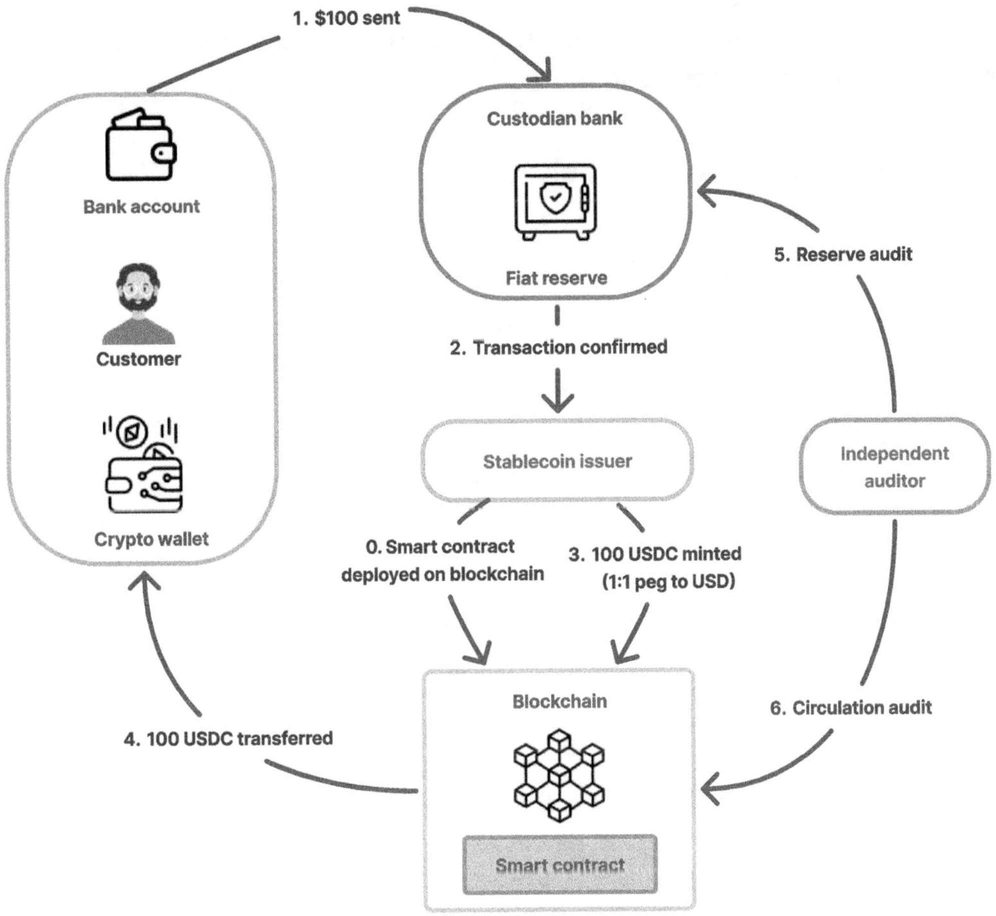

Figure 58.1: Stablecoin minting: from fiat to token.

Minting starts outside the blockchain. A customer sends fiat money to the issuer's banking partner, custodian, or reserve institution. Once the money arrives, the reserve institution confirms receipt to the stablecoin issuer. The issuer then mints the equivalent number of tokens on a blockchain.

If the customer sends $100, the issuer mints one hundred stablecoins, each worth $1.

The customer now holds an on-chain token in a crypto wallet, while the reserve remains off-chain, with the issuer connecting the two.

That is the key architecture of fiat-backed stablecoins. They use blockchain rails for transfer, but the trust anchor is a traditional financial reserve.

The blockchain can display token supply, show wallet transfers, and record minting and burning events. It cannot, by itself, prove that the issuer's bank accounts or custody arrangements hold safe, liquid assets. That proof has to come from outside the chain: attestations, audits, regulation, disclosure, supervision, and trust in the issuer.

Redemption: From Token Back to Fiat

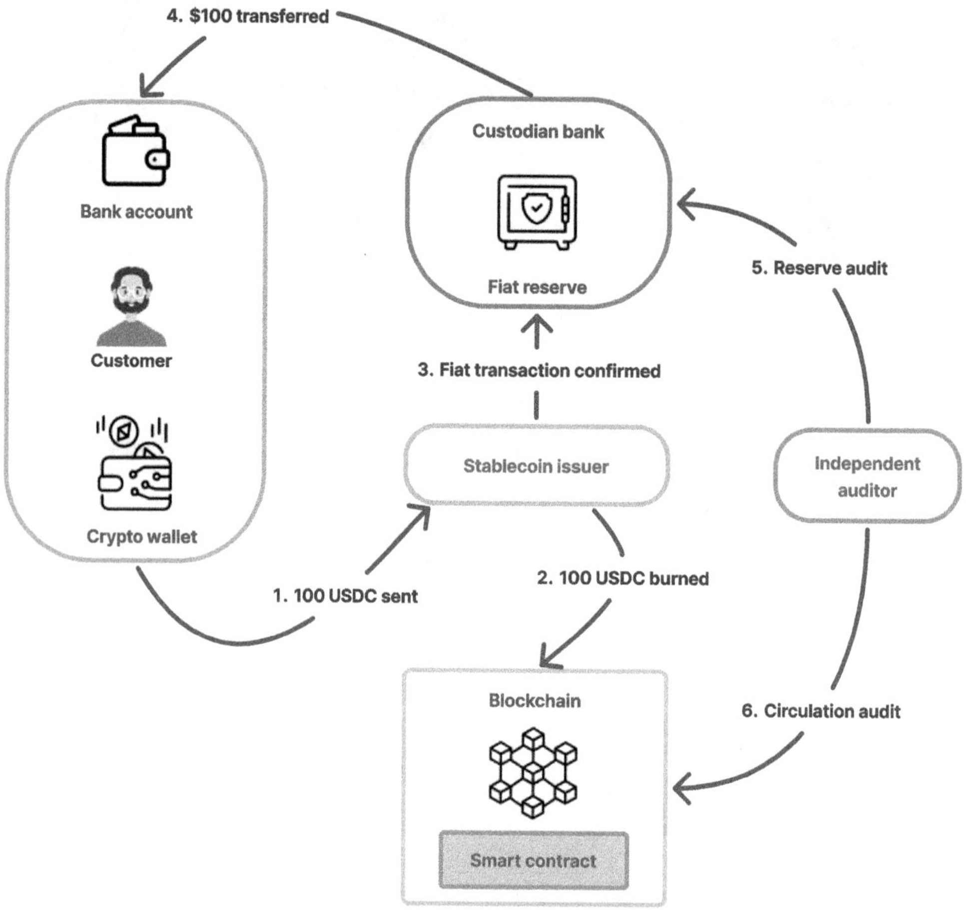

Figure 58.2: Stablecoin redemption: from token to fiat.

Redemption runs the process in reverse.

The customer sends stablecoins back to the issuer. The issuer burns the tokens, removing them from circulation. The issuer then releases the corresponding fiat funds from the reserve and returns them to the customer's bank account.

Burning keeps the token supply aligned with the backing. If one hundred tokens are redeemed, the circulating supply should fall by one hundred. Otherwise, the same reserve base would have to support more tokens than before.

Redemption also helps defend the peg. If a dollar stablecoin trades at $0.98, a market participant may buy it cheaply and redeem it for $1, assuming direct redemption is available. That arbitrage should push the market price back toward $1.

The mechanism depends on confidence in redemption. If redemption is delayed, restricted, expensive, or available only to selected institutions, the market price may not behave like that of a perfect dollar claim.

A stablecoin's stability is therefore not only a market outcome. It is also a promise about how the issuer, reserve, and redemption system operate under stress.

Crypto-Collateralized Models

Some stablecoins are backed not by fiat reserves in bank accounts but by crypto collateral locked in smart contracts.

The reason for this model is independence from a traditional stablecoin issuer. A fiat-backed stablecoin depends on a company, bank accounts, custodians, reserve reports, and redemption promises. A crypto-collateralized stablecoin tries to move more of the mechanism on-chain. The collateral can be visible on the blockchain, smart contracts can enforce the rules, and users can create or redeem stablecoins without having to ask a central issuer to mint or redeem tokens for them.

The basic design is overcollateralization. A user locks crypto assets into a protocol and receives stablecoins in return. The collateral must be worth more than the stablecoins issued.

For example, a user might lock $150 worth of ether into a smart contract and generate $100 worth of stablecoins. The extra $50 is a safety buffer. If the value of ether falls too far, the protocol can liquidate the collateral to repay the stablecoin debt and protect the system.

This is useful in decentralized finance. A user can borrow a stablecoin without selling their crypto holdings. A trader can use the stablecoin in a lending protocol or liquidity pool. A decentralized application can use it as a dollar-like unit of account without depending entirely on a bank-backed issuer. MakerDAO's DAI popularized this model. It showed how a crypto-collateralized stablecoin could be generated against collateral locked in smart contracts. Its collateral design has also changed over time, including both crypto-native and more centralized assets.

The advantage is transparency and programmability. The collateral and many of the rules can be inspected on-chain. The system can automatically manage collateral ratios, liquidations, and repayments through smart contracts.

That changes the risks rather than lowering them by default. The same volatility that makes crypto unsuitable as ordinary money also threatens the collateral behind the stablecoin. If collateral prices fall quickly, the protocol must liquidate positions quickly enough to protect the peg. That process depends on market liquidity, reliable price oracles, and smart contracts that behave correctly under stress.

Governance adds another layer. Parameters such as collateral ratios, accepted collateral types, liquidation penalties, and emergency controls can change over time. A stablecoin that appears decentralized on the surface may also rely on centralized assets or other stablecoins as collateral, bringing some of the same issuer and reserve risks back into the system.

Algorithmic Models

Algorithmic stablecoins try to maintain a stable price without holding a full reserve of dollars, euros, or other safe assets.

The basic idea is to defend the peg through incentives. If the stablecoin trades below $1, the system tries to make it attractive for traders to remove stablecoins from circulation. If it trades above $1, the system tries to increase supply. The design goal is to push the market price back toward $1 through arbitrage rather than through direct redemption from a reserve account.

Suppose a stablecoin is supposed to trade at $1, paired with a second token that absorbs gains and losses. If the stablecoin falls to $0.98, the protocol may let users exchange 1 stablecoin for $1 worth of the second token. In theory, traders buy the stablecoin cheaply, exchange it through the protocol, and make a small profit. That buying pressure should pull the stablecoin back toward $1.

The mechanism works only while the second token has market value and users believe the system can recover. If confidence falls, the trade becomes dangerous. As users rush to sell the stablecoin, the protocol has to issue more of the second token or rely on it more, and the second token's price can fall as well. The system then tries to defend one weakening asset with another.

That is why algorithmic stablecoins are fragile. Their stability depends less on assets held in reserve and more on market confidence, liquidity, and traders' willingness to continue supporting the mechanism during stress.

The failure of TerraUSD in 2022 became a cautionary example. TerraUSD was designed to maintain its dollar peg through a relationship with the LUNA token. When confidence broke, selling pressure hit both tokens. The mechanism that was supposed to restore the peg instead accelerated the collapse.

Calling something *stable* is a design claim, not a guarantee.

Deposits, E-Money, and Money Market Funds

A stablecoin balance can feel familiar because it is denominated in dollars, euros, or another reference currency. Legally and operationally, it is not the same as a bank deposit.

A bank deposit is a liability of a commercial bank. The customer has a claim on the bank. In many jurisdictions, deposits are protected up to a limit by deposit insurance. Banks are subject to capital, liquidity, supervision, resolution, and conduct rules.

E-money is also a privately issued money-like value, but it usually exists under a specific regulatory framework. An e-money institution may be required to safeguard customer funds, keep them separate from its own funds, and redeem balances at par. E-money typically moves through accounts or wallets, not public blockchain tokens.

A money market fund is an investment product. It may invest in short-term assets to maintain stable value, but the investor usually bears investment risk. It is not the same as a payment balance, even if it feels cash-like.

A fiat-backed stablecoin can resemble all three without being identical to any of them. It can feel like a deposit because it is denominated in dollars. It can resemble e-money because it is privately issued and redeemable. It can resemble a money market fund if reserves are invested in short-term securities. The legal treatment still depends on the issuer, jurisdiction, reserve model, redemption rights, and user terms.

Instrument	What the User Holds	Main Backing	Typical Protection
Bank deposit	Claim on a commercial bank	Bank balance sheet	Deposit insurance up to legal limits, depending on jurisdiction
E-money	Claim on an e-money issuer	Safeguarded customer funds	Safeguarding rules, depending on jurisdiction
Money market fund	Investment units	Portfolio of short-term assets	Investment regulation, not deposit insurance
Fiat-backed stablecoin	Token and redemption claim, depending on issuer terms	Reserve assets held by issuer or custodian	Depends on stablecoin regulation and legal structure
Cash	Central bank money	Central bank balance sheet	Direct public money

Compliance and Freezing

Stablecoins inherit the open-transfer character of crypto, but fiat-backed stablecoins are usually not fully censorship-resistant.

Many major stablecoin issuers have administrative controls that allow them to freeze tokens at specific addresses. This may occur due to sanctions, law enforcement requests, hacks, scams, or internal risk policies.

That surprises people who assume all blockchain assets behave like Bitcoin. They do not.

A fiat-backed stablecoin is usually issued by a company. That company has banking partners, regulatory obligations, compliance requirements, and legal exposure. If it wants to maintain access to the traditional financial system, it has to operate within legal boundaries.

The token, therefore, sits between two systems. It moves on a public blockchain, but the issuer can still block specific addresses, refuse redemption, or comply with legal orders.

For regulators, this makes fiat-backed stablecoins easier to integrate into the financial system than fully decentralized assets. For users, it means stablecoins are not neutral bearer instruments like physical cash.

Stablecoin Regulation

Stablecoin regulation is moving from a gray area into formal financial regulation. The shift is easiest to see in the European Union. The Markets in Crypto-Assets Regulation, or MiCA, established rules for crypto-asset service providers and stablecoin issuers. Its stablecoin-related provisions took effect in June 2024, and the broader framework became available in December 2024.

The United States followed with a federal framework for payment stablecoins. In July 2025, the GENIUS Act was signed into law. The important point is not the political branding of the law. Stablecoin issuers are increasingly being regulated like financial institutions, with obligations around reserves, disclosures, redemption, supervision, and compliance.

Regulators care because stablecoins are closely tied to money. A token used for payments, settlement, savings, or cross-border transfers is no longer just a crypto-market instrument. If it fails, users can lose access to funds, counterparties can lose confidence, and stress can spread through exchanges, wallets, payment companies, and trading firms.

The regulatory questions follow naturally from that risk. A framework has to decide who is allowed to issue the token, what assets can be held in reserve, whether reserves must be segregated from the issuer's own assets, whether holders have a legal right to redeem at par, how quickly redemption must happen, who supervises the issuer, whether the token can pay interest, and what disclosures, anti-money laundering controls, and sanctions controls apply.

The answers are not identical across jurisdictions. Some frameworks treat stablecoins closer to e-money. Others place them under payment tokens, crypto-asset, securities, commodities, or special stablecoin regimes. Wallets, exchanges, brokers, and payment processors can also face separate rules because they control access to the token, even if they do not issue it.

Stablecoin regulation is moving away from treating stablecoins as a niche crypto experiment. Once a token is used like money, regulators begin asking the same questions they ask about other forms of money-like value: who stands behind it, what backs it, who can redeem it, and what happens if the promise breaks.

Promises and Constraints

Stablecoins do not remove trust from money. They move it.

With Bitcoin, the main promise is that the ledger can operate without a central issuer. With a fiat-backed stablecoin, the promise is different. The token can move on a blockchain, but its value still depends on something outside the chain: reserves, redemption rights, custody, legal structure, and the issuer's ability to operate under stress.

That is why a stablecoin can feel like digital cash in a wallet while behaving more like a private financial claim. It can move at any time, across borders, and between wallets or platforms. But the holder still depends on the system around the token. Can it be redeemed? Are the reserves liquid? Are they protected if the issuer fails? Can the token be frozen? Does the user have a legal claim, or only access through an exchange? What happens if the wallet provider, blockchain, or off-ramp stops working?

These questions become more important as stablecoins move beyond crypto trading. A trader may only need a dollar-like asset inside an exchange. A business using stablecoins for payments, treasury movement, or settlement needs something closer to financial infrastructure: reliable redemption, clear records, compliance controls, safe custody, and a credible answer when something goes wrong.

Stablecoins make crypto systems more useful by borrowing the stability of familiar money. They also bring back one of the oldest questions in finance: can the promise be trusted?

The same trust question looks different when the digital claim is issued by a central bank rather than by a private company.

Chapter 59: Central Bank Digital Currencies

Cash is public money. A banknote is not a claim on a commercial bank, card network, wallet provider, or payment company. It is a direct liability of the central bank.

A bank deposit is different. The balance in a checking account is a liability of a commercial bank. If the bank fails, deposit insurance may protect the customer up to a limit, but the claim is still with the bank.

That legal distinction is easy to miss in daily life. Cash, deposits, card balances, and wallet balances all appear as spendable value. But the institution behind the balance still shapes the risk. It determines who records ownership, who can restrict access, and what happens if the intermediary fails.

In Chapter 58, we asked that question for stablecoins. A stablecoin can look like a digital dollar in a wallet, but its reliability depends on a private issuer, reserves, redemption rights, collateral, or protocol design.

A central bank digital currency, or CBDC, starts from a different claim. It is digital central bank money.

It is closer to cash than to a bank deposit because the liability sits with the central bank. It is closer to a banking app than to a banknote because it moves electronically.

That combination makes CBDCs important and controversial: public money for a digital economy, built on questions about privacy and state control that cash never had to answer.

Public Money in Digital Form

A CBDC is not cryptocurrency in the usual sense. Bitcoin has no central issuer. A stablecoin is usually issued by a private company or generated by a protocol. A bank deposit is issued by a commercial bank.

A CBDC is issued by the central bank. The easiest way to see the difference is to compare three forms of money.

Form of Money	Issuer	Form	Liability Of	Main Use
Cash	Central bank	Banknotes and coins	Central bank	Physical payments and store of public money
Bank deposits	Commercial banks	Account balances	Commercial bank	Everyday digital payments, savings, transfers
CBDC	Central bank	Digital token or account record	Central bank	Digital public money for payments and settlement

A CBDC is designed as sovereign money in digital form, normally valued one-to-one with the national currency. One digital euro would equal one euro. One digital yuan would equal one yuan.

A rough analogy is a banknote that can move through digital infrastructure. The form changes from paper to electronic record, but the claim remains with the central bank rather than a commercial bank or private issuer.

That legal status is the core distinction. A stablecoin tries to maintain fiat value through reserves, collateral, or market mechanisms. A CBDC has a different legal basis: it is issued as public money from the start.

Central Bank Motivations

Central banks are exploring CBDCs for different reasons. The motivation depends heavily on the country.

In some markets, the argument starts with financial inclusion. If many people lack bank accounts but have mobile phones, a CBDC wallet could provide access to digital payments without requiring a full commercial bank relationship. That promise depends on practical design. A wallet that requires expensive devices, constant connectivity, or complex onboarding will not solve the inclusion problem.

In advanced economies, the concern is often different. Cash use is declining, and more everyday payments are handled by private card networks, mobile wallets, and bank apps. Central banks do not want public money to disappear from daily digital life. A CBDC would preserve access to central bank money even when fewer people use banknotes.

Resilience is another argument. If digital payments depend heavily on a small number of private networks or foreign technology providers, a domestic public payment instrument can look attractive. This is one reason the digital euro is tied not only to payments innovation, but also to European payment sovereignty.

Wholesale settlement is a separate motivation. Banks already settle with central bank money through reserve accounts and real-time gross settlement systems. Wholesale CBDC projects ask whether tokenized central bank money could improve securities, foreign exchange, or cross-border settlement for regulated institutions.

These motivations are not only technical. A CBDC changes the relationship between public money, private payment providers, commercial banks, and citizens. The design questions, therefore, become institutional as much as technical: who issues the money, who distributes it, who keeps the ledger, who sees the transactions, and who controls access.

Retail and Wholesale CBDCs

CBDCs come in two broad forms: retail and wholesale.

A retail CBDC is designed for households and businesses. It could be used to pay in shops, send money to another person, receive government benefits, or make online purchases. The digital euro, China's e-CNY, the Sand Dollar in the Bahamas, Jamaica's JAM-DEX, and Nigeria's eNaira are retail CBDC projects.

A wholesale CBDC is designed for financial institutions. Its users are not shoppers at a checkout. They are banks, central banks, and regulated financial firms. A wholesale CBDC could be used for interbank, securities, and foreign-exchange settlement, as well as for the cross-border movement of central bank money.

Retail CBDC has to work like a consumer payment product. People need a way to get a wallet, recover access if a phone is lost, pay merchants, receive refunds, and understand their privacy rights. The system also has to decide whether balances are capped, whether offline payments are possible, and how fraud or mistaken payments are handled.

Wholesale CBDC has a different test. It has to improve the settlement between institutions. The questions concern tokenized securities, foreign exchange, cross-border central bank money, liquidity management, and whether settlement can become faster or safer without introducing new operational risk.

The public debate usually focuses on retail CBDC because it touches ordinary citizens. The operational value may be clearest in wholesale CBDC, where settlement efficiency and risk reduction are easier to define.

Two-Tier Architecture

Most CBDC designs use a two-tier architecture.

The central bank issues the CBDC. Commercial banks and licensed payment institutions distribute it to the public.

That separation is deliberate. Central banks are not built to run retail customer service for millions of citizens. They do not normally operate consumer apps, handle password resets, onboard small businesses, manage fraud complaints, or run call centers. Commercial banks and payment providers already have that customer-facing machinery.

In a two-tier model, the central bank stays at the foundation. It creates the digital currency and maintains the core ledger and settlement infrastructure. Commercial banks and regulated intermediaries provide wallets, customer interfaces, onboarding, compliance checks, and payment services.

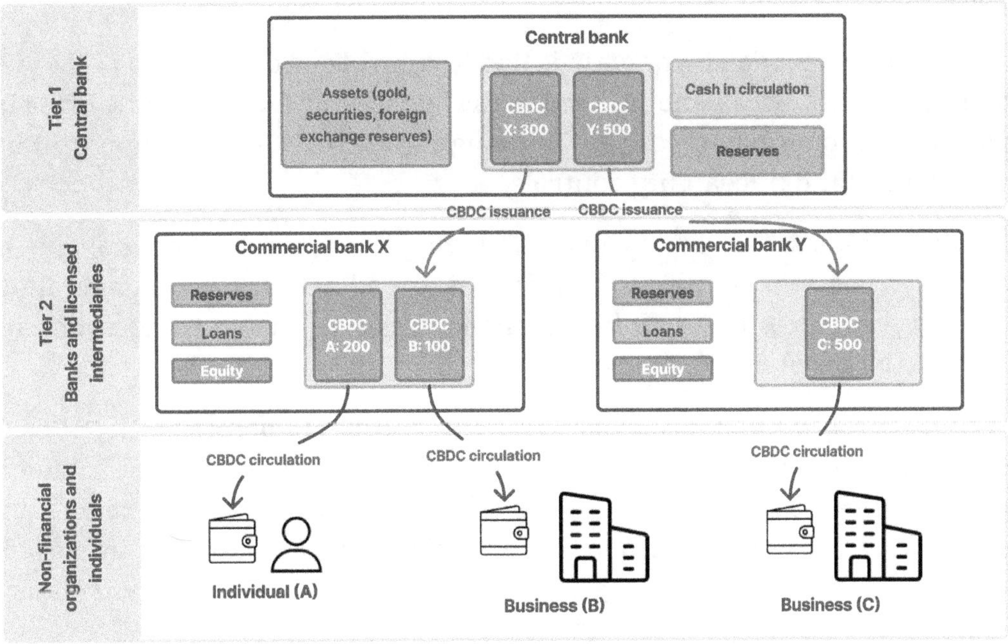

Figure 59.1: The two-tier CBDC model.

This model also protects the role of commercial banks. A direct CBDC account at the central bank could pull deposits away from banks, especially during a crisis. If customers can move money instantly from a commercial bank to a risk-free central bank wallet, bank runs could occur more quickly.

Many CBDC designs include holding limits, tiered remuneration, or other controls for that reason. The goal is usually to provide digital public money without draining the deposit base that banks use to fund lending.

The two-tier model also makes it easier to connect the CBDC to the existing financial system. Banks and payment providers already know how to perform customer due diligence, monitor transactions, manage fraud, provide statements, support merchants, and handle operational exceptions. The CBDC may be new, but the surrounding payment business still needs familiar infrastructure.

Account-Based and Token-Based Models

CBDCs can be designed as account-based or token-based systems.

In an account-based model, ownership is tied to an account identity. The system asks: who is the account holder and what is their balance? This is familiar from bank deposits. Access depends on authentication, identity, and account records.

In a token-based model, ownership is tied to control of a digital token. The system asks: is this token genuine, and is the spender authorized to transfer it? This is closer to a cash-in concept, although most real CBDC designs still include identity and traceability controls.

The difference is not always clean. A CBDC may use token-like technology underneath while still requiring identity-based wallets. A system may allow more privacy for low-value offline payments while requiring stronger identity checks for larger or riskier transactions.

That hybrid design makes privacy difficult. A fully anonymous digital cash system would worry regulators because it could be used for money laundering, sanctions evasion, tax evasion, and illicit commerce. A fully traceable system would worry citizens because it could give the state visibility into every payment.

Many CBDC proposals try to sit between those extremes: more privacy for low-value payments, stronger controls for higher-risk activity, and clear legal limits on who can access transaction data.

Online and Offline CBDC

Digital payments usually require connectivity. A card terminal often needs to connect to the internet for online authorization. A bank transfer needs access to bank systems. A wallet payment usually needs internet or network access.

Cash does not depend on that live connection: a banknote works during a power outage, without mobile coverage, and between two people who do not know each other.

A retail CBDC may need some version of that resilience. Offline CBDC would allow two devices to transfer value without immediate internet access, then synchronize with the main system later.

This is technically hard. The system must prevent double-spending: the same digital value cannot be spent twice while devices are offline. It also has to manage limits, lost devices, fraud, and privacy. Most designs that support offline use impose strict caps on how much can be stored or spent offline.

The digital euro project explicitly includes both online and offline use. The ECB says a digital euro would be stored through a bank or public intermediary and could be used online or offline with a phone or card. The ECB has described 2029 as a possible first-issuance target, assuming the necessary EU legislation is adopted in 2026.

Offline capability is one of the few features that could make a CBDC meaningfully different from an ordinary bank transfer.

Programmability

CBDCs are often described as programmable money. Programmability can mean two different things.

The first is programmable payments. This is not especially controversial. A user, business, or government can schedule payments, automate tax collection, release funds when conditions are met, or integrate payments into smart contracts. Existing payment systems already support some of this through direct debits, standing orders, APIs, escrow tools, and payment orchestration.

The second is programmable money itself. This is more sensitive. It means the unit of money can carry restrictions: where it may be spent, when it expires, who may receive it, or which categories of purchases are allowed.

A government could issue disaster relief funds that expire after three months. A subsidy could be limited to specific merchant categories. A stimulus payment could be designed to encourage spending rather than saving.

Those features may be useful in narrow cases. They also raise serious concerns. Money that can be restricted by purpose, location, time, or identity is not neutral in the same way as cash. It gives the issuer greater control over how money is used.

Privacy and Surveillance

Cash provides strong practical privacy. A person can hand a banknote to a merchant without the central bank seeing the transaction.

Bank deposits provide less privacy. Banks record transactions, and authorities may access records under legal process.

A CBDC could move in either direction.

A privacy-preserving CBDC could imitate some cash properties for low-value payments, especially offline. It could hide transaction details from the central bank and reveal information only under defined legal conditions.

A surveillance-heavy CBDC could give the state direct visibility into payments. Purchases, transfers, donations, and balance movements could become visible or reconstructable through the system.

Most central banks understand this concern. That does not make the problem easy. Privacy depends on architecture, law, governance, and public trust.

The concern, therefore, has to be tested against design choices, not only stated goals. Who operates the ledger? What data is collected? Who can access it? Under what legal process? Can low-value payments remain private? Can users choose other payment methods? Can the rules be changed later?

Citizens will judge a CBDC partly by whether they trust its privacy model.

Adoption around the World

CBDC work has moved from theory to global experimentation, but experimentation is not the same as adoption.

More than 130 countries and currency unions have explored CBDCs, representing almost all global GDP. Many projects remain in research or pilot stages. Only a few countries have fully launched retail CBDCs, including the Bahamas, Jamaica, and Nigeria. For a current country-by-country view, the Atlantic Council's CBDC Tracker follows whether projects are in research, development, pilot, launch, or inactive status: Atlantic Council, CBDC Tracker, https://www.atlanticcouncil.org/cbdctracker/

Some countries have moved slowly, and some have paused or narrowed their work. The United States moved in the opposite direction in January 2025, when a presidential executive order prohibited federal agencies, except where required by law, from taking action to establish, issue, or promote a CBDC and directed existing CBDC initiatives to stop.

This global activity shows broad interest, but it does not prove that CBDCs will become widely used payment instruments.

A CBDC has to compete with existing payment habits: cards, mobile wallets, instant bank transfers, domestic schemes, cash, and private apps. If those systems are fast, cheap, trusted, and widely accepted, a CBDC must offer a clear reason to switch.

For consumers, central bank liability is not usually a selling point at checkout. People care whether payments are accepted, fast, private, cheap, safe, and recoverable. Merchants care about cost, settlement speed, integration, refunds, reconciliation, and customer demand.

Banks look at the same system differently. A CBDC that is overly attractive could pull deposits away from banks and weaken the funding base they rely on for lending. A CBDC that is too limited is not always useful enough for people to adopt. Governments have to decide whether the public benefits justify the cost, complexity, and political risk.

Some launched CBDCs have seen limited uptake for this reason. The hard part is creating a payment instrument that people prefer over the options they already use.

China shows that tension better than any other country.

Digital Yuan

China's *e-CNY*, often called the *digital yuan*, is the world's largest retail CBDC project.

While many central banks are still debating CBDC design, China has operated the digital yuan through large-scale pilots across major cities and use cases. It has not displaced Alipay, WeChat Pay, cards, or bank account payments as the dominant retail rail. Still, it is more than a theoretical project: a live system with large reported transaction volumes.

Official Chinese government reporting said that, by the end of November 2025, e-CNY had recorded 3.48 billion cumulative transactions worth 16.7 trillion yuan, approximately $2.37 trillion.

Even with that scale, the e-CNY operates in a market already dominated by two of the world's most successful private mobile payment systems: Alipay and WeChat Pay. For many consumers, those wallets already work everywhere, offer familiar interfaces, and connect to daily life. A government-issued digital yuan has to compete with that convenience.

The e-CNY is not the same as Alipay or WeChat Pay. Alipay and WeChat Pay are wallet and payment platforms. They move commercial bank money and wallet balances through private ecosystems. The e-CNY is central bank money in digital form.

The ledger level shows the difference. In a private wallet system, the platform and its partner banks maintain customer records and settlement relationships. In e-CNY, the central bank sits much closer to the core record of ownership.

The e-CNY shows both sides of CBDC. It can support digital public money, offline payment capability, and direct state-backed settlement. It can also give the state a more detailed view of money movement than cash ever could.

Whether that is seen as efficiency or surveillance depends on the society, the legal safeguards, and the level of trust in the state.

Digital Euro

The digital euro is the most important CBDC project in Western finance. It is still in preparation, not live.

The ECB presents the digital euro as a complement to cash, not a replacement for it. It is also tied to European payment sovereignty. Europe does not want all digital retail payments to depend on non-European card networks, technology companies, or private wallets.

The ECB says the digital euro would be accessible through banks or public intermediaries and usable online and offline. Its current goal is to be ready for possible first issuance during 2029, assuming the necessary EU legislation is adopted in 2026. The ECB also plans to run a 12-month pilot starting in the second half of 2027, subject to the legislative process.

The project faces serious design constraints. Banks have to absorb implementation costs while considering deposit outflows and the impact on existing payment products. Merchants will judge the system by its fees, acceptance rules, integration work, and reconciliation burden. Citizens need credible privacy protections. Payment providers, meanwhile, have to understand whether the new system supports their role or competes with it.

Those tensions are normal for a project of this size. A CBDC requires more than an app launch. It needs wallets, onboarding, offline access, recovery, merchant acceptance, privacy design, bank integration, and legal rules that people and institutions trust.

Comparison with Stablecoins

CBDCs and stablecoins are often discussed together because both can represent fiat value in digital form. Structurally, they answer different institutional questions.

Dimension	Stablecoin	CBDC
Issuer	Private company or protocol	Central bank
Legal nature	Private money-like claim or token	Public money
Backing	Reserves, collateral, or algorithmic mechanism	Central bank balance sheet and sovereign legal framework
Ledger	Blockchain or permissioned ledger	Central bank or authorized infrastructure
Key benefit	Global reach, 24/7 transfer, crypto ecosystem integration	Public money, legal certainty, domestic payment resilience
Key risk	Reserve, issuer, peg, redemption, wallet, and regulatory risk	Privacy, surveillance, bank disintermediation, adoption, and state control

The difference is institutional. A stablecoin relies on a private issuer, a collateral model, or a protocol. A CBDC rests on the central bank's balance sheet and the state's legal authority.

Neither structure is automatically better. Stablecoins fit naturally into crypto markets, cross-border token movement, and private payment infrastructure. CBDCs are designed to preserve or extend the use of public money in digital form.

Evaluation Criteria

A CBDC is digital public money: central bank money in digital form.

The same term can describe very different systems. A CBDC can be retail or wholesale, account-based or token-based, direct or intermediated, online-only or offline-capable. It can preserve some cash-like privacy, or it can create a payment system with far greater state visibility. It can support programmable payments or embed restrictions into the money itself.

A CBDC should therefore be judged by its architecture, not by the label. The important question is how the system allocates power and responsibility: who issues the money, distributes it, keeps the ledger, sees the transaction, blocks the payment, restores access, and bears the loss when something breaks.

Those choices reveal what a CBDC really is. It may preserve public money in a digital economy. It may improve settlement infrastructure. It may support offline payments or reduce dependence on private rails. It may also expand state visibility into payments, put pressure on bank deposits, or create a payment instrument that citizens do not actually want to use.

CBDCs are not simply the next version of money. They are a design choice about the role of the state in digital payments.

Chapter 60: DeFi and Web3 Finance

Most financial services rely on trusted intermediaries. Banks keep deposits and track balances; brokers provide market access; card networks handle payments and set the rules; clearing houses calculate obligations between institutions. Custodians keep assets safe, and regulators decide what each institution is allowed to do.

This setup exists for a reason. Finance involves money, identity, risk, disagreements, and fraud. Someone needs to keep records, decide who can participate, fix mistakes, block illegal activity, settle disputes, and handle losses when things go wrong.

Decentralized finance, or *DeFi*, starts from a different premise: some financial functions can be run by software on a public blockchain instead of by a traditional institution.

Instead of a bank account, the user has a crypto wallet. Instead of a broker, a smart contract executes trades. Instead of a lending officer, a protocol lends against collateral under rules written in code. Instead of a company ledger, the blockchain records transactions publicly.

This design reshapes finance. It changes who controls access, who holds assets, how transactions are settled, and how rules are enforced. But it does not remove risk. It moves risk into code, collateral, wallets, governance, market prices, and user behavior.

That shift is the central idea of DeFi.

From Web Pages to Wallets

DeFi is not just finance delivered through a website or an app. Online banking, card payments, PayPal, Stripe, and broker apps already did that. DeFi belongs to a different claim: digital assets and transactions can be controlled through wallets, tokens, smart contracts, and blockchain records.

A common shorthand describes the web in three stages: read, write, and own.

Web1 was the read-only web. Pages were mostly static, like online brochures. A user visited a site, read the content, downloaded files, followed links, and left. There was little interaction, no social account layer, and no built-in way for the web itself to handle money. If a payment was made, it was processed via a separate system: card payment, bank transfer, invoice, cash payment, or offline arrangement.

Web2 added writing and participation. Users could create accounts, upload photos, write reviews, stream video, sell products, order food, book rides, and use financial apps. This is the web most people still use every day: YouTube, Instagram, TikTok, Amazon, Shopify, Uber, neobanks, and app-based financial services. But Web2 has a built-in tension. Users create content, data, reputation, audiences, stores, and payment histories, while the platform controls the relationship. The account, followers, transaction records, rules, and access rights sit on servers controlled by a company. Payments became easier in Web2, but they still ran through banks, card networks, processors, wallets, and payment service providers underneath.

Web3 adds ownership. The claim is that assets can live on a blockchain rather than only inside a platform database. A user can hold tokens, stablecoins, digital collectibles, governance rights, or other digital assets through a wallet. The wallet controls the private key. If the user controls the key, they can move the asset without asking the platform to approve the transfer. Smart contracts can then execute transactions according to code rather than platform rules.

This does not automatically make Web3 better; it changes where control and responsibility lie. A platform account can often be recovered if the password is lost, and the platform can reverse or investigate certain mistakes. A blockchain wallet does not always have that safety net, and a confirmed blockchain transaction is usually final.

That trade-off leads directly to DeFi. Web3 gives users direct control over digital assets. DeFi builds financial services around that control.

System Structure

DeFi aims to rebuild financial services as software running on public blockchains.

The services are familiar: exchange, lending, borrowing, asset management, derivatives, stablecoins, payments, and governance. The difference is how the service is accessed and executed.

In traditional finance, access usually begins with an institution. A customer opens an account, passes identity checks, accepts terms, and uses the institution's systems.

In DeFi, access begins with a wallet. A user connects the wallet to a protocol and signs a transaction. The protocol does not need to know the user's name to execute the instruction. It needs to know whether the wallet controls the required assets and whether the transaction satisfies the smart contract's rules.

That makes DeFi open by default. Anyone with a compatible wallet and internet connection can interact with the protocol.

The same openness creates the trade-off. There is no customer support, no dispute process, no suitability check, no complaints team, and no easy way to undo a mistake. The system can be available to anyone because it does not rely on the same gatekeepers. It also lacks many of the protections those gatekeepers provide.

Dimension	Traditional Finance	DeFi
Access	Account opening, KYC, institutional approval	Wallet connection and transaction signing
Ledger	Maintained by banks, brokers, custodians, or market infrastructure	Maintained on a blockchain
Execution	Institutions process transactions	Smart contracts execute rules
Asset custody	Often held by banks, brokers, custodians, or exchanges	Often held directly by the user or smart contract
Risk control	Institutional controls, regulation, audits, legal recourse	Code, collateral, market incentives, protocol governance
Failure mode	Institution failure, fraud, operational outage, legal dispute	Smart contract exploit, lost keys, oracle failure, liquidity collapse

The simplest way to understand DeFi is that it replaces institutional permission with programmable execution.

Smart Contracts

At the heart of DeFi is the smart contract. A smart contract is software deployed on a blockchain. It contains rules and can hold assets. When a user sends a valid transaction to it, the contract executes according to its code.

A simple example is a token swap.

In a traditional exchange, a customer places an order. The exchange matches buyers and sellers, updates internal records, and may rely on custodians, clearing arrangements, and settlement systems as part of its operating model.

In a decentralized exchange, the user connects a wallet and signs a transaction. A smart contract checks the available liquidity, calculates the price, transfers one token from the user, returns another token, and records the result on the blockchain.

There is no human clerk, no broker approval, and no back office team manually updating the ledger. The transaction runs because the code allows it.

DeFi changes the nature of trust. In traditional finance, users rely on institutions, contracts, courts, regulators, and operational controls. In DeFi, they rely on code, governance, validators, wallet security, and the protocol's economic design.

The word *trustless* is often used in DeFi, but it can mislead. Trust has moved from people and institutions into software, cryptography, incentives, and infrastructure.

Smart contracts are the execution layer. On their own, they are just programs that can hold assets and follow rules. DeFi becomes interesting when many of those programs are arranged into recognizable financial services.

Decentralized Exchanges

A decentralized exchange, or DEX, lets users trade crypto assets through smart contracts.

The best-known design uses liquidity pools. Instead of matching one buyer with one seller, the protocol holds pools of tokens supplied by users called liquidity providers. A trader swaps against the pool. The smart contract prices the trade using a formula based on the ratio of assets in the pool.

For example, a pool may contain ETH and USDC. A trader who wants to buy ETH sends USDC into the pool and receives ETH in return. The pool's ratio changes, and the price changes with it.

Liquidity providers earn fees from trades. They also take risks. If the relative price of the two assets changes sharply, they may suffer impermanent loss: a situation where simply holding the tokens outside the pool would have produced a better result.

A DEX reduces the need for a centralized exchange to custody the user's assets. The user trades from their own wallet. But the risk does not disappear. It changes form: smart contract bugs, poor liquidity, price slippage, front-running, fake tokens, and malicious interfaces.

The trade is no longer routed through a conventional intermediary. The user still needs to trust the protocol, the wallet, the token, the price mechanism, and the interface used to reach it.

Oracles

Blockchains are closed systems. A smart contract can read data already on the blockchain, but it cannot automatically know the price of ETH in dollars, whether a shipment arrived, what the weather was, or whether interest rates changed outside the blockchain.

An oracle, such as Chainlink, supplies external data to a blockchain. Price oracles are critical in DeFi. Lending protocols need asset prices to calculate collateral ratios. Derivatives need market prices to settle contracts. Stablecoins may need oracle data to maintain pegs or manage collateral.

If an oracle is wrong, delayed, manipulated, or unavailable, the protocol can make the wrong decision. It may liquidate healthy positions, allow undercollateralized borrowing, misprice trades, or create arbitrage opportunities.

Oracle risk shows a larger DeFi problem. Even if the code works exactly as written, the system can still fail if the data entered into the code is incorrect.

Lending and Borrowing Protocols

DeFi lending protocols such as Aave let users borrow against crypto collateral.

A borrower deposits an asset, such as ETH, into a smart contract. Against that collateral, they can borrow another asset, often a stablecoin. The protocol sets a collateral ratio. If the collateral's value falls too far, the smart contract can automatically liquidate it.

This is very different from a regular unsecured consumer loan. A bank may lend based on income, credit history, affordability, employment, and existing debt. A DeFi protocol usually does not know who the borrower is. It does not rely on a personal promise to repay. It relies on collateral that can be sold if the position becomes unsafe.

DeFi lending is therefore closer to margin lending than to a typical personal loan.

The advantage is speed and access. A user can borrow within minutes without an application process. The constraint is that the borrower usually has to post more collateral than they borrow. To borrow $1,000 in stablecoins, the user often needs to lock up significantly more than $1,000 in crypto assets.

That makes DeFi lending useful for traders, crypto holders, and on-chain financial activity, but much less useful for ordinary consumer credit, where borrowers usually need money because they do not already have sufficient collateral.

The liquidation process can also be harsh. If the collateral's value drops, it can be sold automatically. There is no phone call, no renegotiation, no grace period, and no relationship manager. The code acts because the position crossed a threshold.

Stablecoins as Settlement Money

Stablecoins are the main settlement asset in much of DeFi.

Without stablecoins, users would have to trade, lend, borrow, and measure returns in volatile assets such as ETH or BTC. That makes financial planning difficult. A loan denominated in a volatile asset can become dangerous quickly because the debt itself can change sharply in value.

Stablecoins give DeFi a more stable unit of account. They allow protocols to offer dollar-like trading pairs, dollar-like loans, and dollar-like liquidity without directly using bank deposits.

In Chapter 58, we described several stablecoin models. Fiat-backed stablecoins, such as USDC and USDT, are issued by private companies and backed by reserves. Crypto-collateralized stablecoins, historically associated with DAI-style designs, are generated against collateral locked in smart contracts. Algorithmic stablecoins seek to maintain a peg through incentives and supply mechanisms, and failures in this category have made the risks visible.

Inside DeFi, stablecoins bridge volatile blockchain assets and payment-like financial activity.

That bridge is useful, but it can be fragile. If a stablecoin loses its peg, its reserves are questioned, collateral drops, or regulation changes, the effects can spread through lending markets, exchanges, liquidity pools, and leveraged positions.

Liquidity Pools, Staking, and Yield

DeFi attracted attention because users could earn returns, often described as yield.

Some yield comes from real economic activity. Liquidity providers earn trading fees. Lenders earn interest from borrowers. Validators earn staking rewards for helping secure proof-of-stake networks.

Other yields are less durable. A protocol may distribute governance tokens to attract users. High headline returns often depend on the token's ability to retain value. If the protocol pays rewards in a token whose price collapses, the yield can disappear quickly.

Staking means locking assets to support a blockchain or protocol and earning rewards. In proof-of-stake networks, validators stake tokens to participate in consensus. Users may delegate tokens to validators and receive a share of the rewards.

Yield farming means moving assets across protocols to maximize returns. A user might deposit stablecoins in one protocol, receive a token representing that deposit, and then use that token in another protocol to earn additional rewards.

This ability to combine protocols is one of DeFi's distinctive features. A stablecoin, lending market, exchange, wallet, and governance system can be assembled into new financial products. Developers often describe this as composability: one protocol can become a building block for another.

Composability also spreads risk. If one protocol fails, its effects can propagate to other assets linked to it. What looks like a diversified position can still depend on the same collateral, oracle, bridge, stablecoin, or governance token.

DAOs and Governance

Many DeFi protocols are governed by decentralized autonomous organizations, or DAOs.

A *DAO* is a governance structure where token holders can propose and vote on changes. They may vote on fees, collateral types, risk parameters, treasury spending, protocol upgrades, or emergency actions. The idea is to replace centralized company control with community governance.

In practice, DAO governance can be messy. Token ownership is often concentrated. Founders, early investors, large holders, or professional delegates may have significant influence. Many users do not vote. Some voters do not understand the technical consequences of a proposal. Governance attacks are also possible if an attacker can acquire, borrow, or influence enough voting power.

A DAO can open protocol governance to more participants. It does not guarantee democracy, safety, or accountability.

Bridges and Cross-Chain Risk

DeFi does not live on one blockchain. Assets and applications are spread across networks such as Ethereum, Solana, BNB Chain, Arbitrum, Optimism, Polygon, Avalanche, and others.

Users often want to move assets between chains. That is where bridges come in.

A bridge connects assets or messages across blockchains. In a common model, it locks an asset on one chain and creates a representation of it on another. Other designs use liquidity networks, validators, messaging protocols, or different forms of custody and verification.

Bridges are useful because they connect separate pools of liquidity. They also create some of the largest technical and custody risks in crypto.

A bridge often holds large amounts of locked assets. That makes it an attractive target. If the bridge is hacked or its validation mechanism fails, the asset represented on the other chain may no longer be fully backed.

This is not a minor edge case. Cross-chain bridges have caused some of the largest losses in crypto. They concentrate risk in infrastructure that many users barely understand.

Benefits and Costs

DeFi has real strengths. It gives users open access to financial protocols without a local bank account, a branch network, a credit history, or a broker relationship. A wallet and an internet connection can be enough.

It also makes the activity more transparent. Transactions, contract code, balances, and protocol activity can often be publicly inspected. Traditional finance relies on private ledgers and delayed reporting. DeFi often exposes the ledger directly.

Settlement can be fast. On-chain transactions can settle in minutes or seconds on high-throughput networks. There is no card clearing cycle, correspondent banking chain, or securities settlement window in the traditional sense.

Composability gives developers another advantage. A stablecoin, lending market, exchange, wallet, and identity layer can be connected into new services. This makes DeFi a useful laboratory for programmable finance.

User control is also real. In non-custodial DeFi, users can hold their own assets and transact without relying on a centralized platform to approve withdrawals.

Those strengths come with costs. Smart contract bugs can lead to permanent losses. Once an exploit happens, the blockchain may record the transaction without providing a way to reverse it. Lost private keys can be permanent. A bad wallet approval can empty an account. A fake interface can trick the user into signing a harmful transaction.

Market risk is constant: collateral prices can fall quickly, liquidity can disappear, stablecoins can depeg, governance tokens can collapse, and liquidations can cascade through connected protocols.

Fraud is easier to distribute in an open system. Fake tokens, phishing sites, malicious approvals, rug pulls, and impersonation attacks can reach users directly. Permissionless access makes experimentation easier. It also makes fraud easier.

Regulation remains unsettled. A protocol may be technically decentralized but still attract scrutiny. Developers, front-end operators, governance participants, and major token holders may all face questions about responsibility.

Consumer protection is much weaker than in regulated financial services: a bank customer can complain, a cardholder may have dispute rights, and a brokerage customer may have regulatory protections, while a DeFi user often has none of that. If the transaction was signed and confirmed, the system treats it as valid.

DeFi gives users more direct control, but control is not the same as safety.

Use Cases and Limits

DeFi is not built around the operational requirements of everyday card and bank payments.

Card payments solve a merchant acceptance problem. They provide global acceptance, consumer protections, fraud controls, dispute processes, authorization rules, clearing, settlement, and standardized operating procedures. DeFi does not offer that package in a form that mainstream merchants and consumers can rely on.

Bank payments solve account-to-account money movement at scale. They connect regulated institutions, payroll systems, billers, governments, businesses, and consumers. They operate within legal frameworks that define finality, liability, reversibility, and compliance.

DeFi solves a different problem: permissionless financial execution on public blockchains. That structure can be valuable where the assets, users, and risks already live on-chain. It can provide liquidity for crypto-native assets, support stablecoin markets that operate around the clock, enable collateralized lending without a traditional intermediary, and create programmable financial products that settle directly on blockchain rails.

It is much less suited to ordinary retail payments. Buying groceries, paying rent, running payroll, or disputing a fraudulent transaction requires more than moving value from one wallet to another. Most people do not want to think about gas fees, bridge risks, wallet approvals, slippage, seed phrases, or oracle failures just to buy a cup of coffee.

The harder issues are trust, liability, regulation, reconciliation, and recovery from mistakes.

DeFi can still indirectly influence traditional finance. Banks, asset managers, and market infrastructures are studying tokenized deposits, tokenized securities, smart contract settlement, and blockchain-based collateral movement. They may not adopt public DeFi protocols directly, but they may borrow some of the ideas: programmable settlement, atomic exchange, transparent collateral, and composable financial logic.

The future is unlikely to be DeFi replacing banks. A more realistic path is for regulated finance to adopt selected DeFi techniques that improve settlement, collateral movement, automation, or market transparency.

Chapter 61: AI in Fintech

Artificial intelligence enters finance at a different layer from the systems we have studied so far.

A card network routes messages between issuers and acquirers; a bank ledger records balances and obligations; a payment processor connects merchants, banks, schemes, and technical systems; clearing and settlement determine what gets posted and how money moves. These are infrastructure problems: they define how financial activity is carried out.

AI works around that infrastructure. It helps institutions decide what to approve, block, review, explain, and escalate.

That difference is the key to this chapter. AI increasingly sits as a decision layer across the rails already described in this book. It scores risk, routes work, detects patterns, summarizes cases, and helps institutions decide what to do next.

Every financial institution runs on decisions like these: fraud or normal customer behavior, creditworthy or too risky, legitimate merchant or hidden threat, routine alert or real compliance risk, simple support request or case that needs human assistance.

Across the earlier chapters, we saw these decisions in their own settings: authorization, fraud scoring, KYC and AML, disputes, reconciliation, merchant monitoring, and customer support. AI changes the quality, speed, and scale of those decisions. It changes how they are made, prioritized, documented, and reviewed.

That role is not new. Large issuers, card networks, and processors used machine-learning models for fraud scoring long before the recent generative-AI boom. The newer change is broader reach: stronger models, cheaper computing, better tooling, and large language models have made AI useful across more functions, including fraud, credit, compliance, operations, disputes, support, document review, and product personalization.

Often, AI does not make the final decision. It gives a score, classification, recommendation, summary, alert, or anomaly flag. The outcome may still be decided by a rule engine, a human reviewer, a risk policy, or a regulated process.

In finance, bad decisions have consequences: blocked access to money, approved fraud, unfair credit decisions, missed sanctions risks, or compliance breaches. AI can improve those decisions without moving accountability away from the institution that uses it.

Financial Data for AI

Financial institutions have always relied on data. The change is not that data suddenly appeared. The change is that institutions can process more of it, faster, and across messier formats.

The raw material is familiar: authorization context, account history, authentication results, transaction behavior, onboarding documents, sanctions screening results, support messages, dispute files, merchant websites, invoices, reconciliation breaks, and case notes.

The useful signal is often hidden across several of those sources.

A scam transfer can look ordinary when viewed by amount alone, but different when combined with a new device, unusual timing, recent password reset, and a beneficiary the customer has never paid before. A borrower with a thin credit file may still demonstrate stable income and disciplined cash flow. A merchant that looked normal at onboarding may later show warning signs through refunds, disputes, website changes, and customer complaints.

Rule-based systems still have an important place. Some controls need to be direct, auditable, and easy to explain: block a sanctioned entity, require enhanced review for a prohibited or sensitive merchant category, or apply a clear policy-set threshold.

AI is useful when the decision cannot be reduced to a single rule. A fraud model can weigh device history, merchant category, transaction amount, location, velocity, account behavior, authentication result, and recent customer activity together. No single signal proves the case. The combination changes the risk picture.

That is also where governance becomes important. The institution needs to understand which inputs the model uses, how the output affects the customer, and whether the result can be explained, monitored, and challenged.

Main Techniques

People often use the term AI broadly. In fintech, three families of techniques do most of the work: machine learning, neural networks, and language models.

Machine learning systems learn from historical data. A model is trained on past examples and then used to estimate the likelihood of outcomes for new cases. In payments, that may mean learning from previous fraudulent and legitimate transactions. In lending, it may mean learning from borrowers who repaid and borrowers who defaulted.

The model does not need a human to write every rule manually. It learns relationships from data.

The same learning process that makes the model useful also makes it sensitive to the data it learns from. If historical data contains bias, gaps, bad labels, or outdated patterns, the model can reproduce those problems at scale.

Neural networks are a type of machine-learning model that can detect complex relationships among many inputs. They are useful when the pattern is difficult to express through simple rules, such as when transaction amount, device, merchant, location, velocity, and previous behavior together form a suspicious pattern.

The challenge is explainability. The more complex the model, the harder it can be to explain why it produced a particular result. That becomes a serious issue when the decision affects credit, account access, fraud treatment, compliance review, or customer rights.

Natural language processing, or NLP, handles text. It can read support messages, loan documents, merchant descriptions, complaint narratives, invoices, sanctions information, news, and regulatory filings. It can extract structured data from messy language, classify cases, summarize long documents, and help human teams work faster.

Large language models made NLP much more visible. Their main value in fintech is turning language-heavy work into easier-to-process tasks: summarizing files, extracting facts, drafting responses, comparing documents, routing cases, and helping staff review complex information.

Generative AI and Agentic Workflows

The recent AI boom is mostly about generative AI: models that can produce text, code, summaries, explanations, classifications, and structured outputs from prompts and source material.

In fintech, generative AI is useful for repetitive, language-intensive tasks. A model can summarize a dispute file, draft a customer-support response, extract entities from a merchant website, compare onboarding documents, turn a regulatory update into an internal checklist, or help an analyst understand why a reconciliation break occurred.

The next step is often described as agentic AI. In this model, the AI system not only answers a question, but also plans a sequence of actions, calls tools, retrieves data, drafts outputs, and hands work to a human reviewer.

Agentic AI raises the operational stakes. A chatbot that gives a wrong answer is a problem. An agent that retrieves the wrong account, updates the wrong case, sends the wrong message, or changes the wrong control can create damage before a human notices.

For that reason, agentic AI in finance needs narrow permissions, robust audit logs, human-review thresholds, and clear limits on what the system can do without approval. The more a model can act, the more the institution needs to control the path of its actions.

Fraud Detection and Transaction Risk

Fraud detection is one of the oldest uses of machine learning in payments. Chapter 41 explained the operational problem: the issuer must approve legitimate transactions, block fraudulent ones, and avoid unnecessary declines. AI does not change that goal. It changes how the decision is produced.

A rule-based system might say: decline if the transaction exceeds a threshold, originates from a high-risk country, or involves too many failed attempts. A model-based system can combine many weak signals at once: merchant history, device behavior, transaction velocity, location, amount, time of day, cardholder behavior, authentication result, and previous outcomes. No single signal has to prove fraud by itself. The model estimates risk from the pattern.

That creates new responsibilities. The model has to be trained on reliable data, monitored for drift, tested against false positives, and constrained by policy. A model that blocks fraud but declines too many legitimate transactions damages the product. A model that approves too freely shifts losses into fraud claims and chargebacks.

AI also creates an explainability problem. Fraud teams, compliance teams, merchants, and sometimes regulators need to understand why a decision was made. The answer does not always need to be a full technical explanation of the model, but the institution needs usable reason codes, audit trails, and controls that let humans review decisions when needed.

In payments, AI is therefore not a replacement for authorization controls. It is one layer inside them: a way to turn transaction data into a risk signal, under rules, limits, monitoring, and human accountability.

Credit Scoring and Underwriting

Credit is another major AI use case, and one of the most sensitive. Traditional credit scoring relies heavily on credit history: previous loans, repayment behavior, income, outstanding debt, defaults, and bureau data. That works well for customers with established credit files. It works less well for thin-file customers, new immigrants, gig workers, young people, small merchants, and customers in markets with limited bureau coverage.

AI can widen the data set. A lender may analyze transaction history, income regularity, spending patterns, cash-flow volatility, repayment timing, account balances, business revenue, invoice behavior, or marketplace sales data. For small businesses, a payment processor may be able to underwrite based on actual transaction volume rather than a traditional loan application.

This can expand access to credit. A customer who looks invisible to a traditional bureau may still show stable income, regular payments, and responsible account behavior. A small merchant with a limited formal credit history may still show consistent revenue from card sales or marketplace activity.

In underwriting, that dependence on historical data can also create unfair outcomes. If a model learns from historical lending decisions, it may learn historical discrimination. If certain groups were previously underserved, the model may treat that past exclusion as a risk signal. If alternative data is used carelessly, it can become a proxy for protected characteristics. A model can look neutral while producing unfair outcomes.

That risk turns explainability into more than a technical preference. A lender needs to understand why the model reached its recommendation before deciding whether the result is fair, lawful, and commercially sensible.

A credit decision is not like a product recommendation. If a customer is declined, given a lower limit, or charged a higher price, the institution needs to identify the main reasons. Was the issue unstable income, high existing debt, irregular cash flow, recent missed payments, short account history, or something else? A vague answer, such as "the model scored the applicant too low," is not enough.

Explainability turns a model output into a decision that the institution can review, challenge, document, and defend. In many jurisdictions, customers must receive reasons for adverse credit decisions. Regulators also expect institutions to understand the drivers of credit decisions, monitor outcomes, and test for unfair discrimination.

AI underwriting demands stronger model governance. The more a lender relies on complex data and learned patterns, the more it needs fairness testing, documentation, performance monitoring, human accountability, and a clear process for handling cases where the model may be wrong.

KYC, AML, and Compliance Monitoring

AI does not change the obligation to know the customer, understand the business, screen for sanctions, or monitor suspicious activity. It changes how teams gather, compare, and prioritize the evidence around those obligations.

Models can read documents, extract ownership information, compare identity evidence, screen names, classify cases, and prioritize monitoring alerts. The value is triage. A large financial institution can process millions of events per day, and human teams cannot review them all with the same level of depth.

Sanctions and AML screening also produce large numbers of false positives. Similar names, incomplete data, transliteration differences, outdated records, and noisy transaction descriptions can create alerts that require human review. AI can help group related cases, identify weak matches, summarize evidence, and focus attention on higher-risk alerts.

But compliance AI has a hard boundary. The institution remains responsible for the outcome. A model that reduces false positives but misses a real sanctions match is not a success. A model that produces a helpful summary but hides uncertainty can mislead the reviewer.

For compliance, AI should be treated as triage and decision support. The regulated obligation remains with the institution.

Customer Support and Operations

Financial services produce repetitive customer questions: card delivery, declines, PIN resets, pending payments, disputes, limit changes, refunds, failed transfers, account status, and document requests.

AI can answer many routine questions faster than a human agent when the answer depends on retrieving internal information and explaining it clearly. It can also help inside the operating model. It can summarize a long chat before a human agent takes over, classify a complaint, suggest a response, identify missing documents, and detect when a customer is angry, vulnerable, or confused.

The main risk is over-automation: a customer asking for a card replacement does not need a senior specialist, but a customer reporting fraud after losing rent money may need a human immediately. A customer disputing a transaction should not be trapped in a chatbot loop. A vulnerable customer should not be handled as just another ticket in a queue.

The best support AI distinguishes routine cases from those that require a person's attention.

Disputes, Chargebacks, and Evidence Review

Disputes are a natural fit for AI assistance because they involve documents, timelines, reason codes, evidence packages, and repetitive classification.

In disputes and chargebacks, AI helps teams handle paperwork and timing more reliably within the existing process.

AI can summarize case files, extract key dates, identify missing evidence, match cases to likely reason codes, compare merchant evidence with customer claims, and help prepare evidence packages.

It should not blindly decide every dispute. Disputes affect real money and customer rights. Network rules, local regulations, and evidence standards still govern the process.

AI is useful because it reduces manual work and helps reviewers see the case clearly. It becomes risky when it turns a regulated review process into an automated result that no one can explain.

Merchant Onboarding and Monitoring

In acquiring and payment facilitation, the merchant can pose a risk.

A merchant may be legitimate at onboarding and become risky later. In Chapters 4 and 43, we covered the underlying risks: prohibited activity, transaction laundering, excessive disputes, fake sales, misleading products, and unusual merchant behavior.

AI can help during merchant onboarding by analyzing websites, business descriptions, ownership documents, transaction projections, product categories, adverse media, and sanctions exposure. After onboarding, it can monitor behavioral changes and flag cases that need review.

Acquirers and payment facilitators carry risk for the merchants they serve. A bad merchant can create fraud losses, network fines, regulatory exposure, and reputational damage.

AI can surface merchant-risk patterns earlier. Policy still decides what those patterns mean: which merchants are prohibited, which need enhanced due diligence, which can be approved automatically, and which must be reviewed by a human.

Reconciliation, Exceptions, and Back-Office Work

Not every valuable use of AI is high-profile. In reconciliation and exception handling, the AI angle is operational: matching records, parsing messy references, classifying breaks, and suggesting where to start an investigation.

These tasks are slow because financial data arrives in different formats. Different systems rarely describe the same transaction in exactly the same way. One system may have an authorization ID, another a settlement reference, another a bank statement line, another a merchant order number, and another a customer support note.

AI can help classify exceptions, suggest likely matches, read unstructured references, and route cases to the right team. It can reduce manual work in operations where people spend hours comparing records across systems.

This work is less visible than fraud detection or chatbots, but it can be just as valuable. Financial institutions spend a lot of money moving money and then explaining where it went.

Personalization, Offers, and Financial Insights

AI also changes how financial products are presented to customers. A bank or wallet provider sees patterns that the customer may not notice. It can categorize spending, detect subscriptions, identify salary payments, recognize recurring bills, and spot behavioral changes. From those patterns, it can generate financial insights: a subscription has increased in price, a recurring payment is at risk of failing, cash may run short before rent is due, or a savings goal is falling behind.

This kind of personalization can be useful when it helps customers understand their own financial lives. A good alert gives the customer time to act. A good recommendation can point them to a cheaper account, a better repayment option, or a savings habit that fits their actual behavior. The same machinery can also be used in less helpful ways.

The same data can serve the customer or be used to exploit them. Cash-flow signals can trigger useful support or push more credit. Spending patterns can help someone control subscriptions or nudge them toward more purchases. A trading app can use personalization to educate a customer or to encourage more frequent trading than the customer needs.

That makes personalization different from simple interface improvement. It does more than organize information. It can influence behavior.

The ethical line is not always obvious in each individual case, but the principle is simple: personalization should help customers make better financial decisions, not exploit their weaknesses, stress, habits, or lack of attention.

Investments and Trading

Investment and trading are another major area of AI use.

At the retail level, robo-advisors use customer inputs such as goals, age, risk tolerance, and investment horizon to recommend portfolios and rebalance them over time. The model replaces parts of the standardized work that a human advisor would otherwise do.

At the institutional level, AI can process market data, earnings reports, news, sentiment, macroeconomic indicators, and order-book signals. It can support trading strategies, risk management, portfolio construction, and market surveillance.

The risk is that models can fail under stress. A model trained on normal market conditions may perform poorly when conditions change. When many models respond to similar signals, their actions can reinforce each other. A strategy that looks profitable in testing may stop working when the market structure changes.

In investing, AI does not predict the future. It finds patterns and supports decisions – and stops working the moment those patterns change. The real challenge is knowing when those patterns no longer apply.

Risk Categories

The risks of AI in fintech stem from the fact that financial decisions directly affect people. A weak model can deny credit, block account access, miss fraud, flag the wrong customer, expose sensitive data, or give a confident answer that causes someone to act on bad information.

One group of risks comes from the data used to train and run the model.

A model trained on biased data can produce biased outcomes. This is especially serious in credit, pricing, fraud controls, account access, and collections. If past decisions treated some customers unfairly, the model may learn that pattern and repeat it at scale. If the input data is incomplete or poorly labeled, the model may appear precise while making unreliable judgments.

Privacy faces the same problem. AI systems consume data, and financial data is among the most sensitive. Institutions need strict controls over what data is used, why it is used, how long it is retained, where it is processed, and who can access it.

Another group of risks comes from how models behave over time.

Customer behavior changes, fraud patterns change, economic conditions shift, and regulations get rewritten. A model that worked well last year may perform poorly this year. This is model drift: the relationship between the model's inputs and the real-world outcome weakens. Models need to be monitored, retrained, and retired when performance degrades.

Generative AI adds a more visible problem: hallucination. A chatbot, an analyst assistant, or an operational tool may produce a confident answer that is wrong. In finance, a wrong answer can create customer harm, compliance errors, poor investment decisions, or bad operational actions.

The final group of risks comes from how people and attackers interact with the system.

Explainability is essential because financial institutions need to explain important decisions to customers, regulators, auditors, and internal risk teams. A model that performs well in testing but cannot be explained may be unsuitable for decisions that affect customer rights or regulatory obligations.

Automation bias can make the problem worse. People may trust a model because it sounds confident, because it appears precise, or because challenging it slows down the workflow. Human review only works when the reviewer has the authority, time, and information to disagree.

Security is also different in an AI-enabled system: prompts can be injected, documents can be designed to mislead extraction tools, and fraudsters can test systems until they learn how to bypass them. AI also gives criminals better tools for phishing, social engineering, synthetic identity creation, and document fraud.

The capability is not one-sided. Models that help banks detect fraud can also help attackers write better phishing messages, generate synthetic identities, forge documents, and test stolen data at scale. AI risk is therefore broader than model accuracy. It includes data, oversight, security, accountability, and the workflow design around the model.

AI as Decision and Operations Layer

A serious fintech company should not ask only, "Can we use AI here?" It should first ask what decision the model is influencing.

A model that summarizes an internal policy document creates one level of risk. A model that declines credit, blocks a payment, freezes an account, flags a sanctions match, or sends a customer-facing explanation creates a very different level of risk.

Good AI governance starts with that distinction. The institution needs to know what data the model can use, what output it produces, whether the output can harm a customer, whether regulation requires an explanation, who monitors performance, who can override the model, how errors are detected, and what happens when the model is uncertain.

These controls are becoming more formal. In the European Union, the AI Act has created a risk-based framework for AI systems, including stricter obligations for high-risk uses. Financial firms also remain subject to existing rules on data protection, outsourcing, operational resilience, consumer protection, credit, AML, and governance. The practical lesson is broader than any one regulation: AI does not sit outside the control framework of financial services.

In practice, good AI governance usually includes model documentation, training data controls, bias testing, performance monitoring, audit trails, access controls, human review thresholds, incident processes, vendor oversight, and clear ownership. For low-risk tasks, such as summarizing internal documents, the controls may be lighter. For high-risk tasks, such as declining credit, freezing an account, blocking a payment, or escalating a suspicious activity case, controls need to be much stronger.

AI can make financial services faster, cheaper, more personalized, and more accurate, but it can also make bad decisions at scale. Speed is useful only when the decision remains fair, secure, explainable, and well-managed.

The book began with a simple card payment and followed the machinery behind it: credentials, authorization, clearing, settlement, fees, fraud, disputes, bank rails, alternative payment methods, crypto, digital money, and programmable finance. AI sits across that journey rather than adding another rail to it.

The more finance becomes digital, instant, and data-rich, the more these decisions shape the customer experience. Smarter models will only help if the financial systems around them remain accountable.

Glossary

This glossary gives short working definitions of the main terms used in the book. It is meant as a quick reference, not as a substitute for the fuller explanations in the chapters.

Numbers

3DS (3-D Secure)
A protocol used mainly for authenticating cardholders in online card payments before authorization.

A

ABU (Automatic Billing Updater)
Mastercard's service for updating stored card details for merchants when a card changes.

ACH (Automated Clearing House)
The US bank-transfer system used for batch-based credit and debit payments. ACH is governed by Nacha and operated through FedACH and the Electronic Payments Network.

Acquirer (acquiring bank)
The financial institution that enables a merchant to accept card payments and sends transactions into the card system.

Acquirer markup
The part of the merchant's card fee kept by the acquirer for its services and margin.

ACS (Access Control Server)
The issuer-side 3DS system that evaluates authentication requests and returns the authentication result.

AISP (Account Information Service Provider)
A licensed provider that can access and aggregate payment-account information with the customer's consent but cannot initiate payments.

AML (Anti-Money Laundering)
The legal and operational framework for detecting, preventing, and reporting money laundering and related financial crime.

Arbitration
The final dispute stage in which the payment network reviews the case and issues a binding decision.

ARPC (Authorization Response Cryptogram)
An EMV cryptogram generated by the issuer and returned to the chip to authenticate the issuer's response.

ARQC (Authorization Request Cryptogram)
An EMV cryptogram generated by the chip for online issuer verification of a transaction.

ASPSP (Account Servicing Payment Service Provider)
A bank or account provider that maintains a customer payment account and exposes access under open banking rules.

Assessments (scheme fees, network fees)
Fees charged by a card network to participants for use of its brand, rules, and processing services.

ATC (Application Transaction Counter)
A counter on an EMV chip that increases with each transaction and helps issuers detect replayed or out-of-sequence use.

ATM (Automated Teller Machine)
A self-service terminal that allows cardholders to access banking services, such as cash withdrawals.

Authentication
The process of verifying that a person, device, card, or system is genuine or authorized.

Authorization
The real-time stage in which the issuer evaluates a payment request and returns an approval, decline, or other response. No interbank money movement occurs at this stage.

Authorization code
A code returned after an approved authorization and used to identify and reconcile the approval.

Authorization hold (hold, pending hold)
A temporary reservation of funds, credit, or spending capacity after authorization.

Available balance
The amount the customer can currently spend or withdraw after accounting for posted transactions, holds, limits, and other restrictions.

B

BaaS (Banking-as-a-Service)
A model where licensed banking capabilities are offered to other companies through APIs or platform services.

Balance sheet
A financial statement showing assets, liabilities, and equity at a specific point in time.

Bank transfer
A payment that moves money directly between bank accounts through bank payment rails.

Base II
Visa's proprietary clearing format for submitting card transaction records.

BIC (Bank Identifier Code; SWIFT code)
A standardized code that identifies a bank in international payments.

BIN / IIN (Bank Identification Number, Issuer Identification Number)
The first digits of a payment card number that identify the issuer or card program.

Bitmap
The part of an ISO 8583 message that shows which data fields are present.

Blockchain
A shared ledger where transactions are grouped into linked blocks and maintained across a network.

BNPL (Buy Now, Pay Later)
A financing arrangement that lets a customer split a purchase into scheduled repayments, often offered directly at checkout.

Breakage
The share of loyalty points, vouchers, or stored value that customers never redeem.

C

Capture (batch capture)
The merchant's submission of an authorized transaction for clearing or completion.

CNP transaction (Card-not-present transaction)
A card transaction in which the physical card or payment device does not interact with a terminal, such as e-commerce, in-app, or card-on-file payments.

Card-on-file (CoF, credential-on-file)
A stored payment credential that a merchant can use for later payments with the customer's permission.

CP transaction (Card-present transaction)
A transaction where the card or wallet interacts with a payment terminal at checkout.

Cardholder
The person authorized to use a payment card. The card itself normally remains the legal property of the issuer.

Cash advance
A cash withdrawal using a credit card, usually treated as an immediate loan.

Cashback
A reward that returns a portion of a card purchase to the cardholder as cash or credit.

CBDC (Central bank digital currency)
Digital money issued by a central bank as a liability of that central bank.

CDCVM (Consumer Device Cardholder Verification Method)
Cardholder verification performed on the user's own device, such as a phone, via a biometric check.

CDE (Cardholder Data Environment)
The systems, networks, and processes that store, process, or transmit cardholder data or sensitive authentication data.

Challenge flow
A 3DS authentication path in which the issuer requires the cardholder to complete an additional verification step.

Charge card
A card that requires the full balance to be repaid each billing cycle.

Chargeback
A card transaction reversal initiated through the issuer after a cardholder dispute.

Check digit
The final digit of the PAN, calculated with the Luhn algorithm to detect common data-entry errors.

CIT (Customer-initiated transaction)
A card transaction actively initiated by the cardholder. A CIT can establish permission for later merchant-initiated transactions.

Clearing
The exchange and reconciliation of transaction records after authorization. During clearing, the issuer matches the transaction to the authorization and posts the final charge.

Co-branded card
A card issued with both a financial institution and a partner brand, such as an airline or retailer.

Cold wallet
A cryptocurrency wallet whose private keys are kept offline to reduce exposure to remote attacks.

Commercial card
A payment card issued for business spending rather than personal consumer use.

Contactless transaction
A payment where the card or device communicates with the terminal over short-range contactless technology.

Corporate card
A payment card issued to employees or teams for company expenses.

Correspondent bank
An intermediary bank that helps route payments between banks that do not have a direct relationship.

Credit card
A card that lets the cardholder borrow from the issuer up to a credit limit.

Credit limit (credit line)
The maximum amount of credit the issuer makes available to a cardholder.

Credit transfer
A payment initiated by the sender to push money to a receiver's account.

Cryptocurrency
A digital asset that uses cryptography and distributed ledgers to record ownership and transfers.

Current account
A bank account designed for frequent payments, receipts, and everyday money management. A debit card is commonly linked to this account.

Custodial wallet
A crypto wallet where a third party holds the user's private keys.

CVV (Card Verification Value)
Visa's name for a family of card verification values. Mastercard uses CVC. CVV1/CVC1 protects magnetic-stripe transactions, while CVV2/CVC2 is used mainly for card-not-present checks.

D

DAO (Decentralized autonomous organization)
An organization governed by rules and voting mechanisms encoded on a blockchain.

Data element (DE)
A numbered field in an ISO 8583 message containing a specific item of transaction data. The bitmap indicates which data elements are present.

Data minimization
The privacy principle of collecting only the personal data needed for a specific purpose.

DCC (Dynamic Currency Conversion)
A service that offers cardholders conversion into their home currency at the point of sale.

Debit card
A card that pays from money available in the cardholder's bank account.

DeFi (Decentralized finance)
Financial services built on blockchain protocols rather than traditional intermediaries.

Digital wallet
Software that stores payment credentials or value and lets users make payments digitally.

Direct debit
A payment arrangement where the payee collects money from the payer's bank account under a mandate.

Dispute
A cardholder's formal challenge to a transaction through their issuer.

DPAN (Device Primary Account Number; device token)
A device-specific token used instead of the real card number in mobile wallet payments.

DS (Directory Server)
The 3DS network component that routes authentication messages to the correct issuer system.

E

E-money (electronic money)
Digitally stored monetary value issued against received funds and accepted for payments.

Embedded finance
Financial services placed inside a non-financial product or customer journey.

EMI (Electronic Money Institution)
A regulated institution authorized to issue electronic money and provide payment services without operating as a full bank.

EMV chip
A payment card chip that uses cryptography to make card-present transactions harder to counterfeit.

F

Fallback
Use of a backup acceptance method when the preferred card method fails.

FedNow
The Federal Reserve's instant payment service for real-time payments between participating US financial institutions.

First presentment
The original transaction record submitted through clearing. In a later dispute, it is distinguished from the chargeback and representment stages.

Fixed reserve
A set amount of merchant funds held by an acquirer as protection against future losses.

Float income
Income earned from holding funds before they are spent, paid out, or redeemed.

FPAN (Funding PAN)
The real underlying card number linked to a tokenized card payment.

Frictionless flow
A 3DS authentication path completed without direct cardholder interaction because the issuer assesses the transaction as sufficiently low risk.

Friendly fraud
A dispute or chargeback raised by a cardholder against a transaction they made or authorized, whether deliberately or because of confusion.

G

GDPR (General Data Protection Regulation)
The EU regulation governing how organizations process personal data.

Gift card
A prepaid card or stored-value product used for purchases at a merchant or group of merchants.

GL (General ledger)
The central accounting record where an organization records its financial transactions by account.

H

Hot wallet
A crypto wallet connected to the internet for easier access and faster transactions.

HSM (Hardware Security Module)
A tamper-resistant device used to protect cryptographic keys and perform sensitive operations such as PIN verification and cryptogram validation.

I

IBAN (International Bank Account Number)
A standardized identifier for a bank account used in international and SEPA payments.

iCVV (Integrated CVV)
A chip-related card verification value used to distinguish chip data from magnetic-stripe data.

Interchange fee (interchange)
A fee paid by the acquirer to the issuer for a card transaction.

IPM (Integrated Product Messages)
Mastercard's proprietary clearing message format.

Issuer (issuing bank)
The financial institution that provides the card and decides whether to approve transactions.

K

KYB (Know Your Business)
Checks used to verify a business, its owners, and its risk before onboarding.

KYC (Know Your Customer)
Checks used to verify a customer's identity and assess compliance risk.

L

Loyalty program
A rewards system that gives customers benefits for repeat use or spending.

LPM (Local payment method)
A payment method that is important in a particular country or region rather than globally.

M

Magnetic stripe
The stripe on a payment card that stores static card data for swipe transactions.

MCC (Merchant Category Code)
A four-digit code that classifies a merchant by business type.

MDR (Merchant Discount Rate)
The rate a merchant pays to accept card payments, usually as a percentage of transaction value.

Merchant
A business or seller that accepts payment for goods or services.

Merchant discount fee
The amount charged to a merchant for accepting a card transaction.

MIT (Merchant-initiated transaction)
A card transaction initiated by the merchant without the cardholder participating in real time, under a prior agreement or mandate.

MOTO (mail order/telephone order)
A card-not-present transaction where card details are provided by mail or phone.

MTI (Message Type Indicator)
The ISO 8583 field that identifies the type and purpose of a message.

Multi-currency card
A card that can hold or spend from more than one currency balance.

N

Neobank
A digital-first provider that offers banking products mainly through apps and online channels, often without a traditional branch network.

Net position
The final amount a participant must pay or receive after transactions, refunds, chargebacks, and applicable fees are netted.

Network token
A payment token issued through a card network to replace the PAN in a defined merchant, wallet, device, or payment context.

NFC (Near Field Communication)
Short-range wireless technology used for contactless communication between a card or device and a payment terminal.

Non-custodial wallet
A cryptocurrency wallet in which the user controls the private keys and bears responsibility for securing and recovering them.

Nostro account
A bank's account held with another bank in a foreign currency or market.

O

OCT (Original Credit Transaction)
A card-network transaction that pushes funds to an eligible card account.

ODFI (Originating Depository Financial Institution)
The originator's bank in an ACH payment. It submits ACH entries to an ACH operator.

Offline PIN
A PIN verification method in which the EMV chip checks the PIN locally rather than sending it to the issuer.

Onboarding
The process of signing up and approving a customer, merchant, or business for a financial service.

Online PIN
A PIN verification method in which an encrypted PIN block is sent to the issuer for verification.

Open banking
A framework that lets authorized third parties access bank account data or initiate payments with customer permission.

Overdraft
A bank account facility where spending can exceed the available balance up to an agreed limit.

P

PAN (Primary Account Number)
The card number that identifies the card account for payment routing and processing.

Payment gateway
Software or a service that captures payment details and routes them for processing.

Payment network (card scheme)
The shared card system that provides routing, rules, standards, clearing, and settlement.

Payout
The transfer of card-sale proceeds from the acquirer or payment provider to the merchant after fees, refunds, reserves, and other adjustments.

PCI DSS (Payment Card Industry Data Security Standard)
A security standard for organizations that store, process, or transmit cardholder data.

Pending transaction
A transaction shown before final posting, often while an authorization hold is still active.

PEP (Politically Exposed Person)
A person with a prominent public role who may require enhanced financial-crime checks.

PIN (Personal Identification Number)
A numeric secret used as a knowledge factor to verify the cardholder. A PIN can be verified online by the issuer or offline by the chip.

PISP (Payment Initiation Service Provider)
A licensed provider that can initiate an account-to-account payment from a customer's bank account with the customer's consent.

Posted balance
The account balance after finalized transactions have been recorded. Pending authorization holds may affect the available balance without changing the posted balance.

Pre-arbitration
A stage of dispute where a party challenges the previous outcome before final arbitration.

Pre-authorization
An authorization used to reserve funds before the final amount or completion is known.

Prepaid card
A card that spends from value loaded in advance rather than from a bank account or credit line.

Private-label card
A card accepted only by a specific merchant or merchant group.

Provisioning
The process of adding a card credential to a digital wallet, including issuer verification, token creation, and delivery of the device credential.

PSD2 (Payment Services Directive 2)
The European Union's second Payment Services Directive, which regulates payment services, open banking access, and strong customer authentication.

PSD3 (Payment Services Directive 3)
The European Union's third Payment Services Directive framework, intended to update authorization, supervision, fraud, and consumer-protection rules after PSD2.

PSP (Payment Service Provider)
A provider that bundles one or more merchant payment functions, such as gateway services, processing, acquiring access, fraud tools, and reporting.

PSR (Payment Services Regulation)
A proposed EU regulation intended to harmonize many payment service rules across member states.

Pull payment
A payment initiated by the recipient or merchant under the payer's authorization, such as a card purchase or direct debit.

Push payment
A payment initiated by the sender to move funds to a recipient.

PVK (PIN Verification Key)
A cryptographic key used in PIN generation or PIN verification processes.

Q

QR payment
A payment initiated by scanning or presenting a QR code that carries payment data or a reference used by a wallet, card, or account-to-account rail.

R

RDFI (Receiving Depository Financial Institution)
The receiver's bank in an ACH payment. It receives ACH entries from an ACH operator and posts them to customer accounts.

Reconciliation
The process of matching records from different systems to confirm they agree.

Recurring payment
A repeated payment taken on a schedule under a customer's agreement.

Refund
A transaction that returns all or part of a previous payment to the cardholder.

Representment
A merchant's response to a chargeback by submitting evidence that the transaction was valid.

Reserve
Funds held back to cover possible future losses, chargebacks, or obligations.

Response code
A code returned in a payment message that indicates the outcome of processing, such as approval, decline, or a specific error condition.

Reversal
A message or transaction that cancels the effect of a previous authorization or financial transaction, often after a timeout or processing failure.

RRN (Retrieval Reference Number)
A transaction reference, commonly carried in ISO 8583 Data Element 37, used to locate and reconcile a transaction across systems.

RTP (Real-Time Payments)
The Clearing House's US instant payment network for real-time account-to-account payments.

S

SCA (Strong Customer Authentication)
A European requirement for authentication using at least two independent factor categories.

SCT (SEPA Credit Transfer)
A euro credit transfer scheme for sending payments within the SEPA area.

SCT Inst (SEPA Instant Credit Transfer)
A SEPA scheme for euro credit transfers that completes within seconds.

SDD (SEPA Direct Debit)
A SEPA scheme that allows a creditor to collect euro payments from a payer's account under a valid mandate.

Secure Element
A protected hardware component that stores payment credentials and performs sensitive cryptographic operations on a device.

SEPA (Single Euro Payments Area)
A European payments area that standardizes euro bank transfers and direct debits.

Service code
Card data that tells terminals and issuers how the card may be used.

Settlement
The process of transferring funds between financial institutions to fulfill payment obligations.

Settlement bank (settlement agent)
The bank or central-bank infrastructure through which participants transfer the funds required to settle their net obligations.

Skimming
The theft of card data by secretly reading or copying it from a card or terminal.

Sponsor bank (BIN sponsor)
A licensed bank that provides regulated banking or card-network access for another company.

Stablecoin
A cryptoasset designed to maintain a stable value against a reference asset such as a currency.

STAN (System Trace Audit Number)
A transaction identifier commonly carried in ISO 8583 Data Element 11 and used for tracing within a processing environment.

Statement
A periodic summary of account activity, balances, fees, and payment obligations.

Surcharge
An additional fee charged directly to the customer for using a particular payment or cash-access channel, where permitted.

SWIFT (Society for Worldwide Interbank Financial Telecommunication)
A global financial messaging network used by banks and other institutions to exchange standardized payment and securities messages. SWIFT carries instructions; it does not itself move customer money.

T

Tokenization
The process of replacing sensitive data or an asset reference with a token.

TPK (Terminal PIN Key)
A cryptographic key shared between a terminal and an acquirer for protecting PIN data.

TPP (Third-party provider)
A regulated external provider that accesses account information or initiates payments under open banking rules. AISPs and PISPs are the main categories.

Transaction laundering
Processing payments for one business through another merchant account to hide the true seller or activity.

TSP (Token Service Provider)
The service that creates, manages, and resolves payment tokens. Visa Token Service and Mastercard MDES are network-operated examples.

U

UN (Unpredictable number)
A terminal-generated value used in EMV transactions to help ensure each cryptogram is fresh.

V

VAU (Visa Account Updater)
Visa's service for exchanging updated account information for stored-card merchants.

Virtual card
A payment card issued as digital credentials without requiring a physical card. It can be used online, in apps, or through a wallet.

Void
The cancellation of an approved authorization before it is captured and submitted for clearing. The hold is then released.

Vostro account
A local account that a bank holds on behalf of a foreign correspondent bank.

W

Web3
A broad term for internet services built around blockchain-based ownership, tokens, and decentralized protocols.

X

XS2A (Access to Account)
The PSD2 requirement for account providers to give licensed third parties secure access to payment accounts with customer consent.

Y

Yield farming
Moving cryptoassets across DeFi protocols to earn the highest available rewards or yield.

About the Author

Artem Smirnov is a product leader specializing in card issuing, payments, and fintech infrastructure. For more than a decade, he has worked on payment products across Europe, Asia, and Latin America. His experience spans consumer and commercial card programs, including debit, credit, prepaid, and corporate products, as well as lending and loyalty products, digital wallets, buy now, pay later, Card-as-a-Service platforms, and large card-portfolio migrations. His work has involved banks, fintech companies, processors, and the Visa and Mastercard networks, giving him experience with the technical and operational details of transaction processing, tokenization, fraud controls, accounting, and regulatory requirements.

Much of what he knows about payments was learned through real projects, difficult integrations, and production problems that rarely fit neatly into provider documentation. He wrote this book to make that knowledge easier to acquire and to help readers understand not only how payment systems work, but why they are designed the way they are.

LinkedIn: linkedin.com/in/artem-michael-smirnov

www.ingramcontent.com/pod-product-compliance
Lightning Source LLC
LaVergne TN
LVHW062026051126
851858LV00005B/93